Integrated Ident..y for Gay Men and Lesbians:
Psychotherapeutic Approaches for Emotional Well-Being

FONTENOT BELLONCI

a tomriuʒ inðíu niurt
lré toʒairm trinoit

Integrated Identity for Gay Men and Lesbians:
Psychotherapeutic Approaches for Emotional Well-Being

Edited by
Eli Coleman

Integrated Identity for Gay Men and Lesbians: Psychotherapeutic Approaches for Emotional Well-Being, edited by Eli Coleman, was simultaneously issued by the Haworth Press, Inc., under the title: *Psychotherapy with Homosexual Men and Women: Integrated Identity Approaches for Clinical Practice*, a special issue of the *Journal of Homosexuality*, Volume 14, Numbers 1/2, 1987, John De Cecco, Editor.

Harrington Park Press
New York • London

ISBN 0-918393-38-8

Published by

Harrington Park Press, Inc., 12 West 32 Street, New York, New York 10001
EUROSPAN/Harrington, 3 Henrietta Street, London WC2E 8LU England

Harrington Park Press, Inc., is a subsidiary of The Haworth Press, Inc., 12 West 32 Street, New York, New York 10001.

Integrated Identity for Gay Men and Lesbians: Psychotherapeutic Approaches for Emotional Well-Being was originally published as *Journal of Homosexuality*, Volume 14, Numbers 1/2, 1987.

Cover design by Marshall Andrews.

Library of Congress Cataloging-in-Publication Data

Integrated Identity for Gay Men and Lesbians.
    Psychotherapeutic Approaches for Emotional Well-Being.

    Reprint. Originally published: Psychotherapy with homosexual men and women. New York: Haworth Press, c1988.
        Includes bibliographies and index.
        1. Homosexuality—Psychological aspects. 2. Psychotherapy. 3. Identity (Psychology)
I. Coleman, Eli. II. Title [DNLM: 1. Homosexuality. 2. Psychotherapy. WM 615 P9746]
RC558.P789   1987b   616.85'83406   87-342
ISBN 0-918393-38-8

Dedication

To those who have been in psychological pain and who could have benefited from these newly developed psychotherapeutic approaches.

CONTENTS

Integrated Identity
for Gay Men
and Lesbians:
Psychotherapeutic Approaches
for Emotional
Well-Being

Foreword

We live in an age in which homosexuals and bisexuals are struggling against great odds to achieve positive identities and recognition as individuals and as a valued minority in our pluralistic society. Their task was made somewhat easier by the lifting of the stigma of mental illness by the American Psychiatric Association in 1973, and the subsequent endorsement of that position by the American Psychological Association. As long as the stigma remained, the task of the psychotherapist was seen primarily as that of "curing" the homosexuality. Not only was this impossible, but the consequences of attempting the change in sexual orientation proved to be catastrophic in psychic cost for many.

When homosexuality was officially no longer an illness, there was pressing need to develop new goals and new methods or to adapt well-established methods to the special needs of gay men, lesbians and bisexuals. With the appearance of AIDS, the resources of the gay community were stretched beyond all imaginable limits.

The publication of Dr. Coleman's book meets these needs admirably and could scarcely come at a more auspicious time. It combines a far ranging analysis of the special problems of homosexuals and bisexuals, with the best contemporary psychotherapeutic methods. All psychotherapists, regardless of their own sexual orientation, will find this book indispensable.

Evelyn Hooker, PhD
Research Professor Emeritus
University of California
at Los Angeles

Preface

In 1978, I published a review of psychotherapeutic approaches to the treatment of homosexuality. In this review, many of the psychoanalytic and behavioral approaches which were designed to purge homosexuality from an individual and create heterosexuality were found to be generally ineffective and ethically questionable. The new approach to the treatment of homosexuality was illustrated by a few studies. Its new approach was to assist individuals with predominant same-sex sexual orientations to better individual and interpersonal functioning by acknowledging and helping them consolidate their sexual orientation identity. These new therapies were found to be promising. Further approaches needed to be developed as well as research conducted to prove their efficacy.

Since that time, several books and numerous articles have been published which have continued this development. One of the most significant publications was the special issue of the *Journal of Homosexuality* on "Homosexuality and Psychotherapy" edited by John Gonsiorek, PhD. This was a landmark book which consolidated many of the new treatment methods. This book was published in 1982. Now, five years later, the *Journal of Homosexuality* and The Haworth Press have agreed to publish this current volume which illustrates the fact that there has been a continuing development of these new treatment approaches.

I am very pleased and honored to edit this volume and am very proud of its contents. The articles included here represent incredibly hard work and innovative thinking on the part of these clinician/researchers. I hope that all will find these articles theoretically sound, convincing in the methodology's effectiveness, and moreover practical in its approach to typical psychological problems which the clinician must face daily in working with this population. I truly hope that the articles reflect "the state of the art," are useful in their theoretical conceptualizations, and extremely practical in their suggestions of techniques and methodologies.

I truly believe that the contributing authors are extremely well trained academicians as well as excellent therapists. This is a very unique combination. Bringing their articles together in one single volume, I hope, will be a significant contribution to the field and practical on an everyday level.

I have so many people to thank in helping me with the preparation of this volume. First, I need to thank John De Cecco, PhD, the Editor of the *Journal of Homosexuality*. I was indeed honored when he approached me with this project. John has always been supportive and a true mentor over the years. I am truly grateful to him for his help, support, and confidence in me. This is true, as well, for the publisher of The Haworth Press, Bill Cohen. I thank him for his support and guidance throughout this project.

Next, I need to thank John Gonsiorek, PhD, who edited the first volume on homosexuality and psychotherapy for the *Journal of Homosexuality* and The Haworth Press. John has also been a loyal supporter and encouraged me to pursue this enormous project. I hope that I have been able to continue the work he began with his volume.

I would also like to thank all the contributors to this volume. They were very cooperative in making deadlines and responding to my editorial advice. I appreciate the confidence they had in me and their willingness to take so much time to complete their individual papers.

Next, I would like to thank the staff at the Program in Human Sexuality, my family and friends who have provided me the emotional support and the time away from their needs to complete this project. Without them, I know it would never have been completed.

And, finally, I would like to thank my clients for their inspiration and what they have taught me about themselves and myself in working with them. I hope, in most cases, that their lives and the lives of their loved ones have been enriched by my use of these newer therapeutic approaches. I have certainly been gratified by the growth and improved life experiences which many of them have experienced. It has been an honor to have been a part of their growth process.

Eli Coleman, PhD
Associate Professor and Associate Director
Program in Human Sexuality
Department of Family Practice and Community Health
Medical School
University of Minnesota

Introduction

The significant change over the past 15 years in treatment methods for homosexuality has paralleled dramatic change in homosexual men and womens' lives and changes in society's views of these individuals. These changes reflect a general acceptance of the scientific information refuting homosexuality as an illness. This has allowed therapists to focus upon improving psychological and interpersonal functioning of homosexual men and women rather than changing their homosexual orientation.

A new question has emerged for psychotherapists: Why, exposed to seemingly like environments, have some individuals successfully coped with their homosexuality, while others have labored, suffered, and found a positive identity utterly elusive?

Therapists have begun to realize the following. First, individuals who have had difficulty forming a positive identity have experienced the difficulty because of major psychiatric problems, such as schizophrenia or major depressive illness, independent of their sexual orientation.

Second, are individuals who have experienced difficulty and psychological problems (personality disorders, anxiety, or depressive reactions) because of a variety of external factors. These factors have been defined as: (a) the lack of an accepting and nurturing environment for homosexual expression, (b) myths and misinformation regarding homosexuality, (c) lack of information regarding methods for developing a positive self-identity and improvement of interpersonal functioning, (d) lack of survival techniques for living in a predominately heterosexual and heterosexually-biased society, and (e) lack of healthy role models.

This issue discusses typical problems and treatments for psychological problems, but does not discuss major psychiatric problems. Each of the methods included are designed to maximize potential, improve psychological and interpersonal functioning, and develop a positive self- and sexual identity. Each method is examined from a theoretical point of view to explain underlying psychological principles, illustrated with case presentations, and evaluated for effectiveness by treatment outcomes. Treatment outcomes are described by intended outcome, given the type of client and therapist involved, and are not judged by extrinsic universal criteria.

The issue includes descriptions of typical psychological problems of homosexual men and women and includes a sampling of methods which have been judged effective in treating these problems. The problems chosen are those of individuals with no gross social disorganization or serious psychopathology requiring intensive psychiatric assistance or medication. The problems are not exhaustive but are typical and representative. Areas discussed include: (a) homophobia or internalized shame, (b) lack of positive and integrated self- and sexual identity, (c) conflict with family members, (d) relationship difficulties, (e) sexual dysfunction, (f) compulsive sexual activity, (g) chemical abuse or addiction, (h) AIDS anxiety, and (i) the effects of aging.

While various treatment methods could be used to treat any of the aforementioned problems, only a sampling of methods are included. The methods discussed are: (a) cognitive change; (b) attitude modification; (c) psychoanalytic and psychodyamic relationship enhancement, modeling, simulation, and role-playing; (d) self-help groups; (e) hypnosis; (f) group therapies; (g) client-centered or relationship therapy; and (i) psycho-education techniques. Treatment methods included represent my selection of the most effective and widely utilized for the problems presented.

In selecting articles for this volume, I have tried to choose treatment approaches and techniques which are based upon sound psychological theory and have been researched with homosexual and heterosexual populations. No treatment methods or techniques are included that are so unusual as not to be generally recognizable.

The uniqueness of this issue is the application of accepted psychological methods to this particular population and their psychological problems. The issue is designed to be a comprehensive casebook of typical psychological problems and treatment methods found effective to solve particular homosexual problems.

The articles have been solicited from highly competent clinician researchers. The issue includes articles from clinicians experienced with this population and academically trained in the psychological theories and research upon which they base their therapeutic methods and techniques.

The issue is divided into four areas of commonly presented concerns to the psychotherapist: (a) identity development and resolution of identity and developmental concerns, (b) relationship concerns, (c) family conflicts, and (d) other psychological problems.

IDENTITY DEVELOPMENT

One of the first challenges for the psychotherapist in working with clients regarding concerns related to their sexual orientation is to assess the client's sexual orientation. The first paper included in this section reviews the multitude of methods which have been utilized to assess sexual orientation, and then proposes a new conceptual model and an actual assessment tool.

The second article describes the difficult process faced by adolescents to develop positive and healthy social and personal identities in a relatively hostile environment. Emery Hetrick, MD and Damien Martin, EdD describe the importance of providing a non-threatening, supportive environment that provides accurate information and appropriate peer and adult role models. Through this approach, the risks of maladaptive adjustment are reduced and many of the typical concerns of homosexual adolescents are alleviated and internalized negative attitudes are either modified or prevented from developing. Working with adolescents with predominant homosexual orientations represents an exciting and bold new area for psychotherapists.

Christine Browning, PhD then examines the coming-out process within an adult developmental context. She reviews typical therapeutic issues which surface for the young adult lesbian client and suggests intervention strategies.

For female clients who have difficulty accepting their attractions to other women or their lesbian behavior and identity or both, Joan Sophie, PhD offers therapeutic strategies which have been used successfully by her and her clients to promote self-acceptance and reduce internalized homophobia.

Finally, in this section, Timothy Wolf, PhD and Fritz Klein, MD offer Eriksonian hypnotic and strategic interventions which they have found helpful to their clients experiencing sexual orientation confusion. Case studies are presented which include techniques such as reframing, metaphor, and synesthesia. These methods offer the psychotherapist new and innovative short-term therapeutic approaches for men and women experiencing sexual orientation confusion.

RELATIONSHIP CONCERNS

Until recently, little information has existed in the literature regarding therapeutic techniques effective with male and female homosexual couples. Ken George, PhD and Andrew Behrendt, PhD (cand.) present an overview of four issues which need to be explored by the therapist in working with male couples. These issues are stereotypical male roles, stereotypical sexual roles, homophobia, and sexual dysfunctions. These issues can cause anxiety and stress for the male couple. Consequently, these authors present suggestions for treatment of these issues as they may surface in the process of therapy.

Andrew Mattison, PhD, and David McWhirter, MD, discuss a particularly common problem experienced in male couples: stage discrepancy. Using their theoretical framework, which was presented in their recent book, *The Male Couple*, these authors discuss the difficulties experienced by couples when they are working different developmental tasks of relationship development. This common occurrence is often misunderstood by the couple and adds to their anxieties about their relationship. The authors discuss some factors affecting stage discrepancy, as well as assessment and treatment strategies which they have found to be effective in resolving these problems.

In the next article in this section, Philip Colgan, MA provides the psychotherapist with an understanding of many conflicts in homosexual males in their intimate relationships. Essentially, Mr. Colgan hypothesizes that many homosexual male clients experience identity and intimacy disorders which preclude healthy intimacy functioning. These disorders begin in childhood and can be redressed during any developmental stage. This paper illustrates effective psychotherapeutic techniques designed to form a solid identity based on self-observation and self-valuing. A solid identity and behavioral relearning of intimacy form the bases for satisfying intimacy needs.

Sondra Smalley, MA continues discussion of dependency and identity disorders among homosexual female clients. Resolution of these issues is essential for healthy intimacy expression. Unfortunately, many of Ms. Smalley's lesbian couple clients experience serious lack of individuation in their relationship and become extremely enmeshed. Besides the pain of this stricture on their relationship, this extreme dependency can lead to violence in some cases, as well as termination of the relationship. Sex-role socialization has been a major factor in the development of these problems. Understanding these dynamics and the importance of a healthy balance between individuation and intimacy or closeness is essential for the psychotherapist in working with lesbian couples.

Two papers in this section are devoted to treating sexual dysfunctions among homosexual couples. The first paper is by Marny Hall, PhD, wherein she explains how traditional sex therapy models are often ineffective with lesbian clients presenting sexual problems. Though these behavioral approaches may be found useful later in the process of treatment, the clinician must first address the social and cultural contexts that frame the sexual dysfunctions commonly experienced by lesbian couples.

The second paper on sexual dysfunction describes the causes and treatments of sexual desire discrepancies in male couples. Again, traditional treatment methods of sexual dysfunction need to be altered, given the dynamics of homosexual male couples. Rex Reece, PhD helps translate those techniques which he has found helpful in his clinical practice. This paper is an extremely thorough examination of this problem and techniques for resolution.

FAMILY CONFLICTS

While relationship difficulties have received very little attention, the same is true for family conflicts. This section of the issue explores a number of previously under-studied areas. In the first article, Sue Kiefer Hammersmith, PhD acknowledges that stigma lies at the root of many problems faced by homosexual clients and their families. As a sociologist, she provides the psychotherapist with information from sociological theory and research which help in eliminating myths of homosexuality and reducing the effects of society's stigma. This article offers practical tips for helping clients understand their own or a family member's sexual orientation, for coping with stigma, for reconciling issues of religion and morality, and for determining lifestyle.

In the next article, Timothy Wolf, PhD describes particular issues faced by bisexual men and their spouses. More psychotherapists are becoming aware that a significant number of men and women experience conflict with their sexual orientation within the context of their marriage. Dr. Wolf describes a group psychotherapy method for bisexual men and their wives. This method of treatment appears to be quite helpful to couples experiencing these difficulties. The group provides a supportive environment within which both the needs of the husband and wife can be met. Most previous research has focused on groups for husbands or for wives. This unique methodology offers help for couples who want to maintain their marriages and work together to address the difficult issues this situation presents.

Not all married individuals with bisexual or predominant homosexual orientations decide to stay in their marriages. Many divorce and pursue homosexual relationships and a predominantly homosexual identity. However, many of these individuals have children. This situation presents difficulties for the parents as well as the children. Martha Kirkpatrick, MD reviews the literature on lesbian mother studies. She finds that lesbian mothers benefit from more congenial relations with ex-spouses and include men more regularly in their children's lives than do divorced heterosexual mothers. Coupled lesbian mothers benefit from greater economic and emotional resources than do other groups which live alone with their children. It is important for the therapist to understand the unique stresses these family structures face, but also to understand the advantages which these situations can create. Dr. Kirkpatrick gives many helpful suggestions to psychotherapists working with lesbian mothers or their children or both.

For those working with gay fathers, Edward Dunne, PhD provides a treatment approach for helping them deal with one of their hardest struggles: concerns about revealing their sexual orientation identity to their children. Dr. Dunn describes a time-limited group which helps these

men with this type of problem. Role-playing of disclosure situations is the
main methodology utilized, along with group discussion. Dr. Dunn
presents follow-up data from men who were treated in this fashion.

A number of homosexual or bisexual parents, because of choice or
circumstance, continue to be involved in the parenting of their children in
a significant way. There are many cases in which the homosexual or
bisexual parent retains custody of the children. If they become involved
in another primary relationship, this presents new problems which are
similar to the problems faced by recreated family systems. Step-parenting
becomes a significant problem for many of these new family relationships. David Baptiste, PhD discusses these problems and offers guidelines for therapy with these families.

This section concludes with an article by Joseph Neisen, MA, who
discusses the importance of resources for families with a homosexual
member. Mr. Niesen conducted a mail survey of these families and
reports on the sources of support which they have found. From this
information, Mr. Niesen suggests how psychotherapists might better
prepare themselves for providing services to these families and how they
might better deliver these services.

SPECIAL PROBLEMS

In this section of the issue, a few special problem areas are explored.
One of the most common problem areas is the problem of alcohol abuse
and alcoholism in the gay community. Bob Kus, RN, PhD describes how
Alcoholics Anonymous, as a self-help organization, has been so helpful
to many homosexual men. The high incidence of this problem among
homosexual men cannot be debated. Professional counselors are sometimes reluctant to make use of self-help organizations and are often
unaware of the "inner workings" of these groups. Dr. Kus provides a
helpful insight into this particular self-help organization and suggest how
the professional can better utilize this resource for overcoming alcohol
abuse and alcoholism-related problems.

But if there is any one overriding problem facing homosexual men in
the 1980s, it is the problem of the deadly illness Acquired Immune
Deficiency Syndrome (AIDS). This problem has created innumerable
psychological problems, in addition to the well-known physical ailments.
The psychotherapist is challenged in many ways to help their clients cope
with this dreaded disease which has affected so many homosexual men.
Michael Quadland, PhD, MPH and William Shattls, DSW (cand.)
discuss the AIDS epidemic in the next article, in terms of its effect on
general sexual attitudes and behavior of homosexual and bisexual men,
and then on the issue of control over one's sexual behavior. Many

homosexual men have experienced difficulty controlling their sexual behavior even in light of the evidence that changing sexual behavior patterns is the best preventative measure available at present for preventing contraction of the disease. This leads to a discussion of sexual compulsivity and the debate surrounding this issue. Finally, a group treatment program for homosexual and bisexual men with problems of sexual control is described, as well as outcome findings. This article sheds light on helping homosexual and bisexual men better cope with this serious health threat and aid in the prevention and spread of this disease.

In the following article, Kathy Harowski, PhD addresses the problem of the "worried well," those who do not have AIDS but are terrorized at contracting this illness because they are defined as persons at risk for AIDS because of past or present sexual activity or intravenous drug use. This could also be expanded to those who are asymptomatic for the illness but have tested positive on HTLV-III antibody testing. The "worried well" is an expanding population as the disease spreads throughout the general population and more people become included in high risk categories—not just homosexual men, intravenous drug users, and hemophiliacs requiring blood transfusions. Dr. Harowksi discusses the AIDS epidemic in terms of its impact on the psychological functioning of individuals and their relationships. Treatment strategies which therapists might find useful in working with the worrried well are also presented.

The AIDS epidemic has brought many to begin dealing with issues of death and dying at ages far younger than the average man or woman. But these issues are ones which all must face as a part of growing old, facing inevitable death, and losing loved ones. Richard Friend, PhD concludes this section and the issue with a discussion of the individual and social psychology of aging and the clinical implications for homosexual men and women. One of the unique contributions Dr. Friend has made is the proposed hypothesis of an accelerated aging process among homosexuals. Concerns of aging are often presented to the clinician by relatively young homosexual men and women. Ageist and heterosexist stereotypes and social messages contributed to the phenomenon on accelerated aging. Therapeutic strategies are suggested to assist the homosexual client cope with issues of the normal aging process and the phenomenon of an accelerated aging process which seems to be common among homosexuals.

CONCLUSION

This issue represents some of the most up-to-date treatment methodologies utilized by psychotherapists to assist homosexual and bisexual individuals toward healthier and more positive identities and improved intimate relationships with others. In general, these methods are designed to improve overall psychological functioning by addressing typical psychological problems which many encounter in their lifetimes. Psychotherapists have not always been trained to treat these typical psychological problems. While these problems are not always unique to homosexuals and bisexuals, the social and cultural climate creates unique stresses to dealing with these problems. With an awareness of these issues, along with application of sound psychological theory and psychotherapeutic techniques, many psychotherapists will be more successful in working with this particular population. Consequently, we can improve the overall psychological well-being of the homosexual and bisexual individuals we treat, as well as their family members. This represents a dramatic step beyond simply declassifying homosexuality as a mental illness, and provides effective psychological assistance to many who still suffer society's stigma and the challenges of living in a predominately heterosexual world.

Eli Coleman, PhD

I. *IDENTITY FORMATION*

Assessment of Sexual Orientation

Eli Coleman, PhD
University of Minnesota

SUMMARY. This paper reviews the multitude of methods which have been utilized to assess sexual orientation. The basic assumption of most of the previous methods of assessment is that sexual orientation is determined by one's gender or genitalia and the gender or genitalia of the individual one is attracted to. This assumption is challenged and the complexity of sexual orientation is illustrated. Consequently, a model for assessment of sexual orientation is proposed which includes nine dimensions: current relationship status, self identification identity, ideal self-identification identity, global acceptance of their current sexual orientation identity, physical identity, gender identity, sex-role identity, and sexual orientation identity as measured by behavior, fantasies and emotional attachments, and finally the individual's past and present perception of their sexual identity compared to their idealized future.

The dichotomous or trichotomous categories of sexual orientation (homosexual, heterosexual, and bisexual) is a massive over-simplification of our current understanding of sexual orientation. The clinician, therefore, must have access to more complex and sophisticated assessment methodologies, devices, and to better understand and help the client understand his or her sexual orientation.

Assessment of sexual orientation is important in the treatment of a variety of psychological problems. Conflicts within or between individuals over sexual orientation are quite commonly seen in many cases of

---

Dr. Coleman is Associate Professor and Associate Director of the Program of Human Sexuality, Department of Family Practice and Community Health, University of Minnesota Medical School. Correspondence may be addressed to the author, Program of Human Sexuality, 2630 University Avenue S.E., Minneapolis, MN 55414.

individual psychopathology. These conflicts contribute to psychosexual dysfunctions, relational problems, career indecision, developmental disorders, existential crises, and so forth. Of course, the importance of an extensive assessment of sexual orientation is most important when the client presents with confusion or conflict about his or her sexual orientation. In all cases, the clinician should be well prepared to employ a number of diagnostic and evaluative tools.

TOWARD A MORE THOROUGH, ACCURATE, AND COMPLETE ASSESSMENT

The view that sexual orientation is dichotomous, i.e., heterosexual and homosexual, was dismissed over 30 years ago by Kinsey, Pomeroy, and Martin (1948):

> The world is not divided into sheep and goats. Not all are black nor all things white. It is a fundamental of taxonomy that nature rarely deals with discrete categories and tries to force facts into separated pigeon holes. The living world is a continuum in each and every one of its aspects. The sooner we learn this concerning human sexual behavior the sooner we shall reach a sounder understanding of the realities of sex. (p. 639)

Out of their findings, Kinsey and his associates developed a 7-point scale in which 0 represented exclusive heterosexuality and 6 represented exclusive homosexuality (See Figure 1). Three on the scale indicated equal homosexual and heterosexual responsiveness. Individuals were rated on this continuum based upon their sexual behavior and psychic reactions, i.e., physical attraction to desired partners.

Although this continuum notion better represented the realities of the world, the Kinsey Scale has many limitations for accurately describing an individual's sexual orientation. First, the scale assumes that sexual behavior and erotic responsiveness are the same within individuals. In response to this criticism, Bell and Weinberg (1978) utilized two scales in their extensive study of homosexuality (see Figure 2). They rated their subjects on two scales: one for sexual behavior, and one for erotic fantasies. Their research revealed discrepancies between the two ratings. Paul (1983/1984) reported that discrepancies were found in approximately one-third of the homosexual samples. Most saw their behavior as more exclusively homosexual than their erotic feelings.

While this two-dimensional and continuous view of sexual orientation represented an improvement in assessment of sexual orientation, several clinicians and researchers have recommended additional dimensions.

FIGURE 1.

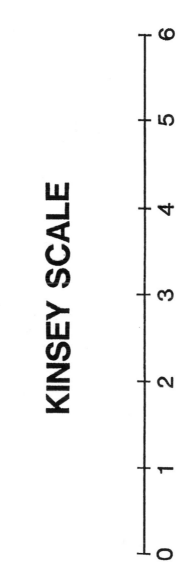

KINSEY SCALE

0   1   2   3   4   5   6

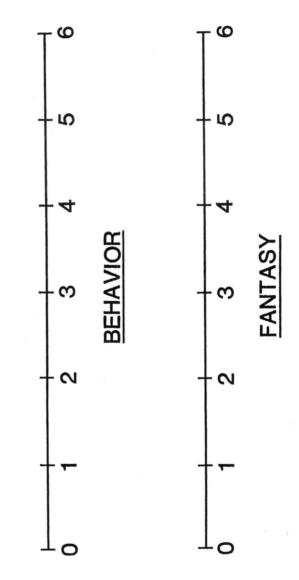

FIGURE 2.

MODIFIED KINSEY SCALE

FURTHER DIMENSIONS OF SEXUAL ORIENTATION, BASED UPON THE BIOLOGICAL SEX OF THE PARTNER

Shively and De Cecco (1977) suggested the conceptualization of sexual orientations embracing physical, interpersonal, and intrapsychic factors. The physical and intrapsychic factors are similar to the notions of Bell-Weinberg that describe the components of sexual behavior (physical) and erotic fantasy (intraspsychic factors). The additional component is an important one: Interpersonal affection refers to associations involving love or affection that may or may not include genital contact. Again, there may be great discrepancies between these three scales within a given individual.

Klein (1978, 1980) and Klein, Sepekoff, and Wolf (1985) went further in outlining other dimensions of sexual orientations. In addition to scales describing sexual behavior, fantasies, and emotional preference, Klein defined other dimensions including sexual attraction, social preference, self-identification, and heterosexual/homosexual lifestyle preference. Therefore, individuals rate themselves on a 7-point scale for seven different dimensions. Klein contended that sexual orientation is not fixed or permanent. Therefore, the Klein Sexual Orientation Grid (KSOG) requires a subject to provide 21 Kinsey-type ratings in a 7 by 3 grid (see Figure 3). This grid shows the 7 dimensions of sexual orientation and provides ratings for the respondents' past and present (as defined by the preceding year) and the individual's ideal choice. Based upon the results of 384 respondents, Klein, et al. (1985) found significant differences between the ranks of the 21 profile variables on the grid. The authors concluded that the KSOG is a reliable and valid instrument (see also Wayson, 1983) that can differentiate sexual orientation by taking into account the meaningful dimension of time as well as other varied dimensions. This grid provides the clinician with a reminder to avoid the simplistic and inadequate labeling techniques used previously.

SEXUAL ORIENTATION BASED UPON THE BIOLOGICAL DICHOTOMOUS SEX OF THE INDIVIDUAL

The previous methods of assessment make assumptions that have been questioned. The basic assumption currently made is that sexual orientation is determined by one's gender or genitalia and the gender of genitalia of the individual one is attracted to. However, many individuals are attracted or oriented to other individuals for reasons other than biological gender.

The assumption of biological gender as the critical variable in determining sexual orientation is based on the biological and deterministic viewpoint that our attractions serve biological purposes (De Cecco & Shively 1983/84). However, humans—and many animal species too—

FIGURE 3.

Klein Sexual Orientation Grid

	PAST	PRESENT	IDEAL
SEXUAL ATTRACTION			
SEXUAL BEHAVIOR			
SEXUAL FANTASIES			
EMOTIONAL PREFERENCE			
SOCIAL PREFERENCE			
SELF IDENTIFICATION			
HETERO/GAY LIFESTYLE			

have shown that attraction can be based upon many other dimensions. Therefore, De Cecco and Shively have suggested a shift from defining orientation based upon one's genitalia to choices that are a reflection of one's personal attitudes and expectations. A number of other researchers have supported this particular shift (Kaplan & Rogers, 1984), and some (Ross, 1984) have even proposed a list of possible meanings or motivations for sexual relationships (See Table 1). Ross believes there are a number of social or demographic variables, such as class, race, income, and religion which may be of equal or greater importance in the analysis of sexual relationships. He believes that any of these variables could be of greater importance in partner choice, but as yet they have not been adequately researched (Ross, 1984, pp. 68–99).

Furthermore, Shively and De Cecco (1977) have broadened the notion of sexual identity to include four distinct components; sexual orientation is only one of the four dimensions. Before considering a person's sexual orientation identity, one's *biological sex* needs to be considered. However, Shively and De Cecco also identified two other important variables: *gender identity and social-sex role identity. Gender identity* refers to the individual's basic conviction of being male or female. This conviction is not necessarily contingent upon the individual's biological gender, as in the case of transsexuals. So, the question arises as to whether a biological male with a female gender identity, who is attracted exclusively to males with male gender and social sex-role identities, is a heterosexual or homosexual individual, and whether it matters that this transsexual is pre-operative or post-operative. It is the author's belief that gender identity can serve as the main criterion variable of sexual orientation.

Moreover, a person's social sex-role is an important aspect of his or her overall identity. Is the biological female with a male gender and social sex-role sexual identity who is attracted to biological males with male gender and social sex-role identities a homosexual or heterosexual individual? Social sex-role could also be used as a criterion variable and might be more important for the individual than the other components.

One biological female colleague stated to me, "I am a biological female with a predominately male gender and social sex-role identity, and I am attracted to males with male gender and social sex-role identities. Therefore, I consider myself, basically, a gay man." From this vantage point, it is clear that the labels homosexual, bisexual, or heterosexual can only be meaningful in the context of, or with an understanding of, the other components of sexual identity (Suppe, 1984).

The four-component model of sexual identity is important in adding to the concepts outlined by Klein (1978, 1980). However, the complexity of sexual orientations goes still further. The concept of sexual orientation needs to be further augmented.

First, Suppe (1984) and others have claimed that qualitative as well as

TABLE 1.

Theoretical Aspects and Meanings of Sexual Relationships

Aspects	Meanings
Reproduction	- continuation of species
Religious	- symbolic of union
Emotional	- extension of love for partner
Release of sexual urge	- release of frustration or libido
Financial	- prostitution
Duty	- socially expected, as in some marriages
Anti-social statement	- rejection of parental/social values
Ritual	- during particular ceremonies symbolic
Hedonistic (Recreational)	- enjoyment
Experimental	- exploration of sexual feelings and behaviors
Relational	- as part of wider social and attitudinal affinities
Dominance	- rape; expression of difference in relative power
Peer-sanctioned	- normative; status-associated
Forbidden or Taboo	- associated with guilt or punishment
Dynastic	- cementing relations between families or groups
Mentor	- teaching sexuality to younger individuals

quantitative descriptors are needed. Bell and Weinberg (1978), who accepted this view, reported on their extensive study of homosexuality. They found that assessment of sexual orientation must take into account the fact that there are many ways of being homosexual. Bell and Weinberg, in their extensive study of homosexuality and through cluster analysis methodology, derived five types of homosexual lifestyle and adaptation:

1. Closed coupleds were monogamous couples in a quasi-marriage.
2. Open coupleds were couples in primary but not monogamous relationships.
3. Functionals were non-coupled, had many sexual partners, and had little regret over their sexual orientation.
4. Dysfunctionals had many sexual partners but were regretful about their sexual orientation.
5. Asexuals had few or no partners and also were regretful about their asexual orientation.

This typology has helped many people understand the diversity of homosexualitites. Note that 29% of the Bell and Weinberg sample were not classifiable according to their inclusion criteria for the five types.

Besides these qualitative descriptions of lifestyles, Bell and Weinberg included a description of psychological adjustment. In their discussion of psychological adjustment, they found that types 1 and 3 were not distinguishable from heterosexual control group subjects, types 4 and 5 were less well-off psychologically, and type 2 subjects were at an intermediate level of psychological adjustment. This classification system is helpful in that it goes beyond simple sexual orientation assessment and looks at lifestyle and psychological adjustment.

So it is important to go beyond descriptors of sexual object-choice orientation to include measures of self-concept, which include self-identification, self-esteem, and self-acceptance.

In this vein, a person's self-identification or identity regarding sexual orientation can be defined as an organized set of perceptions and attached feelings that an individual holds about himself or herself with regard to some social category (Cass, 1983/84). Cass also divided identity into one's *presented* identity, which is the individual's picture of self presented to others with regard to a specific defined category, and the individual's *perceived* identity, which is the image held by another about self with regard to a specific identity. These different aspects of identity can be congruent or incongruent. Cass recognized, and psychotherapists should recognize also, that identiy is a socially constructed concept and is therefore time- and culture-bound.

A person's self-esteem is related to the individual's assessment of his value to himself and to others. It involves the individual's self-comparison to the standards he or she sets for him or herself (Troiden, 1984). Therefore, an individual may have a clear concept of who he or she is but not value that identity. In addition, a person's self-acceptance refers to his or her acceptance of personal identity. A person might be clear about his or her identity, but not accept that identity. These are separate components of self-concept and need to be evaluated separately when assessing sexual orientation. These concepts are basically conceptually confused by researchers and clinicians alike (Cass, 1983/84; Troiden, 1984). Finally, there needs to be more recognition that sexual orientation is not static. It changes infinitely in its complexity. One aspect of change has been described by a number of developmental theorists who have defined various stages of identity development for the homosexual (Cass, 1979; Coleman, 1981/82; Dank, 1971; Lee, 1977; Plummer, 1975; Troiden, 1979; Hencken & O'Dowd, 1977; Minton & McDonald, 1983/84). Admittedly, these models have had heuristic value and do not conform exactly to a definable reality. As with all stage models, they are subject to criticism because they appear to be invariant (Weinberg, 1984), are based upon a mistaken biological model of development (Weinberg, 1984), are inaccurately built upon male models of development (Faderman, 1984), reflect the researchers' own bias, and are not understanding of the constant state of emergence and becoming in human nature (Weinberg, 1984).

In defense of these models, they do serve as heuristic devices to understand better the developmental processes of identity development that do occur in some fashion. These models generally conform to the research data (see Coleman, 1981/82, and Cass, 1984). Obviously, individual variations occur, and these models do not always and everywhere conform to reality. However, they give the individual who is searching for identity integration some guidelines or markers of direction or progress. These models also aid psychotherapists in assisting clients in their growth and development.

It is true that in some models the final stage of identity synthesis is described in terms of the politics of gay identity and fidelity to that set of politics. However, the developmental models of Cass and Coleman describe identity synthesis or true integration, not just acceptance of the "politically correct." Identity synthesis or integration is simply the clarification of identity and matured self-concept, and it is a stage that recognizes fluidity and the nature of change of one's identity (Coleman 1981/82).

As Suppe (1984) remarked, "It seems to me that identity synthesis ultimately involves not only accepting but getting past one's homosexuality" (p. 12).

MAKING CLINICAL SENSE OF THE COMPLEXITY OF SEXUAL ORIENTATION

After reading this far, the clinician is often asking the question, "But what about my client?" The client wants to know whether he or she is gay or straight. Possibly in some future society, the developments that have been discussed with regard to our understanding of sexual orientation will

make the question obsolete. When one considers all the various combinations and constellations of factors, it is easy to see that the labels we
now utilize—homosexual, bisexual, and heterosexual—are becoming
outdated. *And yet*, sexual educators still teach the concepts of the Kinsey
Scale to wide-eyed, astonished audiences. The realitites of the world
today are that these labels still mean something to people, something very
important to their overall self-concept. We may dismiss their attempt at
labeling as futile, and yet the quest will go on.

A more pragmatic approach is needed. First, the clinician must
recognize that labels seem to be an important part of identity development
and psychological well-being at the present time. Further, the meaning of
sexual labels is a summing up of one's sexual and affectional experiences
and interests. It is a personal process, and also a declaration to the social
organization of one's standing within it (Paul 1983/84, p. 56).

While recognizing that these identities are only social constructs and
do not represent some essentiality of sexuality, psychotherapists can help
clients formulate their identity while helping them understand the very
nature of this social construction. As Cass (1983/84) states, " . . . the
concept of the homosexual identity is an unavoidable part of reality, built
into the cultured milieu of the present historical period as part of the
"psychologies" of our time" (p. 120–121). Clinicians must acknowledge that there are many people who perceive themselves as having an
identity that is a rather stable part of themselves, and thus they should not
attack, uncritically, what is a reality for those people (Cass, 1983/84).

Clinicians must also acknowledge that the lack of definition or
integrated identity, or the inability to have authentic relationships, is
negatively correlated to psychological health (e.g., Ross, 1971; Weinberg
& Williams, 1974; Bell & Weinberg, 1978).

Psychotherapists can rest easy in accepting the view that their
conceptualizations of sexual orientation are not any more or less normative
or unscientific than many other mental health classifications—and many
medical ones, too. Notions of sexual identity are unavoidably influenced
by normative standards and are value-laden. This does not mean that we
do not strive for objectivity or scientific rigor. It means simply that we
recognize and acknowledge our limitations and go on from there.

A PROPOSED MODEL OF CLINICAL ASSESSMENT

It seems, at this point in our history, that our assessment of sexual
orientation can be more comprehensive than the older methods previously
discussed. The proposed model rests upon this assumption, as well as on
some pragmatic limitations of the needs of the current clinical population

and the fact that the proposed clinical model does not necessarily lend itself to the needs and requirements of research.

The proposal model is built on a synthesis of the components model offered by Shively and De Cecco (1977), the KSOG (Klein, 1980), the Bell and Weinberg (1978) typologies, and a clinical methodology described by the author (Coleman, in press). As Suppe (1984) argued, the components model, if properly augmented, still furnishes the basis for a theory of sexual identity, and orientation.

The proposed model follows the suggestion by Bell and Weinberg (1978) that:

> Before one can say very much about a person on the basis of his or her sexual orientation, one must make a comprehensive appraisal of the relationship among a host of features pertaining to the person's life and decide very little about him, or her until a more complete and highly developed picture appears. (p. 329)

And, as MacDonald (1984) concludes, we should appreciate by now that there are multiple identities.

Therefore, the proposed model measures nine dimensions of sexual orientation (see Table 2).[1,2] The first dimension is a descriptor of lifestyle or current relationship status. Second, clients are asked to identify their current sexual orientation. Third, they are asked to identify what they would like their sexual orientation identity to be in the future. Fourth, they are asked to give a global assessment of comfort or self-acceptance of their current sexual orientation identity. Beyond these dimensions, the proposed model measures four more dimensions, including the four components of sexual identity—the only way in which sexual orientation identity can be clearly understood, and opens up the broader perspective of ourselves as sexual beings who are not simply defined by our genitalia.

In terms of assessing sexual orientation, the dimensions suggested by Shively and De Cecco (1977) (behavior, fantasies, and emotional attachments) are utilized. The remaining dimensions utilized by Klein (1980) (except for self-identification) are not utilized in a pragmatic effort to simplify and reduce the complexity to some degree. This reduction of variables generally conforms to the research findings of Wayson (1983) and Klein, Sepekoff, and Wolf (1985), although it could be argued that the dimension of social attraction might be added. While Klein (1980) argued for three dimensions over time (past, present, and ideal), past and present are collapsed in this methodology.

While Klein emphasizes that change occurs over time, the clinician is often confronted with the patient's concern regarding the future. It is the comparison of present to the future that yields the most valuable clinical

TABLE 2, Part 1

ASSESSMENT OF SEXUAL ORIENTATION

© Eli Coleman, Ph.D.

1986

Name or Code Number: _____   Age: ____   Date: _____

What is your current relationship status:

O Single, no sexual partners

O Single, one committed partner

O Single, multiple partners

O Coupled, living together (Committed to an exclusive sexual relationship)

O Coupled, living together (Relationship permits other partners under certain circumstances)

O Coupled, living apart (Committed to an exclusive sexual relationship)

O Coupled, living apart, (Relationship permits other sexual partners under certain circumstances)

O Other _____

In terms of my sexual orientation, I identify myself as . . .	**In the future, I would like to identify myself as . . .**
O Exclusively homosexual	O Exclusively homosexual
O Predominantly homosexual	O Predominantly homosexual
O Bisexual	O Bisexual
O Predominantly heterosexual	O Predominantly heterosexual
O Exclusively heterosexual	O Exclusively heterosexual
O Unsure	O Unsure

In terms of comfort with my current sexual orientation, I would say that I am . . .

O Very comfortable

O Mostly comfortable

O Comfortable

O Not very comfortable

O Very uncomfortable

Eli Coleman

TABLE 2, Part 2

INSTRUCTIONS:

Fill in the following circles by drawing lines to indicate which portion describes male or female elements. Indicate which portion of the circle is male by indicating (M) or female by indicating (F).

Example: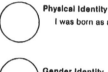

If the entire circle is male or female, simply indicate the appropriate symbol in the circle (M or F).

Example: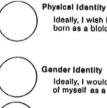

Fill out the circles indicating how it has been up to the present time as well as how you would like to see yourself in the future (ideal).

UP TO PRESENT TIME

Physical Identity
I was born as a biological . . .

Gender Identity
I think of myself
as a physical . . .

In my sexual fantasies,
I imagine myself as
a physical . . .

Sex-Role Identity
My interests, attitudes,
appearance and behaviors
would be considered to
be female or male
(as traditionally defined) . . .

Sexual Orientation Identity
My sexual behavior
has been with . . .

My sexual fantasies
have been with . . .

My emotional attachments
(not necessarily sexual)
have been with . . .

FUTURE (IDEAL)

Physical Identity
Ideally, I wish I had been
born as a biological . . .

Gender Identity
Ideally, I would like to think
of myself as a physical . . .

In my sexual fantasies, I
wish I could imagine
myself as a physical . . .

Sex-Role Identity
I wish my interests, attitudes,
appearance, and behaviors
would be considered
to be female or male
(as traditionally defined) . . .

Sexual Orientation Identity
I wish my sexual behavior
would be with . . .

I wish my sexual fantasies
would be with . . .

I wish my emotional attachments
(not necessarily sexual)
would be with . . .

information. Therefore, the model assesses the ninth dimension to include the individuals' past and present perceptions of their orientation and their idealized future. With this method, the problem of permanence is addressed, as well as yielding an additional measure of self-acceptance.

The other deviation in assessment is the use of circle graphs rather than Kinsey-type (0 to 6) ratings. Instead of individuals placing themselves on a line or adopting a certain number, circles are used that individuals can divide into percentages or slices of a pie (see Table 2). This method yields a graphic illustration of the patient's sexual orientation. If different time periods seem to be relevant given the client's sexual history, other sets of circles can be filled out. It is not necessary to be rigid in using these circles, because their main utility is clinical. The research capability of this method is not known at this time.

Once these circles are filled out, the patient and psychotherapist can discuss the implications, meanings, possible sources of distress, development deficits, and goals for therapy.

CONCLUSION

The labels homosexual, bisexual, and heterosexual seem meaningless when one understands the complexity of sexual orientation. The words "homosexual" and "heterosexual" seem the most limiting. If labels are used, the phrases "predominantly homosexual" or "predominantly heterosexual" are probably more accurate. The word "bisexual" probably should be used more freely to describe someone who has a mixture of same-sex and opposite-sex feelings and experience (see Klein & Wolf, 1985), not someone in the middle of every conceivable Kinsey continuum. In addition, this term recognizes the complexity of variations and combinations of physical, gender, sex-role, and sexual orientation identity. Psychotherapists need to help their patients define themselves, to recognize and value the complexity of their sexual orientation, and to further their overall sexual identity development and satisfaction.

NOTES

1. This assessment device was developed with the assistance, suggestions, and recommendations of many individuals. I would particularly like to acknowledge the revolutionary conceptualization of sexual orientation given to us by Alfred Kinsey and his associates. Further, I would like to acknowledge the research of Alan Bell and Martin Weinberg, John De Cecco and Michael Shively, and Fritz Klein. I would like to thank the staff and consultants of the Program in Human Sexuality, Orlo Otleson for his editorial assistance, and my colleagues of the Society for the Scientific Study of Sex for all of their encouragement and input. Finally, I would like to thank my clients who have found this assessment tool useful in their quest for a better understanding of, and comfort with, their sexual orientation identity.

2. Copies and further instructions of this assessment device may be obtained from the author.

REFERENCES

Bell, A. P., & Weinberg, M. S. (1978). *Homosexualities: A study of diversity among men and women.* New York: Simon & Schuster.

Cass, V. C. (1979). Homosexual identity formation: A theoretical model. *Journal of Homosexuality, 4,* 219–235.

Cass, V. C. (1983/84). Homosexual identity: A concept in need of defense. *Journal of Homosexuality, 9*(2/3), 105–126.

Cass, V. C. (1984). Homosexual identity formation. Testing a theoretical model. *Journal of Sex Research, 20*(2), 143–167.

Coleman, E. (1981/82). Developmental stages of the coming out process. *Journal of Homosexuality, 7*(2/3), 31–43.

Coleman, E. (in press). Bisexuality: Challenging our understanding of human sexuality. In E. Shelp (Ed.), *Sexuality and Medicine.* Manila: E. Reidel.

Dank, B. (1971). Coming out in the gay world. *Psychiatry, 34,* 180–197.

De Cecco, J. P., & Shively, M. G. (1983/84). From sexual identity to sexual relationships: A contractual shift. *Journal of Homosexuality, 9*(2/3), 1–26.

Faderman, L. (1984). The ''new gay'' lesbians. *Journal of Homosexuality, 10*(3/4), 85–95.

Hencken, J. D., & O'Dowd, W. T. (1977). Coming out as an aspect of identity formation. *Gay Academic Union Journal: Gai Saber, 1,* 18–22.

Kaplan, G. T., & Rogers, L. J. (1984). Breaking out of the dominant paradigm: A new look at sexual attraction. *Journal of Homosexuality, 10*(3/4), 71–75.

Kinsey, A. C., Pomeroy, W. B., & Martin, C. E. (1948). *Sexual behavior in the human male.* Philadelphia: W. B. Saunders.

Klein, F. (1978). *The bisexual option.* New York: Arbor House.

Klein, F. (December, 1980). Are you sure you're heterosexual? or homosexual? or even bisexual? *Forum Magazine,* pp. 41–45.

Klein, F., & Wolf, T. (1985). *Bisexualitites: Theory and research.* New York: Haworth Press.

Klein, F., Sepekoff, B., & Wolf, T. J. (1985). Sexual orientation: A multi-variate dynamic process. *Journal of Homosexuality, 11*(1/2), 35–49.

Lee, J. D. (1977). Going public: A study in the sociology of homosexual liberation. *Journal of Homosexuality, 3,* 49–78.

MacDonald, A. P., Jr. (1984). Reactions to issues concerning sexual orientations, identities, preferences, and choices. *Journal of Homosexuality, 10*(3/4), 23–27.

Minton, H. L., & McDonald, G. J. (1983/1984). Homosexual identity formation as a developmental process. *Journal of Homosexuality, 9*(2/3), 91–104.

Paul, J. P. (1983/84). The bisexual identity: An idea without social recognition. *Journal of Homosexuality, 9*(2/3), 45–63.

Plummer, K. (1975). *Sexual stigma: An interactionist account.* London: Routledge & Kegan Paul.

Ross, H. L. (1971). Modes of adjustment of married homosexuals. *Social Problems, 18,* 385–393.

Ross, M. W. (1984). Beyond the biological model: New directions in bisexual and homosexual research. *Journal of Homosexuality, 10*(3/4), 63–70.

Shively, M., & DeCecco, J. (1977). Components of sexual identity. *Journal of Homosexuality, 3,* 41–48.

Suppe, F. (1984). In defense of a multidimensional approach to sexual identity. *Journal of Homosexuality, 10*(3/4), 7–14.

Troiden, R. R. (1979). Becoming homosexual. A model of gay identity acquisition. *Psychiatry, 42,* 362–273.

Troiden, R. R. (1984). Self, self-concept, identity, and homosexual identity: Constructs in need of definition and differentiation. *Journal of Homosexuality, 10*(3/4), 97–109.

Wayson, P. (1983). *A study of personality variables in males as they relate to differences in sexual orientation.* Unpublished doctoral dissertation, California School of Professional Psychology, San Diego, California.

Weinberg, M. S., & Williams, C. J. (1974). *Male homosexuals: Their problems and adaptations.* New York: Oxford University Press.

Weinberg, T. S. (1984). Biology, ideology, and the reification of developmental stages in the study of homosexual identities. *Journal of Homosexuality, 10*(3/4), 77–84.

Developmental Issues
and Their Resolution
for Gay and Lesbian Adolescents

Emery S. Hetrick, MD
A. Damien Martin, EdD
New York University

SUMMARY. The primary developmental task for homosexually oriented adolescents is adjustment to a socially stigmatized role. Although the individual homosexual adolescent reacts with diversity and great resilience to societal pressures, most pass through a turbulent period that carries the risk of maladaptive behaviors that may affect adult performance. Despite individual variation, certain issues have been found to concern most homosexual adolescents. Empirical data from the Institute for the Protection of Lesbian and Gay Youth, Inc. in New York City suggests that isolation, family violence, educational issues, emotional stresses, shelter, and sexual abuse are the main concerns of youth entering the program. If not resolved, the social, cognitive, and social isolation may extend into adulthood, and anxiety, depressive symptoms, alienation, self-hatred, and demoralization may result. In a non-threatening supportive environment that provides accurate information and appropriate peer and adult role models, many of the concerns are alleviated and internalized negative attitudes are either modified or prevented from developing. The authors discuss the effects of prejudice and the impact of negative societal attitudes on the developing social and personal identities of homosexual youths.

All adolescents confront the need to integrate the biological, cognitive, psychological, and social changes that occur during this phase of human development. Sequential physical changes provide the framework for the social and psychological changes, including developing sexuality, that accompany puberty. While the physical changes are usually spoken of as

Dr. Hetrick is Clinical Assistant Professor of Psychiatry, New York University at Gouverneur Hospital, New York City; President and co-founder of the Institute for the Protection of Lesbian and Gay Youth, and the co-founder of Senior Action in a Gay Environment, both also in New York City.

Dr. Martin is Associate Professor in the Department of Communication Arts and Sciences, School of Education, Health, Nursing, and Arts Professions, New York University, and is Executive Director and co-founder of the Institute for the Protection of Lesbian and Gay Youth, New York City.

Correspondence may be addressed to the authors, 144 East 36th Street, New York, NY 10016.

puberty, the culturally dependent psychosocial processes are conceptualized within a somewhat larger framework called adolescence. The physical changes mark the beginning of this period of the life cycle, while the psychological and social aspects that inform the acquisition of independent adult functioning mark the loosely drawn endpoint.

Although biological and cognitive changes provide the framework, many view the development and maturation of psychological and social processes as the hallmark of the adolescent years, with the main task of adolescence being the creation of an autonomous and independent person no longer dependent on others for the management of internal and external affairs. (Brunstetter, 1985). There is no evidence that homosexual and heterosexual adolescents are different in their progress through general biological and cognitive changes. It is in the area of psychological and social development that the homosexually oriented adolescent must deal with issues different from those of the heterosexually oriented adolescent.

This paper will not address general issues of development common to all adolescents except as they relate to the special problems of the homosexual adolescent. Instead, it will focus on the development of the individual within the context of social stigmatization; that is, on the management of what Goffman (1963) has called ''a spoiled identity.'' An important aspect of this management is the "coming out" process described in several works (Dank, 1971; Troiden, 1979; Coleman, 1981/82). This process, which often begins before adolescence and continues throughout life, will not be discussed except as it relates to the issues discussed in this paper.

SOCIAL IDENTITY

Essential to the growth of autonomy as a social individual is the development of the sense of self. This sense of self, laid down from infancy and early childhood, includes not only internal intrapsychic components, but also the management of social roles. Adolescence involves the expansion of this ego identity, particularly in the realm of social roles.

For the homosexual adolescent, such expansion includes a realization that one is a member of a stigmatized minority group, a realization that leads to a denial of what Erikson (1963) defined as ''[t]he accrued confidence that the inner sameness and continuity prepared in the past are matched by the sameness and continuity of one's meanings for others'' (p. 261).

Allport (1958) defines a minority group as any group that suffers from unjustified negative action by the dominant group. Martin (1982b) has addressed the issue of minority status for the homosexually oriented elsewhere; therefore, we will not discuss objections to this concept in this paper. Nevertheless, the importance for this discussion lies in the recognition of society's negative attitudes and actions against the homosexually oriented and their effects on the developing adolescent. Allport (1958) defines these negative actions as occurring in three stages: antilocutions, discrimination, and violence. All three are interdependent. Thus, antilocutions provide the foundation for discrimination; antilocutions and discrimination both precede violence against the group.

Antilocutions are the rhetoric of prejudice, the negative verbal statements and beliefs about the hated group. For example: All Jews are communists; all Catholics must vote the way their priest tells them to vote; all blacks are lazy and on welfare; women cannot be effective workers because of menstruation, and so on. Each represents a negative categorical attitude based on error and overgeneralization. Antilocutions can range from derogatory and trivializing terms like "kike," "nigger," "spick," "faggot," or "dyke," to elaborate scientific theories designed to demonstrate the inferiority or danger of the group. Most people forget that racism was an accepted and respectable scientific theory during the 19th century (Mosse, 1978). Similarly, most do not recognize that psychoanalytic formulations about homosexuality are based largely on discarded hypotheses derived from Social Darwinism (Sulloway, 1979).

Antilocutions against homosexuals cover a wide range of charges. They include beliefs that homosexual men and women are predatory (Kardiner, 1954; Gilder, 1979) unsuitable for the "hard professions" (Voth, 1977; Decter, 1980), unable to form mature non-erotic relationships (Pattison & Pattison, 1980), inimical to the survival of the race (Socarides, 1975), and criminal seducers (Rupp, 1980). Homosexuality and homosexuals supposedly cause anorexia nervosa (Stern, 1962), crime in the streets (christian anti-communism crusade, 1981), the Second World War (Podhoretz, 1977), the Holocaust (Jackman, 1979), and lowered SAT scores (Falwell, 1984). Perhaps the most politically effective allegations, and the most destructive to the homosexual adolescent, are the charges that the homosexual is a danger to the family and to children (Kramer, 1983; LaHaye, 1982; Voth, 1977; Smith & Dilenno, 1979).

A recent book sold in many religious book stores has this to say:

> Most normal people hate and fear homosexual practices both because they fear their own passions, and because they are afraid for their own children. . . . Their fears are not empty. Besides being unnatural and sterile, homosexual acts are a contagious cause of tragedy, and destructive of the natural relationships between the sexes. For heterosexuals reproduce their kind by the use of sex, but active homosexuals multiply by the abuse of sex—by moral

contagion, and by seduction and rape. There are thousands of young boys in large American cities whose services have literally been bought by active homosexuals. It is for these reasons that religious and civil authorities oppose active homosexually (Smith & Dilenno, 1979).

Needless to say, the authors do not mention the many more thousands of young girls "whose services have literally been bought" by "active" heterosexuals. In this they resemble Thomas Aquinas, who taught that heterosexual rape and incest are preferable to homosexuality because rape and incest are more "natural" (Kelly, 1975).

Antilocutions lead logically into the next stage in the acting out of prejudice, discrimination. If one believes a group is dangerous and sick, it is only natural that one must quarantine that group, keep it separate from those who are fearful.

Discrimination against homosexuals takes many forms, of which the following are but a few examples. Immigration laws forbid the entry into this country of homosexuals from abroad; homosexuals are still fired from government jobs and discharged from the military solely because of their homosexuality; teachers, physicians, and other professionals still run the risk of losing their professional rights if discovered to be homosexual; parents can, and do, lose custody of their children because they are homosexual; homosexual couples can be thrown out of their apartments, with no recourse to law; wills have been overturned when a homosexual relationship is involved.

The most devastating acts of social discrimination are those that corrode one's self-worth and self-esteem. For blacks, the signs that said they could drink only from water fountains set aside for their use or use separate toilets were daily reminders that they were considered inferior, even in the basic human acts of alleviating thirst and of eliminating waste products. It is important to note that the incident that triggered the black civil rights movement of the 1950s and 1960s was not a lynching or an act of economic discrimination, but a matter involving humiliation and self-respect. When that one woman refused to move to the back of the bus, she was responding to a need for self-respect. It is the denial of that need that causes the most damage to individual members of minority groups.

While homosexuals may not be forced to use separate toilets or water fountains (although the military does make an issue of shared use of bathrooms as an excuse for keeping homosexuals out of the military), they often suffer from equally corrosive denials of their self-respect and self-worth. The most common perhaps is the daily need to hide an important aspect of their personal and social identity (Martin, 1982a).

Discrimination, coupled with the antilocutions, leads inexorably to the next stage, violence. Violence against the homosexually oriented is endemic, particluarly for the homosexual adolescent. These acts of violence range from the random slap in the school hallway to rape. Cities such as New York, Chicago, and San Francisco have had to set up special rape centers for men who, thought to be homosexual, are attacked sexually. Nor are homosexual women exempt from this violence.

Social role can be defined as a set of expectations for behavior (Heiss, 1981). The sets of behavior demanded for the multiple social roles that each individual performs are learned and enforced through a complex learning and policing process called socialization. Socialization is involved whether the social role is one that is highly approved by society, or one that is seen as a stigma. In the latter case, however, the socialization process is one of stigmatization, whereby both non-stigmatized as well as stigmatized individuals learn what is expected. While this culturally dependent process is primarily sociological in nature, it has implications for the development of stigmatized individuals.

The homosexual adolescent, like adolescents of other minority groups, must deal with the effects of antilocutions, discrimination, and violence. Antilocutions are internalized because of lack of access to accurate information or appropriate role models. They soon learn that knowledge of their sexual orientation may have a negative effect on their treatment in all sectors of society, including the family, school, job opportunities, and so forth. Finally, the homosexual adolescent must deal with the constant possibility of violence (National Gay Task Force, 1984).

As already mentioned, these problems are held in common with other minority groups. But each minority group suffers specific exigencies related to their group. For example, black youngsters may suffer from economic deprivation, while the average white homosexual youngster may not. (It should be noted, however, that homosexuality crosses all sociological differentiators. Thus, no matter the category—black, Jewish, Hispanic, Irish Catholic, priest, and so on,—there are homosexuals within that category.) Hispanic youths may suffer from the conflicting values of opposing cultures, while non-Hispanic homosexual youth may not. But homosexual adolescents have special problems, too. Blacks, Jews, and Hispanics are not thrown out of their families or religions at adolescence for being black, Jewish, or Hispanic; homosexual adolescents are. Even more importantly, other minority adolescents, no matter how terrible the social or economic deprivation under which they may exist, have a chance to develop a sense of the ''we'' versus ''they,'' the very essence of group identity; homosexual young people do not. As Dank (1971) put it:

> It is sometimes said that the homosexual minority is like any other minority group (Cory, 1951; Westwood, 1960); but in the case of early childhood socialization, it is not, for the parents of a Negro can communicate to their child that he is a Negro and what it is like

to be a Negro, but the parents of a person who is to become homosexual do not prepare their child to be homosexual—they are not homosexual themselves and they do not communicate to him , what is is like to be homosexual.

It is in this lack of preparation that homosexually oriented adolescents differ from their heterosexual counterparts, including those in other minority groups.

EFFECTS OF STIGMATIZATION

While the effects of stigmatization on blacks and Jews have been extensively documented (Allport, 1958), very little has been done on the effects of stigmatization on homosexuals. This is surprising because, as early as the 19th century, researchers like Kraft-Ebing (1904/1965), Iwan Bloch (1908/1936), and even Freud (1903) pointed out that many of the problems of the homosexually oriented were caused by societal oppression rather than by homosexuality itself. The following section will outline these effects in broad form. The material is drawn primarily from the authors' experience dealing with homosexual adolescents at The Institute for the Protection of Lesbian and Gay Youth, Inc. (IPLGY) in New York City, a social service agency established to meet the needs of homosexually oriented adolescents and their families.

Presenting Problems

The figures cited below represent the frequency and type of presenting problems on intake of 329 adolescents who came to IPLGY during its first year of operation. The agency serves young people between the ages of 12 to 21. The comparatively high mean age listed results from tallying only those who physically appeared at the agency for a face-to-face interview. Figures do not include those who received telephone counseling alone, a major part of our work. Initially, we tended to have the older adolescent on site for two reasons. First, the older adolescent has greater freedom of movement and is therefore more able to come to the Institute; younger adolescents do not have such freedom and could ask for help only through the telephone. Second, older adolescents had greater access to our initial outreach efforts: advertisements in a local newspaper, referral by other agencies, word of mouth, and so on. During the second year of operation, the data for which is not given here, the mean age had dropped to approximately 16.1. Other demographic figures, especially the ethnic and racial breakdowns, appeared to be the same. Thirty-seven percent of the clients were black, 35% white, 24% Hispanic, 2% Asian, and 2% other (Polynesian, Indian, Arab); 28% were female, 72% were male. The ethnic and racial breakdown appeared to match almost exactly the distribution in the New York City Public High School system; the male-to-female ratio matches that found in most youth-serving social services agencies in New York City. No exact figures for religious affiliation were available during the study for these first clients, but the staff reported a wide range including Roman Catholicism, many Protestant sects, Judaism, including Hasidic and Orthodox Jewish clients, and Islamic and Buddhist clients.

The figures given below represent only presenting problems as elicited at the initial interview; that is, the client stated it as a concern or problem. For various reasons, clients sometimes did not mention certain issues at the first interview. However, once they were engaged in counseling, especially group counseling, some of these issues arose. Therefore, actual figures are much higher for each presenting problem, especially in the areas of family, violence, and sexual abuse. The figures also represent interrelated multi-problem situations. For example, a young person might come to us because he had been beaten by his family, thrown out on the streets, and was homeless. Thus, he would be listed as having presenting problems with family, violence, and a need for shelter.

Isolation. The most frequent presenting problem was isolation. This isolation was often quite extensive and was realized in three major interrelated areas: social isolation, emotional isolation, and cognitive isolation. The socially isolated young person reported having no one to talk to, feeling alone within every social situation, including the family, peers, school, and church or synagogue. Such isolation is usually closely connected to fear of discovery and the concomitant need to hide (Martin 1982a; Hunter & Martin, 1983; Robinson & Martin, 1983). However, even those young people who had a circle within which they could be open—for example, juvenile prostitutes—reported social isolation. In the latter case, the young males in particular felt their contacts with adults were exploitative and that their contacts with homosexual peers, usually other juvenile prostitutes, were competitive. Many young people reported a sexual involvement with adults based more on a need to have some sort of social contact rather than on sexual desire for the older individual.

Emotional isolation, while related to social isolation, is slightly different. In these cases, clients often reported feeling separated affectionally and emotionally from all social networks, especially the family. They may feel afraid to show friendship for a friend of the same sex for fear of being misunderstood or giving away their secretly held sexual orientation; they may feel emotionally distanced and isolated from their families because they must be on guard at all times. Again, in those instances where young people are sexually involved with adults, they often report feeling that sex is the only bond possible with another homosexual person, that they are not valued as separate individuals, and that they have no emotional or spiritual worth other than as sex objects. This depreciation of self, especially when it occurs during adolescence, can significantly impair the development of feelings of self-worth and confidence so necessary to adult functioning. This in turn can feed into a belief that one is unworthy to receive love or affection. Before becoming involved with the Institute, clients often believed that it was impossible for homosexuals to have ongoing committed, loving relationships. Furthermore, the clients often reported a mistrust of their own emotional feelings and the motives of others. The ensuing self-doubt could dampen curiosity and impair growth of exploratory behavior.

Social isolation also leads to two forms of coping behavior that are often detrimental to development of social roles with peers. Young males often discover places where it is possible to make sexual contact, but these contacts do not usually lead to social interactions and networking other than of a sexual nature. As a result, the young male homosexual develops a social pattern in which sexual behavior is an initial stage of social interaction with peers, rather than a behavior that results from interaction on other levels. Young lesbians are so isolated that when they do meet another woman they tend to become locked into fused relationships that do not allow for the development of other friendships or peer networks. While fusion is a difficulty in adult lesbian relationships, it is especially troubling for the teenage lesbian who is deprived of important social learning during a critical developmental stage. While it impossible to state definitely, it may be that fusion in adult lesbian relationships, and so-called "promiscuity" in the adult male homosexual, may be in large part related to socialization processes during adolescence.

Cognitive isolation is directly related to a lack of access to accurate information about homosexuality, including a lack of appropriate role models. The most fundamental information is denied to these young people. It is not surprising, therefore, that the clients often demonstrate an appalling ignorance of what it means to be homosexual, reflecting the basest stereotypes about homosexual people and therefore about themselves.

While not reflected in the figures given here, isolation is also the major presenting problem in the telephone counseling done at IPLGY. In addition to reports that they have no one to talk to, that they must constantly hide, homosexual youths reveal severe cognitive dissonance when requesting basic information. Frequently they ask: "Does this mean I have to be a hairdresser or something like that?" "Will I start messing around with little kids?" "Am I going to get AIDS?" "The Pope hates homosexuals! How can I be a queer?" They report that they are afraid they will be found out; that they want to run away because the pressures of hiding are too much; and perhaps most frighteningly, that they want to kill themselves rather than be a "queer." As will be discussed below, suicide ideation and attempts are sometimes major results of the almost total isolation suffered by homosexual youth.

Family. The second most frequent presenting problem is difficulty with the family. After integration into IPLGY programs, almost all youth state that that they feel distanced and detached from their families. Difficulties can range from fear of rejection by parents to violence and expulsion from the home. Difficulties within the family are clearly linked to stigmatization. Many of the young people who come to us report no difficulties within the family prior to their becoming aware of their homosexuality. The revelation of a homosexual orientation, or the fear of such revelation, often creates a crisis situation. The resolution can lead to the reintegration of the young person after the parents and siblings have reconciled themselves to the sexual orientation of the child. A negative outcome can be reinforcement of secrets, enhanced detachment, and breakdown of communication in the family.

There are times, however, when the young person's attempt to handle their burgeoning sexual identity, rather than the fact of homosexuality per se, may cause family difficulties. For example, some young teenagers, especially males, may begin to be truant in order to make sexual contact. In large part, the truancy seems more related to the social isolation discussed above rather than sexual desire alone. Thus, the young person avoids school to escape the pressures of hiding, the taunts of classmates, or humiliations within the classroom and goes where he need not hide. The parents may be unaware of the reasons for the truancy, or be more upset by the truancy than the sexual orientation per se. Parents have brought their young people to IPLGY, explaining that while they are not happy that their child is homosexual, they are more upset by the delinquent behavior, such as truancy, that may be involved.

Fear of discovery, especially by the family, is also the basis for one problem that is appearing more frequently at IPLGY, the pregnant teenage lesbian. Some young lesbians, out of a need to hide their sexual orientation, may indulge in heterosexual sexual acting out, ranging from simple experimentation to heterosexual promiscuity. They report feeling that their families can more easily accept an unwanted pregnancy rather than a homosexual daughter.

Violence and Suicide. One-third of the clients had suffered violence because of their sexual orientation; 49% of this violence was at the hands of the family. A related but separate finding was that 20% of our clients had either attempted suicide or had strong suicide ideation. The incidence was higher for those who had only telephone contact with IPGLY. This figure, while alarmingly high, is not surprising in light of the report by Bell and Weinberg (1978), who reported that 20% of their respondents attempted suicide before age 20, and Saghir and Robins (1973), who reported that of the six respondents in their study who had attempted suicide, five had done so before the age of 20.

The high percentage of suicide attempts during the teenage years, and the corresponding drop after the teens, is most probably related to the isolation reported above. After graduation from high school, homosexual people are more likely to have the freedom of movement, either at their jobs or in college, to make contact with their homosexually oriented peers.

Emotional Problems. Nineteen percent reported some form of emotional problem, usually involving depressive feelings and anxiety. Eight percent gave evidence of other emotional problems: for example, previous psychiatric hospitalization, taking prescription anti-psychotic medication, involvement in therapy, and so on.

Shelter. Twenty percent presented with shelter problems that ranged from the need for emergency shelter to a need for help in finding alternate housing. The former, a need for emergency shelter, was much more prevalent among young males than females, reflecting to a certain extent the different ways in which discovery of a homosexual orientation is handled within families when the child is male or female. A male child is at greater risk for violent expulsion from the home; a female is more likely to suffer physical and verbal abuse but be kept in the home, at least until graduation from high school.

Job-Related Problems. Job-related problems can be divided into two major areas: difficulties in finding work, and fears of being fired if one is discovered to be homosexual. We found that many young people are afraid to apply for jobs, or have difficulty on the job, because of their perceived need to hide their homosexuality. The fear of humiliation is even stronger than the fear of violence.

Drug Use. Five percent of the clients gave evidence of problems with alcohol, 6% problems with pot, and 9% problems with harder drugs, primarily cocaine. These figures are questionable, however. We have discovered that alcohol abuse is much more prevalent than either marijuana or other drug use, although it is difficult to give a figure. We have also discovered that, as would be expected from other studies, those who abuse alcohol are at much higher risk for suicide attempts.

Because of the skewed nature of this sample population, because of the method of data collection, and because of the present lack of valid long term follow-up studies, it is impossible to make conclusions that would apply to teenage or adult homosexuals. The general impression, however, is that the percentage of drug and alcohol abuse among homosexual teenagers is no greater than that among heterosexual adolescents who apply for services at other agencies.

Sexual Abuse. During the intake interview, 6% of our clients (15 males, 4 females) reported sexual abuse. As mentioned earlier, the actual figures are probably much higher; based on reports of counselors and group leaders, the figure is closer to 17%, with the majority of victims males. Apparently, sexual abuse is not mentioned initially for three reasons: shame, non-recognition of the abuse as abuse, and a feeling that it is not abuse when it happens to one who is homosexual.

Coping Strategies

Homosexual adolescents develop coping mechanisms to deal with the whole process of stigmatization. These strategies may vary both in effectiveness and in the impact they have on the individual, but some may have negative implications for the development of a mature adult sense of self. Space does not permit an extensive discussion of these strategies, but a few are very relevant to an understanding of developmental issues for the homosexual adolescent. It is difficult to say the degree to which an individual may use any of the strategies, or the degree to which a strategy may have a negative effect. For example, aggression against one's group, a strategy related to identification with the dominant group, can range from activities against other homosexual people to repetition of typical antilocutions. Most would agree that the individual who has internalized society's hatred to such an extent that he or she will participate in attacks on the group is much more damaged than the individual who accepts stereotypical negative beliefs. In addition, coping strategies such as being in the closet can be absolutely necessary in certain situations. For example, at IPLGY we strongly recommend to clients who are still in high school that they think very carefully before coming out to their parents. We have seen several instances where a young person, confident of the love of his or her parents, reveals his or her homosexuality and then ends up on the street. Conversely, it is important to note that some do receive support and help from their parents.

Learning to Hide. Perhaps the most important coping strategy for the homosexually oriented adolescent is learning to hide. Goffman (1963) identifies two types of stigmatized individual, the discredited, and the discreditable. The discredited individual is one who is clearly identified as stigmatized. Thus, any individual who cannot hide, like the dark-skinned person in a racist society or the "effeminate" male or "butch" female in a homophobic society, is discredited. Those who can hide, and choose to do so, are the discreditable—that is, those who must live with the constant possibility of discovery. The process by which the homosexual adolescent is socialized to become "discreditable" is discussed in greater detail in another paper (Martin, 1982a). It is important to point out, however, that individuals in such a position must constantly monitor their behavior in all circumstances: how one dresses, speaks, walks, and talks become constant sources of possible discovery. One must limit one's friends, one's interests, and one's expression, for fear that one might be found guilty by association. Again, adolescence is the transitional stage between childhood and adulthood. It is during adolescence that we further expand and develop our management of social identities, an expansion that must include the learning of adult social interactions with others. The individual who must hide of necessity learns to interact on the basis of deceit governed by fear of discovery (Martin, 1982a; Goffman, 1963). Such a pattern has inevitable intrapsychic and social effects, both on the adolescent who must learn to dissimulate, and on the adult who represents the end result of the process.

Self-monitoring, as well as the monitoring of others' reactions, is essential to interpersonal communication and relating. The monitoring of the reactions of others may be either neglected or distorted, however, if one is overmonitoring one's own behavior. In addition, each successive act of deception, each moment of monitoring which is unconscious and automatic for others, serves to reinforce the belief in one's difference and inferiority. Perry, Gawell, and Gibbon (1956) point out:

> The awareness of inferiority means that one is unable to keep out of consciousness the formulation of some chronic feeling of the worst sort of insecurity, and this means that one suffers anxiety and perhaps even something worse . . . The fear that others can disrespect a person because of something he shows means that he is always insecure in his contact with other people . . . now that represents an almost fatal deficiency of the self-system.

The process of deception may hinder the development of nonerotic friendships between members of the same sex. During this transition period between childhood and adulthood, when it is difficult to separate feelings of friendship from erotic feelings, the young homosexual adolescent must be careful not to become too close for fear that the closeness will be misunderstood on either side. This distancing may be interpreted by interested adults, such as parents and guidance counselors, as withdrawal indicative of pathological behavior. Unaware of the actual meaning of the withdrawal, the concerned adults usually do not discuss with the young homosexual issues related to sexual orientation and the social management of homosexuality.

Socialization processes always involve an inculcation of values and a sense of order in the universe, each serving to illuminate and reinforce the other. Lack of access to accurate information, lack of opportunity for non-erotic socialization, and, most important, lack of role models, do not permit an open, balanced evaluation of those values that underlie the predominant sense of order. Therefore, the adult homosexual may develop as conservative and traditional and be steeped in the predominant group values. This may often foster a conflict between those values that deny the individual homosexual's worth and that individual's belief in his or her inherent self-worth, a conflict which can result in alienation, anxiety, and demoralization.

Cognitive dissonance of this depth can be a critical issue for the adolescent. One becomes, in a sense, separate from oneself; a member of, but still separate from, one's primary group. For example, devout Catholic or Orthodox Jewish adolescents have a personal identity closely intertwined with their social identities as Catholics or Jews. Recognition of a homosexual sexual orientation leads not only to a conflict between what they are feeling and what they have been taught about sexual morality, but to a questioning of their sense of self as Catholic or Jewish, as well as a questioning of their sense of belonging to their primary group. That critical faculty of belonging to a primary group, the differentiation between "we" and "they," gets lost. To belong, they must condemn and attempt to repress their developing sexuality; to accept their sexuality, they must cease to belong.

Denial of Membership. Allport (1958) describes several coping strategies that often harm the individual who employs them. They are: (a) denial of membership; (b) identification with the dominant group, including self-hatred; and (c) self-fulfilling negativism. Each is interrelated and each stems from the social processes we have already described. In a society in which even a father can say that the worst possible thing that could happen to his child is homosexuality (Epstein, 1970), it is not too surprising that as a young person slowly begins to realize that he or she is one of "them," that that young person would adopt one or more of these mechanisms.

Denial of membership, hiding one's identity, and dissimulation become an almost inevitable result. Troiden (1979) documented part of this process in his work on the development of a healthy sexual identity in homosexual men. He found that all his subjects went through a phase that he called "dissociation and signification." During this stage, the men recognized certain actions and feelings as homosexual, but denied their significance. Thus, overt homosexual acts became "a phase," "something I would grow out of," "just because there weren't any girls around," and so forth. These respondents had tried to separate themselves from the meaning of their acts, especially as it related to their possible membership in the hated group, homosexuals. These rationalizations and denials of group membership are often reinforced by well-meaning counselors and therapists to the detriment of the individual homosexual.

A common report from our clients is that previous counselors have told them that their homosexual feelings and behaviors do not mean they are homosexual. Various explanations are given: "You are passing through a stage"; You are too young to make up your mind"; "That happens to lots of boys (girls)—it means nothing." Perhaps the most interesting and inane explanation was given to one 14-year-old girl: "You're too pretty to be a lesbian." These comments reinforce the denial of membership in the hated group, partly through confirmation of the belief that to be homosexual is not a thing to be desired. The difficulty with such reinforcement is that it postpones and complicates the whole process of dealing with a stigmatized social identity.

Identification with the Dominant Group. Denial of group membership is intimately intertwined with identification with the dominant group and, thus, with self-hatred. If one believes that heterosexuality is indeed better than homosexuality, then often one may try to become heterosexual. The resulting failure can cause one to hate the homosexual desires that prevent complete identification with the dominant group (Hetrick & Martin, 1984). This self-hatred, also known formally as Ego Dystonic Homosexuality (American Psychiatric Association, 1980), can lead, in turn, to aggression against one's own group.

Self-Fulfilling Negativism. All adolescents must cope with value systems. The homosexual adolescent is faced with the task of examining the values of a society which universally condemns his or her new role. One response is to pare down one's expectations for oneself and limit one's choices to those that fit the stereotype. This in turn may lead to an attitude characterized by what Allport (1958) called a "self-fulfilling negativism." Anything negative in one's life occurs because of one's group membership. Self-fulfilling negativism creates the attitude that one's own efforts mean nothing, that one's race, religion, sexual orientation, or ethnic identity is an insurmountable barrier to achievement. The major problem is that there is often a grain of truth in the fear. But once an individual acquiesces completely in the belief, it becomes self-fulfilling. The attitude can have an effect on matters ranging from educational choices to safe-sex practices. At times, homosexually oriented adolescents will not seek help for an array of problems, ranging from homelessness to medical needs, because they are afraid they will be humiliated or reviled as homosexual (Hunter & Martin, 1983; Robinson & Martin, 1983). Many times this is not the case, for instead they would be treated with professional care and respect. But, nonetheless, the strength of the fear negates the perceived professionalism of those dedicated to helping them.

Gender Deviance. Contrary to the stereotype, the majority of young people who come to IPLGY are not gender deviant in either behavior or dress. At IPLGY the authors have found gender deviance, especially that related to cross-dressing, to revolve around four basic issues: Androgeny, transvestism, cross-dressing as a defense mechanism, and cultural beliefs about masculinity, femininity, and homosexuality.

A small percentage of homosexually oriented adolescents can be described as androgenous. These young people, both male and female, do not cross dress yet are often described as "effeminate" or "butch." Their appearance and behavior does not mimic the opposite sex so much as reflect deviation from gender standards for their own sex.

Some clients appear to be "true transvestites" in that they derive great satisfaction and even sexual pleasure from cross-dressing. Primarily male, they are a very small percentage of all homosexually oriented youth, and are even a smaller percentage of those homosexual youth who do cross dress.

A third group seems to cross-dress, or indulge in other forms of gender-deviant behavior, as a form of defense, including hostile acting out. Thus, a young man who knows that a social worker in an agency is either nervous about, or dislikes him for, his homosexuality will exaggerate gender-deviant behavior, including cross-dressing, as an act of defiance of the accepted norm. This, of course, often interferes with his receiving the services to which he is entitled. Such maneuvers may also be an attempt to enhance threatened self-esteem. Unfortunately, those very maneuvers may become so habitual as to be thought of by some professionals as characterological, and may also contribute to his or her problems in therapy. In addition, gender-deviant behavior that is provocative can interfere with establishing relationships with other homosexual peers.

The question of gender identity, and thus of gender behavior, is further complicated in minority cultures that emphasize machismo. So called deviant gender behavior, especially cross-dressing, in these cultures seems to reflect two related but distinct processes. While these processes apply equally to male and female gender behavior, female deviation from dressing norms and other kinds of gender behavior are tolerated more than deviations by males. Therefore, the following discussion will focus on males, but it must be remembered that it applies to females as well.

In cultures with a highly developed sense of machismo, gender distinctions are rigid and concrete, with little allowance for variation or deviation. One is or is not a man; there are no gradations. The child is raised to believe that to be a male, one must have sexual desire for a female. If the young male does not have such desire, he sometimes reasons that he, therefore, must not be male and wants to be, or basically is, female and must behave accordingly. At IPLGY we have found that many cross-dressers, especially those from black and Hispanic communities, will stop cross-dressing once they are exposed to individuals, peers or homosexual adults, who do not behave as they think a homosexual is supposed to behave, either peers or homosexual adults.

In these cultures with rigidly drawn distinctions between male and female behavior, the stereotype of the effeminate homosexual becomes a social role. Thus, those youngsters who are slightly androgenous, or who choose not to hide, may conform to the culture's expectations and exaggerate deviant gender behavior. Several of our clients report that this serves as a protection in that once they are clearly identified as conforming to the social role of "faggot" or "maricon," they are at less risk for violence.

SUMMARY

Discussions of development often center around changes that occur in interdependent stages. We have focused on specific issues that arise for the homosexual adolescent, rather than on milestones of development. The roots of many of these issues may lie in the pre-adolescent lives of homosexuals, and their results can extend into adulthood. Nevertheless, these issues usually achieve primary importance during adolescence.

We have focused on the interaction of psychological and social factors. The primary issue for the young person is entry into a stigmatized role. The stigmatization process, like most socialization processes, is patterned and rule-governed with generally predictable results. This does not mean, however, that effects on the homosexual adolescent are predetermined. As in all examinations of development, it must be remembered that individuals react, learn, and handle problems differently. Yet although they act as individuals, this does not mean that we cannot identify shared issues, such as social, cognitive, and emotional isolation, but merely that there will be variations. While space does not permit full discussion of the variations, we must stress their importance.

A second danger in focusing on problems and coping strategies is the possibility of giving the impression that homosexuality invariably leads to unhappiness. Studies have shown most homosexually oriented persons develop happy and productive lives, in which as Troiden (1979) puts it, they achieve a homosexual identity where emotionality and sexuality are fused (Weinberg & Williams, 1974; Bell & Weinberg, 1978). Nothing in our discussion should be construed as suggesting that the homosexually oriented, as a group, are less well-adjusted than their heterosexual counterparts. At the risk of redundancy, we repeat that the major developmental issues revolve around their entry into a stigmatized social identity. The fact of stigmatization creates situations and problems that must be resolved. And most homosexual people do resolve them. These resolutions can themselves be viewed in a developmental framework (Martin, 1982a; Hetrick & Martin 1984), and for many they extend well into adulthood.

The problems cited—isolation, family, violence, educational issues, emotional stresses, shelter, and sexual abuse—were empirically derived from the reports of young people who come to IPLGY. The coping strategies that have been found are attempts by some adolescents to survive emotionally and psychologically in a hostile environment. One learns to hide to avoid society's sanctions against being homosexual. Unfortunately, that hiding process is also one of society's punishments. Anxiety, alienation, self-hatred, and demoralization may result; these may be brief in duration or may last into adulthood. Many youth may need only simple remedies, while others may need intensive treatment. At IPLGY these problems often disappear or are ameliorated once the adolescent finds himself or herself in a non-threatening, non-erotic milieu where they can obtain accurate information and can interact and identify with peers.

The opportunity to socialize in a healthy environment—a process that is taken for granted for their heterosexual counterparts—helps homosexual adolescents cope while interacting with others. Therefore, the solutions to many of the problems that homosexually oriented adolescents face are also social in nature. First, they need access to accurate information, including adult homosexual role models. Parenthetically, we might note that adult homosexual role models, as sources of accurate information about homosexuality, would be beneficial to heterosexual adolescents as well. Second, homosexual adolescents need opportunities for socialization with their peers in other than sexual settings. And third, there is a need to counter the antilocutions on all levels. For example, families react with shame and guilt to homosexuality in a child partly because of the widespread belief that homosexuality is the result of bad parenting.

We have not discussed the programs developed at IPLGY to address these problems, for they lie outside the scope of this article. However, our experience with these programs leads us to believe that homosexually oriented adolescents have amazing resilience. Unfortunately, they are one population within the homosexual community for whom programs have not been extensively developed and yet are so needed. Psychotherapists, in conjunction with social service, mental health, and educational institutions, can help develop these programs. The goal is to maximize successful maturation into adulthood and to minimize problems of stigmatization.

REFERENCES

Allport, G. (1958). *The nature of prejudice*. Garden City, NY: Doubleday.
American Psychiatric Association. (1980). *Diagnostic and statistical manual of mental disorders* (3rd ed.). Washington, DC: American Psychiatric Association Press.
Bell, A. P., & Weinberg, M. S. (1978). *Homosexualities: A study of diversity among men and women*. New York: Simon & Schuster.

Bloch, I. (1936). *The sexual life of our times.* (M. Eden Paul, Trans.) New York: Rebman. (Original work published 1908.)

Brunstetter, R. W. (1985). Normal adolescent development. In H. R. Kaplin & B. Sadock (Eds.), *Comprehensive textbook of psychiatry* (Vol. 2) (4th ed.) (pp. 1608–1613). Baltimore: Williams & Wilkins.

Christian Anti-communism Crusade. (1981). *Newsletter,* p. 21. Long Beach, CA.

Coleman, E. (1981/82). Developmental stages of the coming out process. *Journal of Homosexuality, 7*(2/3), 31–44.

Cory, D. W. (1951). *The homosexual in America.* New York: Greenberg.

Dank, B. M. (1971). Coming out in the gay world. *Psychiatry, 34,* 180–197.

Decter, M. (1980, September). The boys on the beach. *Commentary,* pp. 35–48.

Epstein, J. (1970, September). Homo/hetero: The struggle for sexual identity. *Harper's Magazine,* pp. 36–51.

Erickson, E. (1963). *Childhood and society* (2nd ed.). New York: Norton.

Falwell, J. (1984, April 24). Quoted in Flax, E., Falwell packs Irvine for speech on conservatism. *The Daily Pennsylvanian,* p. 1.

Freud, S. (1953). Three essays on the theory of sexuality. In J. Strachey (Ed. and Trans.), *The standard edition of the complete psychological works of Sigmund Freud* (Vol. 7, pp. 123–245). London: Hogarth Press. (Original work published 1905.)

Gilder, G. (1979, April). Letters to the editor. *Commentary,* pp. 4, 8–9.

Goffman, E. (1963). *Stigma: Notes on the management of spoiled identity.* Englewood Cliffs, NJ: Prentice-Hall.

Heiss, J. (1981). Social roles. In M. Rosenberg & R. H. Turner, (Eds.), *Social psychology: Sociological perspectives* (pp. 94–132). New York: Basic Books.

Hetrick, E., & Martin, A. D. (1984). Ego-dystonic homosexuality: A developmental view. In E. Hetrick & T. Stein (Eds.), *Innovations in psychotherapy with homosexuals.* Washington DC: American Psychiatric Press.

Hunter, J., & Martin, A. D. (1983). *A comparison of the presenting problems of heterosexually and homosexually oriented students.* New York: IPLGY, Inc.

Jackman, A. I. (1979). *The paranoid homosexual basis of antisemitism and kindred hatred.* New York: Vantage Books.

Kardiner, A. (1954). *Sex and morality.* New York: Bobbs Merrill.

Kelly, G. (1975). *The political struggle of active homosexuals to gain social acceptance.* Chicago: Franciscan Herald Press.

Kraft-Ebing, R. von (1965). *Psychopathia sexualis.* (12th German ed.) (F. S. Klaf, Trans.). New York: Bell. (Original work published 1904.)

Kramer, R. (1983). *In defense of family: Raising children in America today.* New York: Basic Books.

LaHaye, T. (1982). *The battle for the family.* Old Tappan, NJ: Fleming H. Revell.

Martin, A. D. (1982a). Learning to hide: The socialization of the gay adolescent. In S. C. Feinstein, J. G. Looney, A. Schwartzberg, & A. Sorosky (Eds.), *Adolescent psychiatry: Developmental and clinical studies* (Vol. 10, pp. 52–65). Chicago: University of Chicago Press.

Martin, A. D. (1982b). The minority question. *Etcetera, a review of general semantics, 39*(1), 22–42.

Mosse, G. L. (1978). *Towards the final solution: A history of European racism.* New York: Howard Fertig.

National Gay Task Force. (1984). *Anti-gay/lesbian victimization: A study by the National Gay Task Force in cooperation with lesbian organizations in eight U.S. cities.* New York: National Gay Task Force.

Pattison, E. M., & Pattison, M. L. (1980). Ex-Gays: Religiously mediated change in homosexuals. *American Journal of Psychiatry,* 1553–1562.

Perry, H., Gawell, M., & Gibbon, M. (1956). *Clinical studies in psychiatry.* New York: Norton.

Podhoretz, N. (1977, October). The culture of appeasement. *Harper's Magazine,* pp. 25–32.

Robinson, G., & Martin, A. D. (1983). *A needs survey of professional youth serves on problems and issues in the delivery of services to gay and lesbian youth.* New York: IPLGY, Inc.

Rupp, J. D. (1980). Homosexually related deaths. In W. Curran, A. L. McGarry, & C. S. Petty (Eds.), *Modern legal medicine: Psychiatry and forensic science* [Author: Supply Page Numbers]. Philadelphia: F. A. Davis.

Saghir, M. T., & Robins, E. (1973). *Male and female homosexuality: A comprehensive investigation*. Baltimore: Williams & Wilkins.

Socarides, C. (1975). *Beyond sexual freedom*. New York: Quadrangle.

Smith, H. F., & Dilenno, J. (1979). *Sexual inversion: The questions: The church's answers*. Boston: Daughters of St. Paul.

Stern, J. (1962). *The sixth man*. New York: McFadden.

Sulloway, F. J. (1979). *Freud: Biologist of the mind*. New York: Basic Books.

Troiden, R. (1979). Becoming homosexual: A model of gay identity acquisition. *Psychiatry, 42*, 362–373.

Voth, H. (1977). *The castrated family*. Kansas City, MO: Sheed, Andrews, & McMeel.

Weinberg, M. S., & Williams, C. J. (1974). *Male homosexuals*. New York: Oxford University Press.

Westwood, G. (1960). *A minority: A report on the life of the male homosexual in Great Britain*. London: Longmans, Green.

Therapeutic Issues and Intervention Strategies with Young Adult Lesbian Clients: A Developmental Approach

Christine Browning, PhD
University of California, Irvine

SUMMARY. This paper examines the coming out process within an adult developmental context. Therapeutic issues which surface for the young adult lesbian client include separation from parents, development of social support, exploration of career/vocational goals, and the establishment of intimate relationships. Intervention strategies are suggested which facilitate the coming out process and help the client integrate her sexual orientation within her emerging adult identity.

Specific developmental tasks surface during late adolescence and early adulthood for all women. Some of these tasks represent concerns related to self-definition, autonomy, separation from parental authority, development of competence, and development of intimate relationships. Erickson (1974) notes that integrating adult sexuality into one's personality, as well as learning how to fit into society with its norms and values, is a fundamental aspect of identity development. It is this aspect of identity formation which holds particular significance for the emerging adult lesbian.

When issues of sexual orientation surface during this time of late adolescence and early adulthood, resolution of these developmental tasks become even more challenging. The conflict includes not only the internal struggle of coming out to self, family, and others, but also determining how to live a satisfying and productive life as an adult in a homophobic and sexist society.

Presented in this article are some of the ways in which specific developmental issues may effect the coming out process and the development of a positive lesbian identity. Therapists who understand the

Dr. Browning is Staff Psychologist at the Counseling Center, University of California, Irvine, CA 92714, and is in private practice in Laguna Beach, CA. Portions of this paper were presented at the 92nd Annual Meeting of the American Psychological Association, Toronto, Canada, in August, 1984. Correspondence may be sent to the author at the above address.

developmental context and its limitations are better able to facilitate the coming out process and integration of the woman's sexual identity with other aspects of her identity. Coming out does not end, circumvent, or replace developmental issues, but may obscure or confound critical issues for both the client and therapist.

A brief description of the coming out process will be presented, followed by an elaboration of adult developmental theory. Specific developmental tasks will be examined in relation to the coming out process, and intervention strategies will be described.

THE COMING OUT PROCESS

Coming out to oneself has been described by many authors as a multi-dimensional, continuous process experienced on a cognitive, emotional, and behavioral level. Cognitively, this is a period of identity shifting and a striving for congruence. A woman who recognizes her attractions to other women may try on the "lesbian label" to see how it fits, and then make adjustments in herself or challenge her own preconceptions about the "lesbian label." The emotional component is experienced by the awareness of same sex attraction, which may elicit a variety of feelings such as pleasure, excitement, fear, shame, guilt, or confusion. Women typically experience their initial sexual attractions, emotional attractions, or both, within the context of their relationship with a woman friend.

Behaviorally, women tend to act on their feelings after achieving an intellectual understanding of their attraction. Several researchers (Hedblom, 1973; Riddle & Morin, 1977; Saghir & Robins, 1969) have noted that women tend to emphasize the emotional aspects of their relationships over the sexual expression. This is consistent with traditional sex-role socialization patterns for women that emphasize feelings while downplaying sexual activity. Although physical/erotic attractions tend to be very strong during adolescence, Gramick (1984) suggests that the strong cultural emphasis on heterosexual dating may obscure or delay homoerotic feelings.

Thus coming out to oneself involves a period of time when a woman integrates feelings, thoughts, and sometimes sexual experiences with a new definition of herself as a lesbian and fits this in with her emerging adult identity. The coming out process is similar for many women despite their chronological age. What differs is the relative impact coming out has on identity for an older woman. The younger (17- to 22-year-old) woman is in the process of addressing primary developmental tasks related to self-definition. The older woman may have felt secure in her identity, only later to reevaluate or recycle through the developmental process again in order to incorporate her emerging sexual identity.

ADULT DEVELOPMENT

One challenge posed by this article was to address the problem inherent with theories of adult development. Adult developmental theories have been formulated using a male model. As a result of using male subjects and a male scientific paradigm, psychological maturity and adult identity formation have typically been described as the process of increasing individualization and separation by minimizing attachment to others and emphasizing goals and achievements (Levinson, 1978; Valliant, 1977).

In her study of moral development, Gilligan (1982) provides support for the concept that achieving identity for women involves a relational context. Hence, women's capacity for relatedness, nurturing, and emotionality, while central in identity development for women, is culturally devalued and labeled as less mature or less differentiated. At the same time, there is a societal expectation for women that heterosexual marriage and motherhood represent "the ticket" to psychological maturity and entry into adulthood. Obviously, for the lesbian there is no acceptable way to achieve adulthood as defined by traditional theories and cultural expectations. If she adopts the male-defined adult identity, she must discount her desire for relatedness and adopt a style of increasing individualization. If she rejects the male-defined adult identity and permits herself to incorporate a female relational context with another woman rather than a heterosexual relationship, then she faces the possible consequence of societal marginality, invisibility, or rejection.

It is this dilemma which must serve as the theoretical framework for understanding lesbians in a developmental context. By definition, identity is an organizing function which facilitates the process of integration. Identity emerges when there is perceived discrepancy between one's actual experience (whether feelings, thoughts, behaviors) and the previously held definition of self. For the young woman who is coming out, there is almost always a perceived discrepancy between how she feels, thinks, or behaves and the cultural definition of adult identity. The woman's identity will emerge through the resolution of her perceived discrepancy and how she then chooses to relate to her world.

DEVELOPMENTAL TASKS AND COMING OUT

The most frequent developmental tasks during this period of time are often related to changing relationships with parents, development of peer support/community, exploring career/vocational goals, and establishing intimate relationships.

Parents

Relationships with parents during late adolescence and early adulthood often serve as the backdrop from which the young woman's identity emerges. The process of parental separation involves reevaluating parental values and expectations and adopting those which hold relevance for the woman, while rejecting others not congruent with her self-definition. Most family systems convey strong heterosexual messages; that is, that heterosexual feelings are the only legitimate feelings and heterosexual relationships the only appropriate life goal. Although many families might not actively denounce a homosexual identity as a viable alternative for their children, the absence of discussion of homosexual identitites communicates a negative message.

Societal institutions, of which the family is very influential, assume heterosexuality and permit many opportunities for their children to receive approval and validation for their heterosexual orientation. When heterosexual youth question parental sexual values, the conflict which emerges generally relates to the degree, context, or type of heterosexual *expression*, not that their heterosexual *identity* is itself unacceptable.

The emerging lesbian, however, faces the task of questioning parental values without the security of knowing that her sexual orientation will be validated or accepted. When the young woman compares her parents' values with her own growing awareness of her identity, then the conflict involves a threat to her basic sense of *self*. The task of sorting through the doubts, anxiety, disillusionment, and anger typically felt toward parents at this time thus becomes more intense. It is one thing to rebel against parental values—that is understood and accepted to some degree in our culture—but what the young lesbian anticipates or fears accurately or not is parental rejection of her *personhood* and the subsequent destruction of her relationship with them.

If a young woman avoids coming to terms with changing or redefining her relationship with her parents because of real or imagined fear of rejection, she may not complete her developmental task impeding her ability to develop her lesbian identity. This may result in her parents' continued ability to exert their influence in ways which interfere with her coming out and becoming adult. Writing about identity status, Marcia (1980) describes the process of identity forclosure. This occurs when a person avoids confrontation on controversial issues and acquiesces to parental views because of fear of either disapproval or rejection. Foreclosure prevents achievement of congruence between one's feelings, thoughts, values, and behaviors which is essential in the process of identity formation.

The therapeutic task at this point becomes one of helping the client avoid foreclosure. This can be facilitated by validating the woman's right to her identity as a lesbian and an adult and encouraging her to examine all of her parents' values and expectations, not just those related to sexual orientation; for example, religious, occupational, political, and social attitudes and values. By encouraging the client to affirm her experiences and articulate both similarities as well as differences between herself and her parents, she may be able to see herself as separate from her parents but still be able to maintain a relationship with them. This process may also help her sort out real from imagined parental reactions to her lesbian identity. When she feels secure in her identity and has adequate social support, she may choose to come out to her parents. The motivation to disclose under these circumstances may not be to establish greater distance or parental rejection in order to achieve identity, but instead to achieve greater intimacy or honesty with her parents. In addition, achieving greater congruence between one's values, feelings, and behaviors inherently reinforces increased feelings of internal security, self-confidence, and self-esteem.

Social Support

Adolescents and young adults are in a process of shifting their reliance from parental relationships to peer relationships for validation of their identity. Heterosexual adolescents and young adults have many opportunities to explore their heterosexual identity within a supportive peer group and cultural milieu. Conversely, the emerging lesbian who is seeking validation for her identity may find the process of developing peer support challenging. Heterosexual peers may be intolerant of individual differences, particularly regarding sexual orientation, because they are also trying to understand and incorporate their sexual identity. Until heterosexual peers are secure in their sexual identities, they may be limited in their ability to offer support.

Therapists may help clients by being knowledgeable about the lesbian community and available resources for social support. Sometimes a client will need to learn communication and other social skills to help her feel comfortable in seeking out other lesbians. Frequently, clients may benefit from cognitive therapeutic strategies which examine expectations, assumptions, and irrational fears related to meeting other lesbians. Role playing, rehearsal, and imagery may also be useful interventions to help a client increase her self-confidence and flexibility in new social situations. Without a supportive peer system, a young woman may feel isolated and respond by becoming depressed, chemically dependent, suicidal, or by denying her feelings and adopting a heterosexual identity.

If the young woman has a lover, it is not uncommon for an over-reliance on the other partner to develop in an effort to secure all of the emotional support and validation needed for her identity. If the relationship fails to

meet her needs, she may then question her lesbian identity and self-worth
and reenter a state of confusion about "who she is." Of course, not all
women will respond in these ways as a result of lack of social support. The
coming out process can serve as a catalyst for developing identity because
the woman may come to accept and validate herself, factors critical to
developing adult identity. Therapists, however, are more likely to work
with women who are experiencing the pain of coming out in an unsupportive environment. The therapist must be sensitive to the particular stress
experienced by lesbians as they resolve identity issues. The therapist may
also be in a position to validate her identity, understanding that the final
outcome of achieving identity will be the shifting from a focus on external
validation to a focus on internal validation. As the young woman becomes
more congruent in her feelings, thoughts, and behaviors, she will feel more
confident and able to take personal stands that may or may not be validated
by others. This will allow her to come out to others when she chooses
without the fear that her basic identity is in danger. The ability to disclose
on this level is what de Monteflores and Schultz (1978) have described as
a person's ability to establish contact with her *real* self.

Career/Vocational Exploration

Developmentally, the young adult is seeking ways to gain competen-
cies and be productive in the world. The young lesbian also faces
career/vocational issues, but must consider these issues in the context of
sexist and homophobic attitudes. She must also consider that her
economic security is dependent upon her ability to provide for herself.
Even if she is in a relationship, economic discrimination against women
prevents the average working lesbian couple from earning as much as the
average heterosexual or gay working couple. Anti-lesbian attitudes may
also exist in the workplace which challenge the young adult lesbian to
consider how open she wishes to be about her sexuality and the degree of
acceptance she might experience in a particular field. These are all issues
in addition to the usual career/vocational exploration of values, skills,
interest, and life goals. The therapist may encourage the client not to
"short-circuit" her process of exploration by focusing exclusively on
sexist and homophobic considerations.

Social change is being felt most in the areas of occupational access. A
growing number of companies and professions have adopted anti-
discrimination policies for lesbians and gay men. The therapist can be
helpful in all the traditional ways that help clients integrate career/
vocation into life, while also being particularly sensitive to the lesbian
client's fears and anxieties related to how she can feel productive and
maintain a positive lesbian identity.

Establishing Intimate Relationships

Throughout late adolescence and early adulthood, the nature of intimate relationships depends a great deal upon the degree of development of the individual's identity. Developing intimacy requires the ability to take emotional risks by sharing one's *real* self and establishing a level of commitment between oneself and another. Since women have been socialized to express their sexuality in love-oriented or relational contexts, women are more likely to form couple relationships. As mentioned earlier, the coming out literature supports the concept that women tend to be aware of their emotional/erotic feelings for women prior to acting upon these feelings behaviorally.

Participating in a love relationship with another woman during late adolescence or early adulthood may enhance the development of the individual's adult identity by validating her personhood, reinforcing that she deserves to receive and give love. A relationship can also be a source of tremendous emotional support as the woman explores her goals, values, and relationship to the world. Burch (1982) suggests that because many women couples are rich in relational capacity, they often have the capacity to form deep bonds and experience deep relational satisfaction. Thus, one positive aspect of an intimate relationship can be its support rather than restriction of individual growth and identity development.

On the other hand, intimate relationships can also block the development of identity during young adulthood. When the relationship reflects a premature commitment motivated by fear of loneliness or isolation, it can potentially inhibit the individual's growth. Similarly, when the relationship serves as the exclusive source of validation for the individual's identity, the young adult might feel compelled to inhibit self-expression in order to avoid conflict and potential loss of her partner. Another issue which may surface in lesbian relationships and have an impact on adult identity formation is what Karpel (1976) calls "fusion" and Burch (1982) labels "merger." Both authors describe this process as occurring when one or both of the partners begin to experience difficulty behaving, feeling, or thinking differently or independently from the other partner. Personal autonomy or individualization is perceived as a threat to the relationship.

The therapeutic task when working with an individual who is in a relationship which restricts identity development is to help the client learn how to be separate, by establishing personal boundaries, yet remain emotionally connected within the relationship. For a more detailed conceptualization of merger/fusion and therapeutic intervention strategies see Burch (1982) and Krestan and Bepko (1980).

A necessary component in developing an adult identity which incorporates a positive lesbian identity is the ongoing commitment to understand oneself and to strive for congruence. Intimate relationships which support this activity will serve to enhance identity formation.

SUMMARY

Therapists utilizing a variety of therapeutic interventions can facilitate the adoption of a positive lesbian identity. Understanding the various developmental challenges which face women at all chronological ages and at varying stages of the coming out process will enhance therapeutic interventions. Furthermore, therapists who utilize a feminist perspective in their work can help clients to understand the roots of homosexual oppression, and work toward freeing clients from internalized homophobia which may block the development of an adult identity.

REFERENCES

Burch, B. (1982). Psychological merger in lesbian couples: A joint ego psychological and systems approach. *Family Therapy, 9*, 201–208.

de Monteflores, C., & Schultz, S. (1978). Coming out: Similarities and differences for lesbians and gay men. *Journal of Social Issues, 34*(3), 59–72.

Erickson, E. H. (1974). Youth: Fidelity and diversity. In H. V. Kraemer (Ed.), *Youth and culture: A human developmental approach.* Belmont, CA: Brooks-Cole.

Gilligan, C. (1982). *In a different voice: Psychological theory and women's development.* Cambridge, MA: Harvard University Press.

Gramick, J. (1984). Developing a lesbian identity. In T. E. Darty & S. Potter (Eds.), *Women-identified women.* Palo Alto, CA: Mayfield.

Hedblom, J. H. (1973). Dimensions of lesbian sexual experience. *Archives of Sexual Behavior, 2*, 329–341.

Jay, K., & Young, A. (1979). *The gay report.* New York: Summit Books.

Karpel, M. (1976). Individualization: From fusion to dialogue. *Family Process, 15*, 65–82.

Krestan, J., & Bepko, C. S. (1980). The problem of fusion in the lesbian relationship. *Family Process, 19*, 277–289.

Levinson, D. J. (1978). *The Seasons of a man's life.* New York: Alfred Knopf.

Marcia, J. (1980). Identity in adolescence. In J. Adelson (Ed.), *Handbook of adolescent psychology.* New York: John Wiley & Sons.

Riddle, D. I., & Morin, S. F. (1977, November). Removing the stigma: Data from individuals. *APA Monitor*, [Author: Supply Page Numbers.]

Saghir, M., & Robins, E. (1969). Homosexuality I: Sexual behavior of the female homosexual. *Archives of General Psychiatry, 20*, 192–201.

Valliant, G. E. (1977). *Adaptation to life.* Boston, MA: Little, Brown.

Internalized Homophobia
and Lesbian Identity

Joan Sophie, PhD
Madison Center
South Bend, Indiana

SUMMARY. This paper presents suggestions for therapists working with women who are having difficulty accepting their attractions to other women, lesbian behavior and identity, or both, with the goal of promoting self-acceptance and reducing internalized homophobia. After a discussion of the therapeutic relationship, several coping strategies which have been used successfully by many women are described and therapeutic applications are offered. These strategies include cognitive restructuring, avoiding a negative identity, adopting an identity label, self-disclosure, meeting other lesbians, and habituation to lesbianism. Finally, behavioral indications of success or failure to achieve the goal of self-acceptance are presented.

Recognition and acceptance of lesbian attraction and behavior is a difficult process given the strength and pervasiveness of anti-homosexual attitudes in our society. Hence, it is not uncommon for women to enter therapy with questions and concerns about their sexual orientation and identity. Therapeutic interventions for helping clients with this problem are the focus of this paper. Included are clients who are just beginning to consider relations with women, as well as others who may have been involved in relations with women for some time, but who are still grappling with the issue of a lesbian identity. Regardless of when this problem occurs, the major source of distress is usually the individual's internalized homophobia.

Homophobia has been defined in a variety of ways, from an analogy with other phobias, with the emphasis on fear (Weinberg, 1972), to an analogy with racism or sexism, with the emphasis on negative attitudes of all kinds (Weinberger & Millham, 1979). It is used here in the latter sense. Since the current paper focuses on women, internalized homophobia represents an internalization of negative attitudes and assumptions concerning lesbianism, while societal homophobia refers to the totality of negative attitudes concerning lesbianism expressed by

Dr. Sophie is Staff Psychologist at the Madison Center, P. O. Box 80, 403 East Madison Street, South Bend, IN 46624. Correspondence may be sent to the author at that address.

53

others in the individual's environment, from her immediate friends and family to the institutions of the church, school, and mass media. Internalized homophobia makes consideration of lesbian identity for oneself extremely threatening to the individual's self-esteem.

The problem, then, is to reduce greatly or eliminate internalized homophobia so that a lesbian identity can be considered without loss of self-esteem. Reduction of internalized homophobia to manageable proportions gives the individual a choice which she cannot have as long as internalized homophobia prevails. Most who achieve this goal go on to adopt a positive lesbian identity and lifestyle, while others continue to incorporate an interest in men in their self-definitions and behavior in the form of a bisexual or pansexual identity. The goal of therapy, then, is not the achievement of any particular identity, but the reduction in internalized homophobia which enables the woman to accept her own lesbian desires and experiences and choose her own identity. Below are some suggestions for therapists working with clients on this problem. These suggestions are drawn from my research on women undergoing changes in their sexual orientation (Sophie, 1985), from my clinical experience with lesbians, and from the research literature.

TREATMENT METHODS

The Therapeutic Relationship

The therapeutic relationship is itself a treatment modality, one which can take on special importance for the individual grappling with lesbian identity issues. The therapist is likely to be seen as a representative of society whose reactions may help the client anticipate the reactions of others in her life. The therapist may also be seen as an authority figure whose approval or disapproval carries much weight. In addition, a lesbian therapist, or to a lesser extent a gay male therapist, may serve as a role model for the client. All of these add extra weight to the therapeutic relationship and pose special challenges for the therapist.

One challenge for the therapist is to convey acceptance of homosexuality without minimization of the real obstacles involved. By now there is ample evidence that one can live a healthy, happy, productive life as a lesbian (see, e.g., Adelman, 1977; Hart, et al., 1978), but that doesn't mean it's easy to achieve this goal in a society in which homophobic beliefs still prevail. Wishing to reassure the client, the well-meaning heterosexual therapist may emphasize how attitudes have changed, how acceptable it is now to be lesbian or gay, so that the client feels compelled either to explain how that is not true or to question her own perceptions of societal homophobia. The lesbian or gay male therapist may behave similarly, either for defensive reasons or because it seems that conditions have changed so greatly since she or he came out publicly as homosexual. Change, of course, has occurred, and it has become much more possible now to find the support and sense of community one needs as a lesbian, but that finding is an active process. The community to which the client belongs is likely not to share these positive views of lesbianism; if it did, she would be much less likely to have sought therapy.

It is important for the therapist to be able to acknowledge these negative community attitudes while not agreeing with them. In this way the therapist can model acceptance and valuing of differences among human beings. The coping strategies described later in this paper are useful in helping clients change their beliefs about lesbianism and develop more supportive social networks.

Another challenge is that although disclosure of her sexual orientation to the therapist is apt to be of great significance to the client, this significance may be obscured by her choice of how to disclose. For example, the client may disclose her lesbianism either defiantly or overly casually and then wait for the therapist's reaction before deciding if it is safe to continue on this topic. Or she may indicate that she has something to talk about but be unable to mention what it is. One of my clients spent much of three sessions in this way, then finally revealed her attraction to another woman in the last 5 minutes of a session. However the disclosure is made, it is important for the therapist to realize both how difficult such a disclosure may be for the client, and how important the therapist's response is. There may not be another opportunity to convey non-judgmental acceptance of the client's sexual orientation. If the first attempt fails for the client, she may retreat from the topic or from therapy altogether.

The issue of whether, and how, the therapist's sexual orientation should be disclosed is another challenge for the therapist. The presumption of heterosexuality is so strong in our society that when the client is heterosexual the therapist's sexual orientation is usually not an issue, since the client is apt to presume heterosexuality. The lesbian or bisexual client, however, is less likely to make this assumption automatically. She may instead be very sensitive to the information revealed by the therapist concerning her or his own sexual orientation. Unrequested or unwanted self-disclosures on the part of the therapist may be interpreted by the client as pressure toward the therapist's sexual orientation, or as expressions of discomfort with the client's sexuality. This is particularly apt to occur when the therapist's revelation is made through casual reference to a spouse or children, which may be seen as subtle reminders that the therapist is safely heterosexual. On the other hand, unwanted revelation

of the therapist's lesbian identity may be viewed by the client as a
seductive move. In either case, of course, the client may be perfectly
right. Sexuality is a sensitive issue for all of us, and in this area it is
especially important for therapists to take stock of their countertransference issues (Kwawer, 1980).

However, a therapist's refusal to self-disclose in response to a direct
request for this information may also lead to distrust which can hamper
the therapeutic relationship. For example, one researcher studying lesbian
identity development lost some potential respondents because she refused
to reveal her sexual orientation to them (Spaulding, 1982). The therapy
relationship is likely to be more sensitive to this issue than is the research
relationship. The client has a right to know, if she so wishes, whether the
therapist has experienced the process of coming to terms with a
non-heterosexual identity. Crucial questions for the therapist to consider
are whether the client wants this information, and if so, what it would
mean to her. If her motivation is to assure herself that the therapist has (or
has not) had the experience of recognizing and acting on homosexual
attractions, this is a legitimate concern and can be acknowledged as such
with an honest response to the client's direct questioning of the therapist's
sexual orientation. The meanings of the response can then be explored
with the client. However, if her motivation is based on homophobic and
stereotyped assumptions, or on distorted thought processes due to severe
disturbance, it is probably advisable to risk some distrust by refraining
from responding to her direct questioning.

Sometimes the client may hint that she wants to know the therapist's
sexual orientation. In that case it is often useful to point this out and give
her the opportunity to ask her questions directly. Ambivalence about
whether or not this information is wanted is common, and it is often
useful to explore this ambivalence with the client. It is generally not
advisable to respond to the client's hints with a direct revelation of the
therapist's sexual orientation because despite her hints, the client may not
be prepared to receive this information. Clearly, the issue of therapist
disclosure of sexual orientation is complex and not amenable to simple
answers; each case must be considered individually.

DEVELOPING COPING STRATEGIES

The coping strategies described below are derived primarily from my
research on women who were experiencing changes in their sexual
orientation (Sophie, 1985), although the research literature and my
clinical experience were also used. The purpose of these strategies is to
give the client the benefit of techniques (and to some extent, good
fortune) which have been used effectively by others.

1. Cognitive Restructuring

Cognitive restructuring entails changes in the meanings associated with lesbian or bisexual identity so that these identities take on positive, or at least non-negative, meanings for the individual. Cognitive restructuring is also likely to involve changes in the meanings of the self-concept, of the concept "woman," of religious beliefs and values, and of future expectations. Cognitive restructuring is the basic process which underlies the elimination or reduction of internalized homophobia and its replacement with a positive view of homosexuality. As such, it is probably the major process of coping necessary for acceptance of oneself as lesbian or bisexual. It is the basic process which underlies most of the other coping strategies listed below.

In addition to enhancing cognitive restructuring through the other coping strategies, the therapist can offer some direct assistance through cognitive therapy techniques. Negative stereotypes of lesbians are similar to other irrational ideas and can be uncovered and challenged in the same way in therapy. Specifically, the therapist can emphasize the diversity which exists among lesbians, as among heterosexual women, showing that no stereotype can possibly fit for this diverse group. A feminist analysis of women's roles and stereotypes of women is also useful in this regard.

The elimination of negative stereotypes and the awareness of diversity can be enhanced by referring the client to positive gay and lesbian books which can be found at women's or gay bookstores, or else mail-ordered if no such bookstore is available nearby. Reading alone is not sufficient for cognitive restructuring, but it is a helpful adjunct to other methods.

The therapist may also need to challenge the client's religious beliefs concerning homosexuality, which are frequently a source of great distress for the client. Referral to a member of the clergy of the client's religion who has positive attitudes about sexuality and sexual orientation is recommended when possible, as well as to the gay and lesbian churches, church groups, and synagogues which exist in many cities.

2. Avoiding a Negative Identity

One of the most striking results of my research, and probably one of the greatest differences between the research participants and a clinical population, was that many participants avoided identifying themselves as lesbian, regardless of their experience, until after this identity had become positive, or at least neutral, for them. Thus they avoided a negative identity.

Case Illustration. Jo, a 30-year-old divorced woman, reported that she had had a sexual experience with a woman about 3 years prior to the first research interview. Jo recognized the relevance of lesbianism for herself at the time, identified as the first stage of homosexual identity formation by Cass (1979), but she refrained from identifying herself as lesbian. She said the experience meant more to her than to her friend, who reacted by withdrawing from her. Jo remained married at the time and took no further action on her lesbian feelings. Then about a year and a half later, she became involved in a women's softball team. She quickly discovered that the other team members were all lesbian. She reacted very positively to this and began an exploration of lesbianism (see Coleman, 1981/82) which included going to bed with a couple of women, meeting one who became her lover, and leaving her husband. It was only after these experiences that Jo began to think of herself as a lesbian. Although she was aware of her attraction to women previously, especially after the experience with her friend, Jo did not use the label "lesbian" for herself until she could do so in the positive context of her softball team friends and a relationship with a lesbian/feminist lover.

Other examples could also be given which were very similar. Some of the women did not consider lesbianism for themselves at all until after they had met positive lesbian role models by chance; for example, a college roommate, a work colleague, fellow team members.

This can be used to help clients in therapy, wherein if the client has not yet identified herself as lesbian, the therapist can encourage her to leave the question of identity open while she explores the possibilities for herself. One must bear in mind the great flexibility and variety of experiences actually reported by participants in this and other research, in contrast to the dichotomous view we commonly hold of sexual orientation (see, e.g., Bell & Weinberg, 1978; Shively, Jones, & De Cecco, 1983/84). It is quite possible that the client is neither homosexual nor heterosexual, but some combination of both. This requires a sensitivity to the ambiguity and complexity of sexual orientation on the part of the therapist; both therapist and client must be able to live with this complex understanding of sexual orientation.

Granted, many clients will come to therapy having already adopted a negative lesbian identity. For them it is too late for the therapist to apply the observation that it works better to wait to identify oneself as lesbian until after this identity has positive or neutral meaning. Instead, the therapist has the more difficult task of helping the client change the meaning of lesbianism for herself after she has already accepted this identity with a negative connotation. The other coping strategies described in this paper are useful in this regard, although the entire process is likely to be slower and more difficult for the client who has developed a negative self-concept as a lesbian.

3. Adopting an Identity Label

Adopting an identity label can be viewed as one of the coping strategies individuals use when confronting lesbian identity issues. Different identity labels may be adopted by women at different points in their lives for a variety of reasons. Rather than representing an end of a process, such labels may facilitate coping at the time, but may then be changed later when other needs arise. It is common for women to adopt a bisexual identity temporarily when they are beginning to relate to women because of the lesser stigma of this label and the fact that it allows them to retain some heterosexual advantages while they explore the possibilities of relationships with women (deMonteflores & Schultz, 1978). But other kinds of changes in identity also occur. For example, two women in my research who had adopted lesbian identities previously changed to bisexual, or to no label, during the research in order to allow themselves to reintegrate their attractions to men into their identities. While it is useful to refrain from identifying oneself as lesbian as long as that identity has negative meanings for the individual, it is difficult to remain without a label of any kind for a long period, and doing so can impede further development.

The research participants seemed to be divided into two groups in terms of how they viewed sexual orientation. Some viewed it as a dichotomy and felt that they had to make a choice one way or the other, am I straight or am I gay being a crucial question for them; others emphasized bisexuality or the difficulty of narrowly defining sexual orientation. These differing approaches influenced how they dealt with the process of coming to terms with their own attractions to women. Although the approach taken by a particular woman sometimes changed over time, this did not seem to be an easy change to make. It is useful for the therapist to be aware of these differing views and their impact on the client.

The generalized or bisexual conception of sexual orientation seemed to be particularly useful as a coping strategy at an early stage of considering lesbian relationships. As indicated above, it can enable the individual to avoid some of the stigma associated with lesbianism and to avoid a negative identity. However, if this strategy is maintained too long, it can prevent the woman from entering a lesbian community in which she could find friends and potential lovers. This happened to one of my research participants who after the break up of her first lesbian relationship found herself going out only with men because, although she felt that she was more attracted to women than to men, she did not meet any potential female partners.

The major advantage of the dichotomous view is that it allows the woman to seek out a lesbian community and identify herself with that community. One research participant was quite clear about this advantage and the exigencies of the social world. At her first interview she told me she was bisexual, but that if someone asked, she would say she was gay. She explained that you can't say you're bisexual in the gay community; it sounds like a cop- out. At a later interview she called herself gay, while continuing to maintain that she could relate to men again in the future if she so desired.

The meaning of lesbian identity varies greatly from one person to another. For some the word "lesbian" has a very political meaning. One participant identified herself as gay but said she was not lesbian because she wasn't that radical. Another decided she was lesbian after attending a largely lesbian women's music festival; she was attracted to the political meaning of the identity and said it would not restrict her if she chose to relate to men again in the future. Another who had been very active in the gay movement at her undergraduate campus decided she was bisexual when she realized that she was in love with a gay male friend. And one woman, who had a completely lesbian history up to the age of 31, said she never called herself lesbian because she still wanted to date men and saw her relationships with women as something she was doing, not something she was. The meanings are obviously very personal. And "lesbian" is likely to have personal meaning for the therapist as well. It is a challenge for the therapist to keep open to the client's definitions and confusion, and to refrain from exerting pressure on the client toward labeling herself as "lesbian," "gay," or "bisexual," or adopting any particular definition of these terms, while at the same time challenging the negative connotations of lesbianism for the client.

4. Self-Disclosure

Self-disclosure to people who are important in one's life plays a crucial role in gay self-acceptance (see e.g., Coleman, 1981/82; deMonteflores & Schultz, 1978). All of my research participants mentioned disclosing their feelings toward women to at least some of the people who were important to them, and some stressed the importance of this disclosure and of receiving positive reactions. Self-disclosure is necessary for intimacy in a relationship, for confirmation of identity, and for self-actualization (Graham & Bradmiller, 1981). The reactions of those who are told about one's identity are very important in developing self-acceptance; positive responses promote self-acceptance, while negative responses provide further stress for the individual (e.g., Coleman, 1981/82). As mentioned previously, disclosure to the therapist is itself an important self-disclosure for many clients. The opposite of self-disclosure, keeping this information entirely to oneself, is an affirmation of internalized homophobia, implying that this aspect of oneself is too shameful to disclose to anyone.

But the process of disclosure is fraught with hazards. The outcome depends on to whom one discloses, when, where, and under what circumstances. It also involves handling indirect and accidental disclosures. "Indirect disclosure" refers to providing information, either verbally or behaviorally, which the other person may be able to use to discover one's lesbianism without one directly declaring it. "Accidental disclosure" occurs when there was no intention of disclosing this information to the particular individual who made the discovery. Most lesbians disclose more or less selectively and learn to handle the complications of social interaction in situations where this information may or may not be known (Moses, 1978). But the client who has not yet developed these skills may need help in evaluating the risks involved in disclosing to particular individuals, and encouragement to take some calculated risks in disclosing her lesbianism to selected, valued others (Coleman, 1981/82). She may also benefit from practicing important disclosures before they happen through role plays in the therapy session.

In rehearsing a self-disclosure in therapy, "empty chair" role plays, in which the client plays both parts of the conversation, are particularly recommended, for this method has several advantages over role plays in which the therapist plays a part. First, it enables the client to demonstrate what reactions she expects/fears from the target person, rather than having the therapist guess which reaction is appropriate to the role play. Second, it provides much more information on both the client's relationship with the target person and her assumptions about lesbianism and people's reaction to it. Third, in addition to providing information on her assumptions about the other person's role, playing that role helps the client to appreciate the difficulties of the role for the target person, which in turn may be useful in preventing some degree of hostility in the interaction. The role plays can be amplified by discussing best and worst scenarios for the disclosure. It is also helpful to discuss the longer term implications of disclosure to this target person. Especially when disclosures are made to parents, it is helpful for both therapist and client to keep in mind that the parents will probably also need to go through a process of cognitive restructuring before they can accept lesbianism for their daughter. Finally, it is important to respect the client's decision about to whom it is safe to disclose. If she is positive about her lesbianism, her perceptions of to whom it is safe to disclose will probably be very accurate. Many of the research participants were remarkably good at deciding to whom and how to disclose; and as a result, they got mostly supportive responses, or at least responses which they interpreted positively. Not all parents/bosses/friends/clergy/etc. are alike, and thus the client is in the best position to know how the people in her life are likely to respond to her lesbianism. However, if the client's contacts were primarily with very open and accepting people, she would have been less likely to seek therapeutic help. Therefore, clients are most likely to come from unsupportive environments, and may need help, then, in separating themselves from these environments in order to seek the support they need elsewhere.

5. Meeting Other Lesbians

Interaction with other lesbians who contradict stereotypes and provide positive role models has been found to be crucial for cognitive restructuring. As indicated earlier, reading positive lesbian or gay literature can be helpful in this process, but it is not sufficient in itself (see, e.g., Nemeyer, 1980; Raphael, 1974). This need for contact with lesbians presents the individuals with a paradox: In order to change her views and become self-accepting, she must choose to seek out and interact with those whom, before such change occurs, she considers highly undesirable. Several of my research participants were aware of this paradox; they talked about their inability to accept lesbianism for themselves, or seek out other lesbians, until somehow they did have contact with lesbians which enabled them to begin their cognitive restructuring.

Case Illustrations. Many of the research participants were lucky in finding positive groups of lesbians by chance. Elly found them in her athletic team, Amy had a lesbian roommate and met others through her, and Flo became active in the women's movement and met other lesbians there. Others had to seek out other lesbians deliberately. Sue decided she was lesbian in the absence of a lesbian community and spent several months feeling isolated and miserable. Then she decided that two women whom she knew in the dorm were probably a lesbian couple; in any case, she felt that they were nice women and it would be safe to talk to them about her feelings. Her perceptions proved accurate. They welcomed her news, took her under their wings, and introduced her to their lesbian friends, thus ending Sue's isolation. Whether by chance or design, finding a positive lesbian community or group of friends is extremely important in overcoming internalized homophobia and developing a positive lesbian, or bisexual, identity.

Two problems can occur in this connection. First, the client may have difficulty meeting other lesbians, either because she does not know how to go about finding them, or because her fears keep her from pursuing the possibilities she is aware of. Second, she may meet a group of lesbians but experience this negatively. If the therapy occurs in a city of any size, the first problem is fairly readily resolved since a variety of lesbian resources are likely to be available—lesbian/feminist/gay organizations, women's and gay bookstores, women's centers, bars, and coffeehouses, gay and lesbian churches, and so forth, are found in many cities. But the second problem may prove harder to resolve. A high level of internalized homophobia can lead the client to view negatively the group of lesbians she finds and to over-generalize from any negative encounters she has, thus reinforcing her internalized homophobia. It is important for the therapist to be aware of this process and to help the client counter it by pointing out how her perceptions of the lesbian community she has come into contact with are warped by her negative ideas about lesbians.

Finally, it is important to note that often the only, or major, other lesbian in a woman's life is her partner in a relationship. Although relationship issues are outside the scope of this paper, it is important to keep in mind that the internalized homophobia or either or both partners can greatly interfere with the relationship. At the same time, the nature of the relationship, and the client's interpretation of it, can have a major impact on her development, either reducing or enhancing her internalized homophobia. The therapist can help the client make positive interpretations and refrain from over-generalizing from bad experiences.

6. Habituation to Lesbianism

Habituation is the process whereby lesbianism becomes ordinary rather than unusual. Habituation occurs to one's own behavior and feelings, and to the lesbian subculture, as one becomes accustomed to each of these. While the other methods mentioned above all enhance cognitive restructuring, habituation can be seen as a separate process. One may achieve much cognitive restructuring early in developing lesbian identity, yet still experience the lesbian world as new and strange. Conversely, one can become habituated to the lesbian world without having achieved a full change in one's perceptions and evaluations of lesbianism.

Case Illustration. The last possibility was apparent for Nan, a 34-year-old graduate student who at the time of her interview was involved in a relationship with a man. Nan had interacted in the lesbian world for 13 years while refusing to label herself lesbian because she wanted the social approval accorded to heterosexuality. Her responses showed that she had become habituated to the lesbian subculture, but had not fully changed her conceptions of lesbianism in a positive way. Both cognitive restructuring and habituation are necessary for a positive lesbian identity.

Aspects of habituation are also relevant for those who pursue relations with women but adopt bisexual or generalized identities. These women also need to experience relations between women as ordinary rather than as strange or peculiar. Experience in a relationship, and possibly experience in a group of lesbians, may be as necessary for these women to achieve habituation as they are for those who develop lesbian identities. This could pose a problem for the individual who does not want to adopt lesbian identity, but who may need to participate in the lesbian community in order to find potential partners and to reduce her internalized homophobia. There is little for the therapist to do to aid in this process other than to be aware of the client's need for contact with the lesbian community, and experience in a relationship, in order for habituation to occur.

EVALUATING TREATMENT EFFECTIVENESS

As stated previously, the goal of therapy is the client's acceptance of her attractions to women and achievement of a positive sexual identity, accompanied by a great reduction or elimination of her internalized homophobia. Some behavioral indications that this goal has been achieved are: the client's comfort with her own feelings, relations with women, lesbian fantasies, and so forth; her comfort with, and respect and admiration for, other lesbians and gay men; her ability to form a meaningful relationship with another woman; positive self-disclosures; and her use of a homo-positive reference group (e.g., lesbians, gay men, positive heterosexual friends). Conversely, some indications of lack of success in the client's behavior would include her continuing discomfort with her own feelings, relationships, and fantasies; a preponderance of negative comments regarding gay people; potential relationships with women disturbed by the client's lack of respect for her partner, herself, or the relationship, or her inability to take the relationship seriously; her use of overly confrontational or apologetic self-disclosures; and reliance on a homophobic reference group. It is important to recognize that conflict with the heterosexual world in a variety of forms—conflict with parents, old friends, colleagues, negative comments about the media, frustration with career or school—are not indications of failure to achieve self-acceptance and reduction of internalized homophobia. In fact, these external conflicts are likely to increase as internalized homophobia decreases, at least initially, as the individual becomes more aware of societal homophobia and its negative impact on her life.

REFERENCES

Adelman, M. R. (1977). A comparison of professionally employed lesbians and heterosexual women on the MMPI. *Archives of Sexual Behavior, 6,* 193–201.

Bell, A. P., & Weinberg, M. S. (1978). *Homosexualities.* New York: Simon & Shuster.

Cass, V. C. (1979). Homosexual identity formation: A theoretical model. *Journal of Homosexuality, 4,* 219–235

Coleman, E. (1981/82). Developmental stages of the coming out process. *Journal of Homosexuality, 7*(2/3), 31–43.

deMonteflores, C., & Schultz, S. J. (1978). Coming out: Similarities and differences for lesbians and gay men. *Journal of Social Issues, 34,* 59–72.

Graham, D. L. R., & Bradmiller, L. L. (1981, March). *The self-actualizing lesbian.* Paper presented at the meeting of the Association for Women in Psychology, Boston, MA.

Hart, M., Roback, H., Tittler, B., Weitz, L., Walston, B., & McKee, E. (1978). Psychological adjustment of nonpatient homosexuals: Critical review of the research literature. *Journal of Clinical Psychiatry, 39,* 604–608.

Kwawer, J. S. (1980). Transference and countertransference in homosexuals—Changing psychoanalytic views. *American Journal of Psychotherapy, 34,* 72–80.

Moses, A. E. (1978). *Identity management in lesbian women.* New York: Praeger.

Nemeyer, L. (1980). Coming out: Identity congruence and the attainment of adult female sexuality. *Dissertation Abstracts International, 36,* 6394B. (University Microfilms No. 80-24138.)

Raphael, S. M. (1974). "Coming out": The emergence of the lesbian movement. *Dissertation Abstracts International, 35,* 5536A. (University Microfilms No. 75-5084.)

Shively, M. D., Jones, C., & De Cecco, J. P. (1983/84). Research on sexual orientation: Definitions and methods. *Journal of Homosexuality, 9*(2/3), 127–136.

Sophie, J. (1985). Stress, social network, and sexual orientation identity change in women. *Dissertation Abstracts International, 46,* 949B. (University Microfilms No. 85-10777.)

Spaulding, E. C. (1982). The formation of lesbian identity during the "coming out" process. *Dissertation Abstracts International, 43,* 2106A. (University Microfilms No. 82-26834.)

Weinberg, G. (1972). *Society and the healthy homosexual.* New York: St. Martin's Press.

Weinberger, L. E., & Millham, J. (1979). Attitudinal homophobia and support of traditional sex roles. *Journal of Homosexuality, 4,* 237–246.

Ericksonian Hypnosis
and Strategic Interventions
for Sexual Orientation Confusion

Timothy J. Wolf, PhD
Fritz Klein, MD

SUMMARY. Erickson's utilization approach provides a model of hypnotic and strategic intervention for persons seeking psychotherapy because of sexual orientation confusion. Case studies outline examples of hypnotic and strategic short-term interventions. These cases include the use of metaphor, utilizing resistances, anchoring, and synesthesia.

The hypnotic and strategic interventions of the late Milton Erickson (Rossi, 1980) provide a unique model for the psychotherapist providing services for persons with sexual orientation confusion. Erickson's "utilization" approach rejects the idea that individuals fit into theoretical models and emphasizes and capitalizes on the unique variability and complexity of each person. In the utilization approach, behaviors, attitudes, and resistances have positive potentials which the therapist uses to lead persons toward new feelings and behaviors which emphasize personally autonomous perspectives. Therapy, as described by Erickson, becomes the art of "accepting and utilizing" what a person says and does. In this process a person's thoughts and feelings are reflected back to them in such a way that the person feels accepted and understood. The psychotherapist or hypnotherapist attempts to promote change by working with the person's own thoughts, feelings, and behaviors without imposing his or her own beliefs or theoretical perspectives. The utilization involves using hypnotherapy to tap into the person's unconscious resources.

In the authors' work with persons who are experiencing sexual orientation confusion, Ericksonian hypnotherapy and strategic interventions have been useful, powerful techniques of change. This may be due in part to the unconscious nature of the conflicts many persons experience in the area of sexuality. Traditional "insight" approaches to these problems often leave the client with understanding but little behavioral

Dr. Wolf is a psychotherapist in private practice in San Diego. Dr. Klein is a Diplomate on the American Board of Psychiatry and Neurology, and is Director of the Institute of Sexual Behavior. Correspondence may be addressed to the authors, 4545 Park Blvd., Ste. 207, San Diego, CA 92116.

change. Erickson often commented that insight was often a stumbling block to change in that it reinforced specific behaviors (Haley, 1982). Utilization approaches circumvent the stumbling block by allowing a person in conflict to utilize his or her conscious resistances and unconscious resources in forming new perspectives and strategies.

Persons seeking therapy for sexual orientation confusion present a variety of problems. Some of the major conflicts clients have feared are: (a) confused definitions of homosexuality or bisexuality; (b) difficulties resulting from lack of homosexual or heterosexual experiences (these experiences often too limited to allow them to make healthy choices about their sexuality); (c) difficulties reconciling the incongruity of their attraction and behavior; (d) sexual orientation being a dynamic process (Klein, Spekoff, & Wolf, 1985), a puzzlement over his or her changing sexual orientation over time; (e) conflict about their lifestyle, especially when they are bisexual or married; (f) internalized homophobia (a major source of conscious or unconscious anxiety for persons with sexual orientation confusion); (g) guilt or anxiety associated with internalized religious prohibitions; and (h) stereotyped expectations of sexual orientation which often block healthy understanding of their own complex personal sexual identity.

For those experiencing sexual orientation confusion, the goal is to utilize conscious and unconscious potential resources to integrate an often fragmented sexual identity. This goal is accomplished through hypnosis and strategic interventions which educate, relieve anxieties, change histories, and integrate separated parts of the sexual person. Hypnotic techniques which prove useful are amnesia, post-hypnotic suggestion, time-space distortion, and instruction in self-hypnosis. (For a detailed description of these techniques refer to Yapko, 1984). Strategic intervention makes use of the techniques of metaphor, amplifying deviations, utilizing resistances, prescribing the worse alternative, paradoxical intention (Haley, 1963), anchoring, and synesthesia (Bandler & Grinder, 1979).

In the Ericksonian approach of hypnotic and strategic intervention, emphasis is placed on utilizing treatments which are as brief as possible. The case histories which follow exemplify many of the techniques outlined above within a short-term treatment approach. The first case history describes a one-session intervention.

CASE HISTORY I

David was a 19-year-old college male who presented with complaints about not being able to concentrate and feeling anxious when he had to study. In the initial interview, David also mentioned that he was bothered by his sexual attraction to other men, especially an older executive at his part-time office job. He currently was sexual with women and found his attraction to men in conflict with his attraction to women.

The intervention with David with regard to his academic anxiety included suggestions which would also help David in his conflict regarding his sexual attractions. David was taught self-hypnosis and was able to achieve trance very quickly. After working with David to improve his concentration in his studies, it was suggested that some men and women are sexually attracted to both sexes and that that attraction may be stronger or weaker depending on the person one is attracted to or the time in one's life. Secondly, the part of David that was attracted to men was as valuable as any other part and it was "ok" to allow those feelings of attraction to become conscious when it was comfortable for him to do so. Having those feelings did not mean that he had to act on them. Thirdly, David was told he could choose to act on those feelings or not to act on those feelings. If he chose to act on those feelings, he would do it with someone he trusted and in a safe and healthy manner. David reported in the next session that his anxiety about his college work was now manageable. He went on to say that he had begun to be sexually involved with his work colleague.

This case history showed that the client was able to accept suggestions which allowed him to begin to integrate the divergent aspects of his sexual behavior. This exemplifies brief hypnotic and strategic intervention, in which David did not need consciously to resist the conflicts about his homosexual attractions. In the following case history, both a long-term treatment intervention and a brief hypnotic intervention are described.

CASE HISTORY II

Gary was a 29-year-old white male, born in the South, one of five siblings. He had one older brother and sister and two younger sisters. His father was a machinist, now retired, and his mother was a school teacher. His family was very religious, belonging to the Southern Baptist denomination. In addition, the family practiced temperance.

At the time he entered therapy he was no longer religious, having left the church during his adolescence. He now got along with his parents, though there was a stormy 3-year period when he had rejected his religion. His parents were embarrassed about showing affection with him, though his mother from time to time did so. He got along well with his brother and sisters. He was a B+ student in college, and he had several selling jobs before his present employment with a fine china company, in which he made a good living and earned an above-average salary.

Sex and Relationship History

Gary became aware of sex at an early age through observing animals having sex. At the age of 3 he remembered a boy touching him, and also remembered seeing his father nude in a shower and being attracted to him when he was around 4 years old. At the age of 5 he played around with 12-year-old female cousin. At the age of 7, he and a 10-year-old friend explored each other sexually; his mother caught them and Gary was hit quite severely. From that point on he felt that sex with other males was bad. He had another experience with a boy his own age at the age of 12. He began masturbating at the age of 10–11, and had his first orgasm at the age of 13. In spite of feeling bad about his homosexual feelings, from the ages of 12 to 14 he had three or four more experiences of fondling and touching other boys. He began dating and heavy petting with girls at the age of 16. His first experience of intercourse with a woman was in college at the age of 20, with a girl he dated on a steady basis. From 14 through 19, he had no orgasms (including masturbation). His only sexual outlet during adolescence was nocturnal emissions. The reason for his stopping all sex was that he was afraid that he might be homosexual.

His first relationship with a woman started at the age of 19–20 with Susan. After the first three or four times during which he experienced difficulty in maintaining an erection, sex with her became "super." He continued to fear possible erectile dysfunction, but functioned without difficulty though he did experience retarded ejaculation. He broke off the relationship because he did not want to marry her. He had had sex with two other women during the 6 years prior to entering therapy, a 2-year relationship with one and infrequent sexual encounters over a 3-year period with the other. With both of these women he experienced erectile dysfunction the first few times until he felt comfortable with them.

As an adult, Gary did not experience any sexual contact with another man until the age of 27. This occurred with a friend whom he had known for many years and who was married. Two years later he entered therapy. He had gone to bed with Bill around 10 times over the past 2 years. He always experienced erectile dysfunction with Bill. Their usual pattern of sexual activity involved Gary performing fellatio on Bill and sometimes being the passive partner in anal intercourse.

Course of Treatment

The patient was seen on the average once every 2 weeks for a 3-year period, sometimes weekly for several months, other times not at all for several months. In April of 1982, the therapist moved to San Diego and Gary called him three or four times a year for follow-up therapy sessions by phone. From the beginning, the therapy consisted of exploring Gary's feelings about himself with respect to relationships with both men and women, his fear of being "gay," his phobic behavior toward having sex with men, and the social pressure from society and his family to get married. A variety of therapeutic interventions were used, from being supportive, giving assignments, interpreting dreams, and getting Gary to understand his fears and patterns of behavior. Hypnosis was not used with Gary for this 3-year period.

After the 3 years, Gary had accomplished the following. He met a woman 1 month after the start of therapy and continued to see her and have sexual relations with her over the 3 years. Sex with her "was all right." Again, he at first experienced erectile dysfunction at the start of their relationship which later disappeared almost completely, though his fear of "impotency" continued to bother him. There also were periods during which he experienced retarded ejaculation with her. He continued to see Bill and developed a strong emotional as well as sexual relationship. Finally, his erectile dysfunction disappeared with Bill, though from time to time he would reexperience it when their emotional relationship encountered problems.

From 1982 through 1984, his main preoccupation continued to be his business life. His main emotional concern over those 3 years involved Bill. Their relationship had its ups and downs and when it was rocky, it affected his sexual performance, with him experiencing erectile dysfunction as well as depression. His relationship with Joanie continued to run basically smoothly and was sexually satisfying.

In September 1985, Gary asked for a series of sessions and flew to San Diego for this purpose. Gary had a number of concerns he wanted to address in these therapy sessions. He had married Joanie in June of that year and was having sex with her only once a month and was not able to achieve an ejaculation with her. He felt "out of control." As a result of pressures in many areas of his life, Gary's self-image had begun to deteriorate. In addition, since his problems with Bill had gotten worse in the last number of months, Gary found that any sexual contact with other males was extremely unsatisfying and he was not able to achieve an erection. His old feelings of inadequacy had returned.

Hypnosis

Using the Ericksonian model of hypnosis, and Carter's (1983) method of the "Parts Model," the therapist and Gary investigated and clarified the goals that Gary desired. He wanted to be "sexual" (he felt he stopped "being a star" at the age of 14). The opposing part to achieving this goal was a gut wrenching anxiety that he named "gut fear." The desire of the "gut fear" was to protect him from being gay, which was prohibited by his family, his religion (while growing up), and the society he lived in.

Gary was hypnotized. He proved to be a good subject and entered a deep trance easily. The "gut fear" was visualized as a black rock, a monolith, hard and cold, a rock that he had built. His association to the rock was the Prudential Insurance Rock of Gibraltar.

During several hypnosis sessions, Gary changed the visualized rock into a man, then into himself with a large erection. The therapist continued to stress the intention of Gary's "gut fear," which he had declared to be one of protection. Metaphors were used to create the possibility of being sexual and still feeling secure in different contexts. An example of a metaphor used was the use of dangerous atomic energy verus fusion energy, which was both powerful and safe.

At the end of these sessions, Gary felt completely at peace with himself and found that in imagining future sexual contacts he did not have the "gut fear." He had great difficulty in visualizing and feeling the "gut fear" anxiety that he had felt before the hypnosis. Two sessions were used in "future pacing" to ensure that if in the future he became anxious or could not achieve an erection, he was to use that symptom as a symbol to his wanting change and needing protection.

Bisexual married men and women may experience anxiety and depression associated with the inability to integrate heterosexual and homosexual feelings and behaviors in their married lifestyles. The following case history of Arnold exemplifies a brief intervention for one of these people.

CASE HISTORY III

Arnold, a 35-year-old married man with two children came to therapy because of depression and anxiety which was interfering with his marriage and job. He was an intelligent professional who enjoyed his marriage and children and his current sexual relationships with men. Although he was fairly satisfied with his relationships with his wife and lovers, he was often bothered by guilt, anxiety, and depressive episodes which appeared to be related to his failure to integrate the divergent aspects of his love-life. His history revealed successful compartmentalization of his love relationships and confusion as to why he should feel this way. He revealed an orthodox religious background. In addition, he evidenced dependency needs which were met by his wife and parents.

The intervention with Arnold involved educating him about his sexuality, as well as working with him in trance. Later, the educational aspects of his therapy were also accomplished while he was in trance. During his trance sessions, Arnold was given explanations about the conflicting parts of his sexual feelings and behaviors. On the one hand, there was a part of Arnold who loved his wife and children and enjoyed his heterosexual lifestyle. On the other hand, another part of him yearned for a sexual and emotional relationship with another man. These parts were both valid aspects of his personality just as they are for many men and women who engage in bisexual behavior.

Arnold was further given suggestions that he could choose to give up one or the other of these sexual behaviors, or he could choose to have them both. Whatever decision he made would consider all of the parts of himself. These choices or decisions had to do with being separate and independent, part of trusting one's own judgments regardless of messages from society or family. Arnold learned that growing up means making decisions and choices according to how one feels about his or her needs, rather than just what others expect.

Using these themes in trance, Arnold was able to become more comfortable with his bisexual feelings and behaviors. He chose to remain married and continued his homosexual relationships with far less guilt, anxiety, and depression than before. Although conflicts continued in his marriage, he was able to deal with them in ways which were less detrimental to his relationship with his wife.

Childhood sexual prohibitions leading to repressed sexual feelings as an adult often complicate the quest for an integrated sexual identity. In the case history of Karen, the use of metaphor allowed her to reframe her repressed childhood ideas in light of her adult resources.

CASE HISTORY IV

Karen was a 24-year-old lesbian woman born in Boston. She was one of three siblings of parents who came from a wealthy Boston family. While growing up, she was punished severely on several occasions for mistreating or breaking objects in their large and expensive house. When Karen was 18 she went away to a private college in the West and never returned to live at home.

Although Karen held a responsible job and had a wide circle of friends, she complained that her attempts to be sexual with other women were frustrated and confusing to her. Although she had dated men in college, Karen felt strongly that she wanted to be involved with a woman. At the point where she wanted to become sexually intimate in her relationships, she would invariably find some excuse to break off the relationship. Karen had tried to resolve these fears in her 4 months of "insight therapy." This therapy had allowed her to understand the repressed sexual atmosphere of her childhood, but had not changed the fears which caused her to flee from sexually intimate situations.

Karen was referred to one of the authors after looking for a hypnotherapist. Because she had used self-hypnosis in college as a technique for relaxation, she thought hypnotherapy might help her with her current problem. In therapy she was able to accomplish a deep trance in the first therapy session.

Under hypnosis, Karen was instructed to envision herself walking into the china department of a large department store. Emphasis was placed on the fact that she was no longer a child, but rather an independent adult who was able to move freely about the fragile glass and china objects. After browsing through this wonderful store of frail items, she was told to pick several glass or china objects to which she was attracted. She then was allowed to pick up these items one by one, feeling their lightness and frailty, running her fingers over the textures, and safely placing them back in their place. She was then allowed to choose and purchase any piece to which she was attracted. After the store clerk gift-wrapped a cup and saucer safely and securely in a box, she placed it gently in her shopping bag and took it home.

In the next session Karen was instructed to envision herself at home where she was delighted to find her package in the closet. She carefully removed the package from the dark closet, bringing it into the bright sunlight of her apartment where she very carefully began to unwrap it. Every movement of unwrapping the package was described as a sensuous experience until finally she was able to feel the delicate texture of the cup and saucer she had bought for herself. After filling the cup with tea she was instructed to draw a hot bubble bath in which she would enjoy her tea. Emphasis was placed on the details of pleasure involved in taking a bath and at the same time enjoying the pleasurable contact of drinking the tea (i.e., running her lips around the rung of the cup, enjoying the aroma, licking the smooth insides of the cup).

After four sessions of the author working with her in trance, Karen reported feeling more relaxed in her friendships. She eventually reported that she had a sexual experience with a woman with whom she was now spending her free time.

For the person experiencing conflict with his or her own sexual orientation because of religious prohibitions, the use of reframing and synesthesia are useful techniques. The case of John exemplifies an intervention which utilizes these strategies.

CASE HISTORY V

John was a 29-year-old computer programmer who sought therapy because of his unsuccessful sexual experiences. He grew up in a small midwestern town, the only son in a family of six. His mother and father were strict Catholics and he remembered most of his growing-up experiences revolved around the church and family. Although he began to masturbate at an early age and masturbated regularly, he continued to feel guilt about this activity. His experiences with heterosexual intercourse, although he performed adequately, produced excessive guilt which made these relationships unsatisfactory. Because of his somewhat effeminate appearance, John also remembered constantly being labeled "queer." His recent sexual experiences with men left him with the all too familiar guilt and confusion about his sexuality.

Due to John's high level of anxiety, John was initially instructed in the use of self-hypnosis. After two sessions and a homework tape, John was also able to produce a satisfactory trance. At that time, reframing was used as a technique to change John's negative assumptions about his sexuality into one of positive beliefs. John's bisexual confusion was described back to him as an innate flexibility that he was "lucky" to have. His ability to experience sexually both men and women showed a healthy adaptive capability which would allow him to enjoy both men and women, or to be able to make better choices about future sexual partners. In a similar fashion, his religious upbringing gave him the ability to delay immediate gratifications control impulses, and tolerate frustration, all which are prerequisites for building relationship commitments.

The technique of synesthesia were used to change some of the sensations and images about his religion. While in trance, John was asked to create an image that corresponded to the religious guilt feelings he experienced. One of the images that came up was that of the frowning stern pope pointing a finger down to a place envisioned as hell. John was instructed to change the image to that of a benevolent Pope John XXIII wearing an accepting smile, raising his hand above his head pointing toward heaven. Using this technique of synesthesia, John was able to discard his old negative images and feelings and come to view his upbringing as an asset rather than a liability.

SUMMARY

Ericksonian strategies are effective intervention techniques for persons who seek treatment because of confusion about their sexual orientation and sexual/intimate relationships. These techniques allow the therapist to circumvent resistances evoked by traditional theraputic approaches and produce change within a short-term intervention framework.

REFERENCES

Bandler, R., & Grinder, J. (1979). *Frogs and princes.* Moab, Utah: Real People Press.
Carter, P. (1983). *The parts model.* Unpublished manuscript, International College, Santa Monica, CA.

Haley, J. (1963). *Strategies of psychotherapy*. New York: Grune & Straton.
Haley, J. (1982). The contribution to therapy of Milton H. Erickson, MD. In J. Zeig (Ed.), *Ericksonian Approaches to Hypnosis and Psychotherapy* (pp. 17–40). New York: Irvington.
Klein, F., Sepekoff, B., & Wolf, T. (1985). Sexual orientation: A multi-variable dynamic process. *Journal of Homosexuality, 11*(1/2), 35–49.
Rossi, E. (Ed.) (1980). *The collected papers of Milton Erickson on hypnosis*. (Vols. I–IV). New York: Irvington.
Yapko, M. (1984). *Trancework: An introduction to clinical hypnosis*. New York: Irvington.

II. RELATIONSHIP CONCERNS

Therapy for Male Couples Experiencing Relationship Problems and Sexual Problems

Kenneth D. George, PhD
Andrew E. Behrendt, PhD
University of Pennsylvania

SUMMARY. This article examines four issues that need to be explored by the therapist as possible causes of stress for a male couple: stereotypic male roles, stereotypic sexual roles, homophobia, which includes the "coming out" process, and sexual dysfunctions. These issues can cause anxiety and stress, which may in turn cause relationship problems for a male couple. The role of the therapist is clarified and suggestions for treatment are given.

While there has been relatively little written about therapy for male couples who are experiencing difficulties in their relationship, these couples do seek help when conflicts occur. However, therapists usually have had more experience working with heterosexual couples and sometimes they may not be knowledgeable about the unique issues that effect male couples. The purpose of this article is to describe those issues that need to be examined by therapists as possible causes of anxiety and stress in male couples seeking therapy.

Dr. George is Professor and Chair of the Human Sexuality Program in the Graduate School of Education, University of Pennsylvania. Dr. Behrendt is a lecturer in the same program. Correspondence may be addressed Dr. George, Professor and Chair, Human Sexuality Program, University of Pennsylvania, Graduate School of Education, Philadelphia, PA 19104.

MALE COUPLES

All couples in a healthy relationship, whether homosexual or hetero-sexual, have similar characteristics: The people are committed to each other, share feelings, respect each other, are intimate, and have a capacity to resolve conflicts. Furthermore, in healthy male couples, each man accepts his own homosexuality. This acceptance is necessary for good self-esteem, for he is then more likely to have an appreciation of his partner and an appreciation of himself as a part of a male couple.

Most homosexual men want a loving relationship with a person of the same gender (Harry & Lovely, 1979) and surveys of homosexual men reveal that about half of them are currently involved with a partner (Jay & Young, 1979). McWhirter and Mattison (1984) estimate "that about 2.5 million male couples live in the United States." (p. 149) Dailey (1979) compared homosexual couples, heterosexual married couples, and unmarried heterosexual couples living together. There were few differ-ences between the three groups in terms of the "success" of the relationship or in overall adjustment.

Homosexual men do have positive feelings about love relationships and do have future plans for themselves as a couple (Jones & Bates, 1978), contrary to misconceptions that they are lonely, depressed, or guilty (Williams & Weinberg, 1974). They value their relationships, and do work on them (McWhirter & Mattison, in Anderson 1980). The authors' experiences are in accordance with some of the previous published articles on this topic, e.g., Mendola (1980), Silverstein (1981), and Harry (1976/77). Homosexual men will seek therapy when they recognize they are having difficulties as a couple, provided that (a) identifying themselves as a couple is not precluded by discriminatory practices by the therapist, and (b) they are not treated as if their homosexuality was the cause of their conflict.

CLINICAL MATERIAL

The conclusions presented in this article are based on the authors' clinical experiences with homosexual males who have sought therapy for relationship or sexual difficulties or both during the last 11 years. These men were usually well-educated and in the middle to upper middle socio-economic bracket. They identified themselves as homosexual and as a male couple and recognized that they were having problems. Many of the presenting problems of the homosexual men were similar to the presenting problems of heterosexual clients and couples. The authors, however, have identified four stresses that make working with male couples different than working with heterosexual couples.

AREAS OF STRESS FOR HOMOSEXUAL MEN

Being homosexual and being part of a male couple can bring about unique stresses that are different than the stresses experienced by heterosexual men. In working with male couples, the authors have identified four stresses that need to be explored by the therapist as possible causes of conflict: (a) stereotypic male roles; (b) stereotypic sexual roles; (c) homophobia, which includes the "coming out" process; and (d) sexual dysfunctions. These four stresses are individual issues that each member of the couple may bring into the relationship.

There are three other areas that must also be examined by the therapist: (a) type of couple, i.e., their love style; (2) stage of couple development; and (3) the couple's contract. Because these three areas are discussed by others (See Notes 1, 2, and 3), this article will only discuss the individual issues brought into the relationship that are unique for homosexual men and male couples.

Stereotypic Male Roles

Peplau (1981) states that gender role exerts a greater influence on a relationship than does sexual orientation. In working with male couples, the authors have found relationship problems when one or both of the partners have adopted a rigid stereotypic male role.

The stereotypic male role in our society is to be competitive. Men should be unemotional, the best, in control, strong, capable, and independent. Boys are taught this is how to behave and how to feel (and not feel) in order to be loved, worthwhile, and appropriate men. Boys learn that it would make them feminine if they were tender, caring, or if they acknowledged their weaknesses and needs, and asked for what they want rather than demanded it.

Since both partners in a male couple are men, there is a good possibility that one or both of them have learned a rigid stereotypic male role. Problems may occur in the relationship when one or both men adopt this rigid stereotypic male role. For instance, one of the ingredients for a loving relationship is the ability to communicate, not just behaviors or feelings of anger and control, but needs, feelings of tenderness, and feelings that, once expressed, may leave the man vulnerable. However, what will two men, behaving according to a rigid male stereotypic role, communicate to each other? What kind of loving relationship can exist if both the partners are constantly competing? How can two men in a relationship *both* win? Will they allow themselves to be vulnerable, to let their weaknesses show, and to let the partner see the "real" person? A man who has adopted the societal messages of what a man should be will have difficulty taking these risks. How can a good relationship develop unless risks are taken? A rigid male stereotypic role is a source of conflict for many couples, and especially for couples in which both partners are male.

Stereotypic Sexual Roles

The second issue for male couples is stereotypic sexual roles. The sexual role messages that our society has given to men is that they are "supposed" to be sexually active, experienced, ready and able to perform at any time or any circumstance (Zilbergeld, 1978). Unfortunately, many homosexual men believe these messages. The homosexual male's self-esteem may depend upon his partner perceiving him as masculine and as a good sex partner. How does his partner evaluate his sexual performance? What effect will this have on his self-image; or on his image as a sex partner or as part of the couple? A belief that he must always be desirous and capable of having sex may create considerable stress.

The AIDS health crisis has created further anxiety for homosexual men, including some men in relationships. Each partner may remember his earlier unsafe sex acts and this may cause anxiety. Anxiety may lead to poorer sexual performance and to more insecurity about his sexual role. Also, in newer relationships, the question arises as to how long must the couple practice "safe sex," especially if they are in a monandrous relationship. They must also have "safe sex" with others if they have an open relationship. All of these concerns about AIDS and "safe sex" do cause anxiety and stress in the relationship, feelings should be explored and discussed.

In the authors' experience, most homosexual men prefer a variety of sexual positions and activities. They usually do what feels good and gives them pleasure at the time. Although some homosexual men do have a specific preference, unfortunately, some gay men have equated specific sex acts with masculinity or feminity. The person who is sexually "active" is considered the more masculine sex partner, and the sexually "passive" person is considered the feminine sex partner; this is another sexual role message. Problems can occur when the partners get locked into a specific sexual act because of a role that is being played. Adopting a rigid sexual role can be disastrous to sexual interactions and relationships.

Another stress is caused by "performance anxiety," that is, worrying about performing well. Whatever sexual act they do, they must be "good" at it. They both must ejaculate and have an orgasm. Both must achieve these goals and work hard at doing so. Unfortunately, this often leads to negative results and sex that is not as enjoyable for either partner.

Homophobia

In addition to the normal stresses in our society, the homosexual male is subject to other internal and external stresses due to homophobia, the irrational fear of homosexuality. Homophobia is present in a majority of heterosexual people. What many do not realize is that homophobia is also present among many homosexual males, an issue sometimes ignored by the therapist. Our society has historically viewed homosexuality negatively. Religiously, homosexuality has been considered a sin, laws have made homosexual acts illegal, and, until recently, homosexuality was treated as a mental illness. Most homosexual males grew up hearing derogatory put-downs, such as "queer," "fag," and "faggot." Most homosexual males cannot escape, at least for a period of time, incorporating these negative societal messages into their own self-concepts.

Many homosexual men believe homophobic misconceptions about homosexuality. The first of these homophobic misconceptions is that *sex* between two men is "unnatural" and "immoral." If the homosexual man believes this, he will experience severe conflict in his sexual interactions with other men. The second misconception is that homosexual *relationships* are "immoral and unnatural." If the homosexual man views male relationships in this way, he will have a conflict in thinking positively of his own relationship. The third misconception is that homosexual relationships are short-lived and that homosexual men cannot sustain continued, long-term relationships. If the homosexual man adheres to this belief, this can become a self-fulfilling prophecy which prevents him from forming a lasting relationship with another man. The fourth misconception is that homosexual men have sex with many different partners. If the homosexual man accepts this message, he may act on this belief. He may also feel trapped in a relationship that does not allow him to have many partners. Acting on this belief has caused problems in many relationships.

The authors have found that homophobia is a *crucial* factor to explore in evaluating a homosexual man's acceptance of himself as a person and as a part of a male couple. Homophobia puts extra stress on him and on the couple.

In the "coming out" process, homosexual men examine their own conflicts about being homosexual and living as a homosexual person, and in the process deal with some of the homophobic messages. The authors have identified three stages to the "coming out" process. (There are other models that describe the "coming out" process, e.g. Coleman (1981/82) and Dank (1971)).

The first stage of the coming out process is the acknowledgment of one's own self as homosexual. This realization is usually very traumatic, especially if the man has not challenged some of the societal attitudes about homosexuality. A homosexual man must privately admit his own homosexuality or he will not be able to accept and maintain a relationship with another man.

The second stage is acknowledging homosexuality to other homosexual people and building a support system consisting of other homosexual people. Unless he enters this stage of "coming out," it will be difficult for a homosexual man to meet a "special person."

The third stage, which not all homosexual men attain, is that of sharing the knowledge of one's homosexuality with relatives, heterosexual friends, co-workers, and employers. Often the third stage creates conflicts. It may be that by coming out to others, the homosexual man suffers rejection and abuse. Yet by not coming out, there is the stress of not being true to oneself and having to live a double life, putting on a mask to the world and pretending to be heterosexual. Each homosexual man has to decide for himself with whom he shares his sexual identity.

When the individuals in a couple are at different stages of the coming out process stresses can arise in the relationship. Even if they are at the same stage, there may be problems due to the amount of psychic energy that is devoted to this process. The stage of coming out frequently predicts the psychological healthiness of the individual and the relationship. The more open the members of a male couple are about their homosexual identity, the more adjusted the individuals and the relationship tends to be. The therapist should be aware of the amount of disclosure and its effect upon the couple.

The "candy store" is a term the authors use to identify certain individuals who are not yet ready to be in a one-to-one relationship. The majority of men, homosexual and heterosexual, learn to date as adolescents. At that time, boys are given certain guidelines by their parents and peers, rules on how to behave on a date. This is also the time that many homosexual adolescents start the first stage of the coming out process, as indicated by feelings of being "different," although the overt socializing may be exclusively with girls. Indeed, quite often the adolescent years are spent dating heterosexually.

When the homosexual man enters the second state of the "coming out" process, when he meets other men with whom he can share his sexual identity, it is as if a child enters a "candy store." All of the feelings he has denied expression previously are ready to explode in his sharing with others, and his feelings of isolation begin to disappear. He will begin to date, for the first time, someone to whom he is erotically attracted. He may act as if he is making up for lost time, and just like a child in a candy store, he may want to sample "this one, and this one, and this one." However, unlike during the adolescent years, there are no guidelines and no parents to help with certain decisions, as there were when he was an adolescent.

Many of these men enter the candy store, but do not take the time to go through a dating stage. They meet someone and form a relationship shortly after meeting. This male couple gets an apartment, signs a lease, and buys a dog, all within a short period of time. This couple may enter therapy because they want the relationship to work. However, one or both of the partners may also want his independence and may express a feeling of being trapped. We have seen this issue in couples where one or both have formed a homosexual relationship soon after leaving a heterosexual marriage. It is important for homosexual men to experience the candy store stage of dating prior to forming a one-to-one relationship. One would not encourage heterosexual individuals to marry until they experience dating over a period of time, perhaps with different people. Regardless of his age, a homosexual man in this stage needs to date over a period of time, perhaps with different people. This is a time when a homosexual man can experience and reflect in order to determine his needs in a relationship with another man.

Sexual Dysfunctions

In the authors' work with male couples, there is sometimes an associated sexual dysfunction with one or both of the partners. Homosexual men may experience any number of sexual dysfunctions and the associate problems of those dysfunctions, contrary to the observations of Masters and Johnson (1979). Many male couples have reported to the authors that a previous therapist never asked them to discuss the sexual part of their relationship nor explored the possibility of a sexual dysfunction. A possible explanation for this is that such therapists are uncomfortable discussing sex between two men. Also, some therapists may believe that homosexual men do not have sexual dysfunctions.

The most frequent sexual dysfunction in the authors' practice with homosexual men has been inhibited sexual desire, this in contrast to what has been reported by Masters and Johnson (1979) and McWhirter and Mattison (1978). Inhibited sexual excitement (impotence or erectile dysfunction) was the most frequent dysfunction of the homosexual men seen by Masters and Johnson and by McWhirter and Mattison.

The next most frequent dysfunction found among the authors' clients was inhibited male orgasm (retarded or ejaculatory incompetence), followed by inhibited sexual excitement (impotence or erectile dyfunction), and finally premature ejaculation. Often these sexual dysfunctions were not reported as the initial presenting problem, but were discovered in the course of the first several sessions. The present discussion will be limited to treatment that is specific to homosexual men and male couples, for there already exists a plethora of generalized material about sexual dysfunctions and their treatment.

The following selected clinical cases will illustrate how the previous

three issues, stereotypic male roles, stereotypic sexual roles, and homophobia, relate to sexual function and dysfunction.

Inhibited Sexual Desire

> John and David came into therapy together. David's complaint was
> that John did not want to have sex with him. David did not want to
> go outside of the relationship for sex. John claimed he did not need
> sex and did not want it. He would rather read or watch television.
> Sex was just not enjoyable for him. Otherwise, their relationship
> was healthy.

In the therapists' review of John and David's history, it was evident
that John was experiencing a lot of stress due to his homophobia. In
working with male couples similar to this couple, the therapist needs to
explore with each partner the homophobic messages he has learned, such
as: How does he feel about being homosexual? How do his parents view
his homosexuality? Does his family now accept his partner? What were
his childhood religious convictions? Did anything traumatic happen early
in his life to cause him to be anxious about his homosexuality?

For homosexual men who report a lack of sexual desire, one of the
sources of stress is frequently a traumatic experience early in life arising
out of religious, social, and family taboos against homosexuality.
Consequently, the therapist should examine each man's views about
homosexuality. The homosexual man with inhibited sexual desire usually
has integrated many of the negative societal messages about homosexuality, causing him to be homophobic.

There is another group of men who avoid sex due not to lack of desire,
but to a phobic aversion to sex. These men are different from those men
who lack desire. Generally, they are not homophobic, yet they have
unconscious anger and resentment against men in general. In the authors'
experience, this has been due to an unresolved issue or issues with their
fathers. Therefore, a phobic aversion to getting close to, loving, and
having sex with a man is experienced. However, because they are
homosexual, they have little desire to have sex with women. They avoid
sex until they meet someone special, and then come into therapy because
of this underlying conflict.

Inhibited Male Orgasm

> Tony and John came into therapy because of their constant arguing.
> Tony was very controlling, and John expressed that he frequently
> felt as if Tony was a child. Tony expressed concerns about not being

appreciated. During the third and fourth sessions, when Tony and John were seen separately, both stated that Tony could not ejaculate with anal or oral sex, regardless of whether he was the inserter or the insertee. He did ejaculate through masturbation when he was alone, but never with John. He was a very controlled person. He was no longer religious, but had a strict Catholic childhood and at one time wanted to be a priest.

We have found two attributes common to many homosexual men experiencing inhibited male orgasm. The first is an internal conflict regarding homosexuality; they are homophobic. They believe that homosexuality is wrong and they should not be having sex with a man, and thus they have difficulty getting close to and intimate with another man. The second commonality is they have sexual fantasies of aggression. Associated with these fantasies are fears, fears that they might try to live out their sexual fantasies with another man. Because they need to be in control, to live the fantasies would be unacceptable for they would then be out of control.

Inhibited Sexual Excitement

Larry came into therapy with a history of having had many different sex partners. He rarely could maintain an erection with any of them. When he met Jim, he wanted more than just a "one night stand." The first time they tried to have sex, Larry could not get an erection. The pattern repeated itself on subsequent attempts. Larry was afraid that Jim would not want to have a loving relationship with him if he could not get and maintain an erection. Larry wanted this relationship to work. He finally admitted to himself that he had a sexual problem, and came into therapy.

The major problem is that homosexual men with inhibited sexual excitement usually believe the stereotypic views of masculinity and male sexuality. They have adopted a role and thus experience performance anxiety. How am I doing? How do I compare with his previous partners? What does he think of my sexual ability? Will he tell others I am not very good? Such men are performance-oriented. They spectate rather than participate in the sexual activity, are constantly grading themselves or believe that they are being graded by their partner on how well they are doing sexually, and very rarely abandon themselves in a sexual act. There is little pleasurable involvement. (In such cases, the therapist must check on the amount of alcohol the client consumes. Because gay bars are frequently the only known social meeting place for homosexual men, they may also drink too much).

Premature Ejaculation

When these men come into therapy for a relationship problem, during an early session the partner with the sexual dysfunction will usually state, "I come too quickly to enjoy having sex." This group of men report the same anxieties that heterosexual men report. However, in the authors' practice, premature ejaculation is the least reported of the sexual dysfunctions. Perhaps when two men are sexually involved, the goal is to ejaculate; therefore, they do not as often complain of being "premature."

GENERAL TREATMENT CONSIDERATIONS

The therapist working with a male couple must first examine his or her own views of homosexuality. If the stereotypic homophobic misconceptions identified earlier are believed by the therapist, whether he or she is homosexual or heterosexual, then the male couple should be referred to another therapist.

When a male couple comes for treatment, the therapist must acknowledge them as a couple, not as two unrelated men. They are a couple and it is imperative that they be treated as such. Some male couples have reported to the authors that previous therapists did not treat them as a legitimate couple.

Develop a Support System

If the male couple has not developed a support system, it is important that they do so. This is especially necessary during times of crisis. A support system can acknowledge and affirm two men as a couple, support that heterosexual couples often get from family, church or synagogues, and friends. Also, the therapist should be knowledgeable about the various homosexual organizations in the community that can be used by the couple as resources for developing a support system.

Examine Homophobic Messages

The therapist must have each man examine his own homophobic beliefs. While examining the couple's homophobic beliefs, the therapist should be aware of the amount of disclosure, the stage of coming out, of each of the partners and its effect on them individually and as a couple. The couple must see themselves as a legitimate couple with a sense of permanence.

Identify "Role Expectation" Messages

During therapy, it is important to help the couple become more aware of the "role expectation" messages that they each have received about being homosexual, being male, about sex and relationships. Can they risk affection, or is this considered feminine? Do they believe that homosexual relationships do not work? Did they have sex too soon and then think less of their partner—an extension of a heterosexual notion that she is not "good enough to marry" if she "gave in" too soon? How do they feel about "safe sex"? (Note 4 identifies where to obtain information on "safe sex"). How do they view monandous relationships, or was this chosen because of their fear of AIDS?

Often the basis for therapeutic success is education. It is important for each man to learn that he does not have to: (a) have sex if he chooses not to, (b) ejaculate during the sexual activity, (c) assume the responsibility for how the sexual activity goes, or (d) do any sexual act unless he chooses to do so. The therapist may need to give permission to be sensual, to ask for what one wants, and to receive as well as give pleasure. During therapy, the couple should never be made to believe that their particular sexual activity is "abnormal," "sick," or dysfunctional because it does not meet with an arbitrary standard of "normality." But the therapist does have the responsibility to educate the patient about "safe sex" during the AIDS health crisis.

In understanding that roles are arbitrary, many homosexual men move beyond these limiting behaviors and work toward establishing the kind of relationship that is most suitable for them individually and as a couple. They can then discover their particular needs for affection, intimacy, sex, power, control, dependence, and roles.

CONCLUSION AND SPECIFIC TREATMENT CONSIDERATION

This article discussed stresses that are unique to homosexual men and male couples in order that a relationship therapist can develop an effective treatment strategy. All of this treatment requires time and commitment for therapy. However, when the male couple first comes to see the therapist, it is often because the partners are experiencing a problem, and they may be angry, fighting, and want the conflicts resolved immediately. The therapist can help them by actually utilizing stereotypic male roles to the couples' advantage, i.e. the stereotypic male role of being the decision maker. The therapist should ask them quite bluntly, "What is more important, the relationship or the conflict?", and then allow each of them to be the decison maker. If they both decide that the relationship is the more important, relationship therapy can begin.

NOTES

1. Love styles are discussed in Lee, J.A. (1973). *The colors of love*. New York: Bantam Books.
2. The stages of couple development are discussed in McWhirter, D. P., & Mattison, A. M. (1984). *The male couple*. Englewood Cliffs, NJ: Prentice-Hall.
3. The couple contract is discussed in Sager, C. J. (1976). *Marriage contracts and couple therapy*. New York: Brunner/Mazel.
4. The following pamphlets describe "Safe Sex" and are available by writing to the identified source: (a) *Guidelines and recommendations for healthful gay sexual activities*. National Coalition of Gay Sexual Transmitted Diseases, P. O. Box 239, Milwaukee, WI 53201; (b) *AIDS and healthful sexual activity*. American Association of Physicians for Human Rights, P. O. Box 14366, San Francisco, CA 94114.

REFERENCES

Anderson, S. (1980, February 7). Working relationships. *The Advocate*, pp. 18–21.

Coleman, E. (1981/82). Developmental stages of the coming out process. *Journal of Homosexuality*, 7(2/3), 31–43.

Dailey, D. M. (1979). Adjustment of heterosexual and homosexual couples in pairing relationships: An exploratory study. *The Journal of Sex Research*, 15, 143–157.

Dank, B. M. (1971). Coming out in the gay world. *Psychiatry*, 34, 189–197.

Harry, J. (1976/77). On the validity of typologies of gay males. *Journal of Homosexuality*, 2, 143–152.

Harry, J., & Lovely, R. (1979). Gay marriages and communities of sexual orientation. *Alternative Lifestyles*, 2, 177–200.

Jay, K., & Young, A (1979). *The gay report*. New York: Summit Books.

Jones, R. W., & Bates, J. E. (1978). Satisfaction in male homosexual couples. *Journal of Homosexuality*, 3, 217–224.

Lee, J. A. (1973). *The colors of love*. New York: Bantam Books.

Masters, W. H., & Johnson, V. E. (1979). *Homosexuality in perspective*. Boston: Little, Brown.

McWhirter, D. P., & Mattison, A. M. (1978). The treatment of sexual dysfunction in gay males couples. *The Journal of Sex and Marital Therapy*, 4, 213–218.

McWhirter, D. P., & Mattison, A. M. (1984). *The male couple*. Englewood Cliffs, NJ: Prentice-Hall.

Mendola, M. (1980). *The Mendola report: A new look at gay couples*. New York: Crown Books.

Peplau, L. A. (March, 1981). What homosexuals want. *Psychology Today*, pp. 28–38.

Sager, C. J. (1976). *Marriages contracts and couple therapy*. New York: Brunner/Mazel.

Silverstein, C. (1981). *Man to man: Gay couples in America*. New York: William Morrow.

Williams, C., & Weinberg, M. (1974). *Male homosexuals: Their problems and adaptations*. New York: Oxford.

Zilbergeld, B. (1978). *Male sexuality*. Boston: Little, Brown.

Stage Discrepancy
in Male Couples

Andrew M. Mattison, PhD
David P. McWhirter, MD

CASE EXAMPLE ONE: LOSS OF LIMERENCE

Phil and David sought couples therapy because they both felt that their 2-1/2-year relationship was in trouble. Phil was a 28-year-old physician who had recently started his own private practice. David was 26 and had been a telephone repairman for the last 4 years. It was at Phil's insistence that the appointment had been made. Fidgeting, he sat in the chair and began with a long list of worries. "Things have changed so much and it scares me. Up until recently we did everything together. We shared the same friends, finished each other's sentences, and would spend long hours talking about how things were going for us. Sex was hot and we had lots of it. All of that has changed in some ways."

David chimed in, "Phil is right and somehow I feel like the bad guy in all of this. I think I love him even more than before, but things are different with me. I don't have that need anymore to talk every detail to death. I am beginning to contact friends I had before I met Phil."

As their story unfolded, we learned that David was actively involved in homemaking and remodeling the kitchen and bathroom in their shared house, while Phil was preoccupied with what he saw as a loss of passion in their lives. David was from a mid-western farming family and was by nature quiet and reserved. Phil, an adolescent convert to Catholicism, was from an upper middle class, educated, urban family. It would be difficult to find two men with greater differences in their backgrounds. When they first met, each recently had terminated a 2-year relationship. Both Phil and David vividly remembered "being burned" and left "feeling gun-shy in letting in someone new." Understandably, at the outset each was self-protective in allowing vulnerability and intimacy to grow only in a very controlled way.

Dr. Mattison is Assistant Clinical Professor of Family and Community Medicine at the School of Medicine, University of California at San Diego, and is in private practice. Dr. McWhirter is Assistant Clinical Professor of Psychiatry at the School of Medicine, University of California at San Diego, supervising psychiatrist at the San Diego Department of Mental Health, and maintains a private practice. Correspondence may be addressed to the authors, 4545 Park Blvd., Ste. 207, San Diego, CA 92116.

Discussion

Phil was quite worried about the changes and did not see them for the stage discrepant changes that they were, but as something gone awry with the relationship. He was very much committed to the high blending of stage one, in which he wanted to do everything together and talk every detail out with David in order to feel constantly reassured. He was worried that the decline in sex was an indication that David did not love him as much. He was unsure of how committed David was to the longevity of the relationship. The reality, as the authors saw it, was that they were equally committed to each other and the relationship, but in David's instance the commitment began to take on different characteristics as the relationship matured. David had slipped into stage two and was busy homemaking and finding other ways to establish compatibility with his partner, while Phil was still standing squarely with his feet in stage one, wondering what had happened to the highly limerent relationship (Tennov, 1979) that has so powerfully swept them along for the previous 2 years. This couple demonstrates what we call stage discrepancy.

A WAY TO VIEW CHANGE

Regardless of the differences from man to man, human relationships themselves form separate entities and pass through a series of developmental stages in much the same way that a person grows and develops. The authors have identified six stages (McWhirter & Mattison, 1984) (see Table 1). Each possesses a unique set of characteristics with both positive and negative factors. Couples more through these stages as their relationship grows, although they may find it necessary at times to revert to some characteristics of an early stage. The movement from the first stage to the sixth stage follows somewhat of an orderly pattern and is essential for growth. The importance of this discovery lies in the fact that, prior to this time, many persons believed that they had personality flaws, when the problems that arose really were nothing more than some of the unpleasant manifestations of the various stages of the relationship, like the "terrible twos" or the "feisty fives" of the developing child.

The movement from one stage to the next may appear to the psychotherapist to occur in an even, step-by-step, forward manner. However, many individuals and couples move a few steps backward in the process of moving ahead, an individual may not traverse the stages at the same speed his partner is traveling, and individuals can be dealing with issues of more than one stage at one time. Most importantly, each characteristic in every stage is a process, not an event. Dealing with stage-related issues happens over time, sometimes again and again, and

Table 1

Stages of Relationships

Stage One - Blending (Year One)

    Characteristics
    1. Merging
    2. Limerence
    3. Equalizing of partnership
    4. High sexual activity

Stage Two - Nesting (Years Two and Three)

    Characteristics
    1. Homemaking
    2. Finding compatibility
    3. Decline of limerence
    4. Ambivalence

State Three - Maintaining (Years Four and Five)

    Characteristics
    1. Reappearance of the individual
    2. Risk taking
    3. Dealing with conflict
    4. Establishing traditions

Stage Four - Building (Years Six through Ten)

    Characteristics
    1. Collaborating
    2. Increasing productivity
    3. Establishing independence
    4. Dependability of partners

Stage Five - Releasing (Years Eleven through Twenty)

    Characteristics
    1. Trusting
    2. Merging of money and possessions
    3. Constricting
    4. Taking each other for granted

Stage Six - Renewing (Beyond Twenty Years)

    Characteristics
    1. Achieving security
    2. Shifting perspectives
    3. Restoring the partnership
    4. Remembering

sometimes the process does not stop. We do not think human relationships can be reduced to a simplistic formula like a linear, step-ladder, theory of stages. However, a theoretic model of stages of relationships provides a helpful framework for both couples and the therapist in understanding how relationships and individuals change over time. It is like a map which charts change in direction in the course of a journey. With the application of this model to clinical practice, the therapist can identify and even anticipate those common problems that develop when one partner is in a different stage than his mate. This article reviews some of the more common stage discrepant problems and provides suggestions to psychotherapists in assessing the problems, directions, and strategies for therapeutic intervention.

STAGE DISCREPANCY

Stage discrepancy between partners is one of the most common experiences in relationship development. When one partner experiences characteristics of a stage sooner than the other, stage discrepancy becomes apparent. This is a problem that the authors find so frequently in their clinical practice that much of their psychotherapy with male couples focuses on elucidating and resolving stage-related discrepancies. For example, one may may be individualizing, which frequently occurs in Stage Three, while his partner is deeply committed to the merging to Stage One.

Some Factors Affecting Stage Discrepancy

As with any developing entity, a relationship can be influenced by many factors. Each partner brings to it a unique set of past experiences which can speed up or slow down the movement from stage to stage. Couples with a wide disparity in ages may experience stages at a different pace. A man who has been in previous long-term relationships can find himself moving from Stage One to Stage Two in a few months, while his younger partner, in his first relationship, wants to linger and savor the enveloping feelings of Stage One.

Experiences in previous relationships also can accelerate or brake the forward momentum as time passes. Several emotionally painful experiences can slow down the development of trust for one, while the other easily moves forward with his trust of the partner. A past heterosexual marriage can be a factor which contributes to stage discrepancy early in a male couple's relationship, especially if the formerly married person patterns his expectations of his male partner after those he had for his former wife.

CASE EXAMPLE TWO: DISCREPANCY WITH EQUALIZING

Wil had been married for 7 years, and divorced for 2 years, before becoming lovers with Brad. There was a 6-year difference in their ages and Wil earned considerably more money than Brad; thus, Wil had the idea from the beginning that he was the dominant influence in the partnership. He expected Brad to do certain household chores and naturally follow his lead in the music they played or TV shows they watched. Wil, however subtly, would decide where the couple would vacation and what major purchases they would make. When Brad began to withdraw, lose sexual interest, and spend more time away from home, the couple made an appointment for a couples' assessment.

Discussion

In the evaluation it became quite clear that Wil was completely unaware of how he had been dominating the relationship. Also, Brad was not able to conceptualize what was happening, but he knew that he was not being an equal partner in the relationship. Wil was not working to equalize the partnership, and Brad was beginning to avoid his lover because of his dissatisfaction with the power balance in the relationship. Once the couple began to understand this discrepancy, they began making progress in realigning their relationship.

ASSESSMENT

Making a comprehensive evaluation of the couple and individual is crucial for a successful intervention and outcome. For the authors, this means evaluating the couple in terms of each individual and the well-being of the relationship. The goals of the first session include (a) identifying the presenting problem for each, (b) exploring the development of the relationship, (c) determining expectations from each regarding the relationship and the therapy, (d) evaluating the degree to which each assumes individual responsibility for the difficulties and the motivation for therapy, (e) identifying individual personality traits and potential psychopathology, and (f) identifying background similarities and differences.

Keeping in mind the authors' model of stages of relationships, a detailed history of the development of the relationship is gathered, including: (a) how they met, the early attractions to each other, and when they began to identify themselves as a couple; (b) how they see themselves as similar to each other, and in what ways different; (c) what they like about their partner and what they would like to see changed in him; (d) what they perceive to be their own strengths as well as weaknesses; (e) what makes them feel afraid, and what are their areas of confidence; (f) a history of their sexual behavior and areas of satisfaction, and areas in which they are not satisfied; (g) how they see their particular problems at the time, what they have done in an effort to deal with them, and how they have dealt with their problems in the past; and, finally (h) how each of them thinks his lover would respond to all of those same questions.

Once again, non-stage related issues may affect the forward movement of the relationship when one man is in a different developmental phase then his partner. The following is a list of other issues that are included in the evaluation: (a) dependency needs; (b) ways of maintaining feelings of closeness; (c) anti-homosexual attitudes such as prejudice, ignorance, homophobia, and oppression; (d) chemical dependency; (e) physical illness; (f) role models and an emotional support system; and (g) any psychiatric problems.

Assessment can be accomplished by a team composed of two males, a female and a male therapist, or by a single therapist of either sex. Experience with all these combinations inclines us toward a single therapist because studies in our clinic show the outcome is about the same with any combination, and a single therapist costs less.

After the initial session with the couple, each partner is seen individually for one or two sessions to review his developmental history. The following areas are investigated: (a) his relationships as a child with parents and siblings; (b) the importance and influence of religion in his family of origin; (c) his socio-economic and ethnic background; (d) the way in which tenderness and affection were or were not expressed in his family; (e) how arguments and conflicts were handled within his family; (f) at what age he began to feel different from other boys and his understanding of that (sometimes an awareness of being different from other boys preceeding a conscious awareness of his homosexual orientation.); (g) a careful description of his coming out; (h) a summary of dating, boyfriends, and lover relationships in adolescence and early adulthood; and (i) a thorough sexual history.

Some therapists find it helpful to have the couple hear each other's developmental history as a way of learning more about each other. This can be a very therapeutic approach, especially if each partner is then also given some private time with the therapist.

In the next session, the therapist meets with the couple together and outlines a treatment plan. In this session, the problem areas are reframed for the couple; they hear a new description in terms of stage discrepancy, which explains some of the difficulties that they are experiencing. Providing a cognitive framework for looking at their relationship and the problems that they are experiencing removes some of the emotional pain that each is experiencing, and reduces the blame or the guilt that each may feel and interpret as failure in the relationship. The cognitive realignment or reframing becomes the focus for subsequent therapeutic interactions.

Once the therapist recognizes the stage discrepancies and other mismatches and shares the information with the couple, the real therapeutic work begins. The therapist can assist the couple in learning ways to find compatibility, to make compromises, and to adjust to undesirable habits and personality differences. However, once these discrepancies, mismatches, and differences are pointed out in the assessment, it does not necessarily follow that attitudes and behaviors are going to change. Usually a release of tension occurs because the partners begin to understand the origins and reasons for their difficulties. The therapeutic task is to help them develop skills whereby they can be more accepting of each other, and not necessarily see their differences as flaws in the relationship.

CASE EXAMPLE THREE: REFRAMING BACKGROUND DIFFERENCES

Jim and Peter began therapy as a result of ongoing conflicts they had in handling their finances which led to arguments and feelings of being misunderstood and resulted in their becoming more and more distant from each other. Each contributed to their joint checking account, from which all bills were paid. Peter assumed responsibility for balancing the account and was the more serious one in planning the short- and long-range expenditures with Jim. Peter came from a lower-income family in which any household purchases were budgeted carefully and discussed between his parents before hand. Jim's family was affluent and purchases were made on a whim without consulting with family members. When feeling depressed, Jim would go shopping and buy a new shirt to elevate his spirits; if he did not consult Peter first, Peter would become furious. "How could he do this to us? It's just another sign of his not considering me. And what if I can't make the monthly expenses as a result of his spending sprees?"

Discussion

Once the couple became aware that the real source of their conflict was their background differences, Peter no longer felt so hurt, and Jim now understood what he thought to be Peter's irrational responses when he would buy a shirt without mentioning it to Peter. However, this understanding did not result in change in Jim's behavior or a change in Peter's belief that expenditures should be planned and budgeted. The therapist recommended that Jim set aside some money that would not go into the joint account which he could spend whenever the impulse arose. Peter agreed, and the compromise worked.

CASE EXAMPLE FOUR: MERGING VERSUS INDIVIDUALIZING

A frequent manifestation of stage discrepancy occurs when one man lingers in the high merging and high limerence of Stage One, while his partner is venturing out to reappearance of the individual which is a characteristic of Stage Three. A couple for 2 years, Tim and Jeff had had a torrid, highly limerent relationship for 1-1/2 years when Tim remembered "Jeff's flame began to flicker." Tim maintained high limerence and continued to view Jeff through illusory eyes—"my white knight, no faults, only virtues." In addition, he could not understand Jeff's change in attitude and current anger due to Tim's leaving hair in the bathroom sink, clothes on the floor, and dirty dishes stacked up in the kitchen sink. Jeff was frustrated with these behaviors, even though Tim had always been like that. Tim worried that Jeff didn't love him anymore. Although both agreed to begin psychotherapy with the hope of restoring harmony, Tim expressed his fear "that things were all over for us."

Discussion

After the assessment and during the fourth session, Tim and Jeff each began to understand the stage discrepancy they were experiencing. Couples report considerable relief when this concept is explained to them, just as the man with chest pain is relieved when the physician tells him it is only muscle strain and not a heart attack. With this relief and the consequent reduction in Tim's anxiety and Jeff's annoyances, the therapist focused on methods to improve their skills in getting along better. Tim did not like the change in Jeff's passion, but understood that an enduring relationship is not fueled by limerence forever. Tim ungrudgingly began to be more tidy in an effort to demonstrate his attentiveness. Recognizing Tim's need for reassurance, Jeff made more conscious efforts to be affectionate as an expression of his love, and learned to be more patient with Tim's shortcomings.

The most common stage discrepancy we see occurs when one person is committed to the merging of Stage One and his partner is tending to the reappearance of the individual which usually happens in Stage Three. This discrepancy can be very difficult to navigate in the process of rebalancing, and at a time ripe with the danger of misunderstandings. The relationship can sink the partnership unless each has some awareness about the shoals that lie ahead.

CASE EXAMPLE FIVE: MERGING VERSUS INDIVIDUALIZING

Sean was 21 years old and had been together with John for 2-1/2 years. John helped to bring Sean out of the closet, and this was the first relationship for Sean. John, 34 years old, had had two previous lovers. During their first year, John and Sean did everything together—from laundry to shopping to finishing each other's sentences and enjoying the same friends. They agreed not to disagree. They saw themselves the same in their likes and dislikes, and in fact, they admitted they sublimated some of their own desires and wishes in such a way that, at times, each was not sure what he really liked or wanted to do.

After 2 years, John began recognizing some of the needs he had that were not being fulfilled by Sean. They were very simple needs, and as John saw them most of them were not threatening to the relationship. He began playing tennis again on weekends with some of his old partners; he had stopped playing tennis because Sean did not enjoy the game. He began spending an occasional evening out at dinner with some friends from work. Sean had met John's colleagues, but he found them boring because they only talked about work-related activities which were far afield from Sean's work. Sean made the appointment for the couple to start therapy and was sure that this "must be the beginning of the end."

Discussion

Sean was very committed to the merging of Stage One, while John was moving ahead to the individualizing of Stage Three. After a few sessions with the couple, both were relieved to know that the relationship was not flawed and that this would not be the beginning of the end, but only that they were transversing stages at a different speed. John better understood Sean's concern and made special efforts to reassure him, verbally and by his actions, that he loved him and would not abandon him. On the other hand, Sean did not feel as pained and angered, and stopped insisting that something was wrong. He became more accepting of John spending time with his own pursuits and away from home.

NEED FULFILLMENT

Another important consideration here is the couples' need to understand very early in the therapeutic process that they cannot expect to fulfill or satisfy all of each other's needs. This seems to be one of those age-old beliefs, that couples should expect complete satisfaction and fulfillment from their primary partner. Nothing can be further from the truth, and nothing can be more damaging to a relationship than the belief and underlying expectation that all of one's needs can be fulfilled by one's partner. Thus, when couples understand this idea and begin to look to others to get some of their unfulfilled needs met, much emotional stress in the relationship can be relieved.

CASE EXAMPLE SIX: OVERCOMING FEARS OF ABANDONMENT

Bill was a real estate salesman and Frank a computer analyst. A couple for 6 years, they sought help because Bill complained, "All the romance seems gone. Don't get me wrong, we love and care for each other very much and we have a lot going for us. We own our own home, which we both enjoy working on. We have lots of good friends. We have similar values and lots of the same dreams for the future." Bill was angry as he said, "He used to give me such a big hug when he would come home from work and now it's a peck on the cheek." Frank added, "Yes, the high passion has cooled yet I love and care for Bill in a more enduring way and I have very secure feelings about the ongoingness and security of the relationship." Bill complained that on weekends he was a "computer widow," that Frank would spend hours and hours at the keyboard of his computer. He was highly successful with his career, enjoyed his work very much, and was advancing rapidly. In contrast, Bill saw his own career simply as a job that he did well. "The love and excitement I want from my life is to come home to my Prince Charming." Bill came from an Italian family in which romance and affection were a measure of the vitality of the relationship, whereas Frank came from a more reserved background and shared his caring for Bill in a nonverbal way, such as getting his car fixed for him.

DISCUSSION

Bill was very committed to the blending of Stage One and the homemaking and finding compatibility of Stage Two, while Frank was in Stage Four, increasing his productivity, feeling the safety, serenity, and dependability he had with Bill, and the enjoyment he experienced in collaborating with Bill in designing an extension on their house.

Their therapy initially focused on learning more about each other's background, reviewing their similarities and differences, and getting a much clearer understanding that the relationship was not "on the rocks," as Bill had feared. Bill was clinging to blending and compatibility, with all the safety and closeness that represented for him, and was not willing to take risks, while Frank had traversed that stage. Once they were able to understand that each was in a different stage at the same time, they were able more easily and comfortably to work at effective ways of compromise, and find better ways of compatibility. Specifically, Frank made a more conscious and willing effort to demonstrate more affection, talk less about what went on at work, and even shut down his home computer on Sundays to spend time alone with Bill. Bill developed some hobbies of his own and let go of some of the resentment he felt toward Frank's emphasis on his career.

SUMMARY

Any characteristic in the developmental stages of relationships has the potential for being at the core of a stage discrepancy problem. A few of the more frequently seen stage discrepancies are (a) reappearance of the individual in Stage Three in conflict with the merging of Stage One, (b) reappearance of the individual in Stage Three threatening the dependability of the partner in Stage Four, and (c) the high limerence of Stage One in sharp contrast with the loss of limerence in Stage Two. As a side issue, and as has been stated elsewhere, one of the most common causes for terminating male relationships toward the end of the first year is the loss of limerence. Examples of characteristics in conflict are as numerous as the characteristics in male couples. In some instances, characteristics of later stages appear earlier as symptoms of insecurity, dependency, or difficulty in managing the aging process.

Stage discrepancies often appear as behavioral manifestations, or as symptoms of the difficulties that the couple or individual is having in resolving the stage discrepancy problem. However, the conflicts are often presented to the psychotherapy as problems of: (a) developing or maintaining intimacy; (b) power, competition, or control issues; (c) jealousy; or (d) differences in dealing with expressions of anger or tenderness. Utilizing the framework of stages of relationships and the possibility of discrepancy in the developmental characteristics can give the psychotherapist added understanding of the presenting complaints of male couples, which in turn can lead to a better assessment of the couples' difficulties and the development of new strategies of treatment intervention.

REFERENCES

McWhirter, D. P., & Mattison, A. M. (1984). *The male couple.* Englewood Cliffs, NJ: Prentice-Hall.

Tennov, D. (1979). *Love and limerence: The experience of being in love.* New York: Stein & Day.

Treatment of Identity
and Intimacy Issues
in Gay Males

Philip Colgan, MA
University of Minnesota

SUMMARY. A psychodynamic analysis of the presenting problems of many gay male clients reveals the frequent presence of issues related to identity and intimacy. This paper explores these concepts from the viewpoint of observed clinical phenomena, their likely antecedents, and treatment strategies based on a model of psychological health which balances identity and intimacy.

Identity has been described as a personal construct of self-worth. In this definition, a positive personal construct refers to an internal, innate understanding of oneself as a being whose positive worth is beyond question. When one has formed a positive identity, he consciously or unconsciously defines himself as capable of giving and receiving love, and of making positive contributions to the welfare of others. In short, he can achieve satisfaction in both love and work.

An identity disorder is present in one who lacks adequate formation and development of a positive personal construct of self-worth. This disorder will lead him to form human relationships which perpetuate his lack of self-value. The behaviors which result from his developmental deficit are manifested in intimacy dysfunction.

Intimacy functioning is defined as an affirming interaction between self-affirming individuals. Affirmation has affective components of trust in one another and care for one another's well being, and behavioral components of listening to and responding to the other. Cognitive components are seen in thought processes which affirm the value of the relationship and express faith in its dependability. Healthy intimacy functioning appears to respect the needs of the individuals involved. Consequently, a sense of belonging and affirmation (attachment) occurs

---

Mr. Colgan is Clinical Instructor in the Medical School, Department of Family Practice and Community Health, Program in Human Sexuality, University of Minnesota, 2630 University Avenue, Minneapolis, MN 55414. He is also in private practice as a psychologist and sex therapist. Correspondence may be sent to the author at the above address.

between people who also value and affirm themselves (separation). In this, positive identity and intimacy interact to reinforce each other.

Intimacy dysfunction has been described as a pattern of behaviors which require the identity-disordered male to depend on external agents for a positive sense of self. Examples of external agents, or as Smalley (1982) suggests, addictive agents, include sex, alcohol and other drugs, food, work, gambling, body building, or another person. Dependence on external agents precludes the balance of separation and attachment which appears necessary for emotional health. The imbalance seen in intimacy dysfunction is characterized by interpersonal communication problems, unresolved intrapsychic and interpersonal stress, and behavior patterns designed to cope with the unresolved stress.

In this conceptualization, identity disorders and intimacy dysfunctions represent attempts to return to an original state of well-being. Behaviorally, the attempts have symptoms which can be grouped under patterns of over-separation and patterns of over-attachment.

OVER-SEPARATION AND OVER-ATTACHMENT

Over-separation involves forming and maintaining one's identity at the expense of emotionally satisfying human connections, whereas over-attachment involves a pattern of forming human connections at the sacrifice of one's own separate identity. Both patterns emphasize affective harmony to achieve well being.

Over-separation is clinically characterized by elements of: (a) projection of blame; (b) denial of emotional needs; (c) difficulty of being a recipient, except in prescribed ways; (d) lack of ability to discriminate emotions; (e) emotional divorce; (f) creation of psychological distance by conscious or unconscious means; (g) independence at all costs; (h) preoccupation with outside activities (e.g., work), creation of physical distance (e.g., avoidance of affectionate behavior; extensive travel obligations); (i) alienation/isolation from friends; (j) unconscious or conscious needs for approval/recognition, or both; (k) wariness in interpersonal relationships; and, (l) lack of spontaneity, except when serving other needs.

The goal of over-separation is to control affective expression. Behaviorally, this is manifested in actions taken to preserve independence at all costs. To do otherwise is to risk emotional involvement. The man who displays patterns of over-separation has few skills for emotional interaction. Consequently, he feels under-equipped to be successful in taking emotional risks. To stave off failure, he constructs his behavior to guard his emotional vulnerability. Sometimes, he will have developed an uncanny ability to monitor the affect of others so as to predict their responses and take steps which protect him from exposure to risk. This is coupled with denial of his own affective states, except when they can be displayed to his advantage. These often take the form of sharp outbursts of interpersonal rejection. More common, however, is a practiced denial of affect which becomes so well learned that he becomes numb to his own needs and those around him.

If, however, this adaptive system breaks down, he is flooded with awareness of his emotional needs and may abruptly adopt "over-attachment" behavior patterns. If he succeeds in masking his true emotional needs from his partner, the crisis passes and he escapes exposure. If another person responds to his vulnerability with either smothering (over-attachment) or shaming (over-separation), he will retreat from the threat to his independence with a fierce resolve never again to suffer the embarrassment of letting down his guard. When he is successful in his escape, he can privately excuse his momentary lapse and continue the pattern. When he is exposed, his reaction is dependent on the behavior of the other person. If the other person reacts with the dysfunctional behavior of shaming or smothering, he begins the cycle anew with even greater determination.

By contrast, over-attachment clinically has cognitive, affective, and behavioral elements of: (a) insecure, anxious attachment; (b) difficulties in decision making; (c) toleration of emotional, psychological, or physical insult, or all of these; (d) communication problems centered around the desire to communicate only positive feelings and avoid negative feelings; (e) symptoms of depression (e.g., disorders of sleeping, eating, or both); (f) clinging, nagging for attention; (g) preoccupation with the well being of the other; (h) periodic gestures of grandiose romanticism; (i) neglect of self physically, emotionally, professionally, and so forth.

The goal of over-attachment is to preserve affective harmony. Negative thoughts or feelings are regarded as interfering with affective homeostasis. Consequently, if such thoughts require expression for maintenance of emotional equilibrium, they are often expressed to others outside the relationship, e.g., with friends or a therapist. Behavioral mechanisms are adapted to preserve a feeling of readiness to fall in love, or of being in love. This preservation is essential to stave off fears of not falling in love or fears of falling out of love, fears which though sometimes cognitively recognized, are more often actively denied through regulation of affect.

If the affect-regulatory system breaks down, the individual feels out of control and can explode in unmitigated rage. If the relationship survives this explosion, one using patterns of over-attachment resolves to do everything he can to make the relationship work, i.e., not dissolve.

Over-separation and over-attachment share characteristics of excessive needs for personal and interpersonal affect regulation. In each case, it appears that this need for control is designed to prevent affective involvement which creates unmanageable anxiety. To preserve smooth and efficient interpersonal functioning, men with patterns of over-attachment and over-separation depend on others for cues which inform their behavior choices. Their reactive dependence on others is manifested in the lack of personal choices for pro-active emotional expression.

Lack of affective expression leads to a lack of skills for verbal problem resolution. When conflict arises in the relationship, affective harmony is dependent on emotional withdrawal (over-separation) or self-sacrificial peacemaking (over-attachment). Both choices are reactionary attempts to maintain affective homeostasis. Men may rely on one pattern or the other until fatigue and mounting tension require them to do something different. Often, doing something different means choosing the less-frequently used coping mechanism. Therefore, in one man or in a couple, it is clinically usual to observe periodic swings from over-attachment to over-separation. Further, it is not unusual to observe one man in a relationship assuming a style of over-attachment, and the other a style of over-separation.

A hallmark of both patterns is a lack of alternatives to maintaining affective harmony. The lack of choice has its basis in the inadequate formation and development of a personal construct of self-worth. This deficit is manifested in adult relationships by behavior patterns indicative of intimacy dysfunction.

ETIOLOGY OF IDENTITY DISORDER AND INTIMACY DYSFUNCTION IN MALES

Current theorists (e.g., Johnson, 1985) suggest that optimal identity formation and development represents an ongoing dialogue between one's personal construct of self-worth and the responses of other significant people. As far as can be known, this begins at birth with primitive and preverbal information processing. The development of one's personal construct of self-worth is influenced by the responses of care givers to the infant. Adler (1927) suggests that the infant codes these early parental responses in a way that predisposes him to interpret further human interactions as confirmation of this initial emotional impression. When the responses are consistently negative, the infant's capacity for positive self-valuing is compromised. His identity development becomes disordered. Colgan and Riebel (1981) argue from a family systems perspective that repetition of the parental responses teaches children over time what to anticipate in human interactions. Coleman & Colgan (1986) provide evidence that symptoms of intimacy dysfunction are inter-generationally transmitted in this way.

Johnson (1985) suggests that an infant who is actively rejected by cold or hostile parents will develop adult relationship patterns here described as over-separation. Apparently lacking a basic sense of trust in others, he learns to depend only on himself. He denies the desire to connect emotionally to protect himself from reexperiencing rejection.

Alternatively, Johnson suggests that some children initially form emotional bonds with parents. If those bonds are prematurely interrupted, the infant experiences emotional abandonment, and further emotional development is impaired until those emotional bonds are reestablished with another significant adult. The desire to reestablish these significant emotional bonds is expressed in relationship patterns here described as over-attachment.

It would appear that males have ample opportunity for being rejected or abandoned. For example, Garbarino and Gilliam (1980) report that male babies are more likely than females to suffer physical abuse, and that more fathers than mothers use physical force to discipline. Noller (1978) found that boy-parent dyads had fewer interactions than girl-parent dyads. This study further showed that fathers give more affection to daughters than to sons.

Attachment theorists (e.g., Bowlby, 1975) suggest that anger is an expected response to such rejection or abandonment. Boys, however, are discouraged from verbalizing feelings of anger. They are instead encouraged to take action, often aggressive action (Gleason, 1975). In the present conceptualization, the action can take the form of over-separation or over-attachment.

With a premium placed on action over expression, it appears that affective inexpressiveness becomes an expected part of male development. It is not surprising, then, that young boys are less likely than young girls to admit feelings of fear or anxiety (Lekarezyk & Hill, 1969). And it is not surprising to find that, as adults, males express affect less than females (Haccoun, Allen, & Fader, 1974). This lack of affective expressiveness appears to be a major component of intimacy dysfunction for adult males.

OVER-SEPARATION AND OVER-ATTACHMENT: DEVELOPMENTAL FACTORS IN GAY MEN

Several factors influence the development of over-attachment and over-separation patterns in gay men. Included among them are his relationship with his parents, particularly his father, his gender conformity/non-conformity, particularly in relationship with his peers while growing up, and issues particular to male-male bonding in the development of adult relationships.

Coleman's (1982) five-stage model of the coming out process is a useful framing device for understanding specific developmental tasks of attachment and separation for gay men. At each of Coleman's stages, the gay man encounters significant events which influence his development of identity and intimacy. Each stage holds opportunities for redefining both his relationship to self (separation) and his relationships with others (attachment). At each juncture, he may develop or intensify a dependency disorder. Alternatively, he may continue or resume the natural process of healthy attachment and separation begun at birth. To illustrate these issues, the concepts of attachment and separation are overlaid on the concept of developmental stages as described by Coleman (see Figure 1).

Pre-Coming Out

The pre-coming out stage is characterized by an unconscious awareness of one's value to self and his value to others. For the gay man, this stage will encompass the life span from birth until he begins consciously to recognize his "difference" from other males. His family of origin has great impact on the development of his personal construct of self-worth (identity) and his templates for forming human relationships (intimacy), as discussed previously.

The greatest obstacle to optimal identity development and intimacy functioning is the experience of being rejected or emotionally abandoned by primary care givers. Pre-homosexual boys appear to have ample opportunity for either to occur, especially when the boy is gender non-conforming. Both experimental and retrospective self-report data confirm that parental responses to gender non-conformity pose additional bases of rejection or abandonment for many pre-homosexual boys.

Block (1973) reports that socially well-adjusted, gender non-conforming adult males are reared by parents who are secure in their own identities, provide nurturing home environments, and are involved in the socialization of their sons. Further, the parents were characterized as comfortable with non-traditional sex-role behaviors.

Many parents, however, discourage "sex-inappropriate" behavior (Fling & Manoscvitz, 1972). Apparently, these parents believe Moore's (1984) conclusion that "the culture encourages (affective) inexpressiveness for boys and young men, that significant penalties exist for deviating from the traditional roles, and that men must establish a firm sense of sex role before they can increase their affective responsiveness" (p. 80). In other words, the belief is that boys must develop "separation" before they can incorporate "attachment."

Toward that end, it may be that parents who are insecure about non-traditional sex-role behavior, or who are unaware of the importance of a balance between separation and attachment, will discourage attach-

Figure 1

PRE-COMING OUT

SEPARATION

patterns of self

affirmation

ATTACHMENT

patterns of affirming

connections with others

COMING OUT

awareness of difference

(from other males)

self labeling as

homosexual

(self-acceptance)

awareness of desire

(for other males)

telling others

(acceptance of others)

EXPLORATION

developing a sense of

personal attractiveness

and sexual competence

developing social skills

for establishing sexual

contacts

FIRST RELATIONSHIPS

consolidating identity

establishing intimacy

INTEGRATION

refining and maintaining

separation

refining and maintaining

attachment

ment behavior in a misguided attempt to spare their son the social stigma associated with cross-sex behavior. The attempt is misguided when cross-sex behaviors are misconstrued as "masculine" failures. If gender non-conformity is an expression of individuality, identity development may be compromised by disapproval; if gender non-conformity is an expression of attachment desires, disapproval may compromise intimacy functions. In either case, disapproval of the behavior may be interpreted by the boy as rejection or emotional abandonment. As has been noted, rejection or abandonment of the boy will lead to identity disorder and intimacy dysfunction in the adult.

The rejection or abandonment is more likely to come from adult males than adult females. Feinman (1974) asked college students to rate cross-sex behavior in children age 3 to 8. Male subjects were found to be more disapproving than female subjects. The comparative lack of disapproval of cross-sex behavior by females may be the reason that therapy samples of adult homosexual males cannot be distinguished from non-therapy samples, or for that matter from heterosexual samples, on the basis of mother/son relationships (Bell, Weinberg, & Hammersmith, 1981).

The retrospective self-report data of Bell, et al. (1981) provide clues for understanding the influence of the father/gender-non-conforming son relationship. When comparing clinical and non-clinical samples (ever been in therapy versus never been in therapy), the authors found what appears to be a common thread. The clinical group reported having detached, hostile fathers. This variable is tied to the development of gender non-conformity. The non-therapy sample, however, reported having "negative relationships with father," a factor not tied to the development of gender non-conformity.

Gender conformity/non-conformity in this study is composed of three factors: how masculine or feminine the subjects perceived themselves to be in childhood, and how much they disliked typical boys' activities (e.g., sports), and how much they enjoyed typical girls' activities. The authors point out that development of gender non-conformity may represent a phenomenon not measured by these three factors. Nonetheless, the combination of gender non-conformity with a detached/hostile father apparently distinguishes the therapy from the non-therapy sample.

It may be presumed that because the pre-coming out stage represents unconscious psychosexual development , the gender-conforming boy is reared without the overlay of stress introduced by parent/child interactions related to gender non-conformity. The gender-conforming male who is rejected or abandoned by his father will, however, face difficulties in forming adult bonds with males. Not having experienced an emotional connection with a significant male in his childhood, he will presumably have little positive basis for affective involvement with other males during later developmental stages.

Coming Out

Becoming consciously aware of his difference from other males and ascribing that difference to homosexual feelings signal the beginning of the coming out stage (Coleman, 1982). Together these form the basis for continued development of separation (identity) and desires for attachment (intimacy) for the pre-homosexual boy. At this stage, affective acceptance by self and others represents optimal identity and intimacy development.

It appears that during the coming out stage, responses to gender non-conformity continue to influence the development of patterns of over-separation and over-attachment. At this stage, gender non-conformity may be manifested externally by overt, non-masculine behavior, or internally with awareness of the negative sanctions of the culture regarding homosexuality. For the pre-homosexual boy, awareness of his difference amounts to awareness of his gender non-conformity, regardless of how obvious his difference is to others.

The boy's internal response to his difference is likely to be negative. Bell, et al. (1981) report that in their sample, homosexual men compared with heterosexual men reported having been unhappy during childhood and adolescence primarily because of their [external] gender non-conformity (e.g., not liking sports), and secondly because they felt different sexually [internal gender non-conformity]. This feeling of difference appears to be the case regardless of whether or not one is effeminate.

Gender non-conformity in the presence of heterosexual socialization exacts a psychological cost from the emerging homosexual male. The risks are two-fold: interruption of the continuing process of positive identity formation, including sexual identity, and limited opportunities for healthy expressions of intimacy needs due to the perceived necessity for denial of attachment desires. (See Malyon, 1982, for an excellent discussion of these issues.) The emerging homosexual male who views his difference in a negative sense may suffer from both identity disorder and intimacy dysfunction. Note that the stress introduced by gender nonconformity is overlaid on the sanctions against affective expressiveness for males in general.

The overtly gender non-conforming pre-homosexual male who has not established an identity based on self-worth appears to be at greatest risk for developing problems with attachment and separation. In the absence of emotional reassurance from parents, he is likely to withdraw from the rejection encountered from peers and concurrently to reject himself for the unhappiness caused by his gender non-conformity. Thus, in effect, he may compromise identity and intimacy development.

Not all non-conforming males, however, develop severe identity problems. One may speculate from available data (e.g., Block, 1973) that the gender non-conforming male who has learned from parents to value difference and to value himself will suffer fewer psychological insults to positive identity development. Still, the relatively limited possibilities for peer acceptance and for positive expression of his attachment desires may challenge his developing ability to form intimate relationships.

When the boy is overtly gender-conforming, it would appear that negative labeling by peers is less likely to happen. For this reason, the overtly gender-conforming pre-homosexual male presumably would be more able to keep his emerging sexual identity secret. With this, he may find peer-group validation for his "masculinity," but will serve his needs for a sense of belonging (an intimacy function) only at the cost of secrecy. Lack of emotional nurturing from parents will compound his emotional isolation. If he rejects his homosexual feelings, he will face this affective hurdle during the next phase, exploration. Lack of self-acceptance, as evidenced by his "double life," may lead to over-separation behavior at that time. Alternatively, during exploration, he may well develop patterns of over-attachment as a response to fear of repeating the emotional isolation, perhaps begun in infancy and reexperienced during the coming out stage.

EXPLORATION

The period immediately following completion of primary and secondary schooling appears to offer an opportunity for redirecting earlier patterns of over-attachment and over-separation. For some, this time period means engaging in experiences which repair some of the earlier damage. For others, it means continuation and perhaps intensification of preexisting problems.

Erikson (1959) argues that in late adolescence and early adulthood, the task of the individual is to begin to refine his connections with others in the form of establishing "intimacy," or intense interpersonal affective expressiveness with one other significant person. Toward this end, many men appear to work toward incorporating affective expressiveness (attachment) to complement their already developed masculine behavior (separation) (Moore, 1984). Interestingly enough, it is also during this time (age 18–20) when one symptom of identity and intimacy problems, i.e., heavy drinking patterns, peaks among males (Smith, Apter-Marsh, Buffum, Moser, & Wesson, 1984).

For many gay males, the age period 18–24 offers opportunities for more overtly bridging any existing gaps between sexual feelings and sexual behavior. For such men, this is the time during which same-sex sexual contacts are explicitly regarded as homosexual. The developmental tasks appear to be primarily behavioral in nature; cognitive and affective components appear to assume a secondary position.

Overt gender non-conformity appears to fade in importance for many at this time. They find that wider involvement with gay men reveals peer support not previously experienced. Some apparently see this as a time for experimenting with masculine behavior that was previously inhibited.

For another group of overtly gender-conforming and gender-non-conforming males, any introjected negative sanctions of the culture regarding homosexual behavior will surface. If left unaddressed, these homophobic responses to self and others will compromise completion of the developmental tasks of this stage.

At the exploration stage, over-separation often appears in the form of sexual independence. Men who rely on patterns of over-separation will perpetuate their need for distance from affective expressiveness by establishing skills only in sexual performance. Some of these men apparently become fixated with sexual behavior as an avenue for satisfying their needs for connection with other males. Others protect themselves from losing by insulating themselves from the possibility of sexual rejection by way of alcohol or other drug abuse. More often, drugs and alcohol are used in conjunction with sexual behavior. In these patterns, the healthy development of interpersonal communication skills either outside of sexual relationships or within sexual relationships may be compromised.

Men who have formed patterns of over-attachment will be challenged by the developmental tasks of the exploration period as well. Because the focus is on developing an internal frame of reference for sexual comfort, their proclivity for attachment behavior may prevent full positive development of separation behavior. For example, termination of an "exploring" sexual relationship may be seen as continued proof of their unworthiness to receive love. Not willing to question their ability to give the love they desire, they may question what they did wrong sexually. By this, they threaten the possibility of successfully integrating sexual self-esteem, or healthy separation behavior. An alternative possibility is the internal decision to "do whatever he wants" sexually so as to avoid rejection. In this pattern, he may underdevelop his ability to be sexually assertive. In either case, development of sexual dysfunction is a possible outcome.

An excellent portrayal of how childhood patterns of over-separation and over-attachment resurface for some men in the exploration stage is provided by Silverstein (1981). He refers to men displaying these patterns as the "rejector" and the "suitor," respectively, and ascribes both patterns to unresolved hostility toward the gay man's father. In Silverstein's terms, the rejector acts from a deep sense of anger and hostility toward his father. While claiming to desire love, he rejects would-be lovers as fools because he is ultimately unlovable, as he believes his father thought him. He searches for someone to father him, but repeats the earlier pattern by rejecting his father-lover. Never finding satisfaction and always avoiding rejection, he perpetuates his identity disorder via over-separation.

The other pattern described is that of the "suitor." Having been abandoned by his father, he nonetheless believes in love and is constantly searching for the "right one" to form a romantic attachment with. His idea of romantic attachment is to find another man to fulfill the love his father discarded, at least in his perception. He, too, is constantly disappointed in not being able to find someone who can accept his love. Never finding satisfaction and always experiencing rejection, he perpetuates his identity disorder via over-attachment.

These patterns illustrate the kinds of presenting issues for men who initiate psychotherapy during the exploration stage. Sometimes, the sudden shift in having greater contact with other gay men makes him question his patterns of relating with men. Other times, he initiates therapy out of depression when his period of exploration extends beyond that which is useful for him. In either case, full exploration of attachment and separation issues is best left until his immediate symptoms have subsided. Some men will require only crisis relief in order to retap their own resources. For others, discontinuing therapy after crisis relief actively perpetuates identity disorders and intimacy dysfunctions. Careful assessment of coexisting issues of current life and past history will provide direction for the psychotherapy.

Successful completion of the developmental tasks signals readiness for the next stage. This is revealed in balancing his positive sexual identity (separation) comfortably with interpersonal communication (attachment).

FIRST RELATIONSHIPS

The developmental stage "First Relationships" is described by Coleman as a time when men begin to explore homosexual relationships that combine physical and emotional attraction. The primary task in this stage appears to be the incorporation of affective expressiveness in close relationships. Ideal identity development means developing further skills in affective self-disclosure. Affective responsiveness to one's partner signals further development of intimacy skills.

Expressing affect is challenging for adult males in general. Cosby (1973) concluded that men [affectively] self-disclose less than women. Rosenfeld (1979) found that men choose not to self-disclose for reasons of maintaining control of the impressions given, for fear of being misunderstood, and because self-disclosure is perceived as threatening to relationships.

Affective expressiveness, then, can be seen as a form of gender non-conformity. Narus and Fisher (1982) found that androgynous men will be more affectively expressive than masculine men. Consequently, it may be that the gender non-conforming boy who has successfully navigated developmental tasks in previous stages will find his ability to be affectively expressive is an asset in completing the tasks of first relationships. Similarly, those who have developed a positive sense of self-worth regardless of gender conformity, and have balanced this with interpersonal communication skills, will presumably have an easier time forming relationships which include affective expression.

Men who display patterns of over-separation and over-attachment, however, will be especially challenged during this time, for these are relationship patterns nurtured by one with an underdeveloped positive identity. Consequently, relationship patterns built on such developmental deficits will become more apparent. The less well-developed the man's sense of positive identity, the less likely he will be to learn from his experiences in ways which further his abilities to form satisfying connections with others.

Those who display over-separation will be hesitant to engage in close relationships which require affective expressiveness. Alternatively, the over-attachment inherent in first relationships may be welcome relief after the intense individuation of exploration. In either case, their first relationships may be satisfying so long as affective harmony prevails. This can be achieved fairly easily in the "limerence" phase of a relationship (Tennov, 1979) when similarities are magnified and differences minimized. But problems with intimacy will surface at the end of limerence unless his partner also values affective harmony over affective expressiveness. If his partner requires affective expressiveness, he may well retreat by ending the relationship. If the partner does not require affective expressiveness, he may be in relationship with another man who displays over-separation. More likely, however, this partner displays over-attachment, which also emphasizes affective harmony.

The man who displays over-attachment patterns may find himself "walking on air" in the limerence phase of a relationship. The intense emotional connection may be experienced unconsciously as reestablishing the emotional bond interrupted during infancy or childhood. Consequently, he will do anything to make the relationship work, though unfortunately this is often done at the expense of his attending to needs for separation. Even if the relationship is emotionally painful, he will remain attached until rejected or until he resumes the process of developing an identity based on positive self-worth.

In Coleman's (1982) model of ideal development, men move through this stage via several short-term relationships. In each one, the man refines his identity with greater self-knowledge and self-understanding, and refines his skills for being in an intimate relationship by developing more realistic expectations of his partner. Learning from his experience, he gradually chooses one person who appears to suit his needs. In essence, he learns about balancing identity and intimacy.

INTEGRATION: THE MALE COUPLE

The primary developmental task in integration is reestablishing the balance of separation and attachment in each man, and in the couple. In ideal development, this means the reappearance of individuals who are at the same time emotionally connected with one another.

McWhirter and Mattison (1984) speak of developing a balance between intimacy and individuality as a stage-related phenomenon. In their view, "A major signpost of Stage Four relationships is the balance between individual independence and dependence on the partner. These oppositional push-pull forces strive for homeostasis and in the process provide the high and low emotional punctuations [for keeping their mutual attraction viable and minimizing boredom and stagnation]" (p. 91). The authors argue that this balance is the outgrowth of developmental stages in the life of a relationship.

Integral to these stages is merging, experienced as limerence (Tennov, 1979), when individual identity is sacrificed for the rewards of being a couple. This sets the scene for stage two, nesting, when ambivalence and finding compatibility signal the end of limerence. In stage three, maintaining, the reappearance of the individual engenders risk taking, and developing skills for conflict resolution. These are necessary, in the authors' view, for the later developmental stages which incorporate the behaviors here described as balancing identity and intimacy.

Clinically, it appears that developmental issues which are left unaddressed until this stage in one's life surface primarily under circumstances of crisis. Until the crisis emerges, men have little motivation for addressing any underlying unresolved developmental issues. The crisis can take any form, e.g., career, health, or financial problems. Sometimes, a sense of time passing, or the "mid-life crisis," forms the basis for reconsidering one's intimate connections. Developmental deficits which reappear under crisis form the primary emotional threats to developing an integrated balance of identity and intimacy.

For many men, the safety of the relationship provides the basis for redressing earlier developmental wounds. The emotional connection offered by a history together appears to provide a safety net for the emotional risks of identity redevelopment. This is unlikely to occur, however, without some considerable tension in the relationship. As McWhirter and Mattison (1984) note, insecurity and fear of loss threaten the stability of the relationship when the individual reappears in stage three, maintaining.

For men who have utilized patterns of over-separation and over-attachment, the maintaining stage is a particularly stressful time. Very often the relationship will have achieved some stability inherent in predictability. The predictability of cognitive, affective, and behavioral responses to one another give the men the illusion of comfort. Even relationships characterized by overt, chaotic symptoms of identity disorders and intimacy dysfunctions such as alcoholism have achieved a life of their own, independent of the individuals. While the relationships may appear stressful to outsiders, the men in them are likely to have achieved an adaptive level of stress tolerance that is highly resistant to change, except in the face of crisis.

Psychotherapy at this stage, then, begins with crisis management. Where overt symptoms of dependency disorders are present, e.g., addictions, the focus is on removal of the external agent. Other times, crisis management means helping the relationship stabilize so that issues can be addressed with the full resources of the couple. Clinically, if one man experiences an identity crisis based on unresolved dependency issues, the resulting crisis in the relationship causes the other man to address such issues as well. Clinicians in the field of alcoholism and other drug dependence have recognized the importance of including the other partner in treatment as well for this reason.

Successful psychotherapy at this juncture balances individual and couple's work. For the individual, psychotherapy appears to attend to the redevelopment of his independent sense of positive self-worth. Within the couple, this will mean developing new skills for affective self-disclosure and affective responsiveness. Frequently, interpersonal communication training helps ease the transition to a new level of intimate functioning. Overall, the ability of the individuals to recognize emotional needs, to affectively express these, and to follow through with behavioral changes leads to a more integrated balance of identity and intimacy.

SUMMARY

The efficacy of this model of development for gay men awaits empirical investigation. What remains, however, is that males are at risk for developing identity disorders and intimacy dysfunctions when reared in homes where personal constructs of self-worth are not modeled, taught, and reinforced. The issue of gender conformity/non-conformity provides an overlay of problem possibilities in the presence of peer socialization pressures. The additional overlay of emerging sexual identity may expose some pre-homosexual boys to even greater risk for the development of dependency disorders in adulthood.

It may be that patterns of over-attachment and over-separation seen in adulthood represent extreme responses to usual developmental issues for adult males in general. The sanctions against male affective expressiveness have lead many to believe that only by establishing separation can the man experiment with attachment (e.g., O'Leary & Donoghue, 1978).

Clinical observation, however, suggests that balancing separation and attachment has its roots in childhood and is expressed in each developmental stage during the life span. When this balance is ignored, identity disorders and intimacy dysfunctions are probable outcomes. As Miller (1984) argues: "After the first stage, in which the aim is the development of basic trust, the aim of every other stage [described in prevalent literature] is some form of increased separation or self-development. When the individual arrives at the stage called 'intimacy,' he is supposed to be able to be intimate with another person, having spent all of his prior development geared to something very different" (p.n.a.).

Over the life span, then, each stage presents possibilities for balancing separation and attachment. Optimal identity and intimacy development appears to represent an ongoing dialogue between one's personal construct of self-worth and the responses of others who equally value themselves. At each shift in personal and interpersonal perspective— family interactions, peer involvement, coming in contact with other gay men, establishing first relationships, settling in with one other man—it appears that attachment forms the necessary basis for exploration of the individual. This would account for McWhirter and Mattison's (1984) observation that a balance of independence/dependence in the relationship occurs only after establishing the adult emotional bond.

Yet it appears that optimal development over the life span of the individual gives opportunities for developing this balance much earlier. In childhood, optimal identity and intimacy development appears to begin with emotional bonding to both parents. While the value of the emotional bond with the mother is widely assumed, for men in general and for gay men in particular, bonding with the father appears to be equally vital for optimal development. After this period of attachment gives the child a sense of security, he can experiment with separation behavior. In primary school the need for attachment reappears, this time directed to peers. For many men, but for gender non-conforming men especially, the need for attachment is interrupted by the lack of boys' abilities to be affectively expressive.

The lack of affective expressiveness apparent in patterns of over-separation and over-attachment may not appear to be a problem in the exploration stage. But patterns of relating to other adult gay men which are established during this stage will have full expression in the first relationships and integration stages.

TREATMENT CONSIDERATIONS

The imbalance of attachment and separation, begun in childhood for many men, can be redressed during any developmental stage by resuming the natural process of learning to view oneself as positively worthwhile.

This is best done while in connection with other important people, for from this basis of both attachment and separation, a balance of identity and intimacy is redeveloped.

Clinically, it appears that one who utilizes patterns of over-separation and over-attachment can redevelop his dormant capacity for positive self-worth (identity) by establishing an empathetic relationship with an important adult (intimacy). Within the therapeutic relationship, the therapist can be an instrument in helping the client collect cognitive and affective information about himself. Behavior changes are built on this new data. The self-discovery of positive worth (identity) is enhanced through emotional understanding and acceptance by the therapist (intimacy).

Identity and intimacy are redeveloped in this approach. The focus of therapy will change slightly, but emphasis is placed on the priorities of (1) crisis management, (2) addressing the developmental tasks of the current stage of development, and (3) redressing history. The priorities of current versus past developmental tasks often shift back and forth. The therapist who is alert to this can aid clients by following the clients' lead, except when it appears that either (a) adequate progress toward present goals cannot be achieved without addressing the past, or (b) when emphasis on either present or past seems to be a defense against experiencing affect associated with completing the developmental tasks of the other.

To illustrate treatment concepts, a clinical vignette will be used. "Eric," of course, represents a fictional client.

* * *

Eric is a 27-year-old white male referred by his physician for psychotherapy for recurrent depression. Physical causes for symptoms of fatigue, boredom, lack of motivation, and episodic sleeplessness had been ruled out.

He reported having seen his physician for physical symptoms, but had been disappointed in not being able to find a physical cause. When his physician recommended psychotherapy, he was resentful. Yet, he reported, with his lack of concentration, and the ever-present loneliness, he just didn't know what else to do.

A brief review of his present situation revealed gradual deterioration of mood and energy. While not in what he called "crisis" yet, Eric feared that his lack of energy would jeopardize his career. This, coupled with his increasing boredom with short-term relationships, and his concern over the increasing amounts of alcohol or marijuana he used to feel comfortable in sexual situations, caused considerable anxiety about ever having his life "work out."

Eric's family history was largely unremarkable. The youngest of four, he had been reared in a middle-class suburb with his older brother and two older sisters. Eric described his parents' marriage of 35 years as "probably pretty boring" as they never fought, rarely showed affection to one another, and both seemed to thrive on work and church activities.

An average student and mediocre athlete, Eric achieved a small amount of distinction as a photographer for the school newspaper. He graduated from a university with a degree in business and was currently working as a systems analyst for a multi-national corporation.

His sexual history revealed an early awareness of his homosexuality. To guard against discovery of his feelings, he developed a series of "best friends" with whom he occasionally engaged in mutual masturbation. The introduction of sex play usually ended the friendship as "he wouldn't want to be around me anymore." Eric curtailed his homosexual activities in the last years of high school and dated a girl with whom he had a non-genital, "petting" relationship.

In college, Eric joined a fraternity. While he enjoyed the company of the other men, he kept his sexual orientation secret and did not act on his sexual fantasies, except for rare occasions when he visited gay bath houses. He always feared being seen entering or leaving, and so went only when he "couldn't stand the tension any more."

After college, Eric missed the company of men, but also felt more free "not to answer to anyone." He began meeting men at local gay bars. During the 5 years since college, Eric gained more confidence in his ability to meet men socially, largely to make sexual contacts.

While he reported enjoying sex with men, he didn't feel emotionally close to his sexual partners. His emotional ties were to three good friends he had known for some time. In two of those friendships, sexual relations had been curtailed as the men became better friends. In the third case, they had never been sexual.

Recently, Eric's fright about contracting AIDS had led him to "try to stick it out with one man." His relationship lasted 3 months. Eric reported that despite his efforts to be available to his lover, he felt increasing pressure to get closer than he was comfortable with. Finally, feeling smothered, he left the relationship after a particularly bad fight. Although he continued to function at work, the continuing depression made him fear losing his job. So with the encouragement of his friends, he initiated psychotherapy.

Further exploration of family interactions revealed Eric's sense of having failed his parents. Throughout his life, Eric's father had maintained a "respectful distance" about Eric, including his homosexuality. Eric reported that his father thought Eric's private life was none of his business. Eric reported his mother had "tried to understand, but she didn't get it." He described their reaction to his coming out as "sad, but they didn't say much. That's the way it always was—not much talk." His siblings maintained a *laissez-faire* attitude about him and his sexuality.

Eric reported that he was highly skeptical about therapy. He didn't see how talking about things was going to do any good. But he was "tired of living his life trying to do the right things and having it [a relationship] not work out."

An analysis of Eric's situation from the conceptual viewpoint previously discussed reveals patterns of over-separation traceable to childhood. As an adult, his needs for attachment had usually been separated into sexual and non-sexual relationships. His desire for a more lasting sexual/emotional attachment is seen in his foray into first relationships following a period of exploration.

Therapeutic considerations included Eric's need to be in charge (over-separation) balanced by his goal of making more satisfying connections with men (attachment). The double-bind he expressed in the second session gave clues for the direction of the therapy: Eric felt like a failure for having to see a professional [need for separation], and he feared that he would fail at therapy by "not being good enough" [need for attachment]. To address the former, we agreed that Eric would not be required to change anything he didn't want to; to address the latter, we agreed that failure would be indicated if Eric dropped out of therapy without discussing it with me. I also agreed not to end without discussing it with him, although he had not requested this.

The first step in the change process Eric was to undergo involved learning how to view himself without the debilitating connection with shame (Smalley & Coleman, 1985). Removing the judgment inherent in shame means being able to stand apart from one's behavior, becoming an observer of self—one's thoughts, feelings, actions, and their consequences. This gives a sense of being in control of the change process [need for separation]. Reporting one's observations to an accepting outsider helps diminish the shame by making a psychological bridge with another person (Kaufman, 1974) [need for attachment].

In this process, the therapist assumes a very important role in attending to the client without suggesting what the client should think or feel. In making and reporting his self-observations, Eric was able both to refine his sense of personal identity (separation) and to experience an honest and emotionally communicative relationship with a significant person (attachment).

Eric seemed relieved immediately to have a task orientation: to collect data about himself. Methods for data collection included self-reflection in a written log (Smalley, 1982), enlisting the aid of his three friends by asking them how they saw him, and bibliotherapy. To see that his data collection was uncontaminated, Eric agreed to refrain from using alcohol or other drugs during the course of therapy.

In this way, Eric began to learn about his present patterns of attachment and separation. This lead to increased understanding about his history of identity formation and intimacy expression in his family of origin.

At this point in therapy, Eric reported a great deal of anxiety. He had begun to have feelings of having been "ripped off" by his family. Prior to this, he had felt disappointed but rather accepting of them. He said that he understood that their lives were "less than ideal in the way of relationships." He didn't want to "just go and get mad at them," but felt increasing tension when he visited them. He didn't know what to do, and signs of depression had reappeared.

When Eric began to understand the impact of having grown up largely alone emotionally, he intuitively understood the necessity to redress the past. Still, fear of confrontation, and an internalized hopelessness in relation to parents, provide obstacles which may appear insurmountable. This is especially the case with men who don't have concrete traumatic incidences (e.g., physical or sexual abuse) to use as vehicles for entry. In Eric's case, the return of symptoms was reframed as indicative of what he must have felt as a child. With his adult frame of reference, he was able to understand the reality that as a child he was helpless in the face of a lack of understanding. As an adult, he had other options.

With this self-understanding as a base, clients can begin to be actively and powerfully involved in their adult relationships. Therefore, before redressing his past, Eric and I agreed to start with present tense, so as to have more control over successes. This of course increases the probability of effective and satisfying communication with his parents and siblings.

As is expected from studies of male development (e.g., Gleason, 1975), men will want to take action in response to the now emerging affect. This is especially the case with anxiety about having emotions. The therapist who recognizes this tendency can help the client satisfy the need to take action by encouraging him to do something different: to collect more affective and cognitive data about himself so as to take direct and incisive action that is not re-active, but pro-active. In this, Eric balanced a desire to "separate" through action by attending to himself more closely (forming an attachment to self).

Eric therefore found new routes for information gathering, this time about himself and other men. Toward this goal, he attended a work-sponsored seminar on interpersonal communication. His reading about identity and intimacy—self-help books, books about men and sexuality and about addictive patterns of behavior—increased. In addition, he agreed to explore a support group for gay men struggling with intimacy issues. These steps are designed to fill the developmental gaps created by living with one's sexuality as a secret from everyone, from librarians to peers. Essentially, the client does what he might have done in childhood and adolescence under optimal conditions for identity formation and intimacy expression.

With new cognitive data about himself and about others, Eric began to question some of the assumptions he based his behavior on. And as he began to see his patterns of behavior, he decided to do some things differently. For example, he decided not to have sex with men until he developed some emotional closeness. In addition, he decided that for him to have a satisfying sexual experience, he first wanted to talk with his partner about what the experience might mean emotionally. Although he was able to experiment with this healthy attachment behavior with the reassurance of his therapist, friends, and support group, this was especially challenging for Eric. It meant exposing his romantic desires at the risk of appearing sentimental and being rejected.

It is in the affective exploration of such fears that the therapist becomes of primary importance. While Eric continued to expand his options for male-male interaction, he still needed a "home-base" for expression of the affect which had been subsumed for so long. His discovery that he could experience himself fully in all his feelings in the presence of another important person gave him some of the intimacy he had missed with his parents (Miller, A., 1981).

During this time, Eric reported that he frequently had conversations with me in his head. He found that he could rather accurately predict what I might say in various circumstances. He gradually realized that it was his own voice he was hearing. He began to learn through explicit self-reassurance how to respond to himself in the manner he wished his parents had—with encouragement, support, and gentle confrontation.

To accomplish these goals, clients often find it useful to insert a hiatus in the therapeutic process. Unfortunately, this is sometimes confused with premature termination. The two are distinguished by what both therapist and client understand the interruption to represent. In cases where clients initiate termination just as anxiety begins to appear, it may be very useful to discover explicitly whether interrupting therapy is a "flee" response. If so, client and therapist can work together to find a more useful defense mechanism, and continue therapy. When interruption is not a response to the reemergence of psychodynamic stress, then closure of this portion of therapy is indicated. In such cases, closure which explicitly acknowledges the value of the developmental steps taken is most useful. It is often valuable to assess and acknowledge realistically the further work the client may want to undertake. Both approaches prevent reexperience of emotional rejection or abandonment for the client.

Therapy was terminated by mutual agreement when Eric felt he had the tools to be able to count on himself for nurturance (separation), and the courage to express his needs to others without shame (attachment).

SUMMARY

A balance of a positive personal construct of self-worth (separation) with an active awareness of one's sense of relation to, and being at one with, other beings (attachment) is necessary for a satisfying sense of identity and intimacy. When the personal construct of self-worth is not modeled, taught, and reinforced through emotional connection in the boy, a combination of identity disorder and intimacy dysfunction is an expected outcome.

These developmental issues seen clinically in many males may be complicated in the pre-homosexual male's childhood by his own or others' reactions to his emerging sexual orientation, or both; this is particularly the case with gender non-conformity. The resulting developmental deficits will be manifested in some cases by dysfunctional methods for achieving satisfying relationships with himself and with others through patterns of over-separation and over-attachment.

Therapeutic intervention for men can be directed toward formulation of a solid identity based on self-observation and self-valuing. Identification, acceptance, and expression of needs for human contact in the form of cognitive, affective, and behaviorial relearning form the basis for satisfying intimacy needs.

REFERENCES

Adler, A. (1927). *Understanding human nature* (W. B. Wolfe, Trans.). New York: Greenberg.

Bakan, D. (1966). *The duality of human existence*. Chicago: Rand McNally.

Balswich, J., & Avertt, C. P. (1977). Differences in expressiveness: Gender, interpersonal orientation, and perceived parental expressiveness as contributing factors. *Journal of Marriage and the Family, 38*, 121–127.

Bell, A., Weinberg, M., & Hammersmith, S. (1981). *Sexual preference: Its development in men and women*. Bloomington: Indiana University Press.

Block, J. H.. (1973, June). Conceptions of sex role: Some cross-cultural and longitudinal perspectives. *American Psychologist*, pp. 512–526.

Bowlby, J. (1975). Attachment theory, separation anxiety, and mourning. In A. Silvano (Ed.), *The American Handbook of Psychiatry* (Vol. 6, pp. 292–309). New York: Basic Books.

Cohen, F., & Densen-Gerber, J. (1982). A study of the relationship between child abuse and drug addiction in 178 patients: Preliminary results. *Child Abuse and Neglect, 6*, 383–387.

Coleman, E., & Colgan, P. (1986). Boundary inadequacy in drug dependent families. *Journal of Psychoactive Drugs, 18* (1), 21–30.

Coleman, E. (1982). Developmental stages of the coming out process. In J. Gonsiorek (Ed.), *Homosexuality and psychotherapy: A practitioner's handbook of affirmative models*. New York: Haworth Press.

Colgan, P., & Riebel, J. (1981). *Sexuality education for foster parents*. Minneapolis: University of Minnesota.

Colgan, P. (in press). Treatment of dependency disorders in men: Toward a balance of identity and intimacy. *Journal of Chemical Dependency Treatment*.

Cooper, I., & Cormier, B. (1982). Inter-generational transmission of incest. *Canadian Journal of Psychiatry, 27*, 231–235.

Cosby, P. C. (1973). Self disclosure: A literature review. *Psychological Bulletin, 79* (2), 73–91.

Cytryn, L., McKnew, D., Zahn-Waxler, C., Radke-Yarrow, M., Gaensbauer, T., Harmon, R., & Lamour, M. (1984). A developmental view of affective disturbances in the children of affectively ill parents. *American Journal of Psychiatry, 141*, 219–222.

Erikson, E. (1959). *Identity and the life cycle.* New York: W. W. Norton.

Feinman, S. (1974). Approval of cross-sex role behavior. *Psychological Reports, 35*, 643–648.

Fling, S., & Manosevitz, M. (1972). Sex typing in nursery school children's play interests. *Developmental Psychology, 7*, 146–152.

Garbarino, J., & Gilliam, G. (1980). *Understanding abusive families.* Lexington, MA: Lexington Books.

Gleason, J. B. (1975). Fathers and other strangers: Men's speech to young children. In D. P. Dato (Ed.), Georgetown University roundtable on language and linguistics. *Developmental Theory and Applications.* Washington, DC: Georgetown University Press.

Haccoun, D., Allen, J., & Fader, S. (1974). *Sex differences in response to emotion: A study of peer counseling.* Paper presented at the 82nd annual convention of the American Psychological Association, New Orleans.

Johnson, C., & Flach, A. (1985). Family characteristics of 105 patients with bulimia. *American Journal of Psychiatry, 142*, 1321–1324.

Johnson, S. (1985). *Characterological transformation: The hard work miracle.* New York: W. W. Norton.

Kaufman, G. (1974). The meaning of shame: Toward a self-affirming identity. *Journal of Counseling Psychology, 21*, 568–574.

Lakarezyk, D. T., & Hill, K. T. (1969). Self esteem, test anxiety, stress, and verbal learning. *Developmental Psychology, 1*, 147–154.

McWhirter, D., & Mattison, D. (1984). *The male couple: How relationships develop.* Englewood Cliffs, NJ: Prentice-Hall.

Malyon, A. (1982). Psychotherapeutic implications of internalized homophobia in gay men. In J. Gonsiorek (Ed.), *Homosexuality and psychotherapy: A practitioner's handbook of affirmative models* (pp. 59–69). New York: Haworth Press.

Miller, A. (1981). *Prisoners of childhood* (R. Ward, Trans.). New York: Basis Books.

Miller, J. B. (1983). *The construction of anger in women and men.* Works in Progress No. 83–01. Wellesley, MA: Wellesley College.

Miller, J. B. (1984). *The development of women's sense of self.* Works in progress. Wellesley, MA: Wellesley College.

Moore, D. (1984). *An investigation of changes in affective expressiveness in men as a result of participation in a multimodal psychological intervention.* Minneapolis: University of Minnesota.

Narus, L., & Fisher, J. (1982). Strong but not silent: A reexamination of expressivity in the relationships of men. *Sex Roles, 8*, 159–168.

Noller, P. (1978). Sex differences in the socialization of affectionate expression. *Developmental Psychology, 14*, 317–319.

O'Leary, V., & Donoghue, J. (1978). Latitudes of masculinity: Reactions to sex role deviance in men. *Journal of Social Issues, 34* (1), 17–28.

Robinson, J. (1985). *Sex differences in prosocial behavior: A reexamination.* Unpublished manuscript, University of Minnnesota.

Rosenfeld, L. B. (1979). Self disclosure avoidance: Why am I afraid to tell you who I am? *Communication Monographs, 46*, 63–74.

Silverstein, C. (1981). Man to Man: Gay couples in America, New York: William Morrow.

Smalley, S. (1982). *Co-dependency: An introduction.* New Brighton, MN: SBS Publications.

Smalley, S. & Coleman, E. (in press). Treating intimacy dysfunctions in dyadic relationships among chemically dependent and co-dependent clients. *Journal of Chemical Dependency Treatment.*

Smith, D., Apter-Marsh, M., Buffum, J., Moser, C., & Wesson, D. Socio-sexual issues in the using and recovering alcoholic. *Alcoholism Treatment Quarterly, 3*, 17–32.

Tennov, D. (1979). Love and limerence: *The experience of being in love.* New York: Stein & Day.

Wolin, S., Beannett, L., & Noonan, D. (1979, April). Family rituals and the recurrence of alcoholism over generations. *American Journal of Psychiatry, 136* (4B), 589–593.

Dependency Issues
in Lesbian Relationships

Sondra Smalley, MA

University of Minnesota

SUMMARY. The focus of this paper is dependent relationship patterns or co-dependency in lesbian relationships. Co-dependent relationship patterns are identified, in general, as well as in lesbian relationships. Treatment strategies found to be successful in overcoming these co-dependent issues are illustrated with case studies.

In working with relationship issues with lesbian clients, therapists often have a blind spot related to biases about women in close relationships. I once contacted a colleague who had been a long-time feminist therapist and who had been working with women in lesbian relationships for many years. At lunch I shared my discovery with my friend who calmly said, "Oh, we've all done that, you know."

We both had assumed that lesbian relationships would have few of the characteristics of heterosexual relationships. We thought the bulk of heterosexual intimacy problems centered around male-female sex role conflict. We assumed, albeit not always consciously, that relationships between women would be so different that our therapeutic antenna would short-circuit.

My particular area of specialty has been dependent relationships. Through the years I have worked with both dependent heterosexual and homosexual women and have noticed many similar characteristics. For instance, I must mention dependency as a factor in all relationships. This is an important characteristic of close interaction for all humans as social beings. Inter-dependency is certainly an important part of most lasting relationships.

The focus of this paper is *not* about interdependency, but about dependent relationship patterns or codependency. Codependency describes exaggerated, painful, extreme reactive dependency characteristics (Smalley, 1981). Thus, codependency is a *learned pattern* of behaviors,

Ms. Smalley is a licensed psychologist and a certified chemical dependency practitioner, and is on the Clinical Faculty of the Program in Human Sexuality, Department of Family Practice and Community Health, Medical School, University of Minnesota. Correspondence may be addressed to the author, 185 Windsor Court, New Brighton, MN 55112.

feelings, and beliefs. It often results in self-neglect and is characterized by an external locus of control. Many people have long histories of these codependent patterns in their relationships.

These patterns may be apparent in women, men, and even in children. In each of these populations the stressful relationship patterns are similar. As with lesbian and heterosexual women, I find the differences in co-dependent patterns and interdependency to be one of degree or emphasis, not one of kind (Smalley & Coleman, in press).

The reason for using the term codependency rather than dependency is that it connotes more than fusion. The broader concept includes many of the disguises of dependency, including counterdependency, isolation, controlling, and sacrificing.

To discuss treating lesbian women who are in dependent relationships, I have divided this paper into three parts: (a) codependent relationship patterns, (b) recognizing co-dependent issues in lesbian relationships, and (c) treating codependent issues with lesbian women.

CODEPENDENT RELATIONSHIP PATTERNS

The following assumptions about codependent relationship patterns dictate the treatment considerations and therapeutic techniques to use. First, painful dependent relationship patterns (codependency) are spawned and flourish in high-stress environments. Clients with this pattern are often from high-stress families, e.g., in which alcoholism, chronic illness, mental illness, and obsessive compulsive traits were present. Thus, the family of origin has often been one with an uncomfortable tense climate (McCubbin & Figley, 1983). In adulthood most people with this pattern continue to work and play and love in tense production, friendship, and intimate environments (Wotitz, 1983). Some people with this pattern encounter stress in all of life's areas, others in only some.

Codependent patterns seem to serve a purpose, the most common being to avoid pain. The varying beliefs of codependent individuals seem to support this notion.

> "If I just stay close, I'll be OK."
> "If I just stay distant, I'll be OK."
> "If I just stay in control, I'll be OK."
> "If I just give enough, I'll be OK."

Many people with codependent patterns operate throughout their lives on one or more of these beliefs which become the central organizing principles of their lives.

Many people with this pattern display a great deal of surface maturity. They look and act very responsible, very mature, very adult (Black, 1982); many have appeared this way since childhood. The psychiatric literature has suggested for years that when we observe a very mature little child or a very serious adult, this indicates a person who has not had his or her dependency needs met.

Some of the other characteristics of people with codependent patterns are:

1. *An external locus of control,* tending to focus on people and things outside oneself for validation (Seligman, 1975).
2. *Preoccupation with relationships,* particularly intimate ones, resulting either in extreme avoidance or extreme attachment.
3. *Unseen audiences,* carrying a psychological audience who is always observing one's actions and evaluating one's performance. (Most codependent people also relate to others, particularly in intimate relationships, in the role of critic—one who must be *responsible for* those they love. Smalley, 1981).
4. *High tolerance of inappropriate behavior accompanied by "tolerance breaks."* A puzzling dynamic that results in extremes of acceptance and rage. I believe those who have much of their identity resting on their "selfless image," are most prone to explosive outbursts or panic.

The description of this pattern is dependent upon two important assumptions. First, love is learned; loving and being loved is not a part of one's generic personality, but a learnable skill. Second, codependency is a pattern, not an illness. This pattern is an intricate weaving of many characteristics, which depends upon each person's past learning history.

RECOGNIZING CODEPENDENT ISSUES IN LESBIAN RELATIONSHIPS

Most of my clinical experience has been with white lesbian women from 25 to 55 years old who have come from middle-class or working class families. Each woman has been college-educated, and all live in a large urban center. They have ranged in their coming-out process from only acknowledging their sexual attraction to women, to exploring their sexuality with multiple relationships with women, to having a positive self-concept with lesbianism. The majority of the women I will mention have integrated their lesbian identity into their overall identity.

It has been interesting to note that these codependent women have often chosen partners who have only recently acknowledged their attraction to women. One common characteristic of codependent patterns is psychologically to place one's head higher or lower than the other person's, which creates unequalness or a lack of mutuality from the inception of the relationship. Thus, the relationship begins with a "new" and an "old" lesbian. The following story is a typical example of this.

I saw Martha for 2 years. Martha was a talented, very bright 45 year-old woman who was also a recovering alcoholic with over 10 years of sobriety. For those 10 years, Martha was in a relationship with a woman (Molly) who at first acknowledged her attraction to women, then as the years went on denied it. This denial process interfered with their relationship for many years; sex became non-existent. Martha became more submissive and gave her time, her energy, her love unstintingly. She earned little money, kept house, and read over 12 hours a day. She had fewer lesbian friends over the years. The more Martha talked about her sexual desire or desire for any kind of closeness, the less desire Molly displayed.

With Martha there was a tendency to become submissive in intimacy, whereas Molly, who was less accepting of her lesbianism, tended to be more demanding and talked of needing independent time and distance. Thus, a demanding-deferring relationship dynamic developed. These patterns of codependent lesbians are very similar to others I have seen. Codependent women, like Martha, appear very mature (surface maturity), selfless (high tolerance for inappropriate behavior), concerned about their relationship (relationship preoccupation), and very responsible for their partner (external locus of control). For Martha this relationship served a purpose: the avoidance of mutuality, and thus the avoidance of a very basic anxiety. It also helped her not to focus on herself because the relationship was often dramatic, fast-moving, and attention-getting.

Tumultuous relationships serve the same purpose, namely the avoidance of intimacy, and also the perpetuation of confusion and the push-pull of the undecided. In other words, "Is it really okay for me to have a relationship with a woman?"

Often a committed relationship will experience disturbance until the basic lesbian identity issues have been settled. Beyond that, there are some basic issues around intimacy that must be addressed after the identity acceptance occurs. This is a task for all people—"How do I get close enough without losing my self?" "How do I find my self while intimate?" This is an old dilemma, similar to patting one's head and rubbing one's stomach simultaneously. A lesbian woman has both; some tasks in this process of balancing intimacy and identity are easier and some are harder. Some of the more difficult tasks include:

1. Maintaining a low-stress lesbian relationship in a predominately heterosexual and anti-homosexual society. Holidays, extended families,

work places, traveling, and so forth, can all be stressful in themselves. However, even well-integrated lesbians often cannot integrate their relationships into these activities easily. Many lesbians encounter prejudice and discernment in business offices if one's lover calls on the telephone. Traveling and encountering, or fearing encountering, unfriendly attitudes among hotel staffs can be a concern. Controlling affectionate displays in public is a specific example of the tension-producing aspects of lesbian relationships, many of which are not encountered by their heterosexual couple counterparts.

2. Coming to believe that hurt and pain do not have to accompany intimacy. Many lesbian women have encountered rejection and fear in their families of origin and in their feelings of "differentness" which often leads to caution in commitment. Deciding that comfortable intimacy is possible helps change a life-time pattern for many lesbian women.

3. Intimacy skill development has often been delayed because of the energy-draining task of accepting one's sexual preference. When women have avoided all intimacy, as many have done, there has been little practice in learning who they are in relationships.

4. Usually in the "coming-out" process women develop very strong and important support networks. This is often positive, but sometimes can become a substitute "unseen audience" that must be played to.

There also may be excessive concern with, "What will my friends say about my lover? (this relationship?) and so on." This may heighten an external locus of control and impede a woman's discovery of her own particular individual preference.

At the same time, in developing less dependent, more intimate relationships, lesbian women with integrated identities accomplish some tasks with more ease. For instance:

1. They usually have a higher level of self-awareness. They are more aware of the "I," answering "Who am I when alone in the middle of the night?" more easily. Brochures published by one lesbian and gay resource center focus on increasing trust in one's self, one's self-confidence, and one's survival skills (Lesbian and Gay Community Services, 1984). In feminist literature and interaction, such concepts as owning one's power, asserting one's own rights, and other such boundary-clarifying subjects lend to self-clarity (Kaufman, Harrison, & Hyde, 1984; Gauthier, 1983). The support of women and self-power is more apparent in lesbian clients.

2. In general, integrated lesbian women tend to have more friendships, be more aware of balance in life, and pay attention to self-health and nutrition. In other words, the women's movement has fostered more high-level wellness, and this can be observed in lesbian clients as opposed to others.

3. Lesbian women are less pressured to be "ALWAYS" in a relationship. There are fewer external "SHOULDS," about long-term relationships for the sake of the public or the family.

4. In working with lesbian couples versus heterosexual couples, I have noticed that they are more willing not to use heterosexual marriages as an intimacy role model—although a number at first use this model and are not aware of it. The heterosexual model seems to be one of self-limitations rather than one of self-enhancement or expansion. Also, lesbian couples who engage in power struggles go beyond them with more ease, possibly because there are not the sex-role expectations and complications.

TREATING CODEPENDENT ISSUES WITH LESBIAN WOMEN

The population of codependent lesbian women I am primarily addressing is usually integrated in their work and public identity. They are able to be their own person, to explore, to succeed, to achieve. In contrast, in their relationships there is hesitancy, bewilderment, and confusion in love and intimacy.

I will discuss below some of the treatment considerations and therapeutic techniques in addressing this co-dependent pattern, and will also mention some differences I note in treating heterosexual women with the same codependent pattern.

The main goal of this treatment process is to help women have more comfortable relationships that are self-expanding. The particular skills I see as important are to encourage women: (a) gently but firmly to observe and intervene on their own relationship patterns, (b) learn to lower their stress levels in both self-intimacy as well as in intimacy with others, and (c) learn about relationship development and develop additional interaction skills.

I have used this model in individual and couples therapy, and in psycho-educational groups. Deciding to work with a codependent person alone, or with a relationship, or in a group, depends on the past learning history of the individual involved. A group process is suggested if a woman's anxiety and stress level is low enough that she can listen in a group without engaging in selective inattention or focusing exclusively on others. The goal is for her to learn about her relationship patterns without undue anxiety. Sometimes individual psychotherapy two or three times in the 26-week group process is helpful to clarify and summarize the information. The group process is psychoeducational and non-confrontive, with the goal of encouraging each woman to become more self-confrontive.

Group Format

Phase I. This phase addresses their identity and is concerned with the "I" or the intrapersonal aspect of each person. Many homework assignments are given, such as keeping private log books (with fewer unseen audiences), inner dialoguing, encouraging self-observation of one's inner process, and assessing one's own unique codependent characteristics. Each participant is encouraged to do "parallel play" in the group—not investing in each other, but instead choosing their world for a laboratory, practicing outside the group.

Phase II. This phase addresses their interaction and is concerned with the "ME" or the *interactional* aspect of a person. The question "Who am I in relationships?" is emphasized along with an examination of all aspects of all historically important relationships beginning with the family of origin. Participants are taught about stages in relationships, examining one's ego attachments in relationships, and untangling boundary dilemmas. Again, many homework suggestion are given.

Phase III. The final phase focuses on love and work, both identity and intimacy and their delicate balance. Attachment, separation issues, definitions of love and intimacy, origins of their overt and covert beliefs about love and work, and the issues of endings and launchings are discussed. These groups are called psychoeducational because they are designed primarily with very low stress levels. Humor and permissiveness are also important components. These groups are designed for women to be together without excessive self-disclosure being demanded or expected. The therapist's role is one of a gentle coach who helps design strategies, teaches techniques, and supports and celebrates change.

Although the psychoeducation groups are useful as adjunctive therapy, sometimes I find exclusive individual therapy with a women most beneficial. This is true, especially when her level of awareness about her relationships is especially clouded or confused. Two such women come to mind.

Case Illustration

Sarah reported a history of tumultuous sexual relationships of a few days' duration which always "broke up" with hostility. Sarah was satisfied with her career but not her particular job. She reported having no close friends, but she did have a support network. She had told her parents she was a lesbian several years ago and had what she described as a satisfyingly distant relationship with them. She wanted to have more long-term rewarding relationships with friends.

Ann reported she had not had a sexual relationship for 7 years, at which time she accepted her sexual preference. Before that time she had a few short-term relationships with women. Several months previous to the start of therapy, she had developed a love relationship in which she became submissive. It had abruptly and painfully ended. Ann was satisfied with both her career and her job. She said she had lots of close friends and a wonderful support network of relationships. She had never told her parents she was a lesbian as she knew, "they would have a fit."

The paradoxical pattern of codependency was present in both these women's histories, as they both reported job satisfaction and success coupled with intimacy discouragement.

I began working with Sarah to explore her past experiences with intimacy, beginning with her family. She discovered she had never trusted or been close to her family as she had felt "different" as long as she could remember. She seemed to have adapted a belief, "If I stay distant I'll be okay." I was as though every time she took a risk and tried to get close, it proved to be painful. Her self-fulfilling prophecy was aided by her tendency to choose inappropriate sexual partners—only women who were volatile and abusive.

Ann seldom chose any sexual partners and lived out her belief that, "If I just stay isolated I'll be okay." In the breakup of her only recent relationship, she had tried out the opposite idea, "If I just hold on to you, I'll be okay," but she discovered she wasn't.

Both women shared their belief in the safeness of distance and the danger of closeness in intimacy.

Ann's lover came back and Ann's first response was to reject her. She then reported that she made a conscious choice to stay and see if she could learn more about herself. One of the first things she discovered was when she was no longer submissive she became critical and power-abusive. Sarah noted she treated herself internally the same way and that this pattern had a distancing effect. She began to observe that when she was mean, she told her partner she was aware of this. For the first time, Ann began slowly to decide that her beliefs about danger in closeness were creating much of her tension in her relationship. As she became more self-focused and less self-critical, she became less power-abusive and invasive with her partner. I believe Ann's anxiety and denial around intimacy was so extreme that in a group she would have intellectualized rather than integrated the material.

Sarah called after a period of time and reported she had been in a quiet, satisfying relationship for over a year. She attributed this change to her greater gentleness with herself and others, as well as her continuing self-observations in her log book.

I believe both clients learned the same skill. They became gentler with themselves and firmly encouraged themselves to stay put and choose relationships from which they could learn.

A Couple Case Illustration

Emily and Beth's communication with each other was usually very respectful. They had been seen separately in codependent groups and reported they had gone beyond power struggling, except with one big issue. Emily and Beth were now searching for bonds that were firm connections. They had lived together for 5 years, with Emily's children visiting 3 days a week. Beth stated she wanted to live alone, although she got along well with children. Emily was sad, confused, and afraid that Beth was going away for good, but felt confined and limited.

In the previous 2 years there were periodic painful fights over the issue. In observing all their past relationships, they found neither had ever lived alone; they had gone from family to marriage or lived in relationships. Both had left relationships whenever there were power struggles, each feeling wounded, rejected, and unloved.

They reported they wished to react to their present relationship differently. Each woman was satisfied with her work, her friendships, and her family relationships. Her lesbian identity was integrated into the rest of her life. Neither woman was extremely preoccupied with their relationship and had many friends and interests. This couple benefited from developing their interaction skills to help them reorganize their relationship. First, it was established to each one's satisfaction that they cared for each other and that they were cared about. They stated they had two goals in therapy: (a) to improve their communication skills so that each felt understood, and (b) to become less ego-involved over the resolution of their living situation.

We began by historically reviewing the process of their relationship. They had come together with new intensity that felt secure and safe. For almost 3 years they maximized all of their similarities and minimized their differences. Beth did not tell Emily how overwhelmed she felt living with the children. Emily never shared her disappointment in Beth's passiveness.

Then, 2 years ago, each began to speak up. Beth began to avoid the children; Emily began to ask that Beth speak up more. Beth finally announced that she wished to live alone. Emily found this intolerable. The power struggle was set. Each woman said she clung to her position with her own life. There was no longer the extreme intensity of the positive bonds of the first few years. In the last few months they had begun to be more accepting of their differences. They both felt relieved that the relationship was quieter, but they felt distance was developing between them without the negative bonds. The affectionate ties were apparent, but the task was to create some new connections that were more overt and that fit each person's own intimacy needs.

First, each woman was helped to recognize when her anxiety level was beginning to rise. The task then was to ask immediately for reassurance—

such as "Do You Care About Me?"—and to allow the positive response to quiet the anxiety. As they began to ask for reassurance they reported less anxiety over alternative living arrangements. Emily said she had sometimes dreamed of living alone, but was convinced that would mean the end of the relationship and the loss of Beth. Beth said she had feared adjusting their relationship because change had often meant despair for her.

We also worked on their communication skills. One technique which proved useful for them was to interview each other for information. They designed a routine in which each interviewed the other with no editorializing in their questioning. In taking turns, they each began to feel "heard" and no longer needed the ritual of interviewing.

The pain in most communication is in not being "heard." It is a mistake to believe that each person's position must be fully understood or agreed with in order to have harmony (Chapman & Chapman, 1980). (Many people with codependent patterns seem to have invented "long talks." These "long talks" seem to be devoted to explaining and justifying positions so others can thoroughly *understand*.)

Another useful concept for this couple was for each woman to observe her own demand that *all* her intimacy needs be met in this relationship. For instance, when Emily heard Beth say that she wished to live apart at least for a while, Emily reacted angrily, with panic.

Emily discovered she was thinking, "Beth *must* not live apart *or* I am *nothing*." In asking Emily the question, "Who are You?", she would respond, "Nothing." This response illustrated the characteristic of codependency of defining oneself according to someone else's behaviors. The symbiotic tie—the *OR*—is obvious. Each of these women, with their codependent patterns, was doing this whenever their anxiety level increased around this topic. Hence, the topic was difficult to address. Emily learned to lessen the intensity, but not deny her wishes, by stating, "I prefer Beth not live apart, but if she does, I am somebody."

This form of cognitive re-structuring is an important psychotherapeutic tool in working with codependent people. Emily and Beth began to address and reexamine their belief systems around closeness, distance, and boundaries. They discovered that these self-definitions and needs have been themes in most of the relationships in their lives. Emily and Beth were then able to design a unique relationship agreement that satisfied them, at least for the time being. They were able to develop a comfortable relationship in which they both felt reassurance, but both felt they could expand themselves. Their design represented a unique blend of each woman's honest preferences. They had no models to go by, but having accepted their "differentness" as lesbians, they were more easily able to design a "different" intimacy model. Their model would not necessarily work for others, however.

SUMMARY

In summary, I have tried to address treating lesbian couples with dependency issues as a task that has similarities to treating other couples with dependency problems, while also recognizing some differences. In treating lesbian couples, I have found it easier to work with two women as we share a more common language. In other ways, I find it personally painful when I see, first-hand, the emotional and spiritual violence that this society has caused by telling someone that they are sick or weird. It is obvious that, as Michael Carrera states, "Gay men and lesbian women . . . have been excluded, trivialized, and rendered invisible." (Carrera, 1984).

I believe as lesbian women continue to learn to live in comfortable relationships and deepen their intimacy bonds, they will have done something that the larger society has not done, and that is far from trivial.

REFERENCES

Black, C. (1982). *It will never happen to me*. Denver: M.A.C.

Carrera, M. (1984). Acceptance speech, AASECT Award Dinner. *Journal of Sex Education and Therapy*, 8–12.

Chapman, A. H., & Chapman, M. (1980). *Harry Stack Sullivan's concept of personality development and psychiatric illness*. New York: Brunner/Mazel.

Gauthier, J. (1983). The enhancement of self-esteem. *Cognitive Therapy and Research*, 7, 389–398.

Kaufman, P., Harrison, E., & Hyde, M. (1984). Distancing for intimacy in lesbian relationships. *American Journal of Psychiatry, 141*, 530–533.

Lesbian and Gay Community Services. (1984). *Therapy support and educational group services*. Minneapolis.

McCubbin, H., & Figley, C. (Ed.) (1983). *Stress and the family (Vols. 1 & 2)*. New York: Brunner/Mazel.

Mead, G. H. (1962). In C. W. Morias (Ed.), *Mind, self and society* (pp. 135–226). Chicago: University of Chicago Press.

Seligman, M. (1975). *Helplessness, on depression, development and death*. San Francisco: W. H. Freeman.

Smalley, S. (1981). *Co-Dependency: An introduction*. New Brighton, MN: SBS Publishing.

Smalley, S., & Coleman, E. (In press). Treating intimacy dysfunctions in dyadic relationships among chemically dependent and co-dependent clients. *Journal of Chemical Dependency Treatment*,

Wotitz, J. (1983). *Adult children of alcoholics*. Hollywood, FL: Health Communications.

Sex Therapy with Lesbian Couples:
A Four Stage Approach

Marny Hall, PhD
San Francisco
and
Oakland

SUMMARY. The many factors—social, cultural, psychological—that shape homosexual sexual expression render purely behavioral sex therapy models one-dimensional and ineffective for lesbian clients with sexual presenting problems. Though a behavioral approach may be useful later in the treatment of such problems, the effective clinician must first address the inimical social and cultural contexts that frame lesbian sexual impasses. This paper offers specific techniques, both direct and indirect, designed to illuminate and neutralize these contexts. Additionally, the author presents a sequence of sensate focus exercises tailored to the particular needs of lesbian couples.

HISTORICAL OVERVIEW

When Masters and Johnson (1970) designed a program of behavioral exercises to neutralize sexual fears, they departed from the historic treatment of erotic impasses with verbal psychotherapy alone. Rather than attributing sexual problems to childhood experiences or early trauma, Masters and Johnson targeted performance anxiety, stating that when partners focused on the pleasure of touch instead of the achievement of orgasm, the inhibiting anxiety would dissipate and desire would spontaneously reappear. It had always been there, but was simply masked by anxiety. Though Masters' and Johnson's approach didn't live up to its proponents' early claims of success, their formulations were a useful, radical departure that became part of a new therapeutic dialectic.

Later therapists theorized that perhaps some anxieties should not be skirted, that in fact sexual dysfunction might be appropriate in some cases. To eliminate anxiety behaviorally, these therapists believed, would violate the psychological gestalt of the client. Today, the most common approach to sexual problems is an amalgam which combines behavioral

---

Dr. Hall is a psychotherapist in private practice and is the author of the book *The Lavender Couch: A Consumer's Guide to Psychotherapy for Lesbians and Gay Men*. Correspondence may be addressed to the author, 1015 Elbert Street, Oakland, CA 94602.

exercises with more traditional indepth approaches (Kaplan, 1974; Apfelbaum, Williams & Greene, 1979).

The lesbians who were treated for sexual dysfunction by Masters and Johnson-influenced therapists couldn't claim any more lasting successes than their heterosexual counterparts who followed the same regimen (Masters & Johnson, 1970). When their sexual problems weren't resolved, however, lesbians were more forgiving than were heterosexuals. The serious consideration of their problems outside the traditional context of pathology was worth the time and money spent in the therapist's office. If the counselor wasn't unblocking erotic impasses, at least she[1] was treating a problem which probably had not even been articulated: damage to self-esteem caused by homophobia.

In addition to the healing effect of therapy which focused on clients' presenting problems instead of lifestyle, and legitimized relationships by including *both* partners, the Masters and Johnson approach offered another distinct advantage. Unlike verbal therapy, the results of which always remained ambiguous, the behavioral approach was short-term, focused, and success and failure were immediately apparent. It was, in fact, the failures of behavior therapy with lesbians that forced therapists to look beyond its prescriptions, and to reconceptualize the problem of lesbian sexual impasses.

LESBIAN SEXUAL PROBLEMS

Discrepancy in sexual desire between partners, or the absence in both partners of erotic feelings are the problems reported most frequently by lesbian couples. Though homosexual male couples and heterosexual partners bring parallel problems to therapists' offices, reports of insufficient sexual arousal are less ubiquitous among these populations. The post-honeymoon diminution in ardor reported by couples of all persuasions is both more dramatic and pervasive among lesbian couples. In the first 2 years of lesbian relationships, 76% of lesbians in the Blumstein and Schwartz (1983) study reported having sex once a week or more, compared to 83% of heterosexual married couples. After 2 years, only 37% of lesbian couples still made love at least once a week, compared to 73% of heterosexual couples (p. 196).

There are a number of reasons cited for the plunge in sexual exchanges between lesbians in long-term relationships. Primary among them is a dissolution of individual boundaries, a submergence of self in the larger arena of the relationship. In the beginning, such a commingling of souls is intensely erotic. If each partner does not reclaim herself eventually, however, the relationship becomes stultifying, and the spark of difference that ignites eroticism disappears. According to Kaufman, Harrison, and

Hyde (1984), lesbian relationships sometimes become characterized by "excessive closeness . . . extreme and intense ambivalence, and a failure to establish emotional territorial, temporal and cognitive space for each individual" (p. 530). Burch (1986) describes such relationships as mergers in which the "individual differences may be smoothed over so thoroughly that one or both persons abandon whatever parts of the self that do not fit with the other. This denial of differences may exist only when they are together; at its extreme, one person is unable to think or act in ways the other wouldn't, even when they are apart" (p. 59).

That this pattern is common among lesbian couples is not disputed. The reasons for the merger, however, is the subject of some debate. Psychodynamically oriented clinicians point to the mother-daughter relationship as the prototype for lesbian fusion. Because mother and daughter cannot refer to the palpable physical differences that distinguish mother and son to help with differentiation and individuation, their boundaries vis-à-vis one another always remain more permeable (Chodorow, 1978). Consequently, they are always more likely to "lose" themselves in relationships. According to psychodynamic interpretations, lesbian mergers are devoid of sex because the partners both crave and dread the primal mother/daughter union they have, to some degree, replicated. Physical union, combined with the psychological union they are already experiencing with their partners, overloads the terror side of the primal equation; partners fear they will be reduced to the state of a powerless infant, subject to the whims of the engulfing mother.

Sociologically oriented clinicians (Miller, 1976) claim that women's tendency to fuse comes from gender-bound conditioning. So pervasive are the culturally encoded messages that prescribe women's roles as supportive and self-sacrificing, that the notion of ego boundaries simply doesn't apply. Women's psychic structuring is not modular, as the concept "ego" suggests. It is, instead, affiliative in nature. When two women form a relationship, the affiliation quotient increases exponentially. Such bonding generates a great deal of caring and empathy, but little eroticism. If any spark remained, women's culturally conditioned passivity would guarantee that it would go unfanned.

According to one group of researchers, Hatfield and Walster (1978), it is not fear of the engulfing mother or cultural conditioning, but lack of adrenaline which accounts for the extinction of libido in fused couples. For better or worse, sexuality seems to flourish under conditions of adversity. When there are obstacles to the union—cultural or family opposition, an angry, displaced lover, the necessity for clandestine meetings—passion runs high. When all these obstacles are circumvented and the couple is firmly ensconced in an intruder-proof nest, partners often find erotic feelings have fled. A good skirmish, the threat of another suitor, or a forced separation can be counted on to produce the adrenaline necessary for an erotic resurgence.

Yet another source of de-eroticized relationships not included in any of the categories mentioned above are past sexual encounters (Loulan, 1985), positive or negative, which can generate associations so powerful that they contaminate later expression of sexuality. Ironically, past traumatic experiences such as childhood sexual abuse or rape may be no more inhibiting than the passionate encounters which inaugurated the relationship. Post-passionate sexuality may seem tepid by comparison, and partners may not ''feel'' sexual. What they are actually saying is that they are not feeling ''passionate.''

Systems-oriented social analysts such as Krestan and Bebko (1980) see fusion in yet another light. The existence of the lesbian couple in a hostile, homophobic culture prompts the lesbian couple to adopt an us-against-the-world stance. In order to present a united front, all individual idiosyncrasies must be jettisoned. Merger is the result—a relationship which is a fortress rather than a choice. Within such a fortress there is no need for more union; consequently, the bridging function of sex becomes redundant.

BEYOND MASTERS AND JOHNSON: IMPLICATIONS FOR TREATMENT

If during sex therapy the clinician doesn't continue to address the stigmatizing and entropic effect of homophobia, as well as the myriad effects of women's socialization, psychology, and biology mentioned above, sex therapy will resemble nothing so much as an attempt to start a fire with wet kindling. Sex therapy with lesbians, therefore, extends far beyond the early prescriptions of Masters and Johnson.

As discussed in depth later in this article, part of treatment must address a primary consequence of homophobia: the partners' sense of failure, the feeling that they are flawed, as evidenced by the fact that they do not have an ideal sexual relationship. What the therapist must flush out, and hold up for examination, is the flaw beneath the flaw, the outsider status which partners feel they must constantly compensate or overcompensate for by being a ''perfect'' couple.

An equally critical treatment component is the delineation and modeling of a behavioral style which may seem alien and threatening to both partners: autonomous behavior within the context of the relationship. This is the sine qua non of effective sex therapy. The assignment of touching exercises will be futile unless partners can, on a fairly regular basis, have experiences outside the boundaries of the relationship that are pleasurable, stimulating and engaging, activities which recharge the batteries of partners.

Finally, the exposure and toleration of differences, also described in more detail later, is the other essential element in treatment. If partners can acknowledge differences in sensitive areas, money and status, for example, and discuss the meaning of such differences openly, without trying to redress the imbalance, they will not be as likely to surface in the bedroom disguised as sexual incompatibility.

BEGINNING THE THERAPEUTIC PROCESS: CONCERNS FOR INITIAL SESSIONS

Sex therapy includes four fairly distinct stages: (a) the beginning; (b) the middle, in which the problem is reframed; (c) the segment that includes sensually focused assignments; and finally (d) termination. Each stage represents particular tasks for the therapist. In the first stage, the couple and therapist exchange information which shapes the progress of treatment, helps them articulate initial goals, and establishes the tone of therapy.

Seating

Even if clients have been at loggerheads for months before the therapy session, the threat of coming under scrutiny by an "expert" will activate a well-developed stance in the repertoire of every lesbian couple: us-against-the world. Because such a stance denies differences between the partners, it is important that therapists persist in challenging this pseudo-mutuality wherever it appears. One of the simplest ways of undermining the couples' ersatz alliance is by the seating arrangement. Having partners face each other, rather than sitting side by side, with the therapist positioned as the third corner of a roughly equilateral triangle, facilitates the emergence of the adversarial aspects of the relationship. When the therapist is conducting a mini-individual session within the context of couples therapy, such a configuration makes it easier for the unengaged partner to focus on the active partner, rather than on the therapist's questions or comments. The triangular arrangement also promotes ambiguity about who actually comprises the couple. At any given time, the "couple" may be the therapist and one of the partners. Such temporary alliances between partner and therapist may be useful for unbalancing the merged dyad. By interacting with the therapist, partners demonstrate their ability to be engaged by others—a refreshing message to an overburdened relationship.

Taking the Relationship History

No lesbian relationship has escaped the stigmatizing effect of homophobia. By giving partners an opportunity to tell their story by asking questions designed to expose the warp and woof of the relationship, the therapist not only gets necessary information, she contradicts culturally encoded messages that state that relationships between two women are visible only as targets for derision. Otherwise, they are submerged in oblivion, never entitled to the kudos, gifts, and celebratory rituals that surround heterosexual pairing. The first level of healing, therefore, consists simply in the *telling*, before a sympathetic witness, of the partners' tale.

Every couple will tell several stories. The first, the unfolding of their relationship, will be shadowed by the subtext the partners convey with the feint and parry of their dialogue, i.e., their postural shifts, the comfort or discomfort they display when differences surface, and a variety of other cues. Most therapists are accustomed to decoding the myriad subliminal details that amplify the couples' spoken story.

Just as critical to the process is the subliminal story the therapist tells the clients. How she arranges seating reveals her attitude toward confrontation. The way she structures the session shows how comfortable she is as definer, as initiator. When she doesn't sculpt exchanges, she shows she tolerates ambiguity and passivity; the way she listens demonstrates a certain brand of receptivity and empathy; the way she supports shows a way to be simultaneously close and separate. When she confronts she demonstrates that she can risk opposing. And finally, when she ends treatment, she shows that one can be sad, and at the same time enriched, by the separations that punctuate all relationships. The way she comports herself are treatment elements as vital as any assignment she suggests or verbal insight she offers. If for example the therapist emphasizes the need for each partner to be autonomous, and is chronically unable to end the session on time because she feels she hasn't accomplished enough, her behavior will speak far louder than her words. The effectiveness of sex therapy is contingent upon the degree of congruency between the therapist's words and actions.

With the therapist alternating open-ended and specific questions, a good starting place is the origin of the relationship. How did the partners meet? What state was each in at the time? Were they immediately drawn to each other? For what qualities? Was there a courtship? Who wooed whom? Who was initially less ardent? Were there obstacles? What shifts has each partner noticed over time? Sexual? Non-sexual?

The therapist also needs detailed information about the history of the couple, their previous relationships, family background, sexual history, the ways in which each person relates to friends and co-workers, as well as to her partner.

The intensity of the partners' fears about autonomy, and concomitantly the degree of fusion, will be evident by the partners' interactions during their story-telling. Does one seem to rely on the other for details? How is disagreement handled? Does one partner speak for the other? Does one try to smooth over any differences of opinion? Are differences a source of anger? During the story-telling, the therapist will have an opportunity to delineate individual boundaries by means of structural directives. The therapist's restraining touch on the interrupting partner's knee, combined with a turn toward the interrupted partner and a request that she continue, are interventions as crucial for reinforcing individuation as any interpretation offered or assignment given. One common by-product of story-telling, fighting, is a form of interaction that offers therapists a particularly ripe opportunity for establishing clear boundaries between partners.

Case Illustration Number One

Angie and Meredith came to therapy because they rarely had sex. Each accused the other of sabotaging her efforts to initiate sexual contact. Sex was not the only source of conflict; they fought a great deal, often about little things. In fact, as soon as they came into the therapist's office, they skirmished about who would get the plushier chair. Shortly into the story-telling, their fighting began in earnest.

When Angie didn't agree with the information Meredith was relaying, she interrupted her, shouting, "That's not the way it was at all!"

"That's exactly how it was," retorted Meredith.

Before Angie could escalate the argument, the therapist, turning toward her, and nudging her foot with her own shoe, said, "Wait a minute, Angie. I want to hear your perceptions of those events. First I want you"—and here she turned back to Meredith—"to finish your impressions of what happened." This process of disengaging and refocusing the partners was the therapist's most consistent intervention during the succeeding sessions. The intense but ineffectual struggles by each partner to emerge from the undifferentiated mass of ideas, memories, feelings which compromise the relationship at that moment reveal simultaneously both the fused state and the anguish it generates. By stopping the struggle between the partners, the therapist helps shift the partners' perspective from scarcity—there is never going to be enough time for me—to one of abundance: I can exist; there is enough room for my thoughts, feelings, recollections.

Sex as the Unmentionable Presenting Problem

Those most urgently in need of sex therapy, ironically enough, are often not those clients who ask for such treatment. The couples who, in the course of relationship counseling, don't mention absence of sex as a problem are often the ones who need it the most. It may be that, indeed, it is not a problem. However, therapists find that partners coming in for other reasons will often divulge the fact of infrequent sex after some time in therapy. Even when they do disclose such information, one or both are likely to say that they have come to accept the status quo, that they are quite affectionate, and that the lack of sex is not troublesome. Perhaps some couples are genuinely comfortable with their renunciation of erotic pleasures. It is more likely, however, that in order to preserve the stability of the relationship, they have muffled various disappointments, sex among them, under layers of compromise and denial.

Case Illustration Number Two

Gerri and Sue came to therapy after Gerri had joined Alcoholics Anonymous. For the first 10 years of their relationship, the partners had been perfectly aligned on the matters of alcohol and tobacco. But now, Sue refused to keep their apartment alcohol-free and continued to abuse alcohol herself. In her own defense, Sue said she had stopped smoking recently but that Gerri continued to smoke and keep cigarettes in the house. Sue also felt threatened because Gerri was meeting a whole new group of friends at AA with whom she was beginning to socialize after work. In the past, Sue and Gerri had always socialized as a couple. After the therapist had spent several sessions elucidating the new autonomous paths the partners were taking, pointing out the justifiable fears as well as the strengths it revealed, Gerri said very tentatively that she wanted to talk about something else: They rarely had sex any more.

Helping clients break the conspiracy of silence, exhuming the disappointment buried by denial, is the first step with such couples.

When Sex Therapy Is Contraindicated

There is one presenting problem associated with diminished sexuality that therapists should not tackle: Sex therapy is contraindicated in situations in which one partner is passionately engaged with someone outside the primary relationship. The partner who is torn between affection and loyalty to her primary partner, and passion for the new lover, may come into therapy hoping for the sexual rejuvenation of her primary relationship. Undertaking sex therapy at such a juncture is ill-advised. Sex therapy involves a refinement of one's perceptions of sensual pleasure, tuning into small sensations. Such refinement is impossible when one partner is being swept away by another passionate source. The exercises described later in this article will only serve to heighten the contrast between new and old lovers and to exacerbate the conflict the enamoured partner is feeling. If the couple asks for sex therapy under such circumstances, the therapist should be candid about her assessment that sex therapy might be appropriate in the future, but not at present. Such an assessment doesn't, however, preclude non-sexually oriented couples therapy, probably a good alternative under such circumstances.

THE MIDDLE STAGE:
REFRAMING THE PROBLEM

The work at this treatment stage is the reshaping of the partners' interactions and perspectives, a lengthy process which at times approximates the endless drills one must endure to master a new language.

Normalizing Sexual Frequency

Partners frequently report a decline in the frequency of sexuality within the first year of the relationship, and it is important to ask clients what the diminution means to each individual. By asking such questions, the therapist avoids any alignment with a common premise that may be tryannizing both partners: More is better. If such a standard emerges during the questioning, and partners say they rarely have sex, it is important for the therapist to "normalize" the current sexual frequency. The therapist can do this in several ways. She can ask questions that emphasize quality rather than quantity: Can you remember what it was like last time you had sex? Who initiated? What did you feel? What did you (to the other partner) feel? If sex, despite its infrequency, is satisfying to both, the therapist can guide them through a worst case scenario. What would happen if a month went by and you didn't have sex? Two months? Six months? Such a process generally exposes the role of sex in the partners' lives as compensation for marginal social status. The partners are worthless unless they can maintain a "House Beautiful" version of a lesbian relationship. If the partners don't have sex at regular intervals, they have lost one of their few tickets to respectability. When such standards and aspirations are ferreted out and articulated, their inapplicability and irrelevance become evident. As clients become aware that their attempt to be "normal" by dominant cultural standards is futile, they may experience some hopelessness, even despair. Simultaneously, however, partners may feel a surge of relief. It can be intensely exhilarating to realize that what is normal for oneself is exactly that: what is normal for oneself. Such a revelation releases partners, finally, from the endless pursuit of the chimera of respectability.

Therapists can reinforce this message by citing experiences with friends, clients, research studies, or books like *Surpassing the Love of Men* by Lilian Faderman (1981) that contain descriptions of a great many "normal" relationships between women which are highly erotic, yet totally devoid of overt sexual expression.

The "normalization" of the partners' sexual frequency, if one or both partners are dissatisfied with the quality as well as the number of erotic encounters, frequently requires, in addition to the interventions mentioned above, a temporary prohibition of sex. Such an assignment demonstrates the therapist's indifference to standards of frequency, relieves pressure to perform, and gives everyone time and an opportunity to look at problems which actually belong in other areas of the relationship, but have taken up residence in the bedroom.

Identifying Individual Contributions to the Problem

The therapist must establish an orientation that combats projection and blame, and instead focuses each partner on the ways in which the relationship reflects her own particular psychological thumbprint. Individual therapy, which is frequently an appropriate suggestion by the therapist at this juncture, often enhances this process.

Case Illustration Three

Pen and Kathy had very particular grievances with each other. Despite her unrelenting attempts to be a superb lover, cook, and companion, Kathy complained that she could never please Pen, who always seemed disgruntled, out-of-sorts. For her part, Pen claimed that Kathy wasn't really seeing her for who she was, didn't appreciate her particular tastes. If for example, Kathy went to a lot of trouble to make a fancy meal when she knew Pen preferred simply cooked food, Pen felt invisible. In order to unravel the impasse, the therapist first turned her attention to Kathy. It sounded, she said, as though Kathy were frustrated by her unsuccessful efforts to please Pen. The therapist wondered if there were any other experiences in Kathy's past that paralleled this situation. Kathy said that the current situation reminded her of the many times growing up when she struggled to buoy up the spirits of her chronically depressed mother. After some discussion, the therapist turned to Pen and spent some time exploring how it felt for her to feel so invisible. Pen said that in individual therapy she'd discovered that her parents, who had wanted a son, had never appreciated her for who she was.

Presenting the couple's problems in a new framework, the result of the early family patterns of each partner, interposed between the two another reality besides the escalation of conflicting needs. By presenting the problem as a ''psychological'' puzzle, instead of accepting each partner's version of who is right and who is wrong, the therapist offers the clients a new model. In this alternate model, the more ''puzzle pieces,'' i.e., individual idiosyncrasies, the partners can identify and scrutinize, the more likely they are to reach the goal of more complete understanding. The means to the goal, the amplification of individual differences, and the goal of understanding, itself, is in direct contrast to the clients' framework. According to the partners model, their goal of unity can only be reached by eliminating all the discordant elements, the individual differences that don't fit into a harmonious whole. Since each partner is attached to her idiosyncracies, to prevail, one partner must convince the other that the other's traits, intentions, and behaviors are the *real* source of disharmony and that she must change for the relationship to improve.

It takes both suppleness and firmness on the therapist's part to shift clients from a perspective which censors differences to one that amplifies them. Even when a therapist succeeds in achieving such a shift in one session, the ground gained frequently disappears by the next session. However, if therapists are vigilant in reinforcing this perspective, at some point a critical mass of intervention occurs, resulting in a permanent shift in perspective and, concomitantly, in the couples dynamic.

Articulating Power Imbalances

Certain differences between partners, because they exist in sensitive areas, are too threatening to spark skirmishes. In order to preserve the stability of the relationship, the partners, who may subscribe to lesbian/feminist ideals of equality, believe that such differences must be denied. Suppressed, these contrasts in partners' income or status are likely to reappear, isomorphically transformed, in the sexual arena.

Case Illustration Four

Three years ago, Jamie, a ward nurse, met Sheila, a medical resident, during the night shift in a city hospital. Shortly afterward, they began dating and a year later moved in together. Thereafter they had little sexual contact because, Jamie said, she didn't like Sheila's sexual style. At the point of entering therapy, Jamie described herself as "completely turned off."

Because they pooled their money and friends, their differences in status and income were not evident on the surface. In response to the therapist's probing about these matters, Sheila stated that her overhead expenses—she had started her own practice after her residency—made it difficult to ascertain her actual income, but, she said, it probably approximated Jamie's salary. The same measured, leveling responses met the therapist's queries about future opportunities, friends, and family. (The couple's difference in status and power was mirrored by their families of origin.)

Whether deserved or not, the therapist said, doctors are venerated in our culture. They often have access to large incomes, prestige, and attention from both friends and strangers. Nurses, the therapist continued, are not accorded the same prestige and are, in fact, generally seen as much less than, and handmaidens to, doctors. It was important to look at the way this power difference affected each partner in the relationship.

After several more similar forays into the unmentionable by the therapist, Jamie was able to talk about some of her resentment. She said she could see Sheila basking in the attention she got from admiring friends at parties and it disgusted her. It wasn't unusual after these events for Sheila to want sex.

The surfacing of these differences and the accompanying resentment doesn't signal the partners' readiness for sex therapy exercises; it is simply one step in this direction. If the less powerful partner cannot replace sexual refusal with another power source of her own, either external or intrapsychic, it is unlikely that the imbalance in the bedroom can be corrected.

Assigning Boundary Exercises

Because power imbalances or lack of autonomy often figure in the partners' presenting problem, it is very tempting for the therapist to try to promote individual activities by suggesting a group or a class that one partner or the other might attend. Occasionally such assignments are fruitful; more often they activate the couples well-developed anti-outsider defenses which then further tighten the boundary around the relationship. If the therapist insists on such outside activities, she compromises her effectiveness and it is likely that the couple will drop out of therapy. Such assignments can be made after some time has elapsed in therapy and each partner has established a strong bond with the therapist. The therapist is on safer ground, vis-à-vis independent activity assignments, however, if she is indirect: casually mentioning a group a friend has recommended, and asking parenthetically if they have heard anything about it. If one partner is considering a group, it behooves the therapist to muzzle her enthusiasm, to say incidentally "I'd be curious about your impressions. People sometimes ask me for recommendations and I like having first-hand reports." Inside-the-relationship assignments, if they emphasize distance by exaggerating closeness, are paradoxical[2] and, therefore, need to be so circumspect.

If, for example, partners complain about having a difficult time at home because of constant bickering, the therapist can frame fighting positively, and then assign it. Fighting can be viewed as a vital attempt to clarify one's ideas, stake out one's own cognitive space. It can be seen as a ritual which precedes either engagement or disengagement and contains elements of both. Thus reframed, the therapist can deduce that it is not fighting that is the problem, but rather the irregularity of it. She might suggest that they devise a fight schedule and try it for a week. The schedule should transcend other commitments. If both partners are at work at the appointed time, they should skirmish by phone over a topic selected for potential volatility and its resistance to previous attempts at resolution.

Renegotiating Sex Therapy

As we see from the previously mentioned examples, there are many legs in the sex therapy journey. In contrast to Masters and Johnson's (1970) short term approach, sex therapy, or rather the requisite work preparatory to assigning sensual exercises, may take months, even years. Throughout this time, the therapist must reconnoiter regularly. Are clients moving, even gradually, toward more expression of autonomy and individual differences? If after some sessions, perhaps 10 or 15 (the actual number is best left to the therapist's own discretion), the answer is no, then it is important to renegotiate the original contract with the partners.

Case Illustration Five

It was Erin's and Maria's first relationship. After meeting in college 2 years before, they had moved to the West Coast together. They had both found unsatisfying and isolating jobs. Because all their friends were back East, they had become each other's best friend, support network, political ally; simultaneously, they had stopped being lovers. In an effort to make more friends, both partners joined the same rap group, but they dropped out after a few weeks. Other outreach attempts, supported by the therapist, were equally abortive.

The partners did not present an absolutely united front. Erin couldn't sleep well with Maria and sometimes wanted to sleep alone, but Maria got so upset that Erin shelved her preferences. Maria's one potential friend, an acquaintance who had recently moved out from the same eastern city, wasn't on particularly cordial terms with Erin who, consequently, disapproved of the friendship. Thus, Maria stopped seeing the woman.

The therapist worked paradoxically with the sleeping problem, assigning yet more time together, and worked individually with each partner about the meaning of loss and abandonment. Although these interventions seemed effective initially, at the end of 2 months it was evident that the partners' intense dependency on each other had not shifted.

At this point the therapist proposed renegotiating the original contract of sex therapy. From her perspective, they were as far from tackling any exercises that had to do with their sexual impasse as they had been when they first came in. Sexual intimacy, for better or worse, was a way of bridging distance. Their intimacy, comforting as it was, took the place of sex. It was fine if they continued in therapy, she said, but she wanted to clarify the focus since it had diverged from their initial direction.

The partners decided to stop therapy for a month "to see what would happen on their own." When they came back a month later, they had made some initial steps toward establishing friends outside the relationship. They were still, however, far from being candidates for sensuality exercises.

Reaching the point at which sensuality exercises can be assigned is not critical; what is essential is that sexual presenting problems, and progress, or 'lack thereof, toward resolving them be evaluated regularly. This accomplishes several goals. First, because it is easy, perhaps even necessary, for therapists to get lost in the welter of problems that may emerge during therapy, it is also useful to have some way of resurfacing periodically to take stock. The original presenting problem offers a good compass point by which therapists and clients may get their bearings.

Secondly, taking stock in this way offers clients an opportunity to mention the unmentionable. Afraid to challenge the "expert," the partners, perhaps dubious about certain aspects of therapy or qualities of the therapist, may be keeping their reservations to themselves. By offering the time and space for such misgivings, the therapist emphasizes in yet another way the importance of expressing differences.

Finally, such recesses also give clients the opportunity to stay or discontinue therapy for clearly delineated reasons. If they do leave, these crisp boundaries allow them to make equally clear decisions about returning, which drop-outs without explanation preclude.

The progress of partners may be a three-step forward, two-step back process interrupted entirely at many points. Many of the lesbian clients who come in for sex therapy only make a start in the necessary direction. To lay the groundwork may be more than enough for a beginning course of treatment. Partners who have discontinued therapy may reappear months, even years later, may even come back with different partners, to continue their work.

Such an interval-studded, apparently cumulative process, challenges the usual definitions of therapy and, in fact, may be unique to gay affirmative therapy approaches, or any therapy in which both the client and therapist are members of the same stigmatized group. Such membership demands that the therapist be a cultural, and sub-cultural, commentator, a witness, a priest, a choreographer, a community bulletin board, a codifier of new norms which requires both expert and questing stances. All of these roles suggest a suppleness more characteristic of an acrobat than a clinician. Perhaps the proof that gay affirmative clinicians have in fact been quite skillful in juggling a number of roles is the increased presence in the lesbian community of the norms that had been previously limited to therapist's offices. Groups like Al-Anon—a non-professional support organization for people whose lives have been affected by alcoholism—which emphasize self-care, are well-attended by lesbians, and it is no longer unusual for homosexual women coming into therapy for the first time to be familiar with the notion of autonomy and its relevance to sexuality.

REFRAMING SEXUALITY:
THE STROKING SESSIONS

The third stage of treatment offers partners the opportunity to uncover and express sexually generated feelings which have been unmentionable. In addition, the stroking exercises provide an expectation-free, sensual framework in which partners can explore their physical responses.

The sensuality assignments are complex and involve a number of sequences. Any reluctance to complete them should be honored; such resistance constitutes important feedback for the therapist. The preparatory work may not have been adequately completed, and the therapist and clients should go back and consider how power imbalances are affecting the relationship, as well as issues of merger and autonomy.

The more the therapist can dissociate herself from the role of sexual authority while giving the touch exercises, the less likely she is to stimulate the resistance provoked in most people by "experts" of various stripes. The therapist can do this by occasionally referring to her own sexual fumbling, but never to her triumphs. Another relatively simple authority divestiture is simply to give each partner photocopies of the touching assignments[3]. On paper, the "expert" is disembodied; the therapist, as she goes over her exercises, is simply a guide.

Physical Space

If the sexual impasse is longstanding, the site of it, usually the couple's bedroom, has become saturated with disappointments, anxiety, and feelings of self-doubt. The dismantling of the visual cues that have become conditioned stimuli for these feelings should precede the assignments. Partners should move the site of the exercises to an "uncontaminated" room in the house, or change the bedroom; i.e., move the bed, get new pictures for the walls, new sheets, and so on. For additional association scrambling, the therapist can suggest that, during the exercises, the partners play records they have not become familiar with, use new incense, flowers, and so forth.

Temporal Space

The partners should engage in the exercises when they are relatively free from time pressure; e.g., no exam is pending, no imminent arrival of a long-absent relative for whom the house must be cleaned that afternoon. In other words, the time should not be wrested from a set of other clamorous demands. Equally important, the exercise shouldn't occur at the end of a long uninterrupted period together, at a time when separation and the pursuit of independent activities is called for.

Cognitive Space

Time-outs should punctuate the assignments. During these recesses, which may be scheduled in advance or initiated by either partner during the exercises, partners can investigate, privately at first, and then with their partners, the feelings stimulated by the touching. Before partners get used to calling their own breaks, they can set an egg-timer to go off at five-minute intervals. Active listening techniques should be reviewed in a session to remind partners that if painful memories or disturbing feelings are evoked, the listening partner should make no attempt to "fix" them, even if she is named as the source of such feelings. It is enough simply to adopt the stance of sympathetic listener and recorder. Before or during the breaks, partners may be aware of any number of feelings, including apathy, irritation, aversion, anxiety, painful or pleasurable flashbacks, anticipation, hopefulness. If it is difficult to focus on feelings during these recesses, partners should go into separate rooms for a few minutes. They should have pencils and paper handy in order to record their partner's feelings, as well as their own. When the exercises are resumed, it is useful to notice the effect the break has had. There is no limit to the number of breaks partners may schedule or initiate during the sessions.

Session 1: Stroking

Allocate a time period: 10 or 15 minutes for the front of the body, 10 or 15 for the back. At the beginning of the session, the active stroker should giver her partner a choice of talcum powder, oil, or dry finger stroking. During the session, the passive partner may ask to switch, say, for example, from dry to oil or oil to talcum powder. The passive partner may also ask for changes in pressure, which may differ depending on the area being stroked. Stroking should be long and continuous, without losing bodily contact. Sensitive areas such as breasts, genitals, and so on should be included without special focus. After a break of 10 or 15 minutes, during which time the partners stay in separate rooms, the exercise should be repeated with the active and passive roles reversed.

During the exercise, the clear division into active and passive stances may crystalize discomfort with either role which previously may have been obscured by a more simultaneous approach to love-making. Additionally, if partners have been emotionally merged, past sexual encounters have offered little opportunity for legitimate disengagement. Taking necessary time out during sex to process individual feelings would probably have alarmed the more engaged partner. Instead of taking such necessary space, partners simply avoided sex entirely. This exercise demonstrates an alternative to such avoidance.

Case Illustration Six

During the first stroking session, Susan, who was in the active role, called repeated recesses. She was furious. Stroking Birgitte reminded her of the first few months of the relationship when Birgitte had just laid back and expected her to do everything. Even though Birgitte had responded to Susan's dissatisfaction by becoming an active partner, Susan still felt exploited.

Instead of going on to the second stroking session, the therapist suggested that they repeat the first exercise, with continued stopping. During the next series of interludes from stroking, Susan was equally angry, but this time it was the memory of her father which evoked her rage. During the next therapy session, the therapist focused on the ways Susan had felt exploited by, and responsible for, her father. Though their relationship hadn't been overtly sexual, Susan was convinced that there had been an erotic component in the way he had held and stroked her. The therapist, having ascertained that Birgitte was willing to participate, suggested that Susan evoke, repeatedly and as vividly as possible her father's memory during the next stroking session—his smell, his nearness, the pressure of his hands. The therapist urged Susan to amplify the feelings these memories generated. If the awareness that it was not her father, but Birgitte, who was touching her broke her reverie she was to start again, tapping into memories of her father. Even if she felt relieved after discharging some of her anger during the recesses, she should try again to conjure up his image. The experience with her father was bad enough, but even more destructive, the therapist explained, was the intrusiveness of thoughts about him. Frequent and intense thoughts of him, *initiated by her*, were the antidote to the power he had wielded in the past. In the following stroking session, Susan's anger subsided and both partners were able to deal with other issues which surfaced during the exercises.

In addition to paradoxical interventions, if one or both partners have been raped or sexually traumatized in the past, it is important for therapists to refer clients to adjunct resources: a therapy or support group which focuses on sexual abuse, or individual therapy, as appropriate.

Middle Sessions: Stroking

In these sessions, partners continue to rehearse and become more conversant with a sensual style which, as well as being free of orgasmic focus, allows room for the expression of previously censored feelings.

Continuous stroking, front and back, can be augmented with heavier kneading, rotating motion of buttocks, thigh, squeezing, light pinching, heavier massaging, and moving of shoulder muscles. Also, more attention can be paid to breasts (experiment with lighter strokes, moving and squeezing of tissue around nipples, and include both inner and outer labia, and clitoris in stroking, always moving away with light teasing strokes.

The number of these middle sessions should be determined by the clients' reports. When they are able to initiate stopping sessions for breaks without using a timer, and to move to a sexual plateau and retreat, the final session(s) can be assigned. During the course of these sessions, the therapist should discuss the counterproductive effect of orgasmic focus. Well-intended attempts to free women from Victorian attitudes have resulted in a disproportionate emphasis on a very small part of sexuality, often at the expense of the whole sensual journey. By mistaking orgasm for eroticism, the well-intentioned liberators of women's sexuality have bypassed the wisdom of ages. Much of the "Kama Sutra," a distillation of centuries worth of sexual lore collected a few hundred years A.D., describes ways of avoiding orgasm in order to heighten pleasure. It is important for the therapist to continue to buttress her arguments with examples which deemphasize orgasm. *Under no circumstances should the therapist be seduced into considering orgasm, or lack thereof, as the primary focus of treatment.* If women's orgasmic groups exist in the vicinity, and partners' concerns about orgasm continue, the therapist can offer such groups as a resource.

The subject of fantasies should also be broached before the last stroking sessions. The therapist can invite discussion about the partners' individual experiences with fantasies, and suggest that they each try out a fantasy during the next stroking session. To maximize autonomy, it is good to encourage each partner to maintain the privacy of her fantasies; if partners feel like sharing them, ask that they wait a day or so to see it the desire continues. If partners have trouble giving themselves the latitude to imagine images which seem, for various reasons, taboo, the therapist can suggest they purchase, independently of each other, some fantasy-fodder books.[4]

Final Session: Stroking

The final session or sessions should recapitulate the past sessions and should be considered complete when the partners can move in and out of an aroused state in a fairly relaxed way.

TERMINATING THE THERAPY PROCESS

If the therapist hasn't divested herself of the expert role by the end of the stroking sessions, it is critical that she do so before termination. The effect of the exercises, the information they have generated, and how aspects of them can be integrated into the couple's post-therapy life are matters the partners can consider in the last sessions. Loose ends, if they are not major, are valuable: They give the therapist the opportunity to acknowledge the limits of her effectiveness. A comment like, "That issue is difficult . . . none of the approaches tried here so far have gotten anywhere, although it seemed like you, Mary, were close to something when you mentioned in our last session that . . . ," effectively hands the reins of responsibility for further exploration to the partners.

Before the final session, the therapist may make one final assignment: for the clients to behave for a week exactly as they did before they started therapy. The effect of such an experiment is the framing of lapses, which will be inevitable, as bits of useful information that mark the progress of the couple. Thus, anxiety about "reverting to the old ways" is neutralized.

If the therapist has been seeing the couple for a long time, and feels some attachment, the final session is a good opportunity to share such feelings. Acknowledgments of the partners' progress are important, too, but should be described in terms of their willingness to experiment, to uncover truths which were sometimes painful, rather than described as accomplishments. The parting, sadness and affectionate expressions notwithstanding, should have a feeling of finality in order to underscore the boundary between clients and therapist.

At later dates, partners may want to come back for recapitulations of ground covered in therapy. It is up to therapists to discriminate the need for such tune-ups from the partners' unwillingness to separate from the therapist. In the latter case, the therapist, while acknowledging the depth of the couples' anxiety, should decline further contact.

SUMMARY

This paper is intended to be heuristic, rather than definitive, to reflect refinements forged through trial and error since Masters and Johnson first set forth their theories and findings. More importantly, it is intended to provoke further forays into the paradox, the mysterious oscillation between the poles of passion and dispassion, of lesbian sexuality.

NOTES

1. In the author's experience, gay affirmative, male therapists have been effective with many of the presenting problems of lesbian clients. For practical reasons, however, this effectiveness doesn't extend to the treatment of lesbian sexual problems.

The therapeutic process that addresses such problems must include the dismantling of internalized heterosexual, i.e., patriarchal, norms about "correct" sexual responsiveness. This is a key intervention that frequently requires self-disclosure on the therapist's part and conversancy with the experiences of other women—clients, friends, and lovers. This lore, often accumulated through painful experiences, is gender-specific. A male crossing this gender boundary is analogous, if one could imagine such a situation, to a white therapist coaching a black client in the art of "shinin' them on."

In addition, the behavioral assignments often include discussions of intimate subjects, e.g., vaginal lubrication, vulval and anal stimulation, penetration, and penis fantasies. Taboos about these topics make them difficult for a female therapist to broach with women clients. Any consideration of these topics by a male therapist would increase the discomfort of the lesbian clients enough to make fruitful discussion unlikely. Consequently, it is the author's recommendation that gay affirmative women therapists treat lesbian clients who present sexual problems. The therapists referred to in the paper are therefore denoted by the pronoun "she".

2. For explanations and illustrations of paradoxical therapeutic interventions see the following: Haley, J. (1973), *Uncommon therapy: The psychiatric techniques of Milton H. Erickson*, New York: Norton; Watzlawick, P., Weakland, J., & Fisch, R. (1974), *Change: Principles of problem resolution*, New York: Norton; Palazzoli, M., Boscolo, L., Cecchin, J., & Prata, J. (1978). *Paradox and counter-paradox*, New York: Jason Aronson.

3. For an expanded version of the stroking exercises, write to the Berkeley Sex Therapy Group, 2614 Telegraph Avenue, Berkeley, California 94704. The exercises are included in a collection of monographs entitled *Expanding the boundaries of sex therapy*, authored by Apfelbaum, Williams, and Green (see References).

4. For a variety of sexual fantasies, see Friday, N. (1973), *My secret garden: Women's sexual fantasies*, New York: Pocket Books; Barbach, L. (1985), *Pleasures: Women write erotica*, New York: Harper & Row.

REFERENCES

Apfelbaum, B., Williams, M., & Green, S. (1979). *Expanding the boundaries of sex therapy: Selected papers of the Berkeley Sex Therapy Group*. Berkeley, CA: Berkeley Sex Therapy Group.

Barbach, L. (1985). *Pleasures: Women write erotica*. New York: Harper & Row.

Blumstein, P., & Schwartz, P. (1983). *American couples*. New York: William Morrow.

Burch, B. (1986). Psychotherapy and the dynamics of merger in lesbian couples. In C. Cohen & J. Stein (Eds.), *Psychodynamic psychotherapy with gay men and lesbians*. New York: Plenum Press.

Chodorow, N. (1978). *The reproduction of mothering*. Berkeley, CA: University of California Press.

Faderman, L. (1981). *Surpassing the love of men*. New York: William Morrow.

Friday, N. (1973). *My secret garden: Women's sexual fantasies*. New York: Pocket Books.

Haley, J. (1973). *Uncommon therapy: The psychiatric techniques of Milton H. Erickson*. New York: Norton.

Hatfield, E., & Walster, G. (1978). *A new look at love*. Reading, MA: Addison-Wesley.

Kaplan, H. (1974). *The new sex therapy*. New York: Brunner-Mazel.

Kaufman, P., Harrison, E., & Hyde, M. (1984). Distancing for intimacy in lesbian relationships. *American Journal of Psychiatry, 141*, 530–533.

Loulan, J. (1985). *Lesbian sex*. San Francisco: Spinsters Ink.

Krestan, J., & Bepko, C. (1980). Problems of fusion in the lesbian relationship. *Family Process, 19*, 279–286.

Masters, W. H., & Johnson, V. E. (1970). *Human sexual inadequacy*. Boston: Little, Brown.

Miller, J. (1976). *Toward a new psychology of women*. Boston: Beacon Press.

Palazzoli, M., Boscolo, L., Cecchin, J., & Prata, J. (1978). *Paradox and counter-paradox*. New York: Jason Aronson.

Watzlawick, P., Weakland, J., & Fisch, R. (1974). *Change: Principles of problem resolution*. New York: Norton.

Causes and Treatments of Sexual Desire Discrepancies in Male Couples

Rex Reece, PhD
West Hollywood, CA

SUMMARY. Multiple causes and treatments of sexual desire discrepancies in male couples are catagorized and discussed. Theoretical constructs and examples of such problems are extrapolated primarily from the existing literature on inhibited sexual desire and from clinical experience. Treatment suggestions are based on a well-established multi-level model and adapted to apply more directly to homosexual couples.

Although much has been written in recent years about hypoactive, inhibited, or low sexual desire (Kaplan, 1977, 1979, 1983; Levine, 1984; LoPiccolo, 1980; McCarthy, 1984; Munjack & Oziel, 1980; Schmidt & Arentewicz, 1983a), sexual desire discrepancies have received little attention in professional sex and marital literature. Only Zilbergeld and Ellison (1980) have focused directly on differences in frequencies of desire in heterosexual couples. Levine (1984) has recognized desire discrepancies as one type of desire problem that does not necessarily reflect a deficiency. He mentioned that desire problems range from absent or infrequent through *incompatible levels within a couple*, on to frequent or strong, and up to relentless (p. 84) (italics added). In their discussion, Zilbergeld and Ellison (1980) also suggested that the emphasis on low desire reflects a professional bias toward "more sex is better sex." They focused on desire discrepancies rather than identifying either high or low desire as *the* problem to be treated.

This paper follows that model, emphasizing diagnosis and treatment in terms of desire discrepancies, rather than isolating either high or low desire as the problem. For purposes of this discussion desire discrepancies include differences in the frequencies with which the two men in a committed romantic relationship want sex, and differences in their preferences for time, place, style, role, or activities involved. Most of the

Dr. Reece is a psychologist in private practice in Los Angeles. Correspondence may be addressed to the author, 9229 Sunset Boulevard, Ste. 608, West Hollywood, CA 90069.

discussion is also applicable to those couples who, after a few years, are having sex infrequently and wondering why.

DESCRIPTIONS OF THE PROBLEMS

Although some couples seek therapy specifically for desire discrepancies, others become aware of the need to focus on these issues while in sex therapy, couple therapy, or even individual psychotherapy. However, desire discrepancies are usually conceptualized and treated within the context of the relationship. The discussions of low sexual desire in the literature mentioned earlier were usually presented in the context of a relationship. Zilbergeld and Ellison (1980) have found desire problems almost always to be relationship problems.

Clinical reports of desire discrepancies in male couples sound similar to those descriptions of low desire found in the literature mentioned earlier. The following examples use situations found in that literature, but are altered to make them applicable to male couples.

Kaplan (1983) has pointed out that the partner who is less interested in sex—the low interest partner (LIP)—may participate in sex not because he is interested, but perhaps to reassure himself of his own potency or in order not to hurt or lose his partner. Under such circumstances he may comply with his partner's—the high interest partner's (HIP)—request reluctantly, with an attitude of "let's get it over with." He may be able to respond with an erection and orgasm if properly stimulated, but that may require intense use of fantasy and he may experience little pleasure. He may feel compelled to bathe himself immediately after an orgasm and turn his attention quickly to other activities. Some LIPs may enjoy physical affection such as kissing, touching, and cuddling; others may have developed an aversion even to affectionate touching, particularly if that usually leads to either unwanted sex or yet another sexual rejection of the other partner, both of which results in discomfort. The LIP may avoid sex by bringing work home, becoming busy, tired, depressed, or starting an argument during those times when sex could happen. Schmidt and Arentewicz (1983a) described the LIP's response to his partner's interest in sex as varying among resigned patience, passive resistance, an impulse to escape, fear of failure, annoyance at being molested, aggressive refusal, and disgust.

The HIP's reaction to his lover's pattern of lower interest and response may also vary. Munjack and Oziel (1980) described some HIPs as simply disappointed, and perhaps even able to feel some sympathy for their partner. But if the HIP personalizes his lover's low interest, he may tend to blame, feel threatened, frustrated, hurt, angry, or rejected. Some HIPs may assume his partner's low interest is a result of his (the LIP's) extra-relationship sexual involvements, and therefore initiate or increase the frequency of his own sexual experiences outside the relationship, or else threaten to end the relationship. Kaplan (1977) noted that any particular HIP might react with unthreatened calm on one end of a continuum, to rage and despair on the other which could lead to an obsessive concern and possible termination of the relationship. Schmidt (1983) recognized that the HIP's emotional response can include feeling unattractive and undesirable, "not good in bed," humiliated, diminished as a man, feeling unloved, lonely, afraid of abandonment, or experience an otherwise general loss of esteem.

Some couples enter therapy at a point when sex has all but ceased taking place; they are usually very confused, hurt, angry, and have begun blaming each other. Schmidt & Arentewicz (1983b) discussed how the problem can be maintained and become more severe because of a pattern of relating involving one partner's pushing for sex while the other refuses; the refusal can elicit more demands from one and then reactive withdrawal from the other.

ETIOLOGIES: MULTI-CAUSAL MODEL

Kaplan (1979, 1983) has offered a multi-causal, multi-level treatment model for sexual problems, one which is a useful model for discovering and discussing the causes of desire discrepancies within male couples. The concept of multiple causal levels incorporates the idea that there are often several contributing factors to the problem, and that they may range from simple misinformation about some aspect of human sexual response or behavior to deep transferences within the relationship which unconsciously repeat unresolved childhood conflicts. Such a model considers that the problem may be maintained not only by an interactive pattern based in poor communication skills, but sometimes by complimentary psychological defenses of each partner that ward off deeper anxieties.

Medical or Organic

Desire discrepancy problems are occasionally caused by conditions for either partner which require kinds of intervention other than couple sex therapy. One such area is organic causes of low or absent desire. Medical illness or injury, hormonal imbalances, or the use of certain prescriptive or illicit drugs can certainly affect sexual interest and response. Additionally, during the initial evaluation, depression or severe life stresses must be considered as possible causes or contributing factors. Two of the most common medical causes for homosexual men are alcohol or drug-related problems. These substances may have been a regular and accepted part of their sex lives, particularly in periods of not being couples. Sometimes such a habit or dependency is carried into the relationship, and the chronic or intense use of such substances may decrease interest in sex. And certainly, either having or being with a lover who has AIDS (Acquired Immune Deficiency Syndrome), ARC (AIDS Related Complex), or has tested positive for the HLV antibody is likely to affect one's interest in sex.

Limited Sexual Repertoire

The etiology of decreased frequency of sex or the immediate cause of sexual conflicts for some male couples may be based in one or both partners being limited in sexual activities that are important to the other partner. Or one of the lovers may not particularly enjoy, or may even dislike, a specific activity that the other feels is really important for his own satisfaction. McWhirter and Mattison (1980) have mentioned that in their work with desire phase disorders in male couples, an aversion to specific acts was more the issue than a generalized lack of sexual desire. Preferences for anal or oral sex, a genital focus/orgasm orientation versus more general sensuality, imagination-based (an emphasis on fantasy or role-playing) versus partner-focused sexual interaction, or an "earthy" attitude toward bodily secretions and smells versus a "hygienic" approach to sex are areas of conflict that are frequently mentioned.

Power Differences

Felt differences in power in a relationship can certainly contribute to less frequent sex. Seeing one's partner as having more prestige, whether through age, attractiveness, material assets, education, or social status may cause the "less powerful" partner to withhold sex, control it in some way, or make sexual demands in order to maintain the balance. A partner who feels less emotionally secure or has greater dependency needs sometimes attempts to manipulate the sexual relationship, usually unconsciously, to reassure himself. While the partner who feels less powerful in terms of more superficial status symbols may withhold sex or limit his participation in certain ways, the partner who feels more insecure or dependent is more likely to contribute to conflicts out of his attempts to get reassurance through sex. The former will more likely decline sexual overtures, while the latter will likely want or demand more sex.

Communication Difficulties

As previously mentioned, there can be multiple causes from different levels of conflict that contribute to desire discrepancies. Additionally, problematic communication styles can be not only the genesis of but also maintain a problem at any level as well as exacerbate problems arising from other causes or levels. Problems with initiating and declining sex are frequently observed areas of conflict which may be limited to inadequate communication skills. In their male couples, McWhirter and Mattison (1980) found problems with initiating sex to be more of the issue than a lack of sexual interest. If poor communication is added to most any other issue or combination of issues, from differences in preferred ways of having sex to parental transferences from childhood, the couple is likely to feel frustrated beyond solution.

Intimacy and Dependency Issues

Kaplan (1979, 1983), McCarthy (1984), and Schmidt (1983b) have each discussed that the etiology of sexual desire problems sometimes is based in ambivalences regarding intimacy and fears of dependency. These often overlapping issues are suggested by a history composed of a variation on several themes, although any one of them does not necessarily reflect an intimacy issue. One typical history may include numerous sexual encounters limited to strangers, while another may include repeated short affairs mostly limited either to "unavailable" partners such as married men, men with lovers, or people from out of town, or to "inappropriate" partners. Kaplan (1979) mentioned as examples uncaring partners, partners from an extremely different cultural milieu, or relationships involving the open or more subtle exchange of material rewards for companionship. Intimacy/dependency conflicts are also suggested by the couple's history. Kaplan [1977] emphasized the necessity of a sexual history for the couple, as well as for each individual. For example, if interest in sex declined in connection either with a deepening commitment, symbolized by moving in together or sharing a major financial obligation, or by an experience of increased emotional vulnerability, fears of intimacy may be involved.

McWhirter and Mattison (1978, 1984), Reece and Segrist (1981), and Tripp (1975) have found that some arrangement for extra-relationship sex, whether comfortable for both or not, seems to have been the norm for established male couples. However, outside sex can still reflect difficulties with closeness, depending on the individuals within the couple and their particular relationship issues.

The issue of physical attractiveness can be a clue that intimacy issues are involved—but only a clue. Complaining of no longer being attracted to one's partner can place the problem outside oneself, so that facing one's own fears is unnecessary. On the other hand, as Kaplan (1983) has stated, men traditionally have depended heavily on physical attractiveness. She affirmed that sex therapy can be very helpful, but may not resolve the issue if it is a true lack of attractiveness rather than an intimacy issue.

Negative Attitudes About Homosexuality

Residual negative feelings about homosexuality, conscious or unconscious, may also contribute to ambivalences about commitment. McWhirter and Mattison (1978) have mentioned in their study of sexual dysfunctions in homosexual male couples that those who presented with desire problems seemed to have much difficulty not only with communication, but also with their sexual orientation. Some clients are very aware that if they had a lover, they would have to be more direct and open about their homosexuality, especially with their families and perhaps with employers, co-workers, or heterosexual friends. Others have come to terms with such conscious issues, but may still harbor unrealized and unresolved guilt, shame, or other powerful negative feelings about being homosexual. These ambivalences can be expressed by lessened interest in sex, especially with a lover.

Coleman (1981/82) has written of the popular belief within the gay male subculture that lover relationships do not last. That self-fulfilling prophecy can, for some individuals, contribute either to holding back sexually with a lover lest one become too dependent or, for another, to attaching extra importance to sex as a symbol of bonding within the relationship. For others, as a defense against the feared intimacy, sex may take on, even within the relationship, a primarily recreational feeling in order to avoid closeness. These adaptations may not be compatible with one's partner's desires or needs.

Unresolved Childhood Dynamics

Related deeper causes of differences in desire may center around fears of abandonment or the dynamics of parental transferences being acted out in the relationship. Levine (1984) discussed some roots of desire descrepancies in a way that seems to reflect similar issues for some gay men. For many, sex may be fine with anyone except a loved object because protection against the pain, rejection, abuse, disrespect, torture, harm, or other residue from childhood is vital. It is irrelevant whether the partner is trustworthy; such damaged personalities fear repetition. Sexual desire deficiencies or excesses can result from such histories, compounding relationship difficulties. Schmidt and Arentewicz (1983b) explain that for the person who tries to recreate the early unfulfilling relationship (fuse with the parent substitute: his lover), a low interest in sex allows him to avoid regression to that total dependency which again elicits the fear of loss.

Sexual Guilt or Trauma

There are other, perhaps less frequent but no less serious, contributing factors to desire discrepancies between male lovers. Sometimes "deeper" (meaning learned earlier), rather than residual, negative feelings about being homosexual result from some degree of basic sexual guilt. Masters and Johnson (1970) found a rigid religious background strongly associated with sexual dysfunctions in heterosexual couples. Because homosexual men grew up in the same Judeo-Christian culture, similar values have created similar guilts and inhibitions that are sometimes found in male couples with desire discrepancies. Schmidt and Arentewicz (1983b) added to this the cultural "conspiracy of silence" about sex, parents' typical asexual modeling, and their repudiation of the child's interest in sex to the list of experiences contributing to sexual guilt and inhibition.

Guilt and inhibition for any one individual may also come from some very painful or traumatic experience. A man may have been terribly humiliated when discovered in sexual play as a child, sexually abused as a child, or raped as a young adult. The consequence can be tremendous difficulty participating in specific acts, or with specific persons who may be consciously or unconsciously associated with that past.

Special Problems

Because alcohol and drug abuse seem to be prevalent among the homosexual male population (Fifield, Latham, & Phillips, 1978), someone with such a problem can present a somewhat particular set of difficulties with sexual desire. That person may feel childlike, inexperienced, and frightened of sex—frightened of possible response failures, intense physical and emotional sensations, emotional intimacy, or of what he doesn't know. It is as if developmentally he feels he became sexually stuck at an earlier stage when substances became habitually used with sex. Coleman (1981/82) mentions that repeated association of substances with sex can inhibit the development of intimacy. If now sober, some must pick up where they first began distorting the experience, perhaps years ago. Such fears can certainly inhibit one's sexual participation and contribute to lowered interest or a narrowed repertoire that can differ considerably from one's partner's fantasies and preferences.

Another potentially seriously inhibiting factor for gay couples is the anxiety about whether one has been or will be exposed to the AIDS virus. Some individuals have become so obsessed with the fear of getting the virus or giving it to their partners that sex is next to impossible, even within current educational guidelines for safer sexual practices. Even if the anxiety is not so intense, it may still be high enough for the couple to avoid discussing what they feel comfortable doing now within those guidelines. Certain practices then begin to drop out of their repertoire, or they may decrease their frequency without much understanding of the real reasons. This anxiety or lack of insight leaves much room for hurt, retaliation, and more conflict.

TREATMENT: MULTI-LEVEL MODEL

Not unlike Kaplan's (1979, 1983) multi-causal, multi-level model for etiology and treatment is Annon's (1974, 1975) PLISSIT (Permission-Giving, Limited Information, Specific Suggestions, Intensive Therapy) model, suggesting interventions at different levels, and indicating that some problems can be alleviated without resolving the sometimes deeper conflicts. Arentewicz and Schmidt (1983) have pointed out that even with deeper underlying causes resolved, the symptom often persists; therefore, the symptom still must be treated.

Arentewicz and Schmidt (1983) have stated that the task of the therapist is to compensate for sexual learning deficits, understand both the meaning of the sexual issue to the relationship and the deeper psychodynamic conflicts, separate them from sex, and resolve the negative self-reinforcement mechanism of the couple system. Another important, and perhaps obvious, assumption is that because desire discrepancies have multiple etiologies from different levels, different treatments are required.

Important Therapeutic Conditions

As therapy with a couple who has desire discrepancies begins, at least two conditions are useful to keep in mind in preparing the couple for therapy.

Commitment

The level of commitment must be evaluated and somehow judged "deep enough" before proceeding with therapy. Zilbergeld and Ellison (1980) have stated that success in therapy depends on commitment. It is quite difficult, for example, to be helpful to a couple that makes the relationship contingent on the resolution of the sexual difficulties. That overburdens sex with expectations to fulfill needs that must be met in other ways. Sex therapy itself usually includes experiencing many pleasurable feelings, but also requires confronting many uncomfortable feelings such as anxiety, embarrassment, guilt, anger, and regret. The likelihood is also for increased intimacy. The relationship, therefore, already must be quite strong to withstand such stress.

McWhirter and Mattison (1978) have reasoned that because of the lack of institutional supports (i.e., religion, family, legal) for homosexual men in relationships, stress, such as sexual desire differences, seriously threatens a relationship, rather than being seen as a problem to be solved. Perhaps because sex has been so easily available for most urban homosexual males, the immediate response to a sexual problem in a committed relationship has often been to compensate for the problem by going outside the relationship for sexual satisfaction, or to end the relationship and try to find someone more "sexually compatible." Incidentally, anxiety about AIDS is likely to inhibit that not atypical response to sexual and other problems within couples. Safe-sex education within the community is currently emphasizing fewer sexual partners as a preventative. As a result, it seems likely that more male couples will be motivated to confront their conflicts, rather than avoid them by seeking outside partners or new lovers.

Cooperation and Compromise

The couple entering therapy also needs to be made aware early in the process that an attitude of cooperation will be required. The emphasis cannot be on finding fault and placing blame, but on discovering the destructive system, appreciating the individual issues, performing the tasks, and learning the processes that increase the desired behavior.

Additionally, as Munjack and Oziel (1980) have stated, the basic assumption for success with such couples is their willingness to compromise. Kaplan (1983) believed that each partner must accept that the other is different and make accommodations accordingly. She wrote that therapy cannot change the basic fit, but it can improve the sexual relationship if the commitment and willingness to compromise is there.

Education and Information

The above-mentioned models for treating desire discrepancies suggest that through education and correcting misinformation, many problems can be resolved. There are many, many instances where much can be done with little work, of which the following are two examples. The level of sexual interest, as well as what is arousing or is a turn-off, is different at different times for the same person. Zilbergeld and Ellison (1980) have stated, therefore, that compatibility is an issue for every couple and is not insoluble. Some couples can be helped tremendously by being reminded of this basic fact and encouraged to keep it in mind as they work together. Zilbergeld and Ellison also point out that for some men, having an erection does not always mean that they are interested in sex. Because others are always interested when aroused, they may assume that their partners are also. Clarifying such individual differences can be helpful and done quite economically.

Discovering Individual Motivations

It can also be useful to explore with couples some general purposes of sex, and help them discover some of their individual motivations and whether these can be met within their relationship, and if so, how. McCarthy (1984) lists shared pleasure, the reinforcement of intimacy, and simple sexual or other tension relief as motivations for sex. Levine (1984) includes relief from loneliness, escape from unpleasant preoccupations, and getting to sleep. Schmidt (1983) believes that modern culture overburdens relationships and sometimes sex with emotional and narcissistic needs like warmth, love, and protection, or confirmations that one is worthy of being loved, is masculine, or is significant and indispensible. Levine (1984) believes that some motivations for sex, especially the need to regulate tension states, are more likely to push a partner toward the driven end of sex and create desire discrepancies out of high rather than low drive.

"Having Sex" Versus "Making Love"

A related, and not infrequent, discrepancy that often can be somewhat diffused with explorations of individual motivations for sex and subsequent investigations into developmental patterns is the difference in preferences for genitally oriented, "functional" sex as opposed to prolonged and sensual lovemaking. It can be helpful to have couples learn to distinguish between "having sex," which includes tension relief, and "making love," which includes mutual pleasuring and assurances of love and appreciation.

The reasons for either style are varied, and with some insight, an individual may be motivated to expand his preference to accommodate his partner. Munjack and Oziel (1980) have pointed out that some men are more romantic, while others are conditioned to genital sex. Schmidt and Arentewicz (1983b) have reasoned that because male masturbation is most likely genitally focused and frequent, especially in adolescence, that such training leads to a genital focus rather than tenderness and sensuality. They went further to offer that many men seem to fear gender inappropriateness, and therefore avoid tender, devotional surrender, which might mean passivity and femininity for which they would compensate with genital-centered, explosive sexuality. Without some work, a particular homosexual man who has extensive experiences with strangers in directly sexually oriented settings and who has internalized negative attitudes about homosexuality and difficulties with intimacy may be quite uncomfortable with other than genitally oriented sex. Conversely, without some effort, a relatively emotionally insecure, dependent partner whose sexual needs include reassurances of attractiveness and love, and who feels guilty and inhibited sexually, may not be able to enjoy a sexual relationship that is frequently genitally focused.

Kaplan (1977) illustrated the potential difficulty for a couple if one partner equates sexual desire with love. If one man needs reassurances of love and always assigns that meaning to his lover's sexual interest, that can mean that his desireability is dependent on his partner's desire. Too much of such distorted attribution can lead to what appears to be excess of desire for the man needing reassurance, or low desire for the lover whose interest is needed. Knowing their own, and appreciating the meanings of their lover's individual preferences can give a couple permission to ask for sexual activities that fit their needs or moods of the moment and motivate them to develop a wider repertoire for themselves.

Combating Repetitive, Routine Patterns

Some couples present with little interest in sex because their routine has become just that—repetitive, predictable, and boring. Such couples can sometimes be motivated to work toward expansion of their repertoires if they are made aware of some of the factors that contribute to boring sex. Schmidt (1983) pointed out that it is a mistake to assume that initial intense sex is an indicator of sexual success in a long-term relationship. Even if sexual experiences are tremendous earlier in the relationship, repetition brings predictability and, in turn, lessened excitement and interest. Living together often leads to "warm" sex. He believes that sexual boredom contributes to maintaining the balance between closeness and distance. Sex which is too intense, might compromise autonomy in an otherwise intimate relationship. Stoller (1979) and Tripp (1975) have theorized that intense sex requires some aspect of competition or conflict. If that is true, it would be difficult for some relationships to withstand enough general conflict in order to make sex more exciting.

From another perspective, Schmidt and Arentewicz (1983b) have reasoned that the sexual repertoire of any one couple is restricted first by the mismatch of the particular preferences of each, then by the inhibitions or aversions of each, and further by each partner's mood of the moment. Boring sex can also be a reflection of the growing lack of sharing in the relationship over time. They have found that, contrary to many assumptions, intimacy seems to decrease over time. Routines, habits, and patterns of interaction develop; more is automatic, less is discussed. Because homosexual men are likely to have their own careers, and each man in a couple may be so preoccupied with his own outside life that little gets shared, within the relationship, including the feelings, needs, and frustrations about their own sex life.

Communication and Awareness Techniques

Beyond education, information, permission-giving, explorations of assumptions about sex, and discovering individual sexual needs, most of the work in resolving issues of desire discrepancies gets done through helping each partner become aware of how he is blocked, and in developing ways of creating mutually desired and satisfying experiences as frequently as is mutually agreeable. To achieve these objectives, much parallel work with each partner is necessary, as well as much time spent getting the couple to communicate their feelings about the experiences as they become aware of them. Through assigned behavioral tasks to be performed at home and detailed discussion of these activities in the therapy sessions, the process evolves from each individual discovering or rediscovering his own sexual desires and anxieties, communicating these appropriately to his partner, and both cooperating to accommodate to some degree each other's particular sexual preferences, all to their mutual satisfaction. Levine (1984) proposed that such problems often lie in negotiation rather than desire.

Sensate Focus and Fantasy Expansion

Sensate focus (Kaplan, 1974; Masters & Johnson, 1970; Munjack & Oziel, 1980) exercises are a good place to begin. Depending on the couple's particular issues, variations on these experiences can help them learn to associate comfort, sensuality, adventure, and intimacy with sex. The exercises can help them develop an ability to discover and focus on their own sensations, emotions, and preferences. Reactions to these experiences help refine the issues and determine future tasks. Levay and Kagle (1977) have found that the client's reactions assist them in determining whether the issues include difficulties with experiencing pleasure, intimacy, or cooperation. Having the couple view erotic material, write an ideal scenario, or as Levine (1984) suggested, a "forbidden" scenario to help them relieve their guilt about "perverse" or "kinky" fantasies, or having them remember past experiences that were particularly exciting, can be useful in expanding fantasies and in shaping sexual preferences to include the partner. When done alone, such experiences help clarify individual desires. If done together, or alone then shared, they can facilitate an awareness of differences and begin to suggest ways to cooperate.

Re-Labeling Internal Cues

Zilbergeld and Ellison (1980) have taught clients to relabel internal cues in order to either increase or decrease the desire for sex. They proposed that sometimes the HIP may learn that some of what he has felt as a desire for sex may actually be a need for closeness or reassurance, or a need to diffuse exciting, uncomfortable, or anxious feelings. Such a client can learn to differentiate these feelings from sexual interest, or relabel them and diffuse or express them in some way other than sexually. Conversely, the LIP may be taught to relabel internal feelings such as excitement, restlessness, or even anxiety as sexual desire, then move from some appropriate "getting in the mood" activity to sex. Kaplan (1979) has found that the LIP may have learned to associate negative thoughts and feelings with anticipated sex. She suggested that after identifying such automatic responses, the LIP can replace those "automatic turn-offs" with pleasant anticipatory thoughts and fantasies. For example, the LIP may respond to a sexual overture by focusing on unattractive aspects of his partner's appearance, personality, style of lovemaking, or any negative associations with past sex. Such a habitual response makes him less interested in sex. However, if he can become aware of this process, he may learn to focus his memories, attention, and anticipation on the arousing aspects of his partner and their interaction.

Patterns of Initiating

Another frequent communication difficulty arises in the area of initiating sex and declining overtures for sex. The HIP usually feels as if he has been repeatedly rejected and, as a result of that hurt and anger, eventually stops initiating. The LIP may not have been interested, but he also could be a rather passive person who has always depended on his partner to demonstrate interest first. The LIP may also have declined sex at times because of the very way in which the HIP communicated his own interest. Or the LIP may have needed some time to "get in the mood." The feelings of both partners about their pattern of initiating and rejecting need to be discussed. Often work needs to be done to develop ways of cooperating to create some degree of physical intimacy, even if full participation in sex is not desireable for both partners at the moment. Variations on a possible scenario that incorporate some of these issues might be:

Tom, through verbal innuendos and suggestive touching, signals Bill that he is interested in sex. Since he has been aware of his desire all day or evening, he is ready now. Bill may not have been thinking of sex at this particular time, so he might respond in several ways, any of which could be helpful and break a typical pattern of outright refusal resulting in hurt and loss of interest. For example, (1) "I've got other things on my mind. Would you give me a back rub for a few minutes, and then . . . "; (2) "I'm just too tired now; but let's plan to sleep in and play tomorrow morning"; or (3) "I'm not so interested right now, but I'd be happy to do something with you or for you to get into it and get off if you want. What would you like?"

All of these responses reflect acceptance of the partner's interest. The first gives time and an appropriate activity for the partner who may not have been anticipating sex to get in the mood. The second communicates a willingness to have sex, but at a more mutually agreeable time. (It can be very helpful when declining to suggest a later time, but it is vital to follow through.) The third response offers cooperation for the partner's pleasure, short of full participation.

Cooperating to Expand Repertoire

If some specific sex act is an issue, such as one partner especially enjoying something the other just has not been able to participate in, with motivation, time, and patience much can be done. For example, partner A may feel awkward, inhibited, or self-conscious (and therefore not much aroused) when his lover (B) asks him to add a verbal scenario to their shared masturbation. If A is motivated to become more versatile, they can shape such behavior through several stages. First, they might masturbate while B verbalizes. Then they might audio-tape such an experience and have A listen to it while he masturbates, perhaps alone. Then he may simply make pleasureable, erotic noises and then allow words and phrases to emerge. In each subsequent shared masturbation session, A gradually verbalizes more until perhaps an entire script is developed. This basic shaping process, useful for many specific activities, is best done against a background of recognition that most people have sexual inhibitions or blocks, and that much of what we enjoy doing is learned and therefore alterable to some degree. Of course, each individual's morals, values, and limits must be respected. Results are improved when done without judgment or pressure, but with support and encouragement from both the partner and the therapist, and in an atmosphere of exploration and fun.

Multiple Issues/Treatments

Maintaining Comfortable Levels of Intimacy

Some sexual problems arising out of power issues, disillusionment with the partner, negative feelings about homosexuality, sexual guilt, issues of dependency and intimacy, or parental transferences may be treated within the context of sex therapy. One frequently useful technique for those couples who want more sex but can tolerate no more intimacy is to help them develop alternative ways of having distance outside of sex; for example, spending more free time alone, perhaps away from home, or with one's own friends may be helpful.

Situations Perhaps Needing Deeper, Individual Therapy

Depending on the depth of the conflict, relationship therapy or individual therapy for either or both partners, or some combination of these may be appropriate. For example, one couple may diffuse the power issues by competing in recreational activities or in their careers rather than in sex. In another couple, the younger partner, previously unable to yield to being penetrated anally by his older and more financially secure lover because he associates femininity and dependence with that act, might learn that it is possible for him to be very active and assertive during sex. Yet another couple may include a partner who feels so powerless because of a combination of his circumstances and his basic personality structure that he may need individual psychotherapy before he can feel confident enough not to attempt controlling the other partner through sex.

A partner in one couple may already realize that much of his lover's personality appeal is the lover's likeness to his father, and through brief therapy may thus realize that his discomfort with sex is based in the incest taboo. Just the insight itself, along with the therapist's permission, may free him either to fantasize sex with his father during sex with his lover, or to separate the two completely during sex. Another couple may include a partner whose gay political activism hides his guilt about being homosexual so well from himself that he is unable to enjoy sex with his lover except in distancing or degrading ways unless he undergoes a period of individual psychotherapy.

SUMMARY AND CONCLUSIONS

Desire discrepancies in male couples can arise from simple misunderstandings, deep individual personality conflicts, or a combination of those and other levels in between, and can be perpetuated by poor communication and attempts to maintain balance within the relationship. Treatments for desire discrepancies they depend upon the depth and complexity of the issues, the creativity and flexibility of the therapist, and the commitment and motivation of the partners.

The easy accessibility of sex for homosexual men reduces their motivation to struggle to overcome desire discrepancies in relationships. Yet in light of the AIDS crisis, more are likely to attempt to make sex better at home. It is hoped that psychotherapists will be able to respond adequately to the need for help and direction.

REFERENCES

Annon, J. S. (1974). *The behavioral treatment of sexual problems: Volume 1, brief therapy.* Honolulu: Enabling Systems.
Annon, J. S. (1975). *The behavioral treatment of sexual problems: Volume 2, intensive therapy.* Honolulu: Enabling Systems.
Arentewicz, G., & Schmidt, G. (1983). Psychotherapy. In G. Arentewicz & G. Schmidt (Eds.), *The treatment of sexual disorders* (pp. 59–74). New York: Basic Books.

Coleman, E. (1981/82). Developmental stages of the coming out process. *Journal of Homosexuality,* 7 (2/3), 31–43.

Fifield, L., Latham, T. D., & Phillips, C. (1978). *Alcoholism in the gay community: The price of alienation, isolation and oppression.* Sacramento: California Division of Substance Abuse.

Kaplan, H. S. (1974). *The new sex therapy.* New York: Brunner/Mazel.

Kaplan, H. S. (1977). Hypoactive sexual desire. *Journal of Sex and Marital Therapy, 3,* 3–9.

Kaplan, H. S. (1979). *Disorders of sexual desire.* New York: Brunner/Mazel.

Kaplan, H.S. (1983). *The evaluation of sexual disorders.* New York: Brunner/Mazel.

Levay, A. N., & Kagel, A. (1977). Ego deficiencies in the areas of pleasure, intimacy and cooperation: Guidelines in the diagnosis and treatments of sexual dysfunction. *Journal of Sex and Marital Therapy, 3,* 10–18.

Levine, S. B. (1984). An essay on the nature of sexual desire. *Journal of Sex and Marital Therapy, 10,* 83–96.

LoPiccolo, L. (1980). Low sexual desire. In S. R. Leiblum & L. A. Pervin (Eds.), *Principles and practice of sex therapy* (pp. 29–64). New York: Guilford Press.

Masters, W. H., & Johnson, V. E. (1970). *Human sexual inadequacy.* Boston: Little, Brown.

McCarthy, B. W. (1984). Strategies and techniques for the treatment of inhibited sexual desire. *Journal of Sex and Marital Therapy, 10,* 97–105.

McWhirter, D. P., & Mattison, A. M. (1978). The treatment of sexual dysfunction in gay male couples. *Journal of Sex and Marital Therapy, 4,* 213–218.

McWhirter, D. P., & Mattison, A. M. (1980). Treatment of sexual dysfunction in homosexual male couples. In S. R. Lieblum & L. A. Pervin (Eds.), *Principles and practice of sex therapy* (pp. 321–345). New York: Guilford Press.

McWhirter, D. P., & Mattison, A. M. (1984). *The male couple: How relationships develop.* New York: Prentice-Hall.

Munjack, D. J., & Oziel, L. J. (1980). *Sexual medicine and counseling in office practice.* Boston: Little, Brown.

Reece, R., & Segrist, A. E. (1981). The association of selected "masculine" sex-role variables with length of relationship in gay male couples. *Journal of Homosexuality,7*(1), 33–47.

Schmidt, G. (1983). Introduction: Sexuality and relationships. In G. Arentewicz & G. Schmidt (Eds.), *The treatment of sexual disorders* (pp. 3–8). New York: Basic Books.

Schmidt, G., & Arentewicz, G. (1983a). Symptoms. In G. Arentewicz & G. Schmidt (Eds.), *The treatment of sexual disorders* (pp. 11–33). New York: Basic Books.

Schmidt, G., & Arentewicz, G. (1983b). Etiology. In G. Arentewicz & G. Schmidt (Eds.), *The treatment of sexual disorders* (pp. 34–58). New York: Basic Books.

Stoller, R. J. (1979). *Sexual excitement: Dynamics of erotic life.* New York: Pantheon Books.

Tripp, C. A. (1975). *The homosexual matrix.* New York: McGraw-Hill.

Zilbergeld, B., & Ellison, C. R. (1980). Desire discrepancies and arousal problems in sex therapy. In S. R. Leiblum & L. A. Pervin (Eds.), *Principles and practice of sex therapy* (pp. 65–101). New York: Guilford Press.

III. *FAMILY CONFLICTS*

A Sociological Approach to Counseling Homosexual Clients and Their Families

Sue Kiefer Hammersmith, PhD
Ball State University

SUMMARY. Stigma lies at the root of many problems typically experienced by homosexual clients and their families. Sociological theory and research shed light on the dynamics of stigma and its consequences, both for the stigmatized population and for their heterosexual families and associates. This article summarizes key sociological research on the nature and development of sexual orientation. It considers the dynamics of homophobia and its implications for homosexual youngsters and their families. It offers practical tips for helping clients to understand their own or a family member's homosexual orientation, for coping with stigma, for reconciling issues of religion and morality, and for determining lifestyle. Suggestions for therapist office materials are also included.

Sociologists traditionally have had little to do with either psychotherapy or counseling. Approaching problems on the collective level, rather than the individual level, sociologists typically focus on social rather than personal influences and seek to understand the general pattern rather than the specific case. For sociologists, intervention strategies typically focus on altering broad social factors rather than on individual growth or reconciliation. Too often, the result is a lack of exchange between therapists and sociologists working on the same substantive issues. This

Dr. Hammersmith is Associate Professor of Sociology and Dean of the University College, North Quad 323, Ball State University, Muncie, IN 47306. The author wishes to thank Lee Cooper for a number of astute observations regarding the dynamics of homophobia.

173

article is intended to lessen that gap by providing, for psychotherapists, a sociological perspective and relevant research findings regarding homosexuality.

THEORETICAL OVERVIEW

This article is based on a "labeling," or "interactionist," approach which introduces a clear and unambiguous distinction between the primary phenomenon (homosexual behaviors or feelings) and the secondary phenomenon (stigma). In this approach, homosexuality is not regarded as inherently pathological, immoral, or "deviant" because each of these labels represents a culturally based interpretation. Rather, homosexuality, as well as other forms of so-called "deviance," is viewed as simply stigmatized in the context of a particular historic and cultural tradition. Just as beauty lies in the eyes of the beholder, so does "deviance" (Becker, 1963).

Stigma itself, once it has become culturally embedded, has certain predictable consequences (discussed below). These include stereotypic and global interpretations; social rejection, distancing, and discrimination; "passing"; altered self-concept; development of a special subculture; and what sociologists call "secondary deviation." Although this article focuses specifically on the issue of homosexuality, the consequences of stigma are identified through common patterns observed with respect to a variety of types of "deviance," including juvenile delinquency, crime, mental illness, unwed motherhood, physical disability, deviant occupations, and even witchcraft. [See Rubington and Weinberg (1981) or Weinberg, Rubington, and Hammersmith (1981) for an overview of this perspective and its application to a variety of "deviant" statuses, and Weinberg and Williams (1974) for its application to homosexuality.]

In America, which sociologists and anthropologists regard as one of the more homophobic of the world's cultures, the dynamics of stigma are subtle and pervasive. They provide homosexual youngsters, their parents, and the spouses or children of homosexual persons with a source of anguish and a special set of problems. This article is intended to help the therapist deal with those problems through information-based education.

THE DYNAMICS OF STIGMA

Stigma and Stereotype

Stigma is culturally supported by moral judgment and exaggerated stereotype. In the case of homosexuality, the public has at its disposal a variety of stereotypic images—all negative. These include the sinner condemned to everlasting punishment, the "drag queen," the molester of little boys, and the "diesel dyke." Because such stereotypes present bizarre caricature-type portraits, they inevitably dehumanize the population they presumably represent. They present one-dimensional images, exaggerate the differences between those images and anything the general public could identify with, and transform homosexuality into a global status rather than just one aspect of an adult's life. Such stereotypes are perpetuated by the mass media, special-interest groups, and cultural tradition.

Perhaps the strongest reinforcer of stereotype, however, is the peer group (McGill, 1985). The social dynamics of homophobia seem to demand that people, especially males, dis-identify with homosexuality. Through "fag" jokes, comments about third parties, and affirmation of traditional stereotypes, participants affirm their own gender identity and membership in the peer group. The fact that sexual orientation is "hidden," rather than visible, only serves to reinforce this dynamic. Because sexual orientation is not outwardly visible, an individual generally cannot question anti-gay stereotype, humor, or prejudice—or try to educate one's self on the topic—without jeopardizing one's own reputation and making one's self vulnerable to the very sentiments in question. Within adolescent peer groups, for instance, stereotypes can be voiced, but open discussion and honest disclosure are impeded. The peer culture, then, provides a powerful force for perpetuating anti-homosexual stereotypes and feelings.

By the time one reaches adulthood, an automatic cognitive association between "homosexuality" and exaggerated stereotype is likely to have become internalized, along with a sense of awkwardness and social distancing, even among well-intentioned, reasonable people. Thus virtually no one—neither homosexual youngsters recognizing that orientation within themselves, nor the parents, spouses, or offspring of homosexual persons—is prepared to deal with this issue when it arises.

Stigma and "Passing"

In the case of homosexuality, as well as other forms of so-called deviance that are not highly visible, anyone who does not fit the stereotype can "pass," and only those who fulfill stereotypic expectations or display stereotypic traits become publicly visible. The stereotype takes on a self-validating character because those who fit the stereotype are publicly visible and those who do not fit the stereotype are not recognized. The public tend to grow smug in their assumptions about what they "know." Thus, the general public is deprived of positive, conventional role models who would disconfirm the stereotype. This means that young people may recognize a homosexual orientation within themselves without having any realistic or workable role models of what that means. Parents are likely to meet disclosure with denial, especially if their son or daughter does not fit the stereotype.

Stigma and a Sense of Self

Stigma threatens both self-esteem and one's sense of identity by denying the social and emotional validation upon which those constructs are built. In the case of homosexuality, virtually all homosexual youngsters are reared in heterosexual families, peer groups, and educational institutions. Consequently, they grow up with the same stereotypes and moral judgments as everyone else. Because passing is so pervasive (and for the survival of most people who work with youths, necessary), homosexual youngsters are also deprived of positive, conventional role models. And sex education, such as it exists below the college level, is heterosexually driven; consequently it fails to prepare either homosexual youngsters or their heterosexual associates for dealing with homosexuality.

Having at their own disposal only bizarre stereotypes (e.g., "drag queens," "diesel dykes," or sex offenders), young people are likely to impute a more global significance to their sexual orientation than it warrants. Realistic, positive role models would allow the young person (and his or her parents) to put sexual orientation in perspective: as only one facet of adult life, along with work, leisure interests, friendships, spirituality, and so forth, which one integrates into one's self-concept and sense of identity. Lacking positive role models, such positive integration becomes problematic.

Stigma and Rejection

In social relationships, stigma generally produces a distancing between those with the stigma and those without. The harsher the stigma, the greater the distancing. Thus, the person who discloses an invisible stigma, in doing so, makes him- or herself vulnerable to rejection.

Within the family, where authenticity forms a taken-for-granted basis for mutual regard, trust, and communication, disclosure can become a critical issue. Parents take it for granted that their sons and daughters will be heterosexual, and thus homosexuality poses a dilemma. Homosexual youngsters can keep their homosexuality secret and lose the sense of authenticity which family relationships presuppose, or they can disclose the homosexuality—often in an attempt to achieve honesty, understanding, and emotional support—and face rejection. Likewise, homosexual parents or spouses may feel compelled to reveal their homosexual orientation to family members in order to achieve a sense of genuineness in their relationship, but in so doing may be rejected.

In less intimate relationships, e.g., with friends or co-workers, disclosure also involves risk of rejection. Secrecy, however, brings about a different sort of distancing, in which the homosexual person may appear outwardly to be popular, well-liked, and part of the group, but feel internally alienated and isolated (Bell, Weinberg, & Hammersmith, 1981; Harry, 1982).

Even among professionals, e.g., in the ministry, journalism, or psychotherapy, the sense of awkwardness, defensiveness, and distancing may lead to a sense of rejection on the part of homosexual clients or associates. The author has witnessed situations, for instance, in which professionals, although not consciously homophobic, inadvertently conveyed rejection by displaying discomfort with homosexual persons or the topic of homosexuality. *This discomfort may be manifested in subtle ways—e.g., hurrying, making excuses, professing ignorance about such things, or changing the subject—which the professionals themselves may not recognize as a cue to their discomfort or distancing, but which homosexual persons may be quick to detect.*

Stigma and Subculture

Stigma can also give rise to a sense of special kinship with fellow victims of the stigma, and a sense of community and naturalness only in their presence. Thus, the stronger the social disapproval of a particular condition or behavior, the more attractive a subculture may become as a source of mutual support. In The Netherlands and Denmark, for instance, where homosexuality is more accepted than in the United States, homosexual men show less need to turn to the homosexual subculture for support and are more socially integrated with heterosexuals in friendships, work, and culture (Weinberg & Williams, 1974).

Stigma and Secondary Deviance

There is also a dynamic by which stereotypic expectations become realized in a sort of self-fulfilling prophecy, or "secondary deviance" (Lemert, 1951). One dynamic producing secondary deviance occurs when the larger society limits the support and resources available to the stigmatized group. Having less support and resources at their disposal, the stigmatized individuals then, in turn, behave in a way that supports the stereotype. (For example, with racially segregated education, blacks were treated as less capable, were given fewer educational resources and opportunities, and consequently turned out to be less capable.)

In the case of homosexuality, some of the very traits which the majority decry about homosexual persons or the homosexual subculture are, in fact, consequences of the majority's lack of support and respect for homosexual persons and relationships. For instance, heterosexual society denounces impersonal sex in the male homosexual subculture while at the same time forbidding homosexual men to go through a more personalized process of courtship and establishing a shared household. Heterosexuals denounce what they perceive to be the instability of many homosexual relationships, but withhold from homosexual couples the legal, religious, and social recognition which bolster their own marriages. And heterosexuals often think of homosexuals as psychologically unstable—without recognizing the toll of condemnation, which results in elevated rates of attempted suicide among young homosexuals, as well as alcohol problems stemming from a bar-centered subculture.

As a defensive strategy in the face of stigma, a stereotypic "deviant" role may become the organizing principle around which one organizes one's behaviors, relationships, or group memberships. In other words, in response to stigma and stereotype, those so stigmatized may segregate themselves (e.g., Princeton's gay alumni association) or take on the very roles, characteristics, and behaviors stereotypically—but not necessarily—associated with the stigmatized status or condition.

Thus a young man, just coming out, may adopt an appearance or demeanor which says, "I am gay." (The author's impression is that the same young man, three years later, will most likely have dropped the obvious dress or mannerisms.)

"Camp" and "leather" reflect secondary deviance in a recreational way. The author's impression is that men who engage in these stereotypic roles often do so with a sense of theatricality and humor. Having been sensitized to arbitrary distinctions between masculine and feminine cultures, they poke fun at gender roles by flouting them (through camp, drag) or by exaggerating them (through the leather scene). For the few who do participate in these activities, they represent gender spoofs, not confusion over one's own gender identity (cf., Newton, 1972).

For homosexual youngsters or their families, however, secondary deviance may seem to confirm their worst, stereotypic fears. The mother in Nebraska watching a campy San Francisco Gay Freedom Day march on the evening news, for instance, may feel her worst fears about the homosexual subculture confirmed.

IMPLICATIONS FOR PSYCHOTHERAPY

In a homophobic society, where homosexuality is stigmatized and generally masked, clients are likely to enter therapy or counseling without realistic images or information.

1. Both homosexual clients and their heterosexual families are likely to have been reared on myth and stereotype, with only misinformation and a sense of pathos regarding what it is to be a homosexual man or woman.

2. Homosexual youngsters and their families are cut off from the very persons who could benefit them most namely, positive homosexual role models and relevant support groups (e.g., for parents of homosexuals).
3. The essential condition—homosexuality—becomes confused with secondary adaptations to, or consequences of, stigma.
4. Homosexuality is given an exaggerated and central importance, rather than being viewed as only one facet of life within a broad network of social relationships and activities (cf., Simon & Gagnon, 1967).

Thus, the author urges therapists to supplement their regular psychotherapeutic approach with a strategy of informational education about homosexuality outside the clinical setting. Drawing on popular myth and misinformation, homosexual persons as well as their families are likely to greet the initial recognition or disclosure of homosexuality with confusion, denial, or anger. Informational education is needed to provide a workable framework within which to interpret either one's own homosexual feelings, or a family member's disclosure of homosexuality.

A sociological perspective, based on nonclinical data, is helpful in this regard because: (1) it dispels myths and stereotypes about homosexuality and provides a more realistic (and reassuring) notion of the quality of life homosexual men and women can expect; (2) it provides guidance regarding the lifestyle adaptations associated, outside the clinical context, with social and psychological adjustment; and (3) it helps to focus clients' attention on appropriate questions and time frames.

The discussion which follows is organized around centers of confusion or misinformation. It does not systematically review the literature, but instead goes directly to what the author sees as the crux of the issue and the conclusions best supported by empirical research. These conclusions are based largely on research conducted at the Alfred C. Kinsey Institute for Sex Research, which includes some of the largest-scale research to date on human sexuality. Although some experts may disagree with some of the conclusions presented, the points of view presented are supported by the bulk of available nonclinical data.

THE NATURE OF SEXUAL ORIENTATION

Based on research at the Kinsey Institute (Bell et al., 1981), as well as others' work (e.g., Harry, 1982, 1984; Saghir & Robins, 1973), I would suggest four key points:

1. Sexual orientation is deeply seated, for both homosexuals and heterosexuals.

2. Sexual orientation is most accurately indicated by erotic feelings (e.g., attractions, dreams, desires), regardless of whether those feelings have been expressed in sexual behaviors.
3. Sexual orientation indicates an inner nature which is unlikely to change.
4. Sexual orientation indicates erotic preference and nothing more (i.e., it is not a global statement about the type of person one is).

Parents may try to deny their son's or daughter's disclosure of homosexuality by way of a variety of interpretive strategies that make the claim superficial or invalid. For example; "It's just a passing phase." "How do you know? You've never even DONE it." "Just wait until you meet the right girl/man, then you'll get over this."

Parents need to understand that a statement of one's inner nature and feelings should be taken at face value. The Kinsey Institute study of sexual development (Bell, et al., 1981) found that most of the homosexual males could be distinguished on the basis of their erotic feelings by the time of puberty (around age 13) and most homosexual females by age 15 or 16. Approximately 9 out of 10 recognized their erotic orientation through romantic infatuations, dreams, masturbation fantasies, or simply knowing they were sexually "different" some years before they became (homo)sexually active. When they did become active, the behaviors merely reflected their already-present feelings.

Nor should parents be allowed to discount their son's or daughter's disclosure because the young person has been active heterosexually. Many of the homosexual men and women interviewed by the Kinsey Institute (Bell, et al., 1981) had dated regularly—but usually, they recalled, only because it was expected. Most had engaged in necking, petting, and coitus. These events, however, generally did not carry the inherent satisfaction or meaning they did for heterosexuals. Most of the homosexual subjects in that study, regardless of heterosexual activity or courtship during high school, had diagnosed themselves as homosexuals by late adolescence (see also Coleman, 1982/83b) and "came out" after that point (i.e., virtually none were labeled by others before they so labeled themselves).

Thus, although a claim of homosexuality may seem sudden to parents, it is likely to reflect years of self-recognition on the part of the youngster. Likewise, the homosexual youngster needs to realize that a conclusion which he or she has taken years to acknowledge may also require time for parents to accept. The process of coming out to parents should be regarded as a lengthy one, not to be accomplished with a single announcement (see also Borhek, 1983).

Among adolescents who are confused because they feel both homosexual and heterosexual attractions (perhaps one year having a crush on a boy and the next year having a crush on a girl, or feeling capable of both types of sexual experience), the Kinsey Institute research indicates that homosexuality will be the enduring orientation in adulthood. The heterosexual control group almost never reported this sort of confusion or variability in erotic attractions.

When they reach adulthood, many homosexual men and women enter heterosexual marriages. Although popular stereotype almost always portrays homosexuals as unmarried and childless, several studies have found one in five homosexual men and more than one in three lesbians to have been married (Bell & Weinberg, 1978; Curren & Parr, 1957; Parr, 1957; Saghir & Robins, 1973)—proportions which could decline were the stigma of homosexuality removed.

Homosexuals who marry are often "trying to do the right thing," genuinely fond of their partner, and desiring the rewards of family life (Coleman, 1982/83b). It may reflect their individual values and temperament that those who were heterosexually married also seem to gravitate toward stable, couple-relationships with same-sexed partners.

Despite such attempts to fit the heterosexual mold, however, existing evidence suggests that a predominantly or exclusively homosexual orientation rarely if ever changes in adulthood. For the men and women who recognize themselves as predominantly or exclusively homosexual in their feelings and attractions, that orientation appears to be as deep-seated and enduring as a heterosexual orientation is for the majority.

Marriage clearly does not extinguish homosexuality. A facsimile of heterosexuality may be accomplished at least for a time, but this is not to be confused with an enduring conversion of sexual orientation. Most homosexual men who have been married report homosexual fantasies during intercourse with their wives (Bell & Weinberg, 1978) and that homosexual dreams, fantasies, and attractions continue (Pattison & Pattison, 1980). Many homosexual men and women report involvement with a homosexual lover as the precipitating factor in divorce (Bell & Weinberg, 1978). Others find their sexual outlet in impersonal homosexual encounters or extramarital homosexual liaisons (Humphreys, 1970; Coleman, 1981/82a).

One wonders how many divorces would be avoided if the appearance of heterosexuality, and resulting marriages, were less mandatory in our particular culture. One also wonders about the consequences of such an arrangement for the unknowing heterosexual partner, who may experience sexual intercourse as frequently as other women (Bell & Weinberg, 1978), but not the associated romantic behaviors and personal validation one expects from marriage (S. Hershman, personal communication, August, 1985).

Nor is there persuasive data to show that therapy or religious experience succeeds in changing sexual orientation. Although some short-term changes may be noted (Pattison & Pattison, 1980), research with homosexual men and women in their 30s or older suggests that such efforts eventually break down—again attesting to the enduring nature of sexual orientation (cf., Bell & Weinberg, 1978; Coleman, 1982/83a).

Finally, clients must be made to realize that one's inner sexual orientation is not a matter of choice. It simply IS (see Bell, et al., 1981; Harry, 1984). Within the general population, most are heterosexual, some homosexual, a few bisexual. If psychotherapists can simply convey to clients and to the public this very simple fact, then I believe almost every other issue associated with homosexuality becomes manageable.

One simple device for helping clients understand the nature of homosexuality is simply to erase the rhetorical distinction between the two major orientations. If one simply answers a question about homosexuality as one would answer the same question for heterosexuality, most of the answers are likely to be reasonable and fairly accurate. One mother, for instance, recalled this exchange with her homosexual adolescent daughter.

Mother:	"How long have you known you were homosexual?"
Daughter:	"When did you know you were heterosexual?"
Mother:	"I don't know; I've just always known."
Daughter:	"Precisely."

This linguistic strategy can be useful in conveying to heterosexual clients the irrevocable nature of one's inner sexual orientation and the parallels between homosexuality and heterosexuality. It allows the therapist to ask parents of homosexual youngsters, for instance, to imagine that they were suddenly on a planet in which homosexuality were the norm. Would they change? Would they want to change? How would they adapt? It helps them then to realize that the same sense of interpersonal connectedness and emotional intimacy which they seek in a heterosexual relationship will eventually come to their son or daughter in another type of relationship. Finally, such a linguistic strategy allows the therapist to isolate conceptually distinct—but often confused—issues such as impersonal sex, pornography, or relations between adults and minors. By separating these issues, conservative clients can see that the same standards they apply to heterosexual morality (e.g., sex only within a committed relationship, no pornography) can also be applied within a framework of homosexuality.

THE QUESTION OF CAUSATION

Another crucial issue is "Why?" This question is often a painful one for parents, who tend to assume responsibility for their offspring's sexual orientation. For spouses of homosexual persons, the question may only add confusion to an already painful situation parallel to a spouse's discovery that his or her heterosexual spouse is in love with someone else. For homosexual youngsters in the process of reconciling themselves to their own homosexuality, the question may translate into "Why me?"—almost as it might with the diagnosis of a terminal illness.

One project at the Kinsey Institute was designed to codify and test the major psychological and sociological models of homosexual development. It differed from previous research by using large, nonclinical samples (979 homosexual men and women, and 477 heterosexual men and women), in-depth interviews (2–5 hours), and a path analysis of sequential relationships. The results are published in a two-volume report, *Sexual Preference: Its Development in Men and Women* (Bell et al., 1981).

Somewhat to the researchers' surprise, we found that:

1. Parents and family environment, either during the formative years or during later childhood and adolescence, have remarkably little to do with the determination of sexual orientation.
2. Homosexuality does NOT result from recruitment. People do not become homosexual through seduction, nor from recruitment into the subculture. (Subcultural involvement usually comes some years after the person has recognized him or herself as homosexual).
3. Homosexuality does not develop through social learning or sexual conditioning—e.g., early pleasurable experiences with members of one's own sex, traumatic experiences with members of the opposite sex, or a same-sexed environment.
4. Sexual orientation is not a matter of choice.
5. Sexual orientation is related to some degree to gender differentiation.

Homosexuality appears to emerge rather independently of the causal factors so long espoused in psychiatry, psychology, and sociology. Although this study found some correlations between homosexuality and various factors thought to influence its development, a sequential path analysis showed most of these to be either reflections of an already-established inner difference, or to have virtually no independent effect on sexual orientation.

Dominant mothers, for instance, account for less than 1% of the variation in sexual orientation among males. (Persons with the classic family constellation of dominant mother and weak, absent, or rejecting father were, however, more likely to seek therapy than were those with more "normal" family configurations, no doubt accounting for the tenacity of that model in the clinical fields.)

Differences in childhood and adolescent sexual experiences also continue to be cited in the literature as support for a social learning model (e.g., Storms, 1981; Van Wyk & Geist, 1984). Our path analysis, however, showed that a vast majority of homosexual subjects were differentiated first in their erotic feelings, and only later on the basis of behaviors. Nor does age of puberty and the boy-girl mix of playmates, another variation on the social learning model, influence sexual orientation (Hammersmith, 1982).

Similarly, social isolation and feelings of alienation are more common among homosexual children and adolescents. These appear to reflect inner differences between homosexual and heterosexual subjects, however, and to play no independent causal or reinforcing role in the development of homosexuality.

The one nonsexual factor which we found to be strongly and consistently related to homosexual development was gender nonconformity, with both male and female homosexual subjects scoring as more androgynous than their heterosexual counterparts. Even those with no outward sign of gender discordance tended to recall some measure of gender nonconformity. Harry (1982), using nonclinical samples, and John Money (personal communication), using clinical cases, likewise reported that virtually all effeminate boys grow up to be homosexual. (They do not have comparable data for females.)

Biological and medical research provides clues to erotic differentiation. Homosexual and heterosexual males are biologically distinct and distinguishable in their metabolic responses to estrogen (Dorner, Rhode, Seidel, Haas, & Shoot, 1976; Gladue, Green, & Hellman, 1984; comparable data for females are not available). A variety of studies have shown the effects of prenatal hormones on the differentiation of the central nervous system, with consequences for both sexual orientation and gender-related behaviors, (e.g., Ehrhardt & Meyer-Bahlburg, 1981; Fleming & Rhees, 1980; Imperato-McGinley, Peterson, Gautier, & Sturla, 1979; Wilson, 1979). Finally, homosexuality is reported among other species of animals, for whom our notions of socialization would scarcely apply (Ford & Beach, 1951).

Sociologist Joseph Harry (1982) argued that homosexual males are properly "masculinized" but not fully "defeminized," a conclusion consistent with our finding that both homosexual men and homosexual women are androgynous. Among birds, for whom maleness is the basic model and femaleness is a differentiated version (the opposite of mammalian systems), female-female rather than male-male homosexuality is observed (ethnologist Michael Conover, personal communication, October, 1979).

Given all of the above, I strongly suspect that one's inner sexual orientation is biologically rooted for the vast majority of both homosexuals and heterosexuals. I also suspect that the same factors producing a homosexual orientation account for much of the gender nonconformity (androgyny) noted in homosexual subjects (i.e., if Johnny is naturally not as aggressive as more masculine little boys, then forcing him to play football will not change his inner make-up.)

The crucial implication for psychotherapy is simply that sexual orientation appears to be a given. It is not a matter of choice, and no one is to "blame." Homosexual persons themselves are therefore not to be blamed or condemned, parents need not feel guilty, and spouses did not "fail." The common analogy of homosexuality to left-handedness is comforting, and perhaps not so inaccurate as we would have thought a decade ago. Beyond that, I think therapeutic speculation about why a particular person became homosexual is purely metaphysical and most likely a waste of time.

COPING WITH REJECTION

For many homosexual persons, disclosure results in rejection by family or friends. For others who do not disclose their homosexuality, the fear of rejection becomes a source of worry and psychological stress (cf. Weinberg & Williams, 1974). Empirically, such rejection is patterned. It tends to be displayed more by father than by mothers, more by men (outside the family) than by women, more by blue-collar than by white-collar persons, more by religious fundamentalists, and more by persons who do not have college educations (cf. Larsen, Cate, & Reed, 1983).

Within the family, rejection often lessens over time. It is my impression that rejection is less when disclosure is not sudden—when parents have been given cues over a period of time and, perhaps, formed a suspicion on their own. The apparently greater rejection of fathers may simply reflect the greater difficulty of heterosexual males in general in dealing with homosexuality, or it may reflect mothers' more unconditional acceptance of their offspring. In disclosing one's homosexuality to parents or dealing with a son's or daughter's disclosure, patience, education, and continued communication among family members will be needed.

Psychotherapists are accustomed to helping clients deal with rejection in a variety of forms, for example, divorce, suicide, loss of employment. In many instances, helping a homosexual client deal with rejection may simply call for the approaches used with other sorts of rejection.

Parents may view the disclosure of homosexuality, however, as an unsharable secret for which they cannot get support from the friends or clergy to whom they would normally turn for help. Homosexual clients or their families may therefore need referral to a supportive social network. Most major college campuses, for instance, have homosexual student groups where an adolescent may find information and support.

Many cities have support groups for parents, in which parents who have already gone through the experience of reconciliation with a homosexual child can guide those who are just beginning. Many urban areas have religious or secular support groups for homosexual persons, which often can be located by telephone through a "gay switchboard" or "gay hotline."

Therapists should know in advance what social support resources are available in their own locale. For information on parents' support groups, write (enclosing a business-size, self-addressed, stamped envelope):

> Parents FLAG
> P.O. Box 24565
> Los Angeles, CA 90024

Reading materials may also provide clients with information and a sense that they are not alone, and I suggest that the therapist keep some materials on hand for clients' use. The special "Growing Up Gay" cover story in the January 13, 1986 issue of Newsweek may be good starting material. Other materials are listed at the end of this article.

As adults, homosexual persons may find discrimination in employment or housing, especially in blue-collar culture (although some labor unions have adopted anti-discrimination contract clauses). They may be denied the security clearances required for some jobs. Homosexual men tend to be subjected to more discrimination than homosexual women. Most homosexual adults, however, describe themselves as satisfied with their careers and do not believe their careers have been adversely affected by their homosexuality (Bell & Weinberg, 1978).

Socially, homosexual men and women who are well-educated and in professional positions often find social rejection in the workplace or among friends to be less than they anticipated, especially if they reveal their sexual orientation only after they have established themselves personally. For persons in such situations, any actual rejection may be less costly, psychologically, than the guilt, shame, and worry they may experience as the result of secrecy.

HOMOSEXUAL LIFESTYLES

There is no such thing as a homosexual lifestyle. There are many options and many lifestyles for homosexuals, just as there are for heterosexuals (see Bell & Weinberg, 1978). Sexually, lifestyles range from abstinence to promiscuity, from marital-type relationships to "playing the field." Socially, they range from heavy involvement in the homosexual subculture to virtually no involvement.

Perhaps the most important informational message for clients who are homosexual or families of homosexuals is that sexual orientation does not determine lifestyle. Despite the images presented in the mass media or contained in popular stereotypes, the homosexual person still has autonomy in molding his or her future. The development of talent, interpersonal skills, self-esteem, and values which are critical for heterosexual youth are just as important for homosexual youth. Likewise, decisions and allegiances with respect to career, religion, politics, and recreation are often similar whether one is homosexual or heterosexual.

Clients should be encouraged to recognize that a variety of lifestyles is available to homosexual and heterosexual alike. Moreover, researchers find happy, healthy homosexual men and women in a wide variety of lifestyles (e.g., Bell & Weinberg, 1978; Weinberg & Williams, 1974).

We do know, however, that some lifestyle adaptations are more functional for homosexual persons than others. Stable homosexual relationships and at least some involvement in the subculture appear to be related to positive psychological adjustment (Weinberg & Williams, 1974), as is a positive acceptance of one's own homosexuality (Hammersmith & Weinberg, 1973).

RELIGION AND MORALITY

Our traditional religious condemnation of homosexuality, and the larger concept of sin in Western civilization, is based on a free-will model. In this view, the rule is clear, and persons may choose to either obey or disobey. Nonconformity, then, is seen as both an act of contempt for moral principle and a social example which must be condemned. In America, this view of homosexuality is further exacerbated by a Puritan tradition of anti-sexuality, which has been ameliorated for heterosexuality only within the last 50 years (cf. Gordon & Bernstein, 1970; Weinberg, Swensson, & Hammersmith, 1983).

Because homosexual persons and their families are reared in the same religious traditions as everyone else (Bell, et al., 1981), this moral condemnation may be a key obstacle to their understanding and accepting homosexuality. Help is available, however, within many mainline churches.

Many of the major denominations (including Episcopalian, Lutheran, Methodist, Presbyterian, Roman Catholic, and Unitarian-Universalist) have established special task forces, offices, support groups, or religious outreach programs to provide positive and accepting support for homosexual persons. The Universal Fellowship of Metropolitan Community churches, a Christian church developed especially for homosexual persons, is one of the fastest-growing denominations in the country. Still others (e.g., the Church of the Brethren) have adopted "moral guidelines" which support the integrity and dignity of homosexual relationships. I have been informed by a leading expert on Mormonism that even the family-centered Mormon Church has softened its stand on homosexuality, abandoning a program of behavioral modification after it was discovered that graduates of that program typically married, had children, and then divorced after a few years (historian J. Shipps, personal communication, February, 1983).

When religion poses a problem, my advice for therapists is threefold. First, the concept of sin needs to be addressed, if not by the therapist then by referral to sympathetic clergy (identified in advance). If sexual orientation is not a matter of choice (and there is no consistent body of evidence that it is), then how can it be a sin? It might be noted that the Christian condemnation of homosexuality was an historical evolution, linked to political and economic developments within the church and society (Boswell, 1980; Greenberg & Bystryn, 1982).

Second, materials (brochures, pamphlets, statements of position) may be obtained from mainline denominations, as well as recommended readings dealing with new religious attitudes toward homosexuality. The Unitarian-Universalists, for example, have a brochure entitled "What Jesus Said about Homosexuality." One opens the brochure and finds it blank. Several denominations have materials offering discussions of homosexuality and religion.

Finally, clients who are troubled by the religious question might be encouraged to explore religious reconciliation with sympathetic clergy or religious support groups (e.g., Catholic "Dignity" groups, Episcopal "Integrity" groups). Each therapist, of course, will have to determine resources locally available in his or her own area. A listing of the national headquarters of religious support groups can be obtained by writing (and enclosing a stamped, self-addressed business-size envelope):

Mary Borhek
P. O. Box 13331
St. Paul, MN 55113

CONCLUSION

The informational education advocated here is aimed at achieving three broad goals:

1. Reconciliation, or acceptance of homosexuality as a normal and enduring component of some people's basic make-up.
2. An "unlearning" of popular but undocumented myths, stereotypes, and dehumanizing attitudes toward homosexuality.
3. Helping clients to overcome the negative consequences of stigma.

ADDENDUM
REFERENCE MATERIALS FOR CLIENTS

Growing up gay, (1986, January 13). *Newsweek*, pp. 50–52.

Provides a very sensitive account of one family's story, told from both the parents' and the homosexual son's perspectives, regarding the son's homosexuality and the coming-out process. Reviews current knowledge and attitudes, and includes a short bibliography of readings (p. 52) for parents and homosexual persons. All materials in *Newsweek's* short bibliography are recommended.

Borhek, M. V. (1983). *Coming out to parents*. New York: Pilgrim Press.

A useful book providing insight, first-hand experiences with Borhek's gay son, and survival tips for gay men and lesbians; includes an ample bibliography of readings, organized by topic (grief, information for parents, books about understanding yourself and creating better family relationships, and readings for a more positive religious view of homosexuality). *My Son Eric*, by the same author, tells one mother's story (New York: Pilgrim Press, 1979).

Bell, A., Weinberg, M. S., & Hammersmith, S. K. (1981). *Sexual preference: Its development in men and women*. Bloomington, IN: Indiana University Press.

As an official report of the Alfred C. Kinsey Institute for Sex Research, this research report should relieve parents of their sense of responsibility for their son's or daughter's sexual orientation. Chapters 17 and 19 might be most useful to parents.

REFERENCES

Becker, H. S. (1963). *Outsiders: Studies in the sociology of deviance*. New York: Free Press.

Bell, A. P., & Weinberg, M. S. (1978). *Homosexualitites: A study of diversity among men and women*. New York: Simon & Schuster.

Bell, A. P., Weinberg, M. S., & Hammersmith, S. K. (1981). *Sexual preference: Its development in men and women*. Bloomington, IN: Indiana University Press.

Borhek, M. V. (1979). *My son Eric*. New York: Simon & Schuster.

Borhek, M. V. (1983). *Coming out to parents: A two-way survival guide for lesbians and gay men and their parents*. New York: Pilgrim Press.

Boswell, J. (1980). *Christianity, social tolerance, and homosexuality: Gay people in Western Europe from the beginning of the Christian Era to the fourteenth century*. Chicago: University of Chicago Press.

Coleman, E. (1981/82a). Bisexual and gay men in heterosexual marriage: Conflicts and resolutions in therapy. *Journal of Homosexuality, 7*(2/3), 93–103.

Coleman, E. (1981/82b). Developmental stages of the coming out process. *Journal of Homosexuality, 7*(2/3), 31–43.

Curran, D., & Parr, D. (1957). Homosexuality: An analysis of 100 male cases seen in private practice. *British Medical Journal, 5022*, 797–801.

Dorner, G., Rhode, W., Seidel, K., Haas, W., & Shoot, G. (1976). On the evocability of positive oestrogen feedback action in transsexual men and women. *Endokrinologie, 67*, 20–25.

Ehrhardt, A. A., & Meyer-Bahlberg, H. F. L. (1981). Effects of prenatal sex hormones on gender-related behavior. *Science, 211*, 1317.

Fleming, D. E., & Rhees, R. W. (1980, August). See: A clue to homosexuality? Stress during pregnancy: Feminization and demasculinization of male rats is found in research. *Science Digest*. pp. 69–70.

Ford, C. S., & Beach, F. A. (1951). *Patterns of sexual behavior*. New York: Harper & Row.

Gladue, B. A., Green, R., & Hellman, R. E. (1984). Neuroendocrine response to estrogen and sexual orientation. *Science, 225*, 1496–1498.

Gordon, M., & Bernstein, M. C. (1970). Mate choice and domestic life in the nineteenth-century marriage manual. *Journal of Marriage and the Family, 32*, 655–674.

Greensburg, D. F., & Bystryn, M. H. (1983). Christian intolerance of homosexuality. *American Journal of Sociology, 88*, 515–548.

Growing up gay. (1986, January 13). *Newsweek*, pp. 50–52.

Hammersmith, S. K. (1982). *Sexual preference: An empirical study from the Alfred C. Kinsey Institute for Sex Research*. Paper presented at the annual meeting of the American Psychological Association, August.

Hammersmith, S. K., & Weinberg, M. S. (1973). Homosexual identity: Commitment, adjustment, and significant others. *Sociometry, 36*(1), 56–79.

Harry, J. (1982). *Gay children grown up: Gender culture and gender deviance*. New York: Praeger.

Harry, J. (1984). Sexual orientation as destiny. *Journal of Homosexuality, 10*(3/4), 111–124.

Humphreys, R. A. L. (1970). *The tearoom trade: Impersonal sex in public places*. Chicago: Aldine.

Imperato-McGinley, J., Peterson, R. E., Gautier, T., & Sturla, E. (1979). Androgens and the evolution of male-gender identity among male pseudohermaphrodites with 5a-reductase deficiency. *The New England Journal of Medicine, 300*, 1233–1270.

Larson, K. S., Cate, R., & Reed, M. (1983). Anti-black attitudes, religious orthodoxy, permissiveness, and sexual information: A study of the attitudes of heterosexuals toward homosexuals. *The Journal of Sex Research, 19*, 105–118.

Lemert, E. M. (1951). *Social pathology*. New York: McGraw-Hill.

McGill, M. E. (1985). *The McGill report on male intimacy*. New York: Holt, Rinehardt, & Winston.

Newton, E. (1972). *Mother camp: Female impersonators in America*. Englewood Cliffs, NJ: Prentice-Hall.

Parr, D. (1957). Homosexuality in clinical practice. *Proceedings of the Royal Society of Medicine, 50*, 651–654.

Pattison, E. M., & Pattison, M. L. (1980). "Ex-gays": Religiously mediated change in homosexuals. *American Journal of Psychiatry, 137*, 1553–1562.

Rubington, E., & Weinberg, M. S. (1981). *Deviance: The interactionist perspective* (4th ed.). New York: Macmillan.

Saghir, M. T., & Robins, E. (1973). *Male and female homosexuality: A comprehensive investigation*. Baltimore: Williams & Wilkins.

Simon, W., & Gagnon, J. H. (1967). *Sexual Deviance*. New York: Harper & Row.

Storms, M. D. (1981). A theory of erotic orientation development. *Psychological Review, 88*, 340–353.

Van Wyk, P. H., & Geist, C. S. (1984). Psychosocial development of heterosexual, bisexual, and homosexual behavior. *Archives of Sexual Behavior, 13*, 505–550.

Weinberg, M. S., Rubington, E., & Hammersmith, S. K. (1981). *The solution of social problems: Five perspectives* (2nd ed.). New York: Oxford University Press.

Weinberg, M. S., & Williams, C. J. (1974). *Male homosexuals: Their problems and adaptations*. New York: Oxford University Press.

Weinberg, M. S., Swensson, R. G., & Hammersmith, S. K. (1983). Sexual autonomy and the status of women: models of female sexuality in U. S. sex manuals from 1950–1980. *Social Problems, 30*, 312–324.

Wilson, J. E. (1979). Sex hormones and sexual behavior. *The New England Journal of Medicine, 300*, 1269–1270.

Group Psychotherapy
for Bisexual Men
and Their Wives

Timothy J. Wolf, PhD
San Diego, CA

SUMMARY. A significant number of men and women experience conflict surrounding homosexual expression within marriage. As the media focuses more attention on these relationships, more bisexual men and their wives seek counseling or psychotherapeutic assistance. Based upon the author's research and clinical experience, this article outlines a group psychotherapy strategy for bisexual men and their wives. Relevant research and background data on mixed-orientation marriages are summarized. Treatment strategy explores intervention processes, resistances to treatment, the unique supportive experiences of the group, and qualities of the co-therapists who may provide assistance to bisexual men and their wives.

As the media focuses attention on bisexual men and their relationships with women an increasing number of bisexual men[1] and their wives or women lovers will eventually seek out counseling or psychotherapeutic assistance. As many as 10 percent of married men (Kinsey, Pomeroy, & Martin, 1948) may be dealing with some aspect of homosexual behavior, especially in the earlier years of their marriage. The conflicts with which they deal significantly influence their relationships with wives, children, friends, and homosexual men. Theirs is the quiet anguish of an invisible group of bisexual men who are married. Both they and their wives often feel alone and isolated, with little support or understanding from the gay or straight communities, and few feel free to share their status with even the closest of friends, colleagues, or family. Often because of the closeted nature of their relationships, they receive some of the poorest attention and care from medical and mental health professionals.

Yet, in my clinical practice, there has been an increasing number of bisexual men and their wives who are demanding a new way of thinking about their relationships. Homosexual men who were previously married want to understand the unresolved conflict of their divorce. Married bisexual men are voicing that they are tired of pastors, counselors, and

Dr. Wolf is a psychotherapist in private practice. Correspondence may be addressed to the author, 3549 Camino del Rio South, #D, San Diego, CA 92108.

psychotherapists attempting to change their sexual orientation. As one married man noted, "For 20 years I went to therapy to try to change. I was frustrated, angry, and miserable most of the time. Since I have openly acknowledged my homosexuality, and my wife and I deal with it together, I feel a whole burden has been lifted." Wives are increasingly asking for support from other women. In addition, many couples are wanting to know how they can manage an open relationship where the bisexual husband maintains his homosexual feelings or behavior or both.

My research with 26 couples who maintained ongoing married relationships in which the husband was bisexual (Wolf, 1985), and my clinical practice and group experience over the past 4 years, have yielded much information about these relationships. Traditional approaches may invalidate the unique difficulties and direction of these marriages and offer certain biases which impede resolution or dissolution of the marriage. This paper outlines an intervention strategy for psychotherapy with bisexual men and their wives. It is based on personal research and clinical experience, the recent research of colleagues, and the shared experiences of other therapists.

Besides the original data of Kinsey, et al. (1948), recent data identified a significant number of married men who have homosexual feelings and behaviors. Cook (1983) reported that of the 2,786 self-identified bisexual men surveyed, one-third were married. Masters and Johnson (1979) found that 23 percent of their homosexual respondents had been previously married. The German studies of Danecker and Reiche, as reported by Ross (1979), estimated the proportion of homosexual men who had been previously married at 10 percent. Weinberg and Williams' (1974) study in the United States, Denmark, and The Netherlands placed that figure at 11.5 percent, 5.8 percent, and 7.5 percent, respectively, in those countries. Saghir and Robins (1973) reported 18 percent of their homosexual sample had been married. In the Bell and Weinberg (1978) study, one-fifth of the white homosexual men and a slightly smaller number of their black counterparts had previously been married. Humphreys (1970), in his study of men who frequent public restrooms for homosexual contacts, reported 54 percent of his sample were married. The original Kinsey studies (Kinsey, et al., 1948) pointed out that 2 percent of older men (ages 25 and older) and close to 10 percent of younger married men (ages 16 to 25) had had homosexual experiences in the previous 5 years.

Given these numbers of bisexual or homosexual men who are currently or have been married, it is surprising that until recently few research studies have been devoted to this phenomenon. Studies by Ross (1971), Ross (1979), Dank (1972), Gochros (1978), Latham and White (1978), Coleman (1981/82), Brownfain (1985), Dixon (1985), Matteson (1985), and Wolf (1985) describe bisexual men in married relationships.

Some researchers have attempted to shed some light on the clinical treatment of bisexual men and the women they marry. Bieber (1969) and Imielinski (1969), utilizing an illness model of homosexuality, commented that the husband's homosexuality must be eliminated in order for the marriage to last. Within a similar framework, Hatterer (1974) described the wife of the homosexual man as having "retarded psychosexual and social development" (p. 275). More recently, different models of these marriages have been reported. Ross (1971) described modes of adjustment of marriages between bisexual men and their wives, and Latham and White (1978) outlined patterns of adjustment as well as clinical factors to be considered in psychotherapeutic assessment and treatment. Coleman (1981/82) reported objectives for the group treatment of bisexual men in marriages. Gochros (1985) described the reactions of women who learned their husbands were bisexual. The data of Wolf (1982) reported higher perceived satisfaction in these marriages when the couples participated in counseling.

Although this interest in mixed-orientation marriages has yielded some guidelines for clinicians working with these couples, no one to date has attempted to outline a treatment approach. As more data on these couples becomes available from both clinical and non-clinical populations, a framework of psychotherapeutic treatment can begin to be formulated.

From these studies, it has been learned that homosexual and bisexual men enter into marriage relationships for a variety of reasons which may include social acceptance, family pressure, desire for children, denial of homosexual attraction, ignorance of homosexual attraction, and a perceived lack of intimacy in the gay world. Many also marry with both partners having knowledge of the one partner's homosexual attraction or behavior, and commonly because they are seeking a friend-companion and are "in love" (Ross, 1971; Ross, 1979; Gochros, 1978; Coleman, 1981/82; 1985; Brownfain, 1985; Matteson, 1985; Wolf, 1985).

These men generally enter therapy because of a crisis in their marriage or because of individual stress. The following examples illustrate couples who sought professional assistance.

COUPLE A

The husband in this couple had recently "fallen in love" with a younger man. His wife was apparently unaware of his extra-marital activities. He was referred by a physician because of high blood pressure and complaints of marital tension. The couple had been married 27 years and both partners were in their late 50's. He was a professional, she a housewife. They had married children as well as grandchildren.

COUPLE B

The wife of Couple B contacted this therapist because of communication difficulties, lack of sexual interest, and social withdrawal in the marriage. The husband's homosexual behavior had been openly acknowledged for 3 years. This couple was in their mid-20's; both were successful professionals. They had been married 5 years and had no children. There were plans for a family.

COUPLE C

This couple sought psychotherapy because of an impending dissolution of their marriage. The husband had recently acknowledged his homosexual activities, precipitating a crisis in the marriage. This couple was also in their mid-20's. They had been married for 4 years and were planning to have a family once their careers were established.

Crises in these marriages may have been precipitated by the voluntary disclosure of the husband's homosexual feelings or behaviors to the wife, by patterns of conflict in the marriage because of the husband's continuing homosexual feelings or behaviors, or by involuntary disclosure precipitated by rumor or arrest. The husband may individually suffer from a variety of stressors, which may include confusion about sexual identity and orientation, conflicts regarding role and time commitment in the marriage, overwhelming guilt, anxiety and depression about his homosexual feelings and behaviors vis-à-vis wife and family, sexual dysfunctions with his wife or with other men, and a variety of physiological illnesses which commonly accompany these psychological stresses. Couples who are seen in therapy are most likely those in which the husband has disclosed his homosexual behaviors after several years of marriage.

Unlike the studies of bisexual married men, the studies of women in these marriages are less clear about motivating factors in the relationship. The study of a small number of women in psychoanalysis indicated an attraction to a particular character structure apparently found in bisexual or homosexual males (Bieber, 1969). Gochros (1985), in her study of 33 wives of bisexual husbands, found a profile of a "highly educated, assertive, self-confident, and socially skilled woman who enjoyed a better-than average marriage." (p. 112). Other researchers have speculated on the mutual self-exploration and struggle toward liberation of women and homosexual men and the non-seductive friendship and companionship of the homosexual male (Malone, 1980; Nahas & Turley, 1979). Few of these women had had love or friendship relationships with homosexual men before marriage, and they were generally attracted by the personality characteristics of their husbands which promoted deep friendships and shared intellectual styles (Wolf, 1982; 1985; Matteson, 1985). Gochros (1985) found that "wives struggled less with the homosexuality itself than with problems of isolation, stigma, loss, cognitive confusion and dissonance, and lack of knowledgeable, empathetic support or help in problem solving" (p. 101).

COUPLES GROUP THERAPY

For many reasons which will continue to be addressed in this article, couples group psychotherapy provides a setting for persons in these marriages to work out many of their personal and relationship conflicts. As an illustration, a husband and wife co-therapy team facilitates a group which meets in San Diego twice monthly for 2 hours. The male and female co-therapy team provides a working communication model and allows both husbands and wives a same-sex person with whom to identify. In a single male-therapist setting, the wife can easily feel threatened and dominated by her husband and the therapist. As the group feels the necessity, husbands and wives will break off to form their separate same-sex groups, sharing themes for discussion as a complete group during the last portion of the session. Periodically the group will also meet on their own for less structured social meetings (i.e., a beach picnic). Friendships which are non-sexual are encouraged among group members. A group contact for non-sexual involvement between group members is essential for trust between group members to be established and maintained.

Marital group psychotherapeutic intervention is a workable strategy for these couples for several reasons. The initial task of the clinician when these couples seek treatment is often to slow an often "snowballing" pattern of dissolution in the marriage. Both husband and wife need to be reassured that the marriage need not be terminated because of the husband's homosexual feelings or behaviors. (See Latham & White, 1978; Wolf, 1982, 1985; Brownfain, 1985; Coleman, 1985; Matteson, 1985). This is often best accomplished within a group setting in which other group members can relate to the husband or wife or both about their successful marriage styles or about realistic reasons why these marriages fail. Other group members may also reassure the couple that an adjustment of the marriage to the husband's homosexual behaviors can often take many years.

Since an adjustment to the husband's open acknowledgment of his bisexuality may take many years, lending support to the couple through-out this crisis time may be crucial. Again, the couples group setting may serve many of these needs. This author has found this to be especially true for the wives of bisexual men. Whereas bisexual men find support from other homosexual or bisexual men or gay organizations (i.e., gay fathers groups), the women in these marriages often feel lonely and isolated, reluctant to tell their secret to the closest of friends or family. Her first impulse may be to deny, suppress, or ignore both her husband's disclosure and her feelings about it. If she does become angry, her anger is often mitigated by her confusion about where she stands in the relationship or by her fears of being left emotionally or economically alone. Some women voice the complaint: "I don't know how to compete with another man." Her resulting depressed self-concept may be further depressed by her confusion about her husband's homosexual feelings or behaviors, the loss of fantasies and dreams about her relationship to him, a sense of betrayal and loss, and concerns about her children. As a woman in a support group for bisexual men and their wives put it: "I have only one-half of a husband and he has all of me and someone else too." Other women in the group who are experiencing, or have worked through similar feelings and situations are able to give these women the empathy and strategies they often need.

The husband is often likewise confused about his marital relationship as well as his sexual orientation identity. He is often concerned about his sexual orientation and how to label it; i.e., "Am I gay, bisexual or homosexual?" Often there is an overwhelming sense of guilt about his homosexual feelings or behaviors and how these feelings and behaviors affect his wife and family. There are times when he may sense that, instead of having the best of both worlds, he has the worst of both. His sense of isolation may be precipitated by feelings that he is neither part of or accepted by his heterosexual friends or colleagues or, on the other hand, the homosexual community. As Cook (1983) pointed out: "Bisexual men reap opprobrium from every side" (p. 211). The homosexual or bisexual husband often additionally fears that he will be rejected by his wife and family and fears misinterpretation and lack of acceptance from his friends and colleagues. Suicidal ideation may be present for many husbands who face these dilemmas. In the couples group the husband is accepted as an equal and his identity can be explored and supported. He can benefit from the realistic and more accurate feedback about his feelings and behaviors from men who are empathetic because of having had similar feelings and experiences.

Another topic that a group can effectively address is what I call the "I want my cake and eat it too" syndrome. Many bisexual men whom I have seen individually or in group are myopically caught up in compulsive sexual behavior or infatuated by ongoing romantic feelings about their homosexual relationships. This often leaves them with little empathy for the plight of their wives and children and a lack of motivation to make changes. In such cases, these men appear unable to recognize how destructive in the long run such behaviors can be to their marriage, their self-identity, and the well-being of their children. The group often effectively intervenes in this syndrome, and other husbands and wives will confront the husband about how harmful his behavior is to himself, his wife, and his children. This group confrontation can give the husband accurate feedback about his lack of sensitivity or self-destructiveness. This may be the first time that a husband seriously has to face the negative consequences of some of his actions. Although such confrontation is usually the most difficult part of the group process, with effective therapeutic direction the group setting can provide directions for change which allow a husband and wife more effectively to understand and work together toward resolving—or if necessitated, dissolving—the marriage.

For a husband, the crucial job of understanding and supporting his wife is critical to the maintenance of the marriage (Matteson, 1985), and at the same time can be a difficult task. For the bisexual husband in therapy, it may be equally as difficult to deal with his spouse's process of understanding and accepting his homosexual feelings and behaviors as it was for him to deal with his own. The wife often comes to symbolize what the husband would often like to leave behind; in this context, she may be seen as the focus of his oppression and the target of the brunt of his rage. She also may symbolize his ambivalence—of still wanting the marriage and at the same time wanting a male companion or lover. Whatever the wife may come to symbolize during this time, the husband may find it difficult to give her the time and support she needs to work through her analogous coming out process. Although the husband may feel tired of dealing again with the issues of his homosexual feelings and behaviors, it is also likely he was able to find more support regarding his issues than his wife. Within the context of couples group interaction, both husband and wife may come to understand and support one another.

At the same time that some husbands may be myopically involved in their homosexual relationships, other husbands may not have had the opportunities to explore their homosexual feelings and behaviors. The couples group must often support a husband, and his wife, through his "coming-out" period, during which the husband can begin to accept and integrate his homosexual feelings and behaviors. The bisexual husband has usually failed to integrate his homosexual feelings through the usual process of coming out during which many homosexual men and women develop a healthy and integrated sense of identity (see Coleman, 1981/82). This phase may be an especially crucial one for the marital relationship. For many men who are experiencing their introduction to homosexual sexuality and relationships, the tendency is to immerse themselves in a homosexual lifestyle while at the same time withdrawing from wife and family. As one husband described it: "I felt like a kid in a candy store and I lost my head about everything else." Other men describe it as a period of adolescence. During this time the couples group can suggest ways for the husband to handle his coming out which will minimize harm to his wife and family and can support the wife through this often necessary phase.

Concurrently, the women in the group also may be assisting other wives with issues of independence, economics, isolation, child care, or with deciding whether to leave the relationship. Often the wife's lack of personally autonomous perspective or financial dependence can make the husband's homosexual behavior a "bigger-than-life" issue in the relationship. In the group, women can help each other gain perspective and make choices, the result of which they no longer feel victimized.

The group therapy setting also provides a convenient forum for presentation and discussion of items and issues of an educational nature. Members benefit both from the knowledge of the co-therapists and that of group members. Information about labeling, sexually transmitted diseases, public exposure, time commitment, family, children, religion, homophobia, coming out, myths of bisexuality and homosexuality, and friendship and community support may be invaluable for couples struggling with bisexual issues in their marriages. Within this wealth of shared information, couples may more easily gain perspective and discover valuable alternatives in regard to their feelings and actions.

SUMMARY

Group therapy for bisexual men and their wives provides a supportive framework within which many needs of both the husband and wife can be met, and resistance which may arise in individual or couples therapy may be eliminated or more effectively addressed in such groups. Shared experiences and support for both husbands and wives provide reassurance to couples who may think they are the only ones with such difficulties. Indeed, group therapy has proven to be an effective means of addressing the unique possibilities of bisexual marriages.

NOTE

1. The men in this article will be referred to as bisexual, even though some of them self-identify as homosexual.

REFERENCES

Bell, A. P., & Weinberg, M. S. (1978). *Homosexualities: A study of diversity among men and women*. New York: Simon & Schuster.
Bieber, I. (1969). The married male homosexual. *Medical Aspects of Human Sexuality, 3*, 76–84.

Brownfain, J. (1985). A study of the married bisexual male: Paradox and resolution. *Journal of Homosexuality, 11*(1/2), 173–188.

Coleman, E. (1981/82). Bisexual and gay men in heterosexual marriage: Conflicts and resolutions in therapy. *Journal of Homosexuality, 7*(2/3), 93–103.

Coleman, E. (1981/82). Developmental stages of the coming out process. *Journal of Homosexuality, 7*(2/3), 31–43.

Coleman, E. (1985) Integration of male bisexuality and marriage. *Journal of Homosexuality, 11*(1/2), 189–208.

Cook, K. (1983). The playboys readers' sex survey. *Playboy*, pp. 126–220.

Dank, B. (1982). Why homosexuals marry women. *Medical Aspects of Human Sexuality, 6*, 614–627.

Dixon, D. (1985). Perceived sexual satisfaction and marital happiness of bisexual and heterosexual swinging husbands. *Journal of Homosexuality, 11*(1/2), 209–222.

Gochros, H. (1978). Counseling gay husbands. *Journal of Sex and Marital Therapy, 5*, 142–151.

Gochros, J. S. (1985). Wives' reactions to learning that their husbands are bisexual. *Journal of Homosexuality, 11*(1/2), 101–113.

Hatterer, M. S. (1974). The problems of women married to homosexual men. *American Journal of Psychiatry, 131*, 275–278.

Humphreys, L. (1970). *Tearoom trade: Impersonal sex in public places.* Chicago: Aldine.

Imielinski, K. (1969). Homosexuality in males with particular reference to marriage. *Psychotherapy Psychosom, 17*, 126–132.

Kinsey, A. C., Pomeroy, W. B., & Martin, C. E. (1948). *Sexual behavior in the human male.* Philadelphia: W. B. Saunders.

Klein, F. (1980, December). Are you sure you're heterosexual? or homosexual? or even bisexual? *Forum Magazine*, pp. 41–45.

Kohn, B., & Matusow, A. (1980). *Barry and Alice: Portrait of a bisexual marriage.* Englewook Cliffs, NJ: Prentice-Hall.

Latham, J. D., & White, G. D. (1978). Coping with homosexual expression within heterosexual marriages: Five case studies. *Journal of Sex and Marital Therapy, 4*, 198–212.

Malone, J. (1980). *Straight women/gay men: A special relationship.* New York: Dial.

Masters, W. H., & Johnson, V. E. (1979). *Homosexuality in perspective.* Boston: Little, Brown.

Matteson, D. R. (1985). Bisexual men in marriage: Is a positive homosexual identity and stable marriage possible? *Journal of Homosexuality, 11*(1/2), 149–171.

Nahas, R., & Turley, M. (1979). *The new couple: Women and gay men.* New York: Seaview Books.

Ross, H. L. (1971). Modes of adjustment of married homosexuals. *Social Problems, 18*, 385–393.

Ross, M. W. (1979). Heterosexual marriage of homosexual males: Some assorted factors. *Journal of Sex and Marital Therapy, 5*, 142–151.

Saghir, M. T., & Robins, E. (1973). *Male and female homosexuality: A comprehensive investigation.* Baltimore: Williams & Wilkins.

Weinberg, M. S., & Williams, C. J. (1974). *Male homosexuals: Their problems and adaptations.* New York: Oxford.

Wolf, T. J. (1982). *Selected psychological and sociological aspects of male homosexual behavior in marriage.* Unpublished doctoral dissertation, United States International University, San Diego.

Wolf, T. J. (1985). Marriages of bisexual men. *Journal of Homosexuality, 11*(1/2), 138–148.

Clinical Implications
of Lesbian Mother Studies

Martha Kirkpatrick, MD

University of California, Los Angeles

SUMMARY. Recent surveys of lesbians have revealed that one-third
have been heterosexually married, and one-half of these have had children.
Studies comparing lesbian mothers and their children with divorced
heterosexual mothers and their children provide data of value to clinicians
preparing to evaluate or treat members of this population. Studies show
similarities between the two groups in marital history, pregnancy history,
child-rearing attitudes, and lifestyle. Motherhood, not sexual orientation,
is the most salient factor in both group's identity. Lesbian mothers had
more congenial relations with ex-spouses and included men more regularly
in their children's lives. Coupled lesbians had greater economic and
emotional resources and provided children with a richer family life than did
mothers of either group living alone with children. No difference in
frequency nor type of psychological problem was found in the children.
Children benefited from group discussions to relieve anxiety about changes
in their lives and in their mothers' sexual orientation.

The counseling needs of lesbian mothers and their children are rarely
addressed. Clinical presentations have tended to educate the therapist
primarily about the maturational crisis of young adult homosexuals, i.e.,
"coming out," internal and external homophobia, self-acceptance and
self-esteem, structuring intimate relationships, and so on. In fact, until
recently lesbian motherhood was invisible, not only to the professional
community but to both the heterosexual and homosexual communities as
well. While not a new phenomenon, fear of losing one's children if
identified kept lesbians with children isolated. As their isolation has
become less obligatory through the successes of the Women's Movement
and the Gay Liberation Movement, researchers have learned more about
the lifestyles, parenting styles, and special problems of this group. This
information, while not clinical, can provide the clinician with a base for
understanding the needs of these clients.

We know that most lesbian women have had some heterosexual
experience. In fact, most studies show that about one-third of the lesbian

Dr. Kirkpatrick is Associate Clinical Professor in the Department of Psychiatry. She is in the
full-time private practice of psychotherapy and psychoanalysis. Her mailing address is 988 Bluegrass
Lane, Los Angeles, CA 90049.

samples has been heterosexually married (Saghir & Robins, 1973; Bell & Weinberg, 1978), and a small number of women who identify themselves as lesbians remain married (Ponse, 1978; Coleman, 1985). Of those currently living as lesbians who have been married, about one-half have had children. Estimates of the number of lesbians in the U.S. who are mothers range from Hoeffer's (1979) 3% of the 6.6 million female heads of families, i.e., 200,000, to Martin and Lyons' (1972) 30% of the estimated 10 million lesbians, i.e., 3 million. Almost all of these women had their children during heterosexual marriages, although there is an increasing number of lesbians, both couples and single, who are opting for parenthood by artificial insemination, insemination through friends, or through adoption.[1]

LIFESTYLE

Several comparative studies have shown unexpected similarities between lesbian mothers and single heterosexual mothers (Kirkpatrick, Smith, & Roy, 1981; Hoeffer, 1981; Mandel & Hotvedt, 1980; Golombok, Spence, & Rutter, 1983). While some lesbian women in the cohorts studies had had lesbian relationships prior to marriage and others had not, the great majority had married for the same reasons as the majority of their heterosexual counterparts, i.e., for love of their husband and desire for marriage. The lesbians did not report coerced marriages nor marriages of convenience, but desired marriage. A further surprise was that the marriages were described as no more conflicted than the heterosexual marriages and had endured the same length of time (7–8 years in the U.S. studies and 8–9 years in the English study). In one U.S. study, Kirkpatrick, et al. (1981), the heterosexual women endured stormier marriages but were less likely to initiate divorce, while the lesbians regularly regarded themselves as the initiator of divorce and blamed the failure of the marriage on a loss of intimacy rather than on abuse. The heterosexual women were more likely to have been victims of physical abuse and anti-social acts, and were more bitter about the failure of the marriage and angrier at men. Very few of the lesbian mothers showed antipathy toward men. In Mandel and Hotvedt's (1980) study, 25 percent of the lesbian mothers stated they would consider remarriage.

Several clinical implications arise from this data. The presence of a durable heterosexual relationship in the life of a woman who later has a durable homosexual relationship requires us to consider that sexual orientation may not be, as we once believed, the fixed compass that directs all intrinsic and extrinsic aspects of personality formation. Object preference, i.e., a resolution of the initial bisexuality of infancy, may remain flexible, varying over time, circumstance, and inner equilibrium, thus allowing for a satisfying heterosexual preference at one time in life, a homosexual at another. Other lesbians may have a fragile heterosexual resolution which cannot be sustained under the impact of a disappointing or non-supportive relationship with a man. Possibly for some women, a bisexual identity may develop which integrates both possibilities without compromising gender or sex-role identity. Our study, Kirkpatrick, et al. (1981), and further clinical experience demonstrated to me that these women who were currently living in satisfying lesbian relationships were capable of heterosexual response as well. Some may continue to have strong feelings of attachment toward a previous spouse, and may be depressed or angry when the ex-husband remarries. In some instances, such a reaction may cause the woman to feel guilty, not only toward her current lesbian partner, but also toward the gay community, as if she were unconsciously "disloyal" to or in danger of losing her current identity. The acknowledgement of heterosexual feelings in a lesbian woman no more suggests a mistaken sexual identity than the acknowledgement of homosexual feelings in a heterosexual woman. Such discovery provides a broader understanding and acceptance of one's self and a richer emotional life. The clinician should not assume such feelings presage or require a behavioral change.

Case I

A successful 43-year-old woman accountant entered therapy for recurrent depressive episodes. Prior to an increase in the intensity of her lesbian feelings some 5 years before, she had been married for 10 years and had two children. She had felt herself blossom both professionally and socially and was less subject to depression since her divorce, and her lesbian relationship was stable and satisfying. The current return of her depression was found to have followed a dream about an attractive businessman who she had accompanied on a trip to evaluate a business venture. The dream was manifestly sexual and reminded her of both sexual and social pleasures she had had in her heterosexual marriage. She felt guilty and afraid that her dream "disloyalty" meant she would be unacceptable to her lover and excluded from the gay community. She was relieved to realize that she had a right to all her sexual feelings and that her gay identity could encompass heterosexual fantasies and dreams without being compromised.

ADJUSTMENTS TOWARD MEN IN FAMILY LIFE

An important consequence of the more congenial relationship between lesbian mothers and their ex-husbands than between heterosexual ex-spouses was demonstrated dramatically in the Golombok, et al. (1983)

study. Of 37 children in lesbian households, 12 saw their fathers weekly, 10 often but less than weekly, and 15 not at all, compared with 38 children in the heterosexual single-mother households of whom only 3 saw their father weekly, 13 less than weekly, and 22 not at all. In the Kirkpatrick, et al. (1981) study, the lesbian mothers were found to be more concerned that their children have opportunities for good relations with adult men than were the heterosexual mothers. The lesbian group had more men as family friends and often included male relatives more regularly in the children's activities. Coupled lesbians in particular were the most likely to include men in planned activities and as regular visitors to the household. Contrary to the fears expressed in court, children in households that included the mother's lesbian lover had a richer, more open and stable family life.

The presence of a lover enhanced the family's financial stability as well. Lesbian mothers share with their heterosexual counterparts the lower standard of living of all female heads of households. While lesbians in general tend to have more education and make more money than heterosexual women, this is not true of lesbian mothers. The fear of a custody battle burdens divorced mothers: Lesbian mothers, especially, have legitimate reasons to fear discriminatory court action (Hitchens & Kirkpatrick, 1985), yet the majority of mothers divorced for more than one year complain not of the children's father's intrusiveness, but of his lack of support for the children, both financially and emotionally. Lesbian mothers often have to re-enter the workplace or develop new marketable skills, which entails all the usual problems associated with finding and maintaining appropriate childcare arrangements. These inevitable problems are made more difficult if the community is especially homophobic or the mother fears it will be. In addition, the gay community may be disappointing as a source of comfort or support. Prior to the visibility of lesbian mothers, the gay community was made up of adults pursuing adult activities; thus, a woman with children looked out of place and was often suspect.

DEVELOPING A SUPPORT SYSTEM

In a study of social support systems, Lewin (1981) found that lesbian mothers, no less than the heterosexual mothers, relied on relatives and ex-spouses for support and help with domestic responsibilities. Support did not regularly come from the lesbian community. However, since lesbians with children have become more visible, in many cities lesbian mother's organizations have developed. *Mom's Apple Pie* is a lesbian newsletter published by the Lesbian Mother National Defense Fund (P.O. Box 21567, Seattle, WA 98111) which provides information and can be used by lesbian mothers to contact others in their community. Lists of organizations for gay parents and other valuable resource information can be found in *Gay Parenting*, by J. Schulenburg (1985), and *Considering Parenthood: A Workbook for Lesbians*, by Cheri Pies. (1985).

INTEGRATING NEW PARTNERS

Lesbian mothers, as do other divorced women with children, find their pool of potential new partners is reduced—first, to those who are willing to assume responsibility for a family and, further, to those who respond well in that setting. Neither the experience or expectations of most lesbians includes parenting. Becoming a parent changes and defines lifestyle, irrespective of sexual orientation. The lesbian mother studies noted that for lesbian mothers, no less than for heterosexual mothers, motherhood was the salient identity. Activities, preoccupations, and friendships centered about that role. Some new partners welcome the unexpected opportunity for family life; others resent the instrusion into the private dyadic intimacy they treasure.

The sense of intimacy which is so valued by women seems especially important to lesbians, perhaps inevitably doubled since two women are involved. A common problem in lesbian couples is an intimacy which has become a restrictive fusion, resulting in the loss of a sense of autonomy and individuality. The presence of children can provide some protection against such an unhealthy merger. Unlike the partners in reconstituted heterosexual families, lesbian mothers often have partners who also have full-time custody of their children. Thus, the establishment of supportive and respectful interactions takes thought and patience. The problems of step-parenting may be compounded in such a family. Our study (Kirkpatrick et al. 1981) found children responding to their mother's partner as a big sister, adult friend, or suspect competition for mother's attention, but not as a replacement for father. Little role-playing was found in these families. Family responsibilities worked best when duties were distributed according to time and talent, though maintaining patience and open communication could prove very difficult in an atmosphere of conflicting loyalties.

Case II

Judy (age 22) divorced shortly after her daughter was born, and began a lesbian relationship when her daughter was 18 months old. Her lover was unprepared for the time and planning parenthood required and became increasingly jealous of the child. Judy, in turn, was angry and disappointed in the lack of help and resented her partner for not appreciating the opportunity to enjoy family life. Counseling helped to clarify some aspects of the disappointment. Each partner wished to have a partner who would provide a new parenting experience for her; namely, a mother who would be dedicated to her needs exclusively. As each began to explore their disappointments with their own parents, possibilities for cooperative and satisfying parenting improved and the relationship matured.

Case III

Betty and Jane had been living together with Betty's two daughters and Jane's son for 5 years since the children were school age. They enjoyed family life together and after some years of financial hardship had established a successful business together. As Jane's son approached adolescence, Betty, a feminist activist, accused Jane of raising a "macho creep" and became critical and ridiculing of the boy's developing masculinity. Jane felt confused, torn between loyalty to Betty and "feminism" and her desire to protect and support her son. These issues of competition and jealousy are common complaints brought to therapy and counseling. Yet they are not limited to, nor the consequence of, lesbian relationships. Unfortunately, many lesbian mothers believe the lesbian relationship has caused the trouble or that the situation can only be understood by a lesbian therapist.

All the evidence from current studies indicates that the lifestyle of the lesbian mother is very similar in pleasure, preoccupations, and troubles to that of the heterosexual mother, including the overriding concern about how what she does will affect her children. The difference lies in the lesbian mother's fear that it is her sexual orientation that will adversely affect her children.

PARENTING STYLE

It is helpful for clinicians to know that no evidence supports the myth that lesbians abhor feminine interests and activities. Studies of lesbian mothers have shown the same desire to bear and rear children as the heterosexual comparison mothers. In comparing lesbian and traditional (married) mothers on maternal attitude and self-concept, Mucklow and Phelan (1979) found that the two groups were very similar, found a positive correlation between the child's self-concept and self-esteem and the mother's self-esteem, not the mother's sexual orientation, and concluded that child-rearing style was a complex product of mother's attitudes, values, and personality characteristics, not sexual orientation. Hoeffer's (1981) careful work investigating parent-child interactions found lesbian mothers to be more tolerant of cross-gender play and more supportive of girls developing autonomy and boys nurturant interests. No study found lesbian mothers who hoped their children would be homosexual, but lesbian mothers were more inclined to hold non-sexist views and ambitions for their children and to state they had no preference as to their children's eventual adult sexual orientation. Both groups of mothers were concerned about their children's development and turned equally often to professionals for help.

CHILDREN'S DEVELOPMENT

It is valuable for clinicians and lesbian mothers to know that the comparative studies completed so far have not identified any damaging consequences to the children's development of growing up in a lesbian household. (Golombok et al., 1983; Kirkpatrick et al., 1981: Mandel & Hotvedt, 1980). So far about 135 children have been studied. While this is a small percentage of children being raised in lesbian households, the importance of the studies lies in the comparison with children of divorced mothers who are not lesbians. In all the studies, the effects of parental discord and divorce were clearly evident. By the measures currently available, no difference in psychological development nor gender identity could be identified. In the Golombok, et al. (1983) study more children in the heterosexual group were judged as having significant psychiatric symptoms than in the lesbian group. The cause of this disparity is unclear, but may be related to more two-adult households among the lesbian group.

While these findings are relieving to lesbian mothers, several caveats should be noted. There are no data on children raised from birth in lesbian households; almost all the children in the current studies had lived in heterosexual households during their first 2–3 years, when influences on identity formation are the strongest. Also, there are no comparative samples of adolescents and young adults, although Golombok, et al. includes a few children to age 17. The methods of gender identity and sexual orientation assessment in pre-adolescent children are of questionable validity and are suggestive as best. Finally, we are in need of studies with larger numbers of children, and most particularly longitudinal studies following these children into adulthood.

DISCLOSURE OF THE MOTHER'S
SEXUAL ORIENTATION TO CHILDREN

When and how lesbian mothers should tell their children about their sexual orientation is not clarified by these studies; however, a few comments may be helpful. In our study (Kirkpatrick et al., 1981), we found no identifiable correlation between what mothers believed their children knew and what the child appeared to understand.

Case IV

Sally, age 6, had been raised since she was 18 months old in a lesbian household consisting of her mother, brother, mother's lover, and her mother's lover's daughter of a similar age. Both mothers were well educated, active in their independent professional lives, and active together in the political life of the gay community. The children were surrounded by both male and female adults, mostly homosexual, who openly discussed these interests. The mothers, while not sexual in front of the children, were openly affectionate, and both disclosed the nature of their relationship to the children on many occasions. Nevertheless, Sally, with coy candor, revealed her belief that her mother and one of her close male friends were going to marry. This did not appear to be a lack of cognitive function, but simply a use of her experience to complete an inner picture necessary in her own developmental sequence. The meaning of a mother's lesbianism will vary depending on the age, stage, and sophistication of the child, and certainly on the child's previous relationship with the mother. Children in the same family may react quite differently. One may be proud of his/her mother's courage and honesty and discuss her lifestyle with close friends; while another may be angry and ashamed, fear ridicule, and keep the information secret. The mother must allow for all these reactions and be prepared for changing attitudes with the child's developmental stage. Significant events in the child's later life, i.e., first romance, marriage, introducing in-laws, and so forth, may continue to require a struggle to integrate the mother's unconventional life.

HARASSMENT

Lesbian mothers, as well as the courts, fear the possibility that their children will become targets of ridicule or discrimination. Surprisingly, none of the comparative studies identified such events in their subjects' experiences. Women living in metropolitan communities may be less subject to discrimination than those in smaller or more traditional communities. Hall (1978) describes several instances of harassment and discrimination in her sample, events similar to harassment related to differences in race, ethnicity, or physical characteristics. Knowing the cultural climate of one's community in regard to homosexuality may help the therapist empathize and support a family during such a time. The mother's guilt over putting her children in such a situation may cause her to distance herself from her children or unconsciously invite their rage as appropriate punishment.

CLINICAL EXPERIENCE WITH THE CHILDREN OF LESBIAN MOTHERS

While children of lesbian mothers appear to develop as well psychologically as their counterparts and without confusion in their sense of the gender and role, that is not to say that there is no pain or struggle. The clinical report of the adolescent development of a girl whose mother entered a lesbian relationship when the girl was 13 describes in detail the sequence of events (Javiad, 1983). She reacted first with denial and pre-mature heterosexual activity. Later, though she felt ashamed and feared ridicule, she nonetheless defended her mother against her father's criticism. She experimented with homosexuality and felt fused with her mother, only later to become enraged at her for depriving her of her father. Her mother's acceptance and understanding of her anger and confusion allowed her to begin to separate herself from her mother and clarify her own heterosexual self. Two thoughtful reports from social work experience confirm the frequent occurrence of these reactions (Hall, 1978; Lewis, 1980). Lewis found children verbally accepting of the mother's new identity once the initial shock was over, but often unable to verbalize pain and anger. For younger children the sense of being different and needing to keep a secret was emphasized, an attitude which at times interfered with closeness to peers. She found adolescents to be more concerned about their own sexual development.

Similar to divorced heterosexual mothers, lesbian mothers may experience loss and pain if teenage sons decide to live with father during this period of development. Oedipal issues and issues of identity foster the need for paternal alliance and restraint; understanding this need as appropriate for growth rather than as a personal rejection will help the mother remain close to her son. Lewis found teenage boys were most likely to express rage, but it was mostly directed at the mother's lover. In general teenagers had the most difficulty in accepting the lover. Preparation and discussion with the children about the lover moving in helped. Lewis discovered that interviewing the children in their own home with siblings without the mother present allowed the children to discuss feelings they said they had not discussed when in therapy, and it also provided relief by enhancing communication with siblings. She felt the lack of a peer group who shared these experiences increased the children's pain and isolation. When this was provided, the children made excellent use of it. She encouraged mental health centers and gay community centers to provide such groups.

CONCLUSION

Lesbian mothers have been shown to be very much like their heterosexual divorced counterparts. The therapist should not expect to find differences in the lifestyle, parenting style, or social support system of the lesbian mothers. However, they present special fears of custody battles with public disclosure of their homosexuality and potential loss of their children, and of the possible adverse affects of their lesbianism on their children's development. They often are anxious and uncertain about what and when to tell their children about their sexual orientation, about the introduction of a lover to the household, and about the management of possible discrimination toward themselves or their children.

It is valuable for the therapist and mother to know that no comparative studies have found differences between the children of lesbian mothers and those of divorced heterosexual mothers; gender identity and sexual development are similar in both groups. The presence of a lover in the home, if stable and responsive to the children, often results in a richer family life for the children.

Children do experience shock and surprise at the disclosure of a mother's lesbian relationship. Most children defend the mother against criticism, especially from the father, but often worry how this difference will affect their development and their relationships. Older boys may feel threatened and need reassurance that their developing masculinity is admirable in mother's eyes. A peer group with similar experiences may be very valuable to such children. There are a growing number of support groups in metropolitan areas for children of gay and lesbian parents.

The therapeutic techniques of the therapist may be less important than his/her recognition that the family struggles are related to the usual issues of family intimacy and trust, separation, individuation, envy and competition, and so on, rather than to the deviance of the lesbian mother. Enhancing the mother's self-esteem and understanding of herself in the context of her own family provides the best therapeutic goal.

NOTE

1. Fay Pannor, MSW, who runs a group for unmarried women planning to become mothers in Santa Monica, California, reports that 1/3 to 1/2 of her group's members are lesbians. Personal communication.

REFERENCES

Bell, A., & Weinberg, M. (1978). *Homosexualities: A study of diversity among men and women.* New York: Simon & Schuster.

Coleman, E. (1985). Bisexual women in marriages. *Journal of Homosexuality, 11*(1/2), 87–99.
Golombok, S., Spence, A., & Rutter, M. (1983). Children in lesbian and single parent households: Psychosexual and psychiatric appraisal. *Journal Child Psychology and Psychiatry, 24*, 551–572.
Hall, M. (1978). Lesbian families: Cultural & clinical issues. *Social Work, 23*, 380–385.
Hitchens, D., & Kirkpatrick, M. (1985). Lesbian mothers/gay fathers. In E. Benedek (Ed.), *Child psychiatry & the law, Vol. II* (pp. 115–126). New York: Brunner/Mazel.
Hoeffer, B. (1981). Children's acquisition of sex-role behavior in lesbian mother's families. *American Journal of Orthopsychiatry, 51*, 536–544.
Javaid, G. (1983). Case report: The sexual development of the adolescent daughter of a homosexual mother. *Journal American Academy of Child Psychiatry, 22*, 196–201.
Mandel, J., & Hotvedt, M. (1980). Lesbians as parents. *Husarts and Praktijk, 4*, 31–34.
Kirkpatrick, M., Smith, A., & Roy, R. (1981). Lesbian mothers and their children: A comparative study, *American Journal of Orthopsychiatry. 51*, 545–551.
Martin, D., & Lyon, P. (1972). *Lesbian women.* New York: Bantam Books.
Lewin, E. (1981). Lesbianism and motherhood: Implications for the child custody. *Human Organization, 40*(1), 6–14.
Lewis, K. G. (1980). Children of lesbians: Their point of view. *Social Work, 25*, 198–203.
Mucklow, B., & Phelan, G. (1979). Lesbian and traditional mothers' responses to adult response to child behavior and self concept. *Psychology Reports, 44*, 880–882.
Pies, C. (1985). *Considering parenthood: A workbook for lesbians.* San Francisco: Spinsters Ink.
Ponce, B. (1978). *Identities in the lesbian world: The social construction of self.* Westport, CT: Greenwood Press.
Rees, R. L. (1979). A comparison of children of lesbian and single heterosexual mothers on three measures of socialization. *Dissertation Abstracts International.* Section B: 3418.
Saghir, M. T., & Robins, E. (1973). *Male & female homosexuality: A comprehensive investigation.* Baltimore: Williams & Wilkins.
Schulenburg, J. (1985). *Gay parenting: A complete guide for gay men and lesbians with children.* New York: Anchor Books.

Helping Gay Fathers Come Out
to Their Children

Edward J. Dunne, PhD
College of Physicians and Surgeons
Columbia University

SUMMARY. This paper describes the treatment of seven gay fathers who were concerned about revealing their sexual identity to their children. A time-limited group was established for the purpose of developing strategies to help them past this juncture in their development as gay men. Role playing of specific situations was the modality chiefly employed. Discussions of the effects of internalized homophobia were also held. At the conclusion of the group (eight sessions) all participants rated the experience as "highly useful." Follow-up data are presented at 6 months.

Men who are homosexual and are, or have been, married and have fathered children can be seen as a special sub-group of the gay male population whose needs may differ from those of the larger population. Bozett (1981) succinctly points out the difficulty facing the gay father with respect to the achievement of a positive gay identity: the incongruity between the two identities of father and gay man. If there are few positive role models for the gay male in general, the situation is seriously compounded by fatherhood. This group has been little studied, although it is estimated that upwards of 25% of all gay men have been heterosexually married (Masters & Johnson, 1979).

Coleman (1981/82) has identified five stages in the coming out process which seem to proceed from the initial recognition of one's homosexual orientation. These stages (pre-coming out, coming out, exploration, first relationships, and integration) carry with them certain developmental tasks which must be accomplished in order to move to the succeeding stage. The task of the final stage of integration can be characterized by what Cass (1979) calls the incorporation of the public and private identities into a single unified self. Such a step would seem to require the

Dr. Dunne is a clinical instructor in psychiatry in the College of Physicians and Surgeons at Columbia University, and is an adjunct professor in psychiatry and the co-director of the Center for Human Sexuality at the Downstate Medical Center, State University of New York. Correspondence may be addressed to the author, Family Support Demonstration Project, Box 117, New York State Psychiatric Institute, 722 West 168 Street, New York, NY 10032.

sharing of one's gay identity with one's children, a step fraught with difficulty and rarely achieved by the majority of gay fathers.

Theoretically, the consequence of failure to come out to one's children is an inability to achieve full integration of one's gay identity with one's public identity. On a more practical level, the consequence is likely to be an increasingly inauthentic relationship between the father and his child or children. This inauthenticity in turn produces increased distance between parent and child and may be a major contributor to the failure of some children of gay fathers to achieve full social and emotional maturity. And the cost to the father is equally severe. In order to avoid detection, the father must resort to hiding his gay identity from his children. He is required to monitor his behavior and that of all his gay friends who come into contact with his children. He may decide to forego participation in the gay community for fear of being detected inadvertently, thereby foreclosing on a substantial amount of support and reducing his exposure to, and contact with, positive role models in that community.

Typically, when the issue is raised in therapy many therapists advise against coming out to the children. There are probably as many rationalizations for this advice as there are therapists, but little evidence exists to support the suggestions of dire consequences to the children, provided the father is able to remain in a close enough relationship with his children to foster understanding and acceptance. Those studies which have examined the effects of open gay parenthood on child development (Kirkpatrick, Roy, & Smith, 1976; Green, 1978) have failed to identify any negative developmental consequences attributable to that fact. Yet therapists often seem to align with the children's mother in maintaining the necessity for silence on the issue, and thereby lend credence to the unscientific basis for fear. Against such pressure is it little wonder that few gay fathers actually achieve disclosure?

Yet even when the therapist and the children's mother pose no direct barrier to disclosure, the gay father is seldom comfortable with the notion of coming out to his children. A variety of concerns, for example, the possibility of rejection by the children and fears of wrongly influencing the child's own sexual identity formation, as well as concerns about the loss of esteem in the child's eyes, surface whenever the issue is discussed. These concerns reflect a mixture of internalized homophobia and reality testing, for a child's response can never be perfectly predicted.

A third source of negative impetus to disclosure comes from the gay community itself. Despite the glamorization of "gay daddies" in the gay media, many gay men hold negative attitudes toward those of their "brothers" who are fathers. These attitudes are reflected in the subtle and not-so-subtle remarks and jokes which are a part of the gay culture, to which the father in the early stages of identification with the community may be especially sensitive. The gay father soon learns that children are frequently seen as a liability by prospective lovers; thus, he may decide to hide the fact that he is a father in an attempt to keep both identities separate. Children who are aware of their father's homosexual orientation and who are accepting of it may place demands of time and participation on their fathers which threaten his keeping these two aspects of his life separate.

Possibly the most pernicious aspect of this dilemma is the creation of an additional source of anxiety for the gay father. Fear of accidental disclosure of his sexual orientation is ever present. Anonymity is sought in large cities, in "business" trips away from the children, and in even more painful separations accomplished through relocation. Conversations with their children about sexual matters become skewed because of the presumed necessity to present a "straight" image. Even the child's innocent use of the term "gay" or any of a vast number of such loaded words can raise the anxiety level to the point that the interaction is discontinued abruptly.

There should be little wonder then that gay fathers seeking therapy on their own do not typically present with a request for assistance in this area. Fathers who are in couples therapy with their children's mother may enter treatment with an agreement with her that no moves toward disclosure will be made. It therefore becomes incumbent on the part of the therapist to help the father explore the reasons for his attitudes and hold open the possibility of disclosure.

Therapeutic approaches to this issue must take into account a number of factors, including the amount of support the father experiences in the family, the amount of support he experiences in the gay community, the extent to which the children's mother supports or opposes the disclosure, the extent to which the father is "out" to his extended family, the extent to which the children's anticipated reactions are based upon reality factors, and, finally, the degree and extent of internalized homophobia present in the father.

DESCRIPTION OF THE GROUP

The seven men in this study were volunteers from a large support network for gay fathers, the Gay Father's Forum of Greater New York. The Forum conducts a monthly meeting which is structured along the lines of a self-help group. Members are drawn from the three states surrounding the New York City metropolitan area.

Forum members were asked to volunteer for a special group which would help them explore issues relating to coming out to their children. It was emphasized from the beginning that it was not the purpose of the group to force disclosure. The group was described as a time-limited, structured, and closed, weekly 90-minute meeting. Participants were asked to commit themselves to attend the full eight sessions.

The seven men who joined the group ranged in age from 27 to 54 years (Mean = 43). Five of them were in homosexual relationships of greater than 6 months' duration. The group was occupationally diverse, but was composed mostly of white collar workers. Five members had been in some form of psychotherapy in the past, although only one was currently in treatment. (See Table 1.)

None of the participants was living with his children at the time the group began. Four of the men were "out" to the mother of their children. Those mothers who knew of their former partner's sexual orientation were reported to be generally resigned to the situation, although none had encouraged the father to share his sexual identity with his children. Most of the group members were out to their own parents as well, with varying degrees of acceptance being reported.

Two of the fathers had informal "joint custody" agreements. All but one had fairly easy access to their children, spending upwards of 5 to 10

Table 1.

Description of the seven men who participated in the project.

Father	Age	# Children	Ages of Children	Divorced	Lover
BF	41	2	m20, f17[1]	No	Yes
SB	38	2	m14, f11	Yes	Yes
CJ	54	2	m27, f25	Yes	No
MG	27	1	m8	No	Yes
PC	46	2	m18, f15	Yes	No
WM	40	3	m16, m14, m12	No	Yes
GR	42	1	m16	Yes	Yes

1. m = male, f = female

hours per week with them. Only one father thought his children definitely knew about his sexual identity, having been told by their mother, although he himself had never discussed the matter with them and they had never brought it up. None of the other fathers felt that their children definitely knew, although many expressed the belief that the children probably suspected.

DESCRIPTION OF THE SESSIONS

Each of the eight sessions was conducted in the author's office. The first session was used to introduce each of the members to each other and to outline some of the parameters of the group (attendance, confidentiality, research purpose, and so on). An agenda outlining the remaining sessions was distributed, along with copies of articles dealing with gay fatherhood written for lay audiences (e.g., "Being a Gay Father," by Don Clark, 1979). Members were asked to read the literature before the following session. The second session was used to explore the issue of homophobia. A formal presentation was made by the author in the first minutes of the session, followed by efforts to get each of the men to examine if they had been victimized by homophobia and whether or not there was evidence that they had internalized this attitude, a factor seen as crucial to the ability to recognize the difference between legitimate concerns about the appropriateness of coming out and concerns which were expressive of internalized homophobia. The remaining six sessions were spent in role-playing. A set of situations were drawn up by the author to encourage the exploration of as many different circumstances as the time would allow. These situations were divided into two categories based upon whether or not the action in them was initiated by the father. Those situations in which the father was the initiating actor were labeled "Proactive Situations," while situations which placed the father in the role of respondent were termed "Reactive Situations." It was the task of the members to develop clear strategies for handling both kinds of situations, through the use of role-play and feedback. The specific situations used in this treatment are listed in Table 2.

Group members were asked to develop specific strategies to handle each of the situations depicted in the role-plays. Members took turns enacting roles of various players. In the enactment of the "reactive" situations, the member playing the father was not told the situation until it was "revealed" to him by the other players.

Following each role-play, time was spent exploring the reactions of everyone present to the way the situation was handled and how it felt to be in it, as well as giving feedback to the primary players which would enable them to revise strategies for specific situations. At the end of each

Table 2.
Role play situations

A. Proactive Situations:
    Answering child(ren)'s generic questions about sexuality
    Answering child(ren)'s generic questions about
        homosexuality.
    Telling child(ren) about gay sexuality in general.
    Telling child(ren) about your gay sexuality.
    Telling child(ren) about your lover.
    Encouraging your child(ren)'s mother to help you in dealing
        with your children around this issue.
    Helping your child(ren) deal with schoolmates' attitudes
        about your homosexuality.

B. Reactive Situations:
    Your child(ren)'s mother tells your children about your
        sexual orientation without your consent.
    Your child(ren) saw you being affectionate with your lover.
    Your child(ren) found evidence pointing to your sexual
        orientation but did not say anything to you about it.
    Your child(ren) ask you about a rumor they heard from
        neighbors about your sexual preference.
    Your child(ren) are teased in school about your sexual
        preference.
    Your child(ren)'s mother forbids you to tell your child(ren)
        about your sexual preference.
    Your lover forbids you to tell your child(ren) about your
        sexual preference.
    Your lover insists you tell your child(ren) about your
        sexual preference.
    Your child(ren)'s mother insists you tell your child(ren)
----

session, members were asked to write out their own preferred strategy for the situations played out during that session. These were duplicated and handed out to the members in subsequent meetings to allow everyone to share in the process of developing strategies. Finally, members were asked to express to the group leader what they felt was good about the session, and also how they might suggest things be done differently.

RESULTS

Probably the most striking aspect of this group was the realistic role-play situations. Each of the members reported feeling deeply involved with the situations being depicted; the involvement for those members who were acting roles being the most intense. In describing his reactions to the situation where a father's children discover him being affectionate to his lover, one father stated: "I'd always feared it would feel like that . . . that sick feeling you get in your stomach like you'd been caught stealing or cheating. It was very hard to keep in mind that it was only a play. The [men who portrayed the] kids were so real. I could just hear my daughter asking those obnoxious questions.''

The ability of the group role-plays to engender new thinking about such a situation can be seen in a statement from a father following one of the "reactive" situations: "I never thought I'd be able to handle that one. It seemed impossible at first. Now I think I'd know what to do and wouldn't be caught off guard. I think I'd do it just about the same although my kids are younger.'' Indeed, the very act of playing the roles induced the members to develop strategies to handle situations they previously had only dreaded.

Some of the men were surprised by a few of the situations. They confessed to having never thought that such a scenario was possible, but on further exploration it became evident they had over-simplified the situation. Following the role-play in which the children found evidence of the father's sexual orientation, Bill stated: "I leave stuff in the dresser all the time. I always assume the boys won't look in there. I don't know why, though, because I certainly went 'treasure-hunting' when I was their age.'' Carl played a child whose friends had teased him in school about a rumor that his father was gay. After the role play, Carl expressed surprise that he had never considered that possibility, even though he had heard his own children teasing another child about some parental behavior that they found unacceptable.

One of the more interesting phenomena to emerge in the group was the almost complete inability of these men initially to approach this subject in any but the most grave tones of seriousness. This was strikingly evident in proactive situations where they were charged with the responsibility of actually initiating the discussion. Under these circumstances, the men always opted for an approach which emphasized the seriousness of the discussion and tended to expect their child(ren)'s reaction to be as serious. These role-plays were reminiscent of scenes in which children are told about the death of a parent or grandparent. Repeated attempts on the part of the group leader to get the participants to "lighten-up" were met at first with confusion and misunderstanding. Group discussion revealed that most of the men believed that nothing positive for the children could emerge from disclosure. It was only with great reluctance that they finally agreed to re-play some of the situations from a less "heavy" perspective. Pete's remarks typify the group's reaction to this later experience: "I wasn't nearly as 'preachy' as the last time. Maybe it helps. I felt better, and more secure in myself this time around.'' His response exemplifies how the group process and the role-playing situations served to alter the men's perceptions of themselves and their situations.

As the group developed, other group effects became evident. The men frequently began each session with a brief period of reporting about their

children and their progress; "close call" situations were described the .
most frequently. At the larger forum meetings they sought each other out,
and some developed closer social ties with each other. They began to urge
others to join similar groups, and urge the group leader to extend the
number of sessions or to hold an additional group. They also began to
discuss among each other the relative merits and disadvantages of the
strategies previously worked out. And they began to incorporate portions
of each other's strategies into their own. This group effect became an
important factor in providing the men with the opportunity to work out
conflicts about their own sexual orientation and identity, albeit on a very
limited basis. It should be emphasized here, however, that although most
of these men had previous experience in psychotherapy of one sort or
another, none had ever attempted to deal with the issue of disclosure
openly.

FOLLOW-UP

Each of the participants was interviewed 6 months following the end of
the group. The interview was conducted to determine whether the
participants had disclosed to their children, and also how they had been
helped by the group experience.

At the time of the follow-up, two of the fathers had voluntarily
disclosed their sexual orientations to at least one of their children. Carl
"found himself" in a conversation with his adult son and felt the moment
was right to reveal himself. The son was neither surprised nor shocked,
having felt for some time that his father might be gay. He was pleased
that Carl had shared this information with him. For his part, Carl reported
feeling an immense sense of relief and an increased closeness to his son
following this discussion. Subsequently, their conversations on the matter
had been frank, understanding, and accepting, although both believed it
would not be a good time to disclose to Carl's daughter.

Steve ended one relationship of several months and entered a new one.
When his oldest son asked about this change ("who is this Rob, and what
happened to Phil?"), Steve used the opportunity to disclose his gayness
to him. The son's reaction was initially moderately negative. He would
make cutting remarks about the relationship and about Rob, and would be
certain to point out the possible gay interpretation of any ambiguous
situation. Within a few weeks, however, he began to adjust to the idea of
his father being gay and ceased all hostile remarks. He would talk with
his father about his wishes that his father were not gay, but seemed to
have adopted a more accepting attitude.

Both Carl and Steve reported that their participation in the group had
greatly assisted them in working through these difficult passages with

their children. Each had felt that the actual situation was even more difficult than the role-plays, but both had found themselves using strategies they had seen developed in the group setting. Steve stated that "there were parts of the experience that seemed very familiar and I knew what to do. Later I realized that we had done that in the group and that I was drawing on that experience almost unconsciously." Carl remarked that he "never would have had the guts to get into the discussion" unless he had first practiced it in the group.

Mario was confronted about his sexual orientation by his parents after he and his lover moved in together. Both were initially quite hostile, but Mario reported holding his ground with them and they eventually accommodated the situation. Mario felt that his participation in the group had been of significant help to him in dealing with this familial crisis. He found that he could directly transpose some of the strategies he had acquired to the situation with his parents. Although he believed that it was premature to disclose his sexual orientation to his 8-year-old son, he stated that the group experience had helped him enormously in dealing with his parents because the situation had evoked much of the same emotional response.

Of the remaining four members of the group, one (Bill) planned to disclose in the near future, two (Pete and Chris, did not think the time was opportune, and one (Brendan) felt that because his children already knew as a consequence of their mother having told them, there was no compelling need to discuss the matter with them. All of the participants reported feeling significantly more comfortable with the idea that their children will someday know about their sexual orientation as a direct result of group attendance. Thus, it would appear that dealing openly and directly with this highly emotional issue through the media of role-playing and frank discussions of homophobia served to alleviate some of the anxiety these men experienced in considering revealing their sexual orientation to their children.

SUMMARY AND CONCLUSIONS

The group described above was composed of gay fathers who were interested in working on their concerns about revealing their sexual orientation to their children. A group approach which was both didactic and experiential was developed to assist the participants in identifying and overcoming their own internalized homophobia and give them direct practice in negotiating the vicissitudes of coming out to their children. Specifically, following a session in which the causes and manifestations of homophobia were explored, the participants were guided through a series of role-played situations dealing with both voluntary and involuntary disclosure. All of the members rated the group experience as highly useful at its conclusion. At a follow-up interview 6 months after the completion of the group, two of the fathers had come out to their children and had used group-developed strategies to do so. Another father had come out to his parents, and a fourth was considering disclosure imminently.

It would appear that attendance in the group assisted these men in coming to grips with one of the most difficult transition situations for gay men: coming out to their children. The opportunity to anticipate probable situations through the medium of role-playing had the dual effect of reducing discomfort and anxiety in the present, and of providing a structure for handling the situations when they actually occurred. It is probable that, even absent the direct intention eventually to disclose voluntarily, preparation for the possibility of being confronted by one's children, or by anyone, about one's homosexual orientation probably can serve to reduce the anxiety such a possibility holds. Such a reduction in specific anxiety can greatly assist the gay father in maintaining an authentic relationship with his children and thereby achieving greater integration of his sexual and social selves.

REFERENCES

Bozett, R. W. (1981). Gay fathers: Evolution of the gay-father identity. *American Journal of Orthopsychiatry, 51*, 552–559.

Cass, V. C. (1979). Homosexual identity formation: A theoretical model. *Journal of Homosexuality, 4*, 219–235.

Clark, D. (1979). Being a gay father. In B. Berzon (Ed.), *Positively gay* (pp. 112–122). Los Angeles: Mediamix.

Coleman, E. (1981/82). Developmental stages of the coming out process. *Journal of Homosexuality, 7(2/3)*, 31–43.

Green, R. (1978). Sexual identity of 37 children raised by homosexual or transsexual parents. *American Journal of Psychiatry, 135*, 692–697.

Kirkpatrick, M., Roy, R., & Smith, C. (1981). Lesbian mothers and their children: A comparative study. *American Journal of Orthopsychiatry, 51*, 545–551.

Masters, W. H., & Johnson, V. E. (1979). *Homosexuality in perspective*. Boston: Little, Brown.

Psychotherapy with Gay/Lesbian Couples and Their Children in "Stepfamilies": A Challenge for Marriage and Family Therapists

David A. Baptiste, Jr., PhD
New Mexico State Unviersity

SUMMARY. As increasing numbers of gay/lesbian parents and their children enter into "stepfamily-like" relationships with a gay partner, they are beginning to seek therapy for difficulties peculiar to stepfamily living involving two same-sex partners. This paper focuses on the difficulties experienced by gay parents and children in a step-relationship, and seeks to sensitize mental health professionals to issues specific to intervention with such families. Effective therapy with these families requires that theraplsts be sensitive to their personal biases and prejudices with regard to gay men and women in general and as parents, and be aware that such attitudes can intrude and negatively affect the therapeutic process and its outcomes. Guidelines for therapy are offered.

It seems that the term "gay parent" is a contradiction. I usually think of the term "gay" as being synonymous with being homosexual and I think of being a parent as reflecting heterosexuality. (James Walters, in Voellers & Walters, 1978, p. 149)

There is today a growing awareness that a large number of Americans identify themselves as gay.[1] Because many of these individuals often acknowledge and declare their gay/lesbian identity after years of living heterosexually in marital or commonlaw relationships, many gay men and lesbians are parents. Despite this fact, a large portion of the American

---

Dr. Baptiste is a counseling psychologist/marital and family therapist in the Center for Counseling and Student Development at New Mexico State University, Las Cruces, NM 88003, and is also in private practice. This article is a revision of a paper presented at the Annual Meeting of the American Association for Marriage and Family Therapy, San Diego, CA, October, 1981. The author wishes to thank Frederick Bozett, Robert Garfield, Anthony Jurich, David Weis, Kaye Zuengler, and two gay parents for their helpful comments on earlier drafts of this paper. Correspondence may be directed to the author at the address listed above.

population continues to believe that it is inconceivable and inherently contradictory that a person can be both gay and a parent. The twin act of having and keeping children is still jealously reserved for heterosexual couples.

Despite society's proscriptions against homosexuality and homosexuals as parents, increased numbers of gay, divorced, and never married single parents are retaining custody of their children from previous relationships and are living in "stepfamily" relationships involving children and a same-sex partner. As is true for heterosexual stepfamilies, gay stepfamilies also experience difficulties concomitant to stepfamily living. Although many of these families neither need nor seek therapy, clinical experience has shown that those who do experience difficulties in their relationships are seeking the services of marriage and family therapists in increasing numbers.

Unfortunately, since most mental health professionals tend to have limited experiences in treating gay couples, with or without children (DiBella, 1979), gay stepfamilies may present for many family therapists a significant challenge beyond that encountered in treating heterosexual stepfamilies. Not only must family therapists deal with problems and stresses common to stepfamily living (Visher & Visher, 1979), they must also deal with issues unique to the gay lifestyle. In this regard, since gay families are a unique subset of stepfamilies, their successful treatment requires knowledge in at least two areas: stepfamily relations in general, and specific knowledge about gays/lesbians and their lifestyles.

The purpose of this paper, then, is to: (1) sensitize mental health professionals to the therapeutic needs of gay/lesbian couples and their children who live in stepfamily relationships; (2) present issues specific to intervention with such couples and families; and, (3) offer guidelines for effective therapy.

DEFINITION OF TERMS

Family/Stepfamily

As used here, "family" and "stepfamily" are intended to denote a cohabitive living arrangement involving two same-sex adults and their children, biological, adopted or conceived through artificial insemination, from previous heterosexual relationships, marital or commonlaw. The relationship is characterized by mutual commitment, property sharing, and sexual intimacies similar to that found among cohabiting heterosexual couples with children.

Partner

The term "partner" is similar to the term spouse in that it describes same-sex adults who are involved in a committed marriage-like relationship similar to that found among heterosexual couples in monogamous relationships, marital or commonlaw.

Stepchildren

"Stepchildren" describes children, biological and nonbiological, who maintain a stepchild relationship with a nonsanguine related adult (and sometimes children) while living in a household parented by two same-sex adults.

PROBLEMS OF GAY/LESBIAN STEPFAMILIES

On one hand, gay stepfamilies experience some problems similar to those experienced by heterosexual stepfamilies, e.g., rejection, jealousy, and stepparent-stepchildren conflicts. On the other hand, however, many of the problems these families experience are unknown to heterosexual stepfamilies, e.g., the societal proscription against their lifestyle and its effects upon their relationship with the wider community. As a result, therapy with these families can be a challenging, demanding, and precarious undertaking since their problems are often complex and uncharted and are affected by many factors.

Among factors which contribute significantly to the problems of gay stepfamilies and help to make their situation different from that of heterosexual stepfamilies are the following:

1. Gay men and women are members of a stigmatized group whose lifestyles and relationships are disapproved by a majority of the population.
2. The status and concept of the gay marriage and family neither have precedent nor recognition in law. Furthermore, homosexual marriages and families currently have no identifiable body of laws, and there are not likely to be such laws in the future (Bernstein, 1977).
3. Contemporary community standards have not evolved to the point where a gay lifestyle is acceptable for purposes of rearing children. Consequently, gay parenthood is evaluated as generally unhealthy.[2] This evaluation is motivated by at least four fears: (a) fear, especially in the case of gay fathers, that children might be sexually molested by the parent or the parent's partner; (b) fear that children of gay parents are more likely to become gay adults or develop

"improper" sex-role behavior; (c) fear that children will be harmed by the stigmatizing process that inevitably surrounds such lifestyles; and (d) fear that children living in a gay/lesbian household, but especially with gay men, are more at risk of being infected with Acquired Immune Deficiency Syndrome (AIDS), since it is erroneously believed by many that AIDS is solely a gay male disease.

4. Gay parents often live in constant threat of losing their parental rights; consequently, they conceal their sexual orientation and lifestyle. Discovery or even suspicion that a parent is gay is often sufficient reason for either an ex-spouse, grandparents, or even government agencies (e.g., the courts) to force that parent to relinquish custody of the child(ren).

5. Because of the social stigma associated with homosexuality and the fear of discovery, which lead to the need for secrecy, the usual problems associated with parenthood, whether as a single parent or as a couple, are compounded. For many of these families, the need for secrecy creates a self-imposed isolation that tends to be more pronounced for the children than for the adults (Baptiste, 1982). The feeling of isolation created by the secrecy separates the family from the heterosexual community, is in part a significant contributor to much of the family's relationship difficulties, and severely hinders their ability to deal with conflicts that arise within the relationship.

THERAPY ISSUES OF GAY STEPFAMILIES

The author's experiences with gay stepfamilies have shown that, although each family's circumstances are unique, there are several commonly encountered issues that can be expected; in general, the most common issues are related to: (a) family communication; (b) sex role conflicts resulting from the difficulty partners often experience in living with another person who has been socialized for similar roles; (c) maintaining a sense of family in spite of opposition to their lifestyles; and (d) parent-child relationships (biological and step), as well as stepsibling relationships. Other important issues these families must confront are those related to their legitimacy and institutionalization in society, to being a gay/lesbian parent in a nonsupportive society, and those specific to children in gay families.

Issues of Legitimacy and Institutionalization

Unlike heterosexual stepfamilies, gay stepfamilies are not perceived as a legitimate family form, and are neither supported by nor institutionalized in society. Consequently, many family therapists tend neither to see gay stepfamilies as a family unit, nor to see their problems as a family problem that may have resulted from the relationship between either the two adults or the adults and the children. Instead, there is a tendency to perceive the problems these families bring to therapy as related to either an individual or to homosexuality. By so doing, therapists are more likely to exacerbate the family's problems, since both the unit as well as the focus of treatment are inappropriate.

Contrary to prevailing beliefs about gay family problems, most gay couples with children who seek therapy often present as a marital or family unit in much the same way as do heterosexual stepfamilies with children. Moreover, these families often seek therapeutic assistance for difficulties arising from family living, e.g., children's school problems, biological/stepparent-child relationships, or problems with the Rem SupraSystem (Sager, et al., 1983), rather than for problems stemming from either the adults' homosexuality or individual intrapsychic difficulties. Since this is the case, it is essential for therapists who treat these families to begin to see them as a family unit, and to see their problems as resulting from the interactions of family members, rather than separate intrapsychic problems of unrelated individuals who only share a common residence.

Issues of Parenthood

Regardless of sexual preference and lifestyle, gay parents experience the same problems of parenthood as do heterosexual parents. However, for gay couples with children, parenthood is further complicated by the realities that the partners are of the same sex, and that gay relationships and lifestyles are disapproved by society.

Not only does the heterosexual society disapprove of gays, but gays also often disapprove of and reject gay parents, especially fathers. Whereas having children is a status passage in the heterosexual world, in the homosexual world it is often a stigma, especially for gay males (Bozett, 1981). From the point of view of many gay/lesbian nonparents, the presence of a partner's child(ren) interferes with the dyadic relationship. Nonparent partners often demand that the dyadic relationship be the primary relationship, and that they be first in the other partner's hierarchy of relationships.

Case Illustration. At interview, Pete (never married) and Jim (divorced) had lived together for 6 years. Jim was a "noncustodian" father of three children. The couple's difficulties had arisen when Jim's 15-year-old son Sam moved into the household. Jim welcomed the opportunity to get to know Sam better, since Sam was 5 years old when Jim had left his family. Jim admitted to feeling guilty because he had missed much of his children's growing up. Pete was opposed to Sam moving in. Since Jim did not intend to disclose his lifestyle, Pete considered the compromises needed to maintain the deception too high a price to pay. Pete expressed feeling betrayed. He stated that, although he loved Jim, he would never have coupled with him if he knew he would become a custodial parent. With the therapist's assistance, Pete and Jim negotiated a compromise and Sam moved in. However, Pete and Sam did not get along. Pete had many effeminate characteristics, and Sam's friends quickly made fun of him and insinuated that he was living with a "queer." Although Pete and Jim's relationship did not deteriorate significantly, the stepfather-stepson relationship worsened such that, after only 8 months, Pete gave Jim the option of choosing between Sam and himself. Jim refused to make such a choice, and Pete ended the relationship.

Whereas many gay fathers and some lesbian mothers must deal with being rejected by their gay peers, all gay parents in a step-relationship confront additional burdens related to their role as parents. Many of the issues tend to be similar for gay fathers as for lesbian mothers. But gay fathers face even greater burdens since two unrelated males living together for an extended period find their sexual orientation is viewed with greater suspicion, which is increased by the presence of children in such households. On the other hand, it is societally acceptable for two women, with or without children, to share residence, without arousing similar suspicion about their sexual orientation. Gay fathers are also victims of the societal proscription against men as custodial parents. Such fathers must contend with the belief that children are best cared for by their mothers, regardless of the quality of the mother's caretaking behavior. As a result, gay fathers who retain custody of their children and live in a step-relationship are always fearful of discovery. It should be noted, however, that although society tends to place greater restraints on gay fathers than on lesbian mothers, such women do experience the "double jeopardy" of being lesbian and women, and are subjected to the constraints and discriminations directed at both.

The additional problems attendant to being a parent or stepparent within a gay relationship greatly increase the pressure and stresses in the family and severely hinder the task of reconstituting. Unless partners in such families are able to overcome these problems, they may face a situation that is more conflict-prone than is true for partners in a heterosexual stepfamily. Therapists who treat these families need to be acutely aware of how the special problems of being a gay parent in a society that is nonsupportive of that role can at times affect both the dyadic and familial relationships. Therapists must help gay couples anticipate these issues, and confront and deal with them when they arise.

Children's Issues

Despite recent efforts by the two major mental health associations (American Psychiatric Association, 1974; American Psychological Association, 1975) to have homosexuality viewed less negatively, and the persuasive research evidence that supports the belief that a gay lifestyle is neither deviant nor pathological (e.g., Bell & Weinberg, 1978; Bell, Weinberg, & Hammersmith, 1981; Saghir & Robbins, 1973), the sexual orientation and lifestyles of gay men and women are still viewed as indicators of maladjustment or psychopathology by many members of society. Consequently, even under the best circumstances, children in gay stepfamilies may experience difficulties since it is not easy for them to grow up in a family that is disapproved by society, and to be labeled as pathological or undesirable by association. In this regard, the current national hysteria about AIDS in the gay community has intensified society's disapproval of gays/lesbians, and by extension the children living in such families.[3] As a result, a primary complaint of children living in gay stepfamilies is feeling isolated from peers and their community. This feeling of isolation tends to exaggerate the feeling of difference these children already experience, as well as to accentuate the lack of a shared consciousness of a kind between the child(ren), the bioparent, and the stepparent. Absence of this shared experience often leaves the children without a refuge to which they can turn for assistance in dealing with societal hostility and pressures.

Voellers (in Voellers & Walters, 1978) has observed that children growing up in other minority families, e.g., Black, Jewish, and Mexican-American, can find refuge in the common experiences of the family, who can teach them techniques for dealing with the outside hostility and pressure. On the other hand, most children of gay parents do not share a common experience with their parents. As a result, these children do not have the same refuge as do children growing up in other minority families (p. 156).

Another important issue specific to children in gay stepfamilies is the need for secrecy about the lifestyle of the adults. Even for those children who are informed of their parent's sexual orientation, the need to maintain secrecy for fear of discovery is often burdensome. From the children's perspective, the need for secrecy creates a "closeted" and isolated existence not only for the adults, but also for them (Baptiste, 1982).

Case Illustration. Tammy (age 9), Melissa (age 13), their mother, Kaye, and her partner, Barb (both divorcees) were members of a lesbian stepfamily. At the initial interview, the family had been together for 16 months, and difficulties with Tammy were the primary presenting concern. Kaye had been informed by school officials that, over a 6-week period, Tammy had gradually withdrawn from all verbal interaction with peers and teachers at school and had now ceased talking to anyone at school. Kay and Barb were surprised by the reports because they perceived no change in the frequency of Tammy's verbal communication at home. Although theirs was a lesbian stepfamily, both Barb and Kaye reported that the girls seemed well-adjusted to the home situation and enjoyed a satisfactory relationship with Barb. Initially, Barb was presented to the girls as a roommate. However, after 4 months of persuasion by their lesbian support group, Barb and Kaye disclosed their lifestyle to the girls. The girls were admonished to tell neither their father nor any other person outside the family because they "won't understand." From Barb and Kaye's perspectives, both girls reacted positively and without any perceptible distress to the disclosure.

During the first six interviews with Tammy, she neither looked at, nor talked with, the therapist. However, following the therapist's disclosure that he was aware that her mother was gay, Tammy revealed that she was afraid to speak in school for fear that the facts about her home situation would unsuspectingly "slip out." She believed that if she inadvertently disclosed that she lived in a lesbian household, not only would her mother and Barb be hurt, but she and her sister would have to return to live with her dad; this was something they did not want to do because their dad had a drinking problem and at times had physically abused both the girls and Kaye. At a later session, both Kaye and Barb expressed concern that Tammy's behavior was having the opposite effect of what the request for secrecy was intended to achieve. They had requested secrecy about the family's lifestyle to protect against society's disapproval. Now, however, Tammy's in-school mutism threatened to remove that cloak of protection and expose the family to the disapproval they sought to avoid. During that session, Kay also revealed that she had requested secrecy with regard to the children's father because she feared that if her ex-husband knew of her lifestyle, he would seek and possibly gain custody of the girls.

With the therapist's help, Kay and Barb released both girls from their vow of secrecy about the lifestyle of the adults. The release cleared the way for both girls to express feelings about living in a lesbian stepfamily. Previous to that time, the girls had never really been given an opportunity to express their feelings about living in such a family. After 10 therapy sessions with the family, Tammy returned to school and resumed talking with peers and teachers. Barb and Kay continued for 10 more weeks, their therapy focusing upon issues related to being gay in a straight world, living as a lesbian couple, and living in a "stepfamily" relationship.

Because of the need for secrecy, many children, especially adolescents, are often reluctant to bring home friends and dates for fear of discovery. Visits to the homes of friends, as well as the homes of noncustodial parents and grandparents, also may be fraught with similar anxieties because there is always the possibility of being asked prying questions about one's family. For those children, especially adolescents who may be experiencing normative developmental difficulties, the added problems attendant to living in a gay stepfamily can at times cause confusion, depression, and even open rebellion when they are unable to adapt and cope with the secrecy necessary to living in such families.

Difficulties in the stepsibling relationship where both partners are custodial parents are frequently aired in therapy. And although many of the issues tend to be similar for gay as for heterosexual stepfamilies, e.g. altered ordinal position, competition, and sexuality, there are special difficulties attendant to the "stepsib" relationship in gay stepfamilies. In this regard, the term "stepsib" as it applies to children in gay stepfamilies is illustrative. In hetereosexual stepfamilies, nonsanguine sibs are stepsibs. However, in gay stepfamilies, because legal ties are absent and children are often not aware that they are in a step-relationship, the appellation "stepsib" is not only inappropriate but confusing. Much of the confusion results from the children's perception of the nature of their relationship with their parent's partner and his/her children. Often the partner is presented to the children as "just a roommate" who shares residence with the family for economic reasons, or as a relative or friend. As a result, the partner's children are, by extension, perceived by the children in the same light as the partner. Frequently, however, parents (biological and step), in their desire for increased family cohesion, will request that their children behave toward their partner's children in a manner similar to that expected for stepsibs in heterosexual stepfamilies; e.g., babysit for, or escort to a social event outside the home.

Unfortunately, because of the children's lack of commitment to a "stepsib relationship," parental requests for fraternal cooperation between the two sets of children are resented and often rejected by the children. Clinical experience with children from these families have shown that while they may behave fraternally toward the partner's children in the home, they are often reluctant publicly to identify the partner's children as stepsibs. In therapy, these children complain that public identification of the partner's children as bonafide stepsibs requires much explanation; such explanations tend to be an embarrassment that intensifies feelings of being different. Furthermore, since the relationship of the couple is often a secret in the community, publicly referring to the children of one's parent's partner as stepsibs removes the veil of secrecy and exposes the family to negative sanctions from the community. As a result of the ambiguity, children experience much difficulty in relating to the children of their parent's partner, even when they are aware that the adults are living in a gay relationship.

THERAPISTS' ISSUES

For a number of reasons, family therapists who treat gay stepfamilies face some obvious complexities that are not to be found in treating heterosexual stepfamilies. The first of these pertains to the need to rethink the concept of the family because neither the gay family structure nor relationship fit the societally accepted views of the nuclear family. Second, there is the need to perceive the family as a unit and to see its problems as a family problem, not as a homosexual problem or the individual problems of persons who only share common residence. Third, there is the need to overcome the family's suspicions toward the therapist because he or she might be perceived as heterosexual. Given the traditionally negative attitudes of many heterosexual therapists toward gay men and women and gay parents, much of this suspicion has been valid. Fourth, therapists need to be aware that there are currently no models nor therapy guidelines for gay family relationships upon which therapists, heterosexual or gay, can draw to guide interventions with gay stepfamilies. Among other issues that therapists who treat these families must confront are societal and cultural value issues and atypical forms of transference and countertransference. Some of these are briefly discussed below.

First, as part of society, all therapists are aware of, and some are affected by, the proscriptions against homosexuality and maintain their own special impressions of homosexual relationships. Thus, because therapy reflects the therapist's own values, these impressions, whether positive or negative, can affect the treatment outcome for gay stepfamilies. If the therapist lacks understanding of his or her level of comfort and acceptance of gay men and women, their lifestyles, and their right to be parents, the therapist's discomfort and perhaps nonacceptance of the family will be sensed by the clients, whether or not this is openly conveyed. It is important, then that in such situations therapists directly acknowledge their feelings and deal with them, or refer the family to a non-homophobic therapist more knowledgeable of gay/lesbian issues. If not confronted, this value discrepancy could lead to subtle manipulations unfair to the family, which, in turn, may cause the family to terminate therapy prematurely and maintain a negative opinion of therapists in general.

Second, therapists who work with gay stepfamilies must, more often than therapists who work with heterosexual stepfamilies, deal with the partners' competition and rivalry for the therapist, as well as their attempts to seduce the therapist psychologically and sexually (Walker & White, 1975). From clinical experiences with these families, the author has found that this situation varies according to the sex of the partners and the sex of the therapist, although in therapy involving a male therapist and a lesbian couple, one or both of whom may be bisexual, competition for and seduction of the therapist have been observed. Usually, however, it is the male therapist working with a gay male couple who may find that the partners compete indirectly to seduce him, overtly or covertly. Gay/lesbian partners may also develop a form of sibling rivalry and vie for the same-sex therapist's attention, having placed the therapist in a parental role (Walker & White, 1975, p. 5).

Case Illustration. In working with one gay male couple—Charles and Don, who consulted the author because of difficulties in their relationship as a part of a stepfamily, seduction of and rivalry for the therapist, by each in turn, became significant issues in therapy. Seduction took some obvious and not so obvious forms. For example, in the presence of Charles, Don would comment about some physical characteristic of the therapist, e.g. "you know you have beautiful eyes", or he would reminisce about his former black lover (the therapist is black). In response, Charles would comment, "your (the therapist) wife is lucky to be married to you. You understand people's feelings so well," or he would remark to Don "Now he would not get mad at Robbie (his son), he has children too. He understands children." Both Charles and Don, individually and as a couple, repeatedly invited the therapist to dinner at their home. Rivalry for the therapist's attention tended to be more subtle than the seduction. Initially, Don would "drop in" without an appointment to discuss some issue(s) specific to parenting. Despite repeated reminders to schedule appointments, Don's drop-in visits continued until the therapist abruptly ended them because of Don's behavior during the hour. Ostensibly, he wanted to discuss parent-child relationships. In actuality, however, he attempted to use his drop-in sessions to forge an alliance with the therapist and "dump" on Charles. Suggestions that he discuss these issues in conjoint sessions with Charles were ignored. After these sessions were revealed to Charles, he in turn dropped in at least three times until he too was stopped. Following cessation of the drop-in sessions, rivalry took the form of monopolizing the conversation with the therapist during the therapy hour, and offering small gifts, e.g., a book either one thought the therapist "would like to read," or from Charles, an acknowledged good cook, a recipe "your wife might like to try."

Third, believing that children in gay stepfamilies are either unwilling or unfortunate members of such families, some heterosexual therapists may tend to be less understanding of the parents and more empathic with the children. As a result, they may uncritically accept the children's claim that their negative behaviors stem from intrapersonal conflicts specific to living in a gay stepfamily. Furthermore, such therapists often will, wittingly or unwittingly, align with the children, and may even validate and sanction their negative behaviors. It is important to recognize, however, that although children in gay families do experience some problems specific to living in such families, e.g., de facto isolation created by the need for secrecy, many of their behaviors are common to all children at a particular developmental stage, as well as to children who live in stepfamilies, regardless of the adult's sexual orientation. Moreover, if the children involved are adolescents, they may be seeking control and displacing their anger with self onto the parental figures (Osman, 1972).

Finally, another problem that increases the challenge of working with gay stepfamilies is conflict stemming from the partners' difficulties in resolving their sex-role differences, regardless of their manifested commitment to a gay lifestyle. Unfortunately, many heterosexual therapists still believe that partners in gay families assume dominant and submissive sex roles. As a result, therapists often structure therapy in an attempt to help partners maintain these stereotypic roles. Contrary to this belief, however, such polarization of roles among gay partners in a committed relationship is rare. Instead, partners in gay families tend to emulate the sex-role patterns similar to those of egalitarian heterosexual couples in the society.

GUIDELINES FOR THERAPY

The author's experience in working with gay stepfamilies has resulted in an appreciation of the complexity of the tasks and an awareness of some of the difficulties that therapists encounter. Despite the difficulties inherent in working with these families, a marriage and family therapy orientation similar to that used with heterosexual stepfamilies can be useful. However, because these families are composed of two men or women rather than one man and one woman, techniques of conventional marriage and family therapy must be modified to their special situations.

Over the years, the author has found a systems model that incorporates behavioral techniques to be successful with these families. Using this approach, the initial focus of therapy is on the family and understanding that system. The second phase of therapy incorporates the insights into the family system by means of a behavioral approach. The primary goal of therapy is to help the family assess and change maladaptive behaviors through "doing." Other important goals of therapy are: (a) to help individual members clarify their relationships; (b) to help members clarify and understand their own behaviors and interactions; and (c) to improve communication using, as leverage, the special nature of the relationship.

The key to effective therapy with gay families is an understanding of the impact of stepfamily living upon the gay relationship. Equally important is an understanding of the impact of the societal biases regarding gays as members of society and as parents, as well as the impact of the Rem SupraSystem (Sager et al., 1983), e.g., ex-spouses, upon the family's intrapersonal relationships. Therapists who treat these families should be clinically skilled and have the requisite experience in working with stepfamilies in general, and gay couples, with and without children, in particular. Therapists who lack the requisite skill and experience should refer the family to a therapist better suited to treat them, or else consider including a co-therapist.

Because the number of gay couples with children who are seeking therapy appears to be increasing,[4] many marriage and family therapists will at some time encounter a gay stepfamily. Consequently, the following guidelines are offered.

1. *Be knowledgeable of and comfortable with homosexuality as a valid lifestyle.* It is important that therapists, regardless of their sexual orientation, have more than a cursory knowledge of the gay culture, especially in terms of family roles, values, relationships, and the place of children as defined by that culture. They must also be knowledgeable of, and comfortable with, homosexuality as a valid sexual preference and lifestyle, and must have freed themselves of the conviction that a gay orientation is either pathological, regressive, or immature. Heterosexual therapists who have a deep conviction that the heterosexual lifestyle is superior to all others, and conduct therapy with gay families from that value premise, will not be of any help to gay stepfamilies. Similarly, homosexual therapists who are unaccepting of gay men and women as parents will not be of any help to these families. Bozett has asserted that therapists who are unable or unwilling to shed their homonegative attitudes, beliefs, and values should not accept gay men and women as clients. To do so would be fraudulent. (F. Bozett, Personal Communication, August 8, 1983.)

2. *Resist the temptation to be overinquisitive or patronizing of the family.* It is important that therapists of all persuasions not treat the family as though it were a laboratory specimen. Neither the adults nor the children in these families should be treated as though they were handicapped because the family is a gay one. Instead, the inherent assets of both the couple's and the family's relationship should be emphasized. Overabsorption in either the pathology of the family's relationship, or the adults' personality and lifestyle, can result in therapists ignoring the family's assets, while emphasizing issues not immediately important to the family, e.g., homosexual concerns.

3. *Be prepared to deal with fears of being stigmatized for working with gay clients.* Heterosexual therapists need to deal with their fears of being stigmatized, or of compromising their reputations, by working with gay families. Often heterosexual therapists who treat gay families may be accused by certain colleagues and others of encouraging homosexuality

or even of being gay if their goal is not to change the sexual orientation of their client(s), or to get the children out of such families. In the author's experience, while many people may be accepting of two gay men or two lesbians living together without children, they tend to be less accepting of gay men and women, especially gay men, as custodial parents. Regardless of the gender of the gay parents, however, many members of society feel that therapists should work to remove children from gay households. Therapists who refuse to behave accordingly may be perceived to be encouraging homosexuality and not behaving in the best interest of the child(ren).

4. *Be able to communicate understanding and acceptance to the family.* Therapists, heterosexual and gay, who are understanding and accepting of the family and the couple's lifestyle, as well as the couple's right to be parents, will probably be more effective in diminishing the family's initial defensiveness and suspicions, and may also lessen the chances of being spontaneously rejected. Defensiveness and hostility can destroy rapport, increase the chances of greater negative feelings toward the therapists, and lead to premature termination of family therapy.

5. *Gain exposure to functional gay stepfamilies and a variety of gay persons.* Ideally, therapists, especially heterosexual ones, should be familiar with and have experience with a variety of well-functioning gay couples who are not clients, as well as with a variety of functional gay stepfamily lifestyles. These families can serve as models/norms against which the therapist can compare the functioning of the family in therapy.

6. *Avoid "pseudo-insight."* It is important that therapists, regardless of their sexual orientation, avoid the pseudo-insight of attributing all the family's problems, especially those involving children, to the fact that the family is a gay one (Bolman, 1968). Therapists must recognize that many of these families' problems may be unrelated to the sexual preference and lifestyle of the adults. Indeed, many of the adults' problems may stem from personality differences, or simply be problems that are to be found in any stepfamily or dyadic relationship. Likewise, many of the children's problems may stem from either normative developmental issues or concerns common to stepfamily living, regardless of the adults' sexual orientation.

7. *Be guided by the family's sense of need.* It is important that therapists let the family's sense of need guide the therapeutic process, rather than redefine the therapeutic goals from the therapist's own value position; e.g. the therapist emphasizing the homosexual/intrapsychic pathology issues to the exlcusion of relationship—parent-child or dyadic—issues; what may be comfort to the therapist may be disservice to the family. In addition to dealing with interpersonal aspects of the family's relationship, attention also must focus on the intrapsychic

dynamics of individual members, as well as on the typical kinds of marital conflicts that are found in heterosexual marriages, whether initial or remarriage. Clinical strategies must also include an ability to identify and deal with other relationship issues specific to gay persons.

8. *Be aware of the Rem SupraSystem's impact upon the family and be sensitive to societal pressures against their lifestyles.* The family relationships of gay stepfamilies, like that of heterosexual stepfamilies, are also influenced by the Rem SupraSystem (a network of different individuals and functionally related people [subsystems], e.g., parents, former spouses/lovers, from previous relationships, marital and nonmarital, who impinge on the stepfamily [Sager, et al., 1983]). From a therapeutic point of view, the Rem SupraSystem can be a positive or negative force for or against the family and the therapist. Consequently, the impact of its members upon the family must not be ignored. Additionally, therapists' awareness of the societal attitudes toward gays in general, and toward gays as parents, and how these might be reflected in the family's interactions, can be helpful in increasing therapeutic effectiveness with gay stepfamilies.

9. *Be familiar with and utilize gay community organizations and resources to the benefit of the families.* For some families, a gay parents' support group may be more effective than a professional therapist in providing invaluable information about how to be a gay parent in a straight world. For others, such groups may be a beneficial adjunct to therapy.

CONCLUSION

Gay stepfamilies are a unique subset of stepfamilies. The problems they bring to therapy are affected by the realities that the partners are of the same sex and that there are external constraints to such relationships. As a result, therapy with these families can be demanding and challenging because of the absence of appropriate guidelines for intervention. In spite of the difficulty inherent in treating such families, heterosexual therapists can be successful with them.

Effective treatment of gay stepfamilies requires that therapists be sensitive to the additional burden stepfamily living places upon the gay relationship, be equally sensitive to their own personal attitudes, feelings, and beliefs about homosexuality, homosexuals, and homosexuals as parents, and be cognizant of how these can intrude and negatively affect both the therapeutic process and its outcomes. Therapy with gay stepfamilies may be challenging, but therapists can be sure they will have an intriguing, eventful, and meaningful experience along the way.

NOTES

1. For the purposes of this paper, the term gay is used generically to denote a predominantly homosexual orientation of either sex. The term lesbian will be used to refer to concerns specific to female homosexuals.

2. Although this situation is changing slowly, this attitude was poignantly emphasized by Royal Switzer, a Massachusetts state representative, during debate on an amendment to bar the placement of foster children in homes posing a psychological or social threat to them. Gay/lesbian homes are perceived as posing such a threat. Switzer stated, ''to knowingly place children with individuals who are known homosexuals is not in the best psychological interest of the children'' (*Sun News*, Las Cruces, NM, May 24, 1985).

3. A recent (December 1985) national poll revealed that although the nation's sympathy for homosexuals has increased (compared to 1973), most Americans continue to disapprove strongly of homosexuality. (*Sun News*, Law Cruces, NM, December 20, 1985)

4. Based on personal experiences with these families and the reports of colleagues in a variety of geographic locations throughout the United States.

REFERENCES

American Psychiatric Association (1974). Position statement on homosexuality and civil rights. *American Journal of Psychiatry, 131*, 497(a).

American Psychological Association. (1975, January 24). Press Release.

Baptiste, D. (1982). Issues and guidelines in the treatment of gay stepfamilies. In A. Gurman (Ed.), *Questions and answers in the practice of family therapy* (Vol. II, pp. 225–229). New York: Brunner/Mazel.

Bell, A. P., Weinberg, M., (1978). *Homosexualities.* New York: Simon & Schuster.

Bell, A. P., Weinberg, M. S., & Hammersmith, S. K. (1981). *Sexual preference.* Bloomington, IN: Indiana University Press.

Bernstein, B. (1977, January). Legal and social interface in counseling homosexual clients. *Social Casework, 58*, 36–40.

Bolman, M. (1968). Cross-cultural psychotherapy. *American Journal of Psychiatry, 124*, 1237–1244.

Bozett, F. (1981). Gay fathers. *Alternative Lifestyles, 4*, 90–107.

DiBella, G. (1979). Family psychotherapy with the homosexual family. *Community Mental Health Journal, 15*, 41–46.

House adopts ban on homosexual placement. (1985, May 24). *Sun-News* (Las Cruces, NM), p. 6A.

Osman, S. (1972, June). My stepfather is a she. *Family Process, 11*, 109–218.

Poll indicates Americans disapprove of homosexuality; sympathy increased. (1985, December 20). *Sun-News* (Las Cruces, NM), p. 6A.

Sager, G., Brown, H., Crohn, H., Engel, T., Rodstein, E., & Walker, L. (1983). *Treating the remarried family.* New York: Brunner/Mazel.

Saghir, M., & Robins, E. (1973). *Male and female homosexuality.* Baltimore: Williams & Wilkins.

Visher, E., & Visher, J. (1979). *Stepfamilies.* New York: Brunner/Mazel.

Voeller, B., & Walters, J. (1978, April). Gay fathers. *The Family Coordinator*, pp. 149–157.

Walker, J., & White, N. (1975, June). The varieties of therapeutic experiences: Conjoint therapy in a homosexual marriage. *Canada's Mental Health*, pp. 3–5.

Resources for Families
with a Gay/Lesbian Member

Joseph H. Neisen, MA

University of Minnesota

SUMMARY. An exploratory mail survey was conducted with families having a gay/lesbian member, inquiring as to where they had received information about gays and lesbians and their lifestyles, and where they found support since their family member came out. The sample population was a 90-member support group, "Families and Friends of Gays and Lesbians." Responses to open-ended questions gave a personal account of these families' concerns, needs, and wants, which suggested answers as to how those in counseling professions might better prepare themselves to provide services to these families by making themselves more available and accessible to families.

It has been estimated that approximately one in four to five families have a member or members who on some level is or are dealing with his or her own homosexuality (National Gay Task Force). Initially all individuals are part of some type of family system. As more individuals continue to "come out" to their families, that is, to acknowledge a homosexual orientation, more families are faced with issues of coping and adapting to their family member's homosexuality. Concomitantly, with the misunderstanding and uneasiness often surrounding homosexuality combined with the fear instilled by the AIDS epidemic, there will be an increased need to provide these families with educational and supportive services. Due to the lack of empirical studies about families with gay and lesbian members, an exploratory study to provide information as to how some of these families cope and adapt is an important research step. There are studies that examine homosexuality in light of recent research (Gonsiorek, 1982). However, no studies have been found that examine homosexuality from the perspective of the impact on the family, their needs, wants, and concerns. Anecdotal works (Clark, 1977;

Mr. Neisen is Primary Therapist at the Pride Institute, Eden Prairie, MN, and a doctoral student in the Department of Family Social Science, University of Minnesota, 290 McNeal Hall, 1985 Buford Avenue, St. Paul, MN 55108. The author wishes to thank Jack DeVine and Gerhard Neubeck for their guidance in formulating the research project, Janice Hogan and Paul Rosenblatt for their help in reviewing this manuscript, and Jan Greenberg for his assistance with the data analysis. Correspondence may be directed to the author at the above address.

Fairchild & Hayward, 1979; Silverstein, 1977) indicate possible implications for families and do suggest means to cope and adapt. (See Appendix for suggested reading list for families.) Nonetheless, no empirical studies in this area have been conducted.

For many families, a member coming out places additional stressors on family functioning. Based on McCubbin and Patterson's (1983) work in family stress theory, finding support is crucial to successful family coping and adaptation. Family stress theory, more specifically the Double ABCX model and the Family Adjustment and Adaptation Response (FAAR) advanced by McCubbin and Patterson after their reformulation of Hill's (1949) ABCX family crisis model, provide a framework from which to address the issue. The Double ABCX model identifies factors that affect family attempts to adapt. These include: (a) the stressor and ensuing hardships, (b) existing and expanded resources of which social support is an integral component, (c) the family's perception of the situation, and, (d) the balance achieved on both a member-to-family fit and the family-to-community fit. The FAAR focuses primarily on the process components of a family's attempts to adapt. McCubbin and Patterson (1983) identify three stages of adaptation as a family responds to a crisis situation: (a) resistance, (b) restructuring, and (c) consolidation. Resistance employs family strategies of avoidance and elimination. Restructuring involves the family's willingness to redefine and address the situation. Consolidation refers to the achievement of a healthy balance in the member-to-family fit and the family-to-community fit.

Not all families reach a crisis stage as they deal with their member's homosexuality. Some families, however, may refuse to address the issue and remain stuck in the resistance stage. Over time some of these families may reassess the situation and begin restructuring. At a later point, they may even reach the consolidation stage of adaptation.

The present study provides information about families, typical of the sample population, that already are making efforts to cope and adapt in response to their member's coming out, and are likely to be in the restructuring stage of adaptation. A major focus of the study centers on these families' existing and new resources and support and the subsequent impact on family coping and adaptation. More specifically, it addresses family efforts to adapt from the vantage point of available and accessible sources of information and support.

METHOD

Questionnaires were mailed to the 90 members of a support group "Families and Friends of Gays and Lesbians" (FFOGL) in the Minneapolis/ St. Paul area. FFOGL is one chapter of more than 60 similar family-oriented support groups across the United States. The Minneapolis/St. Paul chapter of FFOGL is basically a self-run support group in which members are given the opportunity to raise questions and share with each other any concerns and feelings they might have in regard to a family member's homosexuality. Two co-facilitators from Family Support Services of Lesbian and Gay Community Services of Minneapolis are present as adjunct members to respond to any inquiries members might present. Some families had only one member involved in FFOGL, while others had several. Overall, 60 families were represented in the support group.

A cover letter and follow-up postcard explaining the purpose of the research and ensuring anonymity were sent to all members to encourage their participation.

RESULTS

The return rate was 43% ($N = 39$). The demographic data indicate that the sample population might well describe a good cross section of American parents. They were caucasian (100%), christian (82%), well-educated in terms of years of formal education (39% had a college degree), and lived in an urban or suburban setting (82%). Generally speaking, the respondents were middle-aged parents (72% were between the ages of 51 and 70) of a gay or lesbian child now in their mid-twenties (mean age = 26). Sixty-seven percent of the respondents were the mother of a gay or lesbian child, whereas 26% were the father. This is comparable to the makeup of the group in which 24% were male and 76% were female; thus, representation from the group based on sex was similar to the number of respondents based on sex. Five percent of the respondents were the sister of a gay or lesbian family member. The gay or lesbian member had come out to their family on the average of slightly over 2 years ago. Four respondents (10%) had both one gay male and one lesbian female family member. Two respondents had two lesbian family members, and one respondent had two gay male family members.

Seventy-four percent of the respondents had been FFOGL members for between 6 months and 3 years, while 30% of the non-respondents had been members for less than 3 months. Respondents attended monthly FFOGL meetings at a much higher rate than non-respondents. Thirty-one percent of the respondents reported they had attended monthly meetings 10 to 12 times in the past year, whereas of the non-respondents 43% had not attended at all. Eighty-seven percent of the 39 respondents said that at the time of the study they felt comfortable with their gay or lesbian member's sexual preference.

Members surveyed were asked to respond to what degree (a lot, quite a bit, only a little bit, none) the information they received about gays and lesbians and their lifestyle came from different sources of information (see Table 1).

Table 1 indicates that most respondents received their information about gays and lesbians and their lifestyles from printed materials such as books and newspapers, and from gay and lesbian acquaintances other than family members. Only limited amounts of information were received

Table 1

Availability of Information Sources About Gays/Lesbians

Information Sources	Level of Information			
	a lot	quite a bit	only a little bit	none
Printed materials (books, newspapers, etc.)	47	42	11	0
Acquaintances with gays/lesbians other than family members	34	34	14	18
Counselors/therapists	13	13	45	29
Television, films, movies	2	11	63	24
Clergy/ministers	5	8	16	71
Friends and relatives	3	0	34	63

Note. The values represent percentages of respondents.

(in descending order) from all of the following: (a) counselors/therapists, (b) television, films, and movies, (c) clergy/ministers, and (d) friends and relatives.

A second set of questions asked to what degree the respondents used a variety of sources of support. The four possible responses were: (a) all the time, (b) often, (c) seldom, and (d) never (see Table 2).

Table 2 indicates that most respondents used their own family members as the major source of support in dealing with issues concerning their family's gay or lesbian member. Support groups other than FFOGL were the source of support reported to be used second most often; The rate of use, however, was a steep drop from the first most used source of support. Seventy-seven percent used their own family members "all the time" or "often" as a source of support. Twenty-nine percent used support groups other than FFOGL "all the time" or "often." Even with the second most used source of support, 53% still reported "never" using support groups other than FFOGL. Respondents reported a high rate of "never" using all sources of support except their own family members.

Open-ended questions provided the opportunity for respondents to express themselves more freely as to their concerns, wants, and needs. Since some participants gave more than one response, percentages stated are of responses, not respondents. Respondents were asked what kinds of things they would like to see more available for families that are dealing with issues concerning a gay/lesbian family member(s)' sexual preference. The total number of responses was 45. Forty percent of the responses indicated a need for more information and education about gays and lesbians from a variety of sources. One respondent stated, "I would like to see more television coverage of the realistic side of gay [and] lesbian life." Twenty-four percent of the responses asked for more visible, publicized, and accessible sources of support. A respondent wrote, "I wish our parent group (FFOGL) was more visible . . . there must be lots of hurting, confused families . . . especially parents." Another stated a desire for "positive role models who can afford *not* to be closeted . . . both gays and parents." Twenty percent indicated the need for more support groups. Eleven percent were requests for more knowledgeable professionals, e.g., clergy, doctors, counselors, mental health workers, and so on. One respondent stated, "I would like to see pastors, school counselors, [and] physicians more knowledgeable for people especially in crisis." Another responded, "Counselors who have sufficient knowledge, or at least enough to know what they don't know, to be able to counsel a gay person effectively." And a mother stated: "I went to the Mental Health Center and to the Church as soon as I learned my son was gay. Neither facility had any literature to give to me. The counselor and clergy alike were compassionate but professed lack of knowledge on the subject."

Table 2

Availability of Support Sources for Families With a Gay/
Lesbian Member(s)

Support Sources	Level of Support			
	all the time	often	seldom	never
Own family members	24	53	21	2
Support groups (other than FFOGL)	18	11	18	53
Friends	0	18	40	42
Counselors/therapists (other than school counselors)	0	14	43	43
Clergy/ministers	2	11	24	63
Other relatives	3	10	26	61
Community agencies (other than gay/lesbian identified agencies)	3	5	16	76
Family physicians	0	3	24	73
School/school counselors	0	3	2	95
Neighbors	0	0	3	97

Note. The values represent percentages of respondents.

Respondents were asked what has been helpful in coping with their gay or lesbian family member's sexual preference. The total number of responses was 65. Twenty-five percent indicated that FFOGL provided help in their efforts to cope. One parent stated, "FFOGL and meeting other parents. [I] found out we are all normal and interesting/loving people . . . [it] helped with feelings of guilt." Another parent replied, "knowing you're definitely not alone and being able to listen and share experiences with others in the group." Seventeen percent acknowledged learning more about gays and lesbians as being helpful in their attempts to cope and adapt. Fourteen percent indicated that getting to know other gays and lesbians was helpful, whereas another 11% pointed to open communication with their gay or lesbian family member as having facilitated efforts to cope. One respondent replied, "The more familiar one becomes the easier it is to accept. Meeting my gay brother's friends helps show that gays are just ordinary people." Another stated, "Meeting my son's partner and growing to like him very much because he is a fine young man as is my son." A father responded: "Openess, discussion, getting to know his lover, meeting his gay friends in general . . . all my involvement with gays [has been helpful]. All the gay people we have met have been loving and supporting and willing to talk to us. They have saved us from much unnecessary anguish."

Respondents were also asked, knowing what they now know, what things would have been helpful as they were growing up to prepare themselves to deal better with the issues they have faced concerning their gay or lesbian family member's sexual preference. The total responses equaled 38. Seventy-six percent of the responses pointed to more education and more accurate information about homosexuals that is neither stereotypical nor prejudicial. One respondent stated, "If I had been informed that gay people were not sick." Another responded:

> [With] more education . . . people could be brought into a greater understanding. If I had known openly gay people I would have seen they are no different from anyone else. The subject was so taboo . . . no one even talked about it. Obviously something so horrible it couldn't be talked about, must be bad, etc. Education and exposure to gay people would have been helpful.

A father replied, "*All* matters on sexuality should have been more open and not so private. Although society has come a long way, we have a long way to go before we become more comfortable with sexuality issues, our own sexuality." Another respondent stated, "More knowledge of homosexuality. Like most everyone else, I had fear of the unknown. Thinking they were to be feared, they were strange. Very wrong." Fifteen percent indicated that more exposure to openly homosexual individuals would have been helpful. One mother replied:

> , I could have been so well prepared for this if I had known about homosexuality as I was growing up. As I look back on it, I had many friends and relatives in the area who [were] probably [homosexual]. Yes, 10%. Living with them was so natural. I wish I would have known I was living with gays and lesbians and all was so normal and natural.

DISCUSSION

Adequate education and sources of information are needed to facilitate healthy family adjustment as a family learns to cope, adapt, and meet the demands placed on the family system as a member comes out. Family stress theory acknowledges that successful family adaptation is affected by adequate resources, such as accurate information and social support. McCubbin and Patterson (1983) state that " . . . inadequate resources might well contribute to a negative definition of demands to a state of distress, and to coping directed at avoidance of demands" (p. 25). The level of adaptation, from nonadjustment to maladjustment, is partly determined by the existence of, or lack of, these same resources and social support. Concomitantly, successful restructuring involves family systems maintenance as a coping strategy (McCubbin & Patterson). To improve family efforts to cope successfully and adapt and maintain family stability while doing so, it follows that improved resources for education and accurate information about homosexuals and their lifestyles are needed to facilitate successful adaptation and systems maintenance.

The question arises as to whether or not respondents simply did not make efforts to use available sources of information and support, or that such sources were just not available. Respondents, however, were assumed generally to be in the restructuring phase of adaptation for organizational membership implies they were already making efforts to find support. The strategies of elimination and avoidance that typify those families in the resistance phase of adaptation were not evident. Rather, respondents were making attempts to cope and adapt and were reaching out for assistance in doing so. It seems likely that respondents would have been using more sources of information to gain accurate information, and finding more sources of support if, in fact, there were sources available to provide accurate information and support. Such sources cannot be considered as available when they do not have accurate information or when they are perceived to lack accurate information. Nor can they provide support if they are perceived as not being supportive. Providing accurate information in itself may be a supportive measure. Perhaps only limited amounts of support can be provided without having accurate information to accompany it. More sources of accurate information are needed, as are more sources of support, especially sources of support that can provide the objective, stereotype-free information such families are asking for. "Families who have and are able to develop sources of social support (e.g., kin, friends, work associates, church, etc.) are both more resistant to major crises and are better able to recover from crises and restore stability to the family system" (McCubbin & Patterson, 1983, p. 15).

In addition to the necessity for available, well-informed sources of social support, the results of the present survey also raise the issue of the accessibility of sources of support. Both are needed (McCubbin, et al., 1980, 1981). If social support is not available for these families (perhaps professionals do not have accurate information, thereby curtailing possible attempts to provide support), then it is obviously not accessible. But if social support *is* available but not accessible (i.e., professionals who have accurate information about gays and lesbians and are competent to provide supportive services, but families are not aware or do not perceive that this might be the case), then it does limited good as few families are able to utilize the available support. Again, considering that the respondents were likely to be in the restructuring phase, it does not appear to be that well-informed sources of support were available but not accessible, but rather that well-informed sources of support were extremely limited in both availability and accessibility. Considering that 43% of the respondents "seldom" used counselors/therapists for support, and another 43% "never" used counselors/therapists for support, this points to the need for counselors and psychotherapists to be more available and accessible. Seventy-six percent of the respondents reported "never" using community agencies, other than gay/lesbian identified agencies, for support, suggesting that whether or not these agencies were prepared to offer supportive services to these families, these families perceived most community agencies as unavailable and unaccessible to help meet their needs. And, though traditionally speaking the clergy and family physicians have been primary sources of support for families, similar perceptions of the unavailability and unaccessibility of the clergy and family physicians are indicated, as respondents also reported a very high rate of "never" using these two sources. For helping professionals who do have accurate information about gays and lesbians and their lifestyles, this finding points to the greater need for them to make themselves more accessible and visible so as to be able to provide the supportive services needed by these families. For professionals lacking education and current information about homosexuals and their lifestyles, the first step is to acquire this information and become knowledgeable in order to be considered as available to provide informational and supportive services to these families when needed.

In light of the dual levels of adaptation, the individual-to-family fit seems primarily completed for these families, as the majority of them reported using their own family members as a source of support. In addition, most families reported feeling comfortable with their gay or lesbian member's homosexuality. Questions about the individual-to-family fit for those families in the *resistance* phase do arise, however. Those families in the resistance phase might typify families in which a member has recently come out and the family response is to avoid this new information. Since 30% of the non-respondents had been FFOGL members for less than 3 months, and 43% of the non-respondents had not attended any monthly FFOGL meetings in the past year, it suggests that many of the non-respondents might have been in this resistance phase. How a family responds to a member's homosexuality determines whether a healthy or unhealthy individual-to-family fit transpires. And a family's response is partly determined by the resources available to them. This would seem to indicate the even greater need to have accessible and visible sources of information and support for these families in the resistance phase, in order to facilitate a healthy individual-to-family fit. The use of supportive services can help maintain family stability as such families address the issue. Lack of accessible and available sources of accurate information and support may stall families in the resistance phase and disrupt stable family functioning, whereas these same families, with adequate sources of information and support, might otherwise be able more successfully to restructure and maintain family stability. More accessible and available sources of support—that is, well-informed sources of support—are needed to help these families effectively cope and adapt. Properly informed helping professionals can facilitate a healthy individual-to-family fit.

It is important to consider not only how the lack of accessible and available resources for families impacts a family's reaction to a member's coming out, but also the ensuing ramifications for the individual's own coming out process. Coleman (1981/1982) has identified five developmental stages in the coming out process for the individual. These are: (a) pre-coming out, (b) coming out, (c) exploration, (d) first relationships, and (e) identity integration. The individual may come out to his or her family in the coming out stage, or perhaps at a later point, in the integration stage in which a more concerted effort is made to incorporate both public and private aspects of one's life. In whatever stage the individual does come out, the availability and accessibility of supportive services may be crucial to fostering a healthy individual-to-family fit. Supportive services for families might facilitate the process of healthy identity integration for the individual. Concomitantly, the benefit for the family may be family systems maintenance during the process of learning to cope with and adapt to their member's homosexuality.

The family-to-community fit, on the other hand, is very weak, as evidenced by the extremely limited support in the community for these families. Outside of their own families, there appears to be a paucity of support in the larger community, except for support groups such as FFOGL. Even then, the visibility of groups such as FFOGL is questioned. McCubbin and Patterson (1983) reiterate that a major determinant of successful family adaptation is the achievement of a healthy fit on both the individual-to-family level and the family-to-community level. Well informed educators and clinicians might facilitate a healthier family-to-community fit by being more accessible and available to these families. Educators and clinicians may be the crucial link that provides these families with support in the community. On one level, these professionals might be the only source of support within the larger community for some of these families. Considering that respondents in the present study reported a high rate of "never" and "seldom" using friends and relatives for support, there appears to be an emphatic need for professionals to fill this void. Perhaps because of the social ambiguity or the stigma often attached to homosexuality, or both, there may be a hesitancy to use friends and relatives for support, whereas professionals may be viewed as a "safe" source of support—as long as they are perceived as available and accessible. Professionals might help families expand their sources of support by directing them to support groups such as FFOGL, or by starting new support groups so that these families have more contact with other families in the community.

On a second level, educators and other helping professionals might become more involved in actively providing more accurate information about homosexuality, gays and lesbians, and their lifestyles to the larger community so that the community as a whole becomes more knowledgeable. With a fearful and misinformed public, the opportunity for these families to achieve a healthy family-to-community fit is stifled, which, in turn, stymies successful family coping and adaptation. Pilisuk and Parks' (1983) statement exemplifies the necessity of the community in taking partial responsibility for fostering and obtaining a healthy family-to-community fit. "If it made limited sense to treat an individual and then send that individual back to a pathology inducing family, it makes limited sense to treat the family and send it back to a dysfunctional community (p. 137). This statement reiterates the respondents' overwhelming expression of the need for more education and accurate information about gays and lesbians and their lifestyles, and helping professionals of all kinds to be more knowledgeable about the same.

SUMMARY

This study points to the respondents' expression of the need for counselors and psychotherapists to become better informed about homosexuality, and gays and lesbians and their lifestyles. These professionals need to be more available and more accessible for families experiencing difficulty in addressing the issue of a family member's homosexuality. As a greater number of families continue to face issues surrounding their member's coming out, from a preventive mental health perspective, it would appear to be essential for counseling and educational professionals to meet the challenge. Open discussion in regard to homosexuality is most often lacking. Breaking this taboo, this fear of communication and dialogue, may be a beginning step in providing these families with the supportive services they need. Offering these families educational and supportive services can help prevent a family crisis and alleviate the problematic nature many families face as a member comes out. Kantor and Lehr (1975) acknowledge the importance of families having the opportunity to attain what they need to maintain healthy family functioning. "Few conditions are neither more pathetic or tragic than an awareness of what is wanted or needed, combined with the lack of ability or freedom or confidence to attain it" (p. 49). Counselors and psychotherapists can assist these families in meeting the demands placed on the system as they deal with their family member's homosexuality and coming out in a time in which homosexuality continues to be widely misunderstood.

APPENDIX
Suggested Reading List for Families

Borhek, M. (1983). *Coming out to parents: A two-way survival guide for lesbians and gay men and their parents.* New York: Pilgrim Press.

Clark, D. (1977). *Loving someone gay.* New York: New American Library.

Fairchild, B., & Hayward, N. (1979). *Now that you know: What every parent should know about homosexuality.* New York: Harcourt, Brace, Jovanovich.

Kantrowitz, B., Greenberg, N., McKillop, P., Starr, M., & Burgower, B. (1986, January 13). Growing up gay. *Newsweek*, pp. 50–52.

Kelly, M. (1985, November 1). Teen-age homosexuality. *The Washington Post*, Sec. B, p. 5.

National Gay Task Force. (1972). Twenty questions about homosexuality. Available from author, 80 5th Ave., New York, NY 10011.

Reese, M., & Abramson P. (1986, January 13). One family's struggle. *Newsweek*, pp. 55–58.

Silverstein, C. (1977). *A family matter: A parent's guide to homosexuality.* New York: McGraw-Hill.

REFERENCES

Clark, D. (1977). *Loving someone gay.* New York: New American Library.

Coleman, E. (1981/82). Developmental stages of the coming out process. *Journal of Homosexuality*, 7(2/3), 31–43.

Fairchild, B., & Hayward, N. (1979). *Now that you know: What every parent should know about homosexuality.* New York: Harcourt, Brace, Jovanovich.

Gonsiorek, J. (1982). An introduction to mental health issues and homosexuality. *American Behavioral Scientist, 25*(4), 367–384.

Hill, R. (1949). *Families under stress.* New York: Harper & Row.

Kantor, D., & Lehr, W. (1979). *Inside the family.* San Francisco: Jossey-Bass.

McCubbin, H., Joy, C., Cauble, A., Comeau, J., Patterson, J., & Needle, R. (1980). Family stress, coping, and social support: A decade review. *Journal of Marriage and the Family, 42*, 125–141.

McCubbin, H., Joy, C., Cauble, A., Comeau, J., Patterson, J., & Needle, R. (1981). Family stress, coping, and social support: Recent research and theory. In C. Davidson (Ed.), *Systematic assessment of family stress, resources and coping: Tools for research, education, and clinical intervention* (pp. 149–198). St. Paul: Department of Family Social Science, University of Minnesota.

McCubbin, H., & Patterson, J. (1983). The family stress process: The double ABCX model of adjustment and adaptation. *Marriage and Family Review, 6*(1/2), 7–37.

National Gay Task Force. (1972). *Twenty questions about homosexuality.* Available from author, 80 5th Ave., New York, NY 10011.

Pilisuk, M., & Parks, S. (1983). Social support and family stress. *Marriage and Family Review, 6*(1/2), 137–156.

Silverstein, C. (1977). *A family matter: A parent's guide to homosexuality.* New York: McGraw-Hill.

IV. SPECIAL PROBLEMS

Alcoholics Anonymous
and Gay American Men

Robert J. Kus, RN, PhD

The University of Iowa

SUMMARY. Self-help groups can be powerful tools for self-change. Thus, counselors and other professionals are wise to consider referrals to such groups when possible. In this article, the nature of self-help groups is explored in general, and Alcoholics Anonymous (A.A.) in particular. A.A. was chosen because it is the "grandparent" of all 12-Step groups, it has proven effective over time, and because of the pandemic incidence of alcoholism among homosexual American men. Therefore, professionals should be well aware of this invaluable resource for the treatment of alcoholism. This article explores the homosexual alcoholic man in relation to A.A., as well as how professionals may be supportive of the gay A.A. member. Finally, some suggestions are provided about how rural homosexual alcoholic men might be better treated.

In 1985, people from all over the world gathered in Montreal, Quebec to celebrate the 50th anniversary of the founding of Alcoholics Anonymous. This event was important for many reasons. First, A.A. claims that the organization has saved untold numbers of lives. Before A.A.'s founding, alcoholism was seen as untreatable and always fatal. Although no cure seems evident, it can be arrested. A.A. has proven to be a very effective way of doing so. Further, the members of this powerful social movement describe finding a spiritual way of living which can be used by all people. Second, the celebration of A.A.'s birthday was important in

Dr. Kus is a nurse-sociologist specializing in the fields of gay studies and alcohol studies and is Assistant Professor in the College of Nursing, The University of Iowa, Iowa City. Correspondence may be addressed to the author, 110 Hackberry Street, North Liberty, IA 52317.

that A.A. has been the prototype of self-help groups. Many other self-help groups have modeled their groups after A.A. By studying how A.A. works, one can get a better understanding of the power inherent in the entire self-help movement.

Finally, A.A.'s birthday held a special meaning for American homosexual adults, for alcoholism is believed to be the number one health problem among both male and female homosexuals, afflicting between 25–33% of this population (Fifield, 1975; Lohrenz, Connelly, Coyne, & Spare, 1978; and Saghir & Robbins, 1973). Thus, today millions of American homosexual alcoholics have a source of help not available before 1935.

This article will take a brief look at self-help groups in terms of their functions and limitations, and further, a look at the roles professionals can have in relation to them. Next will be an exploration of one self-help group, A.A., in detail; specifically, A.A.'s history, purpose, membership, types of groups and meetings, and its literature.

This article will also profile the homosexual alcoholic man and see how he is both similar to, and different from, other alcoholics. Because this article is based on homosexual men's research, the discussion is limited to gay American men; what is said about these gay men is not necessarily true for lesbian Americans or lesbians in other countries.

To follow will be an examination of the homosexual alcoholic's initial encounters with A.A. and how the professional can be of assistance, a look at homosexual groups of A.A. in terms of their positive aspects and possible limitations, and consideration of how alcoholics can experience A.A. through time as a spiritual way of life.

Finally, a look will be taken at the special needs of rural homosexual alcoholic men and some suggestions offered as to how they can be better treated. At the end of the article, the reader is provided with resources from which to get further information.

SELF-HELP GROUPS: A BRIEF OVERVIEW

The Nature of Self-Help Groups

Self-help groups are groups in which the members provide their own source of help. Professionals are rarely involved in the facilitation of these groups. By their definition, they are self-run and self-facilitated. Although there are different types of self-help groups, they usually subscribe to certain underlying assumptions.

One, there is the belief that only "fellow travelers" (Goffman, 1963) can be truly understanding of one who has "been there." Not only doesn't one have to "reinvent the wheel" in describing one's experiences with fellow travelers, but one is less likely to be able to engage in dishonesty with persons who have experienced the same problem. Traditionally, self-help groups have been formed because helping professionals have lacked the desire, knowledge, or time to be of help to people with a particular problem.

Two, there is usually the belief that one's problem is too much to solve by oneself. But in group, there is strength. As Eller and King (in press) point out, individuals' differences are transcended in self-help groups so that unity builds a power base that is collectively sustained and useful.

Three, there is the belief that one can always improve, and with the group's help, self-improvement is possible.

Four, for the individual to change, the individual is the primary therapist, not a counselor or other professional. Counselors and other professionals are merely assistants providing tools which help the individual to engage in change. The belief that the individual must always be the primary therapist in the psychosocial realms is difficult for some Americans to accept. Many Americans are prone to believe in professionals' "magic" to do something to "fix them." Thus, they erroneously see psychosocial professionals' works much as they see pills or surgery. One just sits back and lets others do something to fix them. "Magical thinking" is not supported by self-help groups.

Five, self-help groups usually place a great deal of emphasis on sharing of self with others to show that one's problems are not unique, but rather, are common to group members. Thus, rigorous honesty is called for. Members are expected to discuss what life was like before coming to the group, what happened to lead the person to the group, and what life is like now with the group's help.

Six, self-help groups try to replace "negatives" with "positives." Rather than simply eliminating the unwanted behavior, the group member would replace this with a quality life state which involves freedom from the unwanted behavior, plus happiness resulting from engaging in a program of recovery. For example, parents who beat their children are shown in groups such as Parents Anonymous not only how to cease such behavior, but also how to discipline their children with love and responsibility.

Types of Self-Help Groups

Self-help groups are usually formed to help members deal with a single issue such as alcoholism, internalized homophobia, compulsive gambling, and so on. While some are free, others cost money. Usually, 12-Step programs are free. Self-help groups may also be classified on the basis of whether they see themselves as life-long or merely temporary. Groups such as Alcoholics Anonymous are seen as life-long, for alcoholism is a life-long phenomenon, while a group focusing on internalized homophobia may see itself as time-limited.

The type of self-help group most relevant for our discussion here is that known as the 12-Step group. Based on the 12 Steps of recovery established by A.A., these groups value anonymity and other A.A. traditions. And although they are formed to help members overcome a particular problem, such as compulsive gambling, these groups see their program of recovery as a life-long one which is a spiritual way of life. Thus, although a young man might go to an A.A. meeting initially to learn how to abstain from alcohol, that is not necessarily why he would continue to attend A.A. meetings over time. Rather, people often continue going to 12-Step meetings not only to share their experiences, strength, and hope with the newcomers, but also because they see the 12-Step program as a concrete way of achieving increased spiritual growth. Some of the more well known Twelve-Step groups include Alcoholics Anonymous, Narcotics Anonymous, Gamblers Anonymous, Overeaters Anonymous, Valium Anonymous, Cocaine Anonymous, Parents Anonymous, Sexaholics Anonymous, and Sex Addicts Anonymous. In addition to these, there are also 12-Step programs for those who are in relationships with members of the above-mentioned groups, and who have life problems based on their unhealthy relationships with members of these groups. For example, the non-alcoholic lover of an alcoholic may become a "co-dependent." He may engage in behaviors such as rescuing the alcoholic from his drinking by making excuses for his lover's drinking. He may also experience a host of psychosocial and biophysical symptoms reflecting this unhealthy relationship (Whitney, 1982). Thus, he may greatly benefit from a 12-Step group geared to him, such as Al-Anon family groups.

Limitations of Self-Help Groups

The value of self-help groups, and especially the 12-Step-based ones, have demonstrated their worth mainly by the number of groups which have been established and the increased number of people who make use of them. But these groups also have certain limitations which must be recognized.

First, they are not professionally run or facilitated groups. Because of this, such groups do not pretend to have the answers for all of life's situations or problems. Thus, an A.A. group is not usually equipped to deal with a variety of serious psychological or psychiatric disorders. While the groups do not try to be "all things to all people," some individuals try to forego necessary psychological or psychiatric care and simply depend upon the self-help group.

Second, self-help groups require the rigorous honesty of their members, for it is through the honest sharing of self that both self and other members can achieve insight. Because alcoholism, like other compulsive disorders, is rationalized by denial, rigorous honesty often eludes the member. When the member is not able to be honest with self and fellow group members, the effectiveness of the program is greatly diminished.

Third, self-help implies that persons who join these groups want to change. Not only does the member want to eliminate negative behaviors, but he or she also wants to replace them with new, positive behaviors. For some people, this is too much. They refuse to abandon faulty ways of thinking or acting, and they refuse to engage in the prescriptions of the group, such as engaging in prayer and meditation.

Fourth, members may misinterpret what the group says. This is very likely when the member harbors hostile feelings about recovery in the first place. It is because of this that helping professionals must know the nature of the group's beliefs so that misinterpretations can be corrected immediately if the group member is a client in therapy. For example, a young man angry about being alcoholic, and angry about the idea of abstinence from alcohol, might tell his therapist that the A.A. group tells him he can never drink again for as long as he lives. On the surface, this is true. But the wise therapist would ask if, in actuality, the group talked about not drinking for "today," for these 24 hours, rather than "forever." This would probably be the case. Likewise, the client may say that A.A. said he could never take medications again. This, too, would be highly unlikely. Thus, misinterpretation of what members of self-help groups say can also limit their effectiveness for the individual member, and this possibility points out the necessity of helping professionals being thoroughly familiar with the teachings and slogans of such groups.

Finally, members going to self-help groups may engage in "magical" thinking. Instead of seeing themselves as their own primary therapist, they enter the group expecting the group to "fix them" and become angry when the "group didn't work for me." This will be discussed later when we address the issue of whether A.A. can "work for" everyone.

In sum, there are limitations of both self-help groups and their members. It is helpful, therefore, for the professional to know these and be able to address them in therapy.

The Role of Helping Professionals in Relation to Self-Help Groups

Helping professionals such as nurses, social workers, physicians, clergy, counselors, and others may play an important role in relation to self-help groups. But to play effective roles, two things are necessary. First, professionals need to know what self-help groups are available, what they can and cannot offer, and who can be a member. Further, they need to know the nature of the group to counteract any misinterpretations of the client. Second, they must possess enough self-confidence in their professional skills to be willing to "let go." Often clients will grow significantly upon practicing a self-help program, whereas they experienced little growth while in professional therapy. Only a self-confident professional will be pleased to see this positive change.

Thus, the role of helping professionals in relationship to non-professional self-help groups involves three elements. One, they may encourage the founding of such groups where there are none. It takes only two persons to have a self-help group. So if two clients present with the same difficulty and express a wish for a self-help group, the professional may get these clients together to form such a group or provide information on how to start a self-help group. Two, they may make referrals to such groups. Often clients lack knowledge of community resources, knowledge which the professional possesses. Referrals benefit not only the client, but add new lifeblood to the group. And because one of the beliefs in self-help groups is that by helping others one helps oneself, referrals provide new opportunities for group members to grow by sharing self with the newcomers. Three, helping professionals may provide support for clients, especially in the initial encounter with the self-help group. Often the client is ashamed, fearful, or angry when going to a self-help group. The professional can provide reassurance that these feelings will subside in time, and can give the client positive feedback for his or her continued attendance and for "working the program" prescribed by the group.

Summary and Conclusions

In summary, self-help groups are powerful tools for persons wishing to engage in change. Such groups help individuals rid themselves of negative ways of thinking and acting, and replace these with new, positive, ways of thinking and acting. While there are limitations to self-help groups, many of the limitations are due to members who are unwilling to follow the program of the group. Helping professionals need to know all they can about such groups in order intelligently to refer clients, to correct misinterpretations clients may have about the groups, and to support clients' attempts to make themselves available to the programs the groups have to offer.

Because it would be impossible to discuss all self-help groups in depth, this article will now look at the "grandparent" group of them all, Alcoholics Anonymous. This group is chosen for specific discussion because all helping professionals dealing with homosexual men are wise to be thoroughly familiar with it because of the extremely high incidence of alcoholism among homosexual American men.

INSIDE ALCOHOLICS ANONYMOUS

A Brief History

The origins of A.A. have been recounted in the biography of one of the co-founders of A.A. After many years of alcoholic drinking, broken promises to his wife Lois that he'd never drink again, and repeated hospitalizations, New York business person Bill Wilson entered Towns Hospital under the care of Dr. Silkworth. There, he waited for the end, for insanity or death. However, a strange phenomenon happened which would forever change the course of alcoholism treatment. Here is the story recounted in Bill's biography, *Pass It On* (Alcoholics Anonymous, 1984):

> Now, he and Lois were waiting for the end. Now, there was nothing ahead but death or madness. This was the finish, the jumping-off place. "The terrifying darkness had become complete," Bill said. "In agony of spirit, I again thought of the cancer of alcoholism which had now consumed me in mind and spirit, and soon the body." The abyss gaped before him.
>
> In his helplessness and desperation, Bill cried out, "I'll do anything, anything at all!" He had reached a point of total, utter deflation—a state of complete, absolute surrender. With neither faith nor hope, he cried, "If there be a God, let Him show Himself!"
>
> What happened next was electric. "Suddenly, my room blazed with an indescribably white light. I was seized with an ecstasy beyond description. Every joy I had known was pale by comparison. The light, the ecstasy—I was conscious of nothing else for a time.
>
> "Then, seen in the mind's eye, there was a mountain. I stood upon its summit, where a great wind blew. A wind, not of air, but of spirit. In great, clean strength, it blew right through me. Then came the blazing thought 'You are a free man.' I know not at all how long I remained in this state, but finally the light and the ecstasy subsided. I again saw the wall of my room. As I became more quiet, a great peace stole over me, and this was accompanied by a sensation difficult to describe. I became acutely conscious of a Presence which seemed like a veritable sea of living spirit. I lay on the shores of a new world. 'This,' I thought, 'must be the great reality. The God of the preachers.'
>
> "Savoring my new world, I remained in this state for a long time. I seemed to be possessed by the absolute, and the curious conviction deepened that no matter how wrong things seemed to be, there could

be no question of the ultimate rightness of God's universe. For the first time, I felt that I really belonged. I knew that I was loved and could love in return. I thanked my God, who had given me a glimpse of His absolute self. Even though a pilgrim upon an uncertain highway, I need be concerned no more, for I had glimpsed the great beyond." (pp. 120–121).

Bill had just had his 39th birthday. He never drank again.

But Bill's freedom was based not only on his unusual spiritual experience, but also had roots in the Oxford Group, a movement emphasizing absolute purity, honesty, unselfishness, and love. Bill was particularly attracted to the principle of honesty.

To say Bill had freedom doesn't mean that he was no longer tempted to drink. On the contrary. In June of 1935, Bill traveled to Akron, Ohio on business. Feeling the need to talk to another alcoholic, for sharing his story with other alcoholics is what he believed kept him sober, he picked the name of a clergyman at random out of the Akron telephone directory, a Rev. Walter F. Tunks. After telling Rev. Tunks his desire to speak to another alcoholic, he was given the names of 10 men who might be able to give him the name of a fellow alcoholic.

Bill called all 10 of these without luck. However, the last man referred him to Henrietta Seiberling, a member of a prominent Akron rubber industry family. When Bill introduced himself as a "rum hound from New York" and told her of his search for another alcoholic, Henrietta had him come immediately to her 65-room mansion called Stan Hywet Hall (which means "Rock is found here" in Welch). There, she also invited an Akron physician suffering from alcoholism, Dr. Bob Smith.

On June 10, 1935, Bill gave Bob a bottle of beer and talked to him about what he had found, that by sharing one's self, one could stay sober. That bottle of beer was the last alcohol Dr. Bob would ever consume. Therefore, it is June 10, 1935 which is celebrated as the birthday of A.A. Since that date, A.A. has grown phenomenally throughout the world. In the United States, virtually no one is far from an A.A. group.

Purpose

The purpose of A.A. is to help members solve their common problem, alcoholism, and to help others recover from alcoholism. This is done through the fellowship of A.A. in which members share their "experience, strength, and hope" with one another.

Membership

The only requirement for membership in A.A. is a desire to stop drinking. While members were reluctant to accept homosexuals and blacks in the early days of A.A., today A.A. is composed of people of every nationality and race, all religions and those who have none, homosexuals, bisexuals, and heterosexuals, young and old, obscure and famous, rich and poor.

The term "loner member" refers to those A.A. persons who do not attend A.A. meetings. Often such persons are away from any A.A. group, such as soldiers sent away or sailors at sea for many months. Such members can still live A.A. and share themselves with other A.A. members via telephone or letters.

"Working the Program"

A.A. is not a series of meetings to attend; it is a way of life to be lived. This way of life is often referred to by members as "working the program." In a current research study being conducted by this author on how homosexual American men of A.A. go about "working their program," it appears that working the program involves five activities.

First, working the 12 Steps of A.A. is the basic foundation of working one's program. (These steps are listed later.) Second, regularly attending A.A. meetings is seen as very important in maintaining high quality sobriety. Third, reading A.A. Conference-approved, as well as non-Conference, literature is seen as important. The former is "official" literature of A.A. and is so marked by a triangle enclosed within a circle. This literature is also identifiable by the fact it is published by Alcoholics Anonymous World Services, Inc. Examples of Conference-approved literature include *Alcoholics Anonymous* (Alcoholics Anonymous, 1976), more commonly known as the Big Book, *Twelve Steps and Twelve Traditions* (Alcoholics Anonymous, 1952, 1953), written by co-founder Bill W., *Living Sober*, which was written by a gay man, Barry L., and other books and pamphlets. Many A.A. members find non-Conference approved literature also useful. For example, many use daily meditation books written especially for A.A. members. Many A.A. members include spiritual and inspirational readings as part of working their program.

Fourth, recalling A.A. slogans when one begins to be overwhelmed by everyday life is seen as another aspect of "working the program." For example, when members find their lives getting too stressful, they may bring to mind such A.A. slogans as "Easy Does It," "One Day at a Time," or "Live and Let Live." They also may bring to mind sayings such as H.A.L.T.—don't get too hungry, angry, lonely, or tired.

The fifth and final way of working the program involves engaging in non-A.A. activities which are the result of working the program of A.A. For example, many gay men find that by conscientiously working the 12 Steps, they begin to see being gay as a positive aspect of self rather than a negative one. Further, they may find that to be a responsible gay person, one should involve self in gay liberation activities. Such activities, whether registering gays to vote, visiting gay AIDS patients in a hospice, or doing volunteer counseling for fellow gay men, are seen as part of working the program.

Clues or symptoms of not working the program have been identified as feelings of overwhelming stress, depression, feelings of hopelessness, feelings of resentments, and so on. In A.A. jargon, these feelings are called "stinking thinking" or being on the "pity pot." Such clues must be taken seriously, for they're the clues indicating the beginning of an alcoholic relapse if not checked.

The 12 Steps of A.A.

The foundation of working the program involves the 12 Steps of A.A. Every helping professional would be wise to learn these steps and explore how they're achieved, for they're the building blocks of the A.A. program. The 12 Steps are (Alcoholics Anonymous, 1976):

1. We admitted we were powerless over alcohol—that our lives had become unmanageable.
2. Came to believe that a Power greater than ourselves could restore us to sanity.
3. Made a decision to turn our will and our lives over to the care of God *as we understood Him.*
4. Made a searching and fearless moral inventory of ourselves.
5. Admitted to God, to ourselves and to another human being the exact nature of our wrongs.
6. Were entirely ready to have God remove all these defects of character.
7. Humbly asked Him to remove our shortcomings.
8. Made a list of all persons we had harmed and became willing to make amends to them all.
9. Made direct amends to such people wherever possible except when to do so would injure them or others.
10. Continued to take personal inventory and when we were wrong promptly admitted it.
11. Sought through prayer and meditation to improve our conscious contact with God *as we understood Him,* praying only for knowledge of His will for us and the power to carry that out.
12. Having had a spiritual awakening as the result of these steps, we tried to carry this message to alcoholics, and to practice these principles in all our affairs (pp. 58–60).

On the surface, it would seem this is a very simple spiritual program of living. And it is. However, as A.A. members are quick to point out, "this is a simple program for complex people." Many books and pamphlets and talks have been developed elaborating how to practice the 12 Steps of A.A. Thus, perhaps it's more difficult than imagined at first glance. For example, being "entirely ready to have God remove all these defects of character" is not so easy. By looking closely at the 12 Steps, one might come to the conclusion that they could serve as a spiritual foundation for virtually anyone, alcoholic or not. And this leads to the question, "Does A.A. work for all alcoholics?"

A.A. is neither a pill nor a surgical procedure performed upon a human. It is a way of life to be lived. Thus, the real question is not whether A.A. can "work for" all alcoholics, but rather, can all alcoholics live A.A.? The Big Book (Alcoholics Anonymous, 1976) answers this question in this way:

> Rarely have we seen a person fail who has thoroughly followed our path. Those who do not recover are people who cannot or will not completely give themselves to this simple program, usually men and women who are constitutionally incapable of being honest with themselves. There are such unfortunates. They are not at fault; they seem to have been born that way. They are naturally incapable of grasping and developing a manner of living which demands rigorous honesty. Their chances are less than average. There are those, too, who suffer from grave emotional and mental disorders, but many of them do recover if they have the capacity to be honest. (p. 58).

The A.A. Traditions

While the 12 Steps are the basic building blocks for the individual's recovery, the 12 Traditions (Alcoholics Anonymous, 1952, 1953) are the basic building blocks for A.A. as an organization. They are:

1. Our common welfare should come first; personal recovery depends upon A.A. unity.
2. For our group purpose there is but one ultimate authority—a loving God as He may express Himself in our group conscience. Our leaders are but trusted servants; they do not govern.
3. The only requirement for A.A. membership is a desire to stop drinking.
4. Each group should be autonomous, except in matters affecting other groups or A.A. as a whole.
5. Each group has but one primary purpose—to carry its message to the alcoholic who still suffers.

6. An A.A. group ought never endorse, finance, or lend the A.A. name to any related facility or outside enterprise, lest problems of money, property, and prestige divert us from our primary purpose.
7. Every A.A. group ought to be fully self-supporting, declining outside contributions.
8. Alcoholics Anonymous should remain forever nonprofessional, but our service centers may employ special workers.
9. A.A., as such, ought never be organized; but we may create service boards or committees directly responsible to those they serve.
10. Alcoholics Anonymous has no opinion on outside issues; hence the A.A. name ought never be drawn into public controversy.
11. Our public relations policy is based on attraction rather than promotion; we need always maintain personal anonymity at the level of press, radio, and films.
12. Anonymity is the spiritual foundation of all our traditions, ever reminding us to place principles before personalities. (Alcoholics Anonymous, 1952, 1953).

Types of Groups

A.A. groups may be general or specific. A general group is one in which all alcoholics are most heartily welcomed. Specialized groups, on the other hand, although they technically must welcome any A.A. member, are by local custom "geared" for certain "types" of A.A. members. For example, a community might have non-smokers' or women's A.A. groups. Certainly, a smoker could attend the non-smokers' group just as a man could attend the women's group. However, courtesy calls for the special nature of the group to be honored. In small towns, one usually only finds general groups. In large cities, however, specialized groups abound and could include groups as esoteric as a Jewish lesbian non-smokers' A.A. group. Specialized gay men's groups and gay/lesbian groups will be discussed later in this article.

The Meeting: Types

Just as there are different types of A.A. groups, there are different types of meetings. The basic classification is whether the meeting is closed or open. A closed meeting means that only A.A. members, i.e., anyone who desires to stop drinking, should attend. An open meeting, on the other hand, means that the meeting is open to the general public, such as family and friends of the A.A. member, students of nursing or social work out to learn more about A.A. in order to be more helpful to their clients, or anyone interested in learning more about A.A.

Besides being classified on the basis of who is welcome, meetings can be classified on the basis of the content of the particular meeting. For example, some meetings are "Step meetings" in which one of the 12 Steps is discussed. "Beginners' meetings" are designed for new A.A. members and for those exploring whether or not they are indeed alcoholic. A "speaker's meeting" is one which features a speaker who shares his or her story in depth with the group, and often this person is from a group other than the group in which they're speaking. Other meetings may be devoted to a particular issue, such as sexuality. Finally, at times groups discuss issues affecting the welfare of the group. The decisions reached by the group are called "group conscience." These are not part of the meeting per se, but usually "group conscience" is held following regular meetings.

The Meeting: Format and Content

At a typical meeting, members are first welcomed by the evening's leader who addresses him or herself by name and says, for example, "Hi, my name is Lance and I'm an alcoholic." (Increasingly, many A.A. members also say they're "addicts"; the person who abuses solely alcohol is becoming rare.) The group then responds with "Hi, Lance!" Lance then asks the members to pause for a moment of silence for the "still suffering alcoholic." After the moment of silence, Lance leads the group in the first three lines of the Serenity Prayer, "God grant me the serenity to accept the things I cannot change, courage to change the things I can, and wisdom to know the difference."

Next, Lance, or someone he asks, will read the Preamble of A.A. The Preamble reminds people that A.A. is a fellowship of men and women who are there to help each other solve their common problem. It also reminds the members that A.A.'s only requirement for membership is the desire to stop drinking, that A.A. has no dues or fees, that A.A. is not aligned with any sect, denomination, politics, organization, or institution and neither supports any causes nor engages in controversy. The Preamble finally reminds all that the purpose of A.A. is to stay sober and to help other alcoholics achieve sobriety.

Following the Preamble, Lance or another person reads "How It Works," which is a few pages from the Big Book and which includes the 12 Steps of A.A. Lance would then ask if there are any visitors or newcomers to the group. If there are, they're given the opportunity to introduce themselves and say anything they'd like to say.

Next, the leader asks if there is any special topic anyone would like to discuss, topics such as gratitude, humility, prayer. If the meeting is a "Step meeting," the leader would remind the members what Step the group is to discuss that day. Usually, the leader of the evening's meeting then gives a "lead" or personal remarks. Following this, members are given the chance to say whatever they'd like to say. The remarks members make usually reflect what life was like before, what happened to bring them to A.A. (referred to as their "bottom"), and what it's like now in "sobriety." In large meetings, not everyone always gets a chance to talk. To provide an opportunity for all to talk, some groups have established candlelight meetings on weekend nights which have a set starting time but no set ending time. Sometimes such meetings are referred to as "midnight" meetings.

Following the body of the meeting, announcements are made which might be of interest to the group. For example, "round-ups" which are like conventions of A.A. members, might be announced, or requests for signing up to clean a club house might be made if the group has a club house.

Next, the leader asks if anyone is celebrating an A.A. "birthday" or special date marking one's sobriety. Medallions ("chips") commemorating 30 days of sobriety, 60 days, 90 days, 6 months, and yearly birthdays are presented. A special medallion, called the "desire chip," is given to any persons who say they would like to stay sober for 24 hours; this chip is usually given to persons attending a meeting for the first time or for persons returning to A.A. following a relapse.

Next, members are reminded that, although there are no dues or fees in A.A., each group is self-supporting based on contributions from the members. Thus, a basket is passed around for donations, the typical donation being a dollar. These donations go to pay rent on the facility, for medallions, and for refreshments.

Most meetings then close by members standing in a circle either holding hands or having arms around each others' waists and reciting the Lord's Prayer or the Serenity Prayer. Following the prayer, which indicates the end of the meeting, members often say to new members, "Keep coming back; it works!"

After meetings, members often socialize among themselves while cleaning up the meeting facility, or meet more informally at a local restaurant. The importance of after-meeting get togethers should not be underestimated, for it is here that new friendships are established, bonds with other A.A. members are formed, and A.A. wisdom is shared.

THE GAY ALCOHOLIC

Before looking at initial encounters in A.A., it might be wise to say a few words about how homosexual alcoholics are similar to, and different from, other alcoholics, in particular heterosexual ones.

Similarities

All alcoholics by definition suffer from the disease of alcoholism. This disease is one which can negatively affect all aspects of the physical, mental, and spiritual health of the victim. Ultimately, it is potentially fatal. How severely one is affected, and how many aspects of one's being are affected, depends in large part on one's "bottom." Persons who stop drinking in the early stages of the disease, before alcohol has caused much damage to them in terms of job, relationships, and so on, are said to have "high bottoms." Persons who have experienced catastrophic calamities, such as loss of their jobs, home, family, and health, are said to have "low bottoms." Those in between are described to have experienced "medium" bottoms. But "bottoms" are relative; all persons coming to A.A. are in pain, and each person's pain is felt acutely whether one has come from "Skid Row" or is a teenager who has felt impairment in their social and family relationships.

All alcoholics seem to experience a number of similar symptoms. For example, alcoholism may negatively affect one's leisure time (Kus, 1986b), friendship circles, job or school performance and satisfaction, relationships with others, finances, mental, physical, sexual, and spiritual health. Gay alcoholic men, like other alcoholics, often experience these same symptoms which result in feelings of low self-esteem, denial, self-pity, and of being overwhelmed by life in general. But there are some differences.

Differences

Unlike the heterosexual alcoholic, the gay man coming into A.A. is usually severely self-homophobic (Kus, 1985b). Indeed, research has shown that this internalized homophobia may very well explain the etiology and the high incidence of alcoholism in gay American men. As Kus discovered, alcoholic drinking begins long before the man ever steps into a gay bar. Attending gay bars does not lead to gay alcoholism. Kus has also found that a positive gay identity can only be achieved by gay men alcoholics after sobriety has been achieved and experienced through time. Even gay men who are out and living openly gay lifestyles, if they are alcoholic, have usually only developed a facade of a positive gay identity. Alcohol serves as a denial and coping mechanism for their internalized homophobia.

Also, gay men have life-long feelings of being "different" which are experienced long before they recognize their homosexual identity (Coleman, 1982; Kus, 1985a). As will be seen later, this sense of "different-ness" has some profound implications for A.A.

First, gay alcoholics are often angry at God for being created homosexual. (Kus, 1985c). Second, they often experience estrangement due to their sexual orientation. Third, their inhibitions are lowered due to their alcohol abuse. However, because of the sexually transmitted disease Acquired Immune Deficiency Syndrome (AIDS) and the high incidence of AIDS among gay men, among other reasons, their sexual activity is sometimes perceived as "sick," "perverted," or "unhealthy"—reinforcing homophobic sentiment (Kus, 1985d).

Finally, we know little of the biological differences between gay men and other men. While biochemical differences are continually searched for (Gladue, Green, & Hellman, 1984), these differences never seem to be replicated (Gooren, in press). Are gay men more prone biochemically to alcoholism than other men? Are their immune systems biologically weaker? Only time will tell just how much gay men are biologically different from other men and how this relates to the disease of alcoholism. Nevertheless, research is needed to pursue the answers to these questions.

INITIAL ENCOUNTERS WITH A.A.

Gay alcoholics, like other alcoholics, get to A.A. by a variety of paths. Some refer themselves. Others are referred by helping professionals, lovers, spouses, employers, or alcoholic treatment centers. Regardless of the path taken to get to A.A., the path is rarely an easy one. Getting to a first A.A. meeting causes many pain and fear. While referral to A.A. is a simple process, it is not always easy to encourage a client to get there. After all, the main defense or rationalization of an alcoholic is denial. One denies for any number of reasons: fear of a life of abstinence, the stigma of the disease itself, the feeling of failure which one might experience if admitting to alcoholism. The professional, however, can help the client overcome some of the typical objections of why "A.A. isn't for me."

Typical Objections and Possible Therapeutic Interventions

Objections gay alcoholics may give to avoid A.A. are the same made by other alcoholics. Although the list of possible objections is theoretically limitless, there are at least nine common ones which professionals are most likely to hear.

1. "I'm just too busy to go to A.A. meetings." A good response by the therapist might be, "If you've decided this might be helpful, how can you make time for your meetings?"
2. "Oh, I've been to A.A. meetings before and saw guys who went to the meetings and then went right out to a bar and got drunk after the

meetings." This may indeed have been observed. But many alcoholics did not go to the bar. The professional might point out that not everyone finds A.A. to be helpful, especially initially, but that many persons do recover if they continue attending the meetings.

3. "I can't go to an A.A. meeting! Someone might recognize me! What would it do to my reputation!" The therapist might point out that "if others recognize you there, you'll recognize them. It's doubtful they would want to tell others you've been there any more than they would want you to tell others they were there. A.A. believes very strongly in the principle of anonymity. Therefore, don't let your fear prevent you from recovery."

4. "I've had friends go to A.A. and now they're A.A. junkies." This objection reflects hurt, and anger, and fear. First, the client may be hurt as his A.A. friends no longer have time for him; alcohol-based lives are not very attractive to newly sober alcoholics (Kus, 1986c). Further, this objection may indicate anger over the perceived "rejection" by the A.A. friends; "just who do they think they are?" Finally, this objection may indicate fear: If my friends are in A.A., and Lord knows they drank much less than I do, what does that mean for me? The professional can help the client see that he is not being rejected by the A.A. people because of something intrinsic, but rather that the A.A. friends have a new way of life. The professional might also take the opportunity to explore here how much of the client's leisure time is alcohol-related. For example, does he avoid parties where alcohol isn't served? Does he avoid restaurants which don't serve alcohol? Can he go dancing at a gay bar without drinking alcohol and still have fun? If answering honestly, the client may be surprised at some of his responses, and he may begin to see that his "A.A. junkie" friends aren't rejecting him for himself, but rather because they don't want to be around a drunk.

The client may also be told that especially in the early days of recovery, many people find that daily attendance at A.A. meetings is critical—"90 meetings in 90 days" is often encouraged in fact. However, in time, many A.A. members find they don't need to attend so many meetings. In short, the client needs to know that his commitment to A.A. doesn't have to be daily attendance at meetings, nor does it mean he is committing himself to attend "forever."

5. "A friend of mine went to A.A. and it didn't work for him." Acknowledge that. Many people don't find A.A. helpful, but it has worked for many where other treatments have failed. "It couldn't hurt to give it a try. Find out for yourself. Go to six sessions and then let's talk."

6. "I can't handle the God stuff. I'm not into religion." This rhetoric reflects not only misinformation which the professional needs to clear up, but it may also indicate deep feelings of estrangement or anger on the part of the gay man.

As for the misconceptions, it can be explained that A.A. is not a religion and is not aligned with any religion. Spirituality is something all people have; religion is not. An atheist can be a member of A.A. and achieve quality sobriety. The notion of "God" is whatever one chooses the notion to be. For some, "God" or a "Higher Power" is the A.A. group itself. For others, God is the conception taught by the Judeo-Christian religions. For others, "God" is a force. And for some, "God" is self. (Kus, 1985c)

But this objection may indicate more than misinformation; it may indicate feelings of rejection, "God hates gays and therefore rejects me," or feelings of anger, "How could you be so cruel to create me gay?" How these feelings can be dealt with will be discussed in the section on gay groups of A.A.

7. "I can't stand sitting listening to a bunch of drunkalogs. I have enough problems myself without listening to drunks' war stories." Drunkalogs, or the "how it was like before A.A." stories of alcoholics, can be very frightening to the new A.A. person; mirrors often are. And one thing is certain: no matter how unique a person's drunkalog is, there is often enough in it to hit home for any other alcoholic in the room— drinking before parties in case there's not enough booze there, hiding alcohol around the house, using breath mints to hide alcohol on one's breath, and so on. Thus, one person's drunkalog is often another person's mirror.

And yet A.A. groups composed of persons who sit around and only talk about their "war stories" often miss the importance of the other aspects of A.A. or dealing with their present feelings. Not all groups are effective. Telling clients that they should "shop around" can alleviate their fears of getting stuck in an unproductive group.

8. "I tried it before and didn't like it." This objection might indicate a lack of understanding of A.A. in that the person seems to believe that A.A. equals meetings rather than a way of life. It also might indicate an unrealistic view of "first impressions." Finally, it may reflect a good judgment of a particular group. The professional might explore with the gay man what, specifically, it was about A.A. he didn't like. Does he see A.A. as meetings rather than a way of living? Does he know that each A.A. group has its own "flavor," and that perhaps the one he came in contact with wasn't the one for him but another one might be?

9. Finally, alcoholics may have specific objections. "The meetings are too smokey" is a good example. Others might be complaints about the location of the meeting, the fact that the building is too hot, too cold, or too far from home. Virtually all such complaints might be realistic, but often can be "red herrings" to cover the real issue of the client's denial system. Sometimes the objections can be overcome simply by suggesting the client go to a non-smokers' meeting. If this is not available, suggest

to the client that he explore with the group a rule allowing only one or two to smoke at a time, or keep the door open and sit by the door. Have non-smoking and smoking sections where possible. In short, the client is encouraged not to let externals prevent recovery.

On another level, the professional might have to confront the client's denial system. For example, the therapist might say, "Those complaints provide you with a good excuse to avoid looking more directly at your alcoholism. You sound like you might be afraid of this."

The Role of the Sponsor

For many alcoholics, having a sponsor in A.A. is seen as useful. A sponsor is similar to a guide, a guide "to help one travel on an unknown path."

Like the helping professional, the A.A. sponsor chosen by the new member must be willing to listen, to answer questions, and to provide information about the Steps, Traditions, and logistics of the organization. In the early days of sobriety, the gay man might feel the need to contact the sponsor on a daily basis. The feelings which had been anesthetized by alcohol for many years often come to the surface and may be quite baffling, overwhelming, and painful. Thus, the sponsor should be able to reassure the man that this is normal, to provide emotional support, and to explain that, in time, the pain often subsides (Kus, 1986a).

Further, the sponsor should be willing to give the man positive reinforcement whenever possible. He may also make helpful suggestions to the new A.A. member, such as to attend more than one meeting per week, to listen more than talk, to get to know other A.A. members, and to read the Big Book. The sponsor often provides practical assistance for the new A.A. member, such as giving him rides to the meetings, introducing him to the other members, and socializing with him after meetings.

GAY GROUPS OF ALCOHOLICS ANONYMOUS

Background

As early as 1945, A.A. co-founder Bill W. realized that quite often gay and bisexual men of A.A. were having difficulty in maintaining sobriety and "living the program." At a lunch with three women and a gay A.A. man named Barry L. of New York, Bill wondered whether or not there should be special gay groups of A.A. He asked Barry L. how much sobriety he had attained. Barry replied that he had been sober for 11 months. Bill told Barry to come back when he had achieved 18 months of sobriety and discuss whether there should be gay groups. Barry never went back for that talk with Bill (L., 1985).

Also during this period, A.A. was faced with accepting not only gay men, but also blacks. The debate about whether to admit all persons to A.A. who had a desire to stop drinking was, in large part, ended by Dr. Bob. Faced with whether to admit all persons who had a drinking problem, Dr. Bob said, "What would the Master do in a situation like this? A man is a member of A.A. if HE says so, not if WE say so" (L., 1985). Thus, the third tradition of A.A. was formed: The only requirement for membership in A.A. is a desire to stop drinking. Thus, gays and blacks were welcomed, at least on a philosophical level.

But many gay men felt they needed special groups. Some felt both overt and covert homophobia in regular A.A. meetings. Others felt A.A. members seemed to preach the non-uniqueness of members too much and that, indeed, the differentness felt by gay men needed to be dealt with, not ignored (Bittle, 1982).

In any case, gay men's groups of A.A. were formed, as were groups for lesbian women and mixed groups of gay men and lesbians.

Gay Groups of A.A.: The Positives

Gay groups have many positive aspects or functions. First, the gay alcoholic man seems to establish trust with other members more quickly than in a regular A.A. group. Second, he can talk about his feelings of being "different." He will find that, indeed, he is not "terminally unique." Rather, he is like all alcoholics. But unlike heterosexual alcoholics, his feelings of being different stemming from his gay self are not only valid, but are shared by the other gay members. Third, gay groups can also alleviate much of the gay man's internalized homophobia. The most effective way of reducing homophobia is to meet and get to know gay persons (Kus, 1985a). Fourth, by getting to know gay alcoholics who have attained sobriety, the new gay member can begin building a new support system (Kus, 1986c). Fifth, and perhaps most importantly, the gay group can help the new gay A.A. member see how the A.A. program is applicable not only to alcoholism, but also to the gay man's sexual identity. For example, Kus (1986d) found that many gay men accept their gay self in a positive light by working on the 4th, 6th, and 7th Steps of A.A. In the 4th Step, many men list "homophobia" or "self-hate" as a character defect. In the 6th Step, these men ready themselves for their "Higher Power" or God to remove these defects of character, and in the 7th Step, they ask their Higher Power to remove these shortcomings. This process has enabled clients to recognize their homophobia as a character defect and to overcome it.

Another example is the notion of being powerless. One cannot change one's alcoholism any more than one can change sexual orientation. The Serenity Prayer asks that one be able to accept the things which cannot be changed, to change the things which one can, and the wisdom to know the difference. Putting these together, the gay man may move more quickly toward accepting his gay identity, rather than viewing it as a negative aspect of self. And unless the gay alcoholic can come to see his gay identity as positive, maintaining sobriety over time will be most difficult to achieve, and serenity, or the peacefulness arising from "quality sobriety," will be virtually impossible to achieve. It is important in this method that the client not view his homosexuality as an illness, for it is internalized homophobia, or non-acceptance of the homosexuality, which is negative.

Another example is that as the gay man learns to accept his sexual orientation in a positive way, he often finds himself thanking his "Higher Power" for this gift, a gift which he had previously seen as a curse (Kus, 1985c). Putting this together with the Serenity Prayer's dictum to "change the things I can," many gay men use their new-found gay self-acceptance to work for the goals of improving their life, as well as working for the improvement of the lives of other gay men, whether alcoholic or not.

But although there are many positive aspects of gay groups, there can also be some limitations.

Gay Groups of A.A.: The Limitations

First, many gay men, because they are homophobic when initially addressing their alcoholism (Kus, 1985b), often dread going to gay A.A. meetings. They may be having great difficulty accepting their alcoholism, and they also are having a difficult time letting others know of their gay identity. Thus, going to gay A.A. groups may be more difficult for the client beginning to address his alcoholism than going to a regular A.A. group.

Second, if the gay man only goes to gay groups, the homogeneity of the group may be oppressive. This is especially apparent in small towns where the total membership of the gay A.A. group is typically small. It's not too long before one not only knows everyone's stories, but also one learns nothing new. In short, by not attending other meetings in addition to gay group meetings, the gay alcoholic may not get a well-rounded perspective.

Third, romantic entanglements may be problematic in gay groups, just as they are in non-gay groups. One phenomenon which can occur is known as "13th Stepping." This refers to an older (in terms of time in A.A.) member having sex with a new A.A. member. If this relationship doesn't develop positively, and it usually doesn't, the new A.A. member is often left feeling used and abused, and he consequently may leave A.A. or the gay group. In other situations, two men of a gay group may form a relationship which may then eventually dissolve. This can cause discomfort for each of the partners as well as the entire group, and oftentimes one or both end up dropping out of the group.

Unfortunately, not enough is said in many A.A. groups about the problems which result from developing sexual intimacies with other group members. Too often these intimacies are tolerated, or may even be encouraged, by certain groups. The professional can be helpful in pointing out the problems of developing such intimacies with group members and encourage clients to use A.A. groups as support groups, not as places at which to form sexual intimacies.

Fourth, in new gay groups, the length of sobriety members have might be fairly short. Thus, new A.A. members might have a difficult time finding a sponsor or others who can provide necessary answers or role modeling.

A Note to Professionals

First, the professional can encourage gay alcoholic clients to attend some gay A.A. meetings. This should be advised given the needs of the particular client. The professional should also encourage him to attend non-gay meetings as well as gay ones. This can provide the client a more well-rounded perspective, and it will show him that much of what he experiences is quite similar to what lesbians, bisexuals, and heterosexuals experience. For example, problems with a spouse are quite similar to problems with a gay lover. Attending other meetings helps alleviate the problems of "ghettoizing" the gay man. Surrounded in a ghetto of other gay men limits the client's positive identity development (Coleman, 1981/1982). And finally, the professional should know as much as possible about alcoholism, as well as internalized homophobia, which these groups can be helpful in treating.

A NOTE ABOUT RURAL GAY ALCOHOLICS

Often gay alcoholic men in rural areas have no gay A.A. groups to attend in their communities, and these men may feel especially isolated. Thus, certain suggestions are provided here which may be of help.

First, rural gay men need to keep in mind that it takes only two people to make a meeting. Thus, quite often gay groups can be formed where they have not existed before. Second, most rural gay men are within traveling distance to a gay A.A. meeting. Many attend regular A.A. meetings in their rural communities on weekdays, and then attend a gay meeting on weekend evenings in a distant town. Third, rural gay men need not rely on gay A.A. groups to help them with the gay self-acceptance. On the contrary, they can attend regular A.A. groups for help in alcoholism, and then use other non-alcoholic gay support systems to help them eliminate their homophobia and develop a positive and integrated identity. Fourth, if there are no other gay men in his community or if he doesn't know any, the gay man would do well to read literature which presents an accurate picture of gay men and their lifestyles. This is available by mail from gay bookstores in many American cities. Finally, rural gay men might consider corresponding with their gay alcoholic brothers who live in larger cities. Writing to a gay A.A. group will likely draw a response.

SUMMARY AND CONCLUSIONS

This article examined the nature of self-help groups in general and Alcoholics Anonymous in particular, and how A.A., as a self-help group, can be of tremendous help to gay alcoholic men. Because A.A. has been a very effective form of treatment for alcoholism, and alcoholism is pandemic among gay American adult men, counseling professionals have a very useful resource as an adjunct to their psychotherapeutic efforts. Finally, helping professionals can be of assistance to gay alcoholic men with regard to A.A. groups, including those gay alcoholic men living in rural areas.

APPENDIX A:
FOR FURTHER INFORMATION

Alcoholics Anonymous World Services, Inc.
Box 459
Grand Central Station
New York, NY 10163

CompCare Publications
Box 27777
Minneapolis, MN 55427

Hazelden Educational Materials
Pleasant Valley Road
Box 176
Center City, MN 55012-0176

National Association of Lesbian & Gay Alcoholism Professionals (NALGAP)
1208 East State Blvd.
Fort Wayne, IN 46805

REFERENCES

Alcoholics Anonymous (1976). *Alcoholics anonymous, 3rd edition.* New York: Alcoholics Anonymous World Services, Inc.

Alcoholics Anonymous (1952, 1953). *Twelve steps and twelve traditions.* New York: Alcoholics Anonymous World Services, Inc.

Alcoholics Anonymous (1984). *Pass it on: The story of Bill Wilson and how the A.A. message reached the world.* New York: Alcoholics Anonymous World Services, Inc.

Bittle, W. E. (1982). Alcoholics Anonymous and the gay alcoholic. *Journal of Homosexuality, 7*(4), 81–88.

Coleman, E. (1981/1982). Developmental stages of coming out. *Journal of Homosexuality, 7*(23), 31–43.

Eller, M. & King, D. J. (in press). Self-help groups for gays, lesbians, and their loved ones. In R. J. Kus (Ed.), *A helping hand: Assisting your gay and lesbian clients* (working title). Boston: Alyson Publications.

Fifield, L. (1975). *On my way to nowhere: Alienated, isolated, drunk.* Los Angeles: Gay Community Services Center & Department of Health Services.

Gladue, B. A., Green, R., & Hellman, R. E. (1984). Neuroendocrine response to estrogen and sexual orientation. *Science, 225,* 1496–1499.

Goffman, E. (1963). *Stigma: Notes on the management of spoiled identity.* Englewood Cliffs, NJ: Prentice-Hall.

Gooren, L. (1986, Sept. 18). LH regulation and gonadal function in homosexual, transsexual and heterosexual individuals. Paper presented at the annual meeting of the *International Academy of Sex Research, Amsterdam, The Netherlands.*

Kus, R. J. (1985a). Stages of coming out: An ethnographic approach. *Western Journal of Nursing Research, 7,* 177–198.

Kus, R. J. (1985b, June). *Gay alcoholism and non-acceptance of gay self: The critical link.* Paper presented at the conference Nursing Research—Hawaii '85, Honolulu, Hawaii.

Kus, R. J. (1985c, September). *Gays and their higher power: An ethnography of gay sobriety.* Paper presented at the first conference of the National Association of Lesbian and Gay Alcoholism Professionals, Chicago, Illinois.

Kus, R. J. (1985d, November). *Sex and sobriety: The gay experience.* Paper presented at the National Symposium of Nursing Research: Advancing Clinical Practice, San Francisco, California.

Kus, R. J. (1986a, June). *The Alcoholics Anonymous sponsor and gay American men.* Paper presented at the 32nd International Institute on the Prevention and Treatment of Alcoholism, Budapest, Hungary.

Kus, R. J. (1986b, April). *Sobriety, leisure, and gay American men.* Paper presented at the annual meeting of the Iowa Academy of Science, Waverly, Iowa.

Kus, R. J. (1986c). *Friends and sobriety: The gay experience.* Unpublished manuscript.

Kus, R. J. (1986d). *Working the program: An ethnography of gay sobriety.* Research project funded by an NIH Biomedical Research Support Grant.

L., Barry (1985, July). *Historical perspective: Homosexual men and women in A.A.* Paper presented at the International Alcoholics Anonymous Conference, Montreal, Quebec.

Lohrenz, L., Connelly, J., Coyne, L., & Spare, K. (1978). Alcohol problems in several midwestern homosexual communities. *Journal of Studies on Alcohol, 39,* 1959–1963.

Saghir, M., & Robbins, E. (1973). *Male and female homosexuality.* Baltimore: Williams & Wilkins.

Whitney, S. (1982). The ties that bind: Strategies for counseling the gay male co-alcoholic. *Journal of Homosexuality, 7*(4), 37–41.

AIDS, Sexuality, and Sexual Control

Michael C. Quadland, PhD, MPH
William D. Shattls, DSW (cand.), ACSW

SUMMARY. The AIDS epidemic is discussed in terms of its effect on general sexual attitudes and behavior of homosexual and bisexual men, then, in particular, on the issue of control over one's sexual behavior. Problems encountered in the formulation of the concept of sexual control are discussed along with relevant theoretical constructs. A group treatment program for homosexual and bisexual men with problems of sexual control is described, along with findings and discussions regarding the effect of such treatment on sexual behavior.

BACKGROUND

By the summer of 1981 information compiled from reports of health agencies around the country indicated that some aberrant medical phenomenon was developing in the homosexual communities of several major cities. On July 3, 1981 the New York Times printed an article announcing a "Rare Cancer Seen in 41 Homosexuals." In October 1981 the Centers for Disease Control (CDC) in Atlanta declared that an epidemic existed. As the statistics from the CDC began to coalesce, a startling and grim picture emerged. Acquired Immune Deficiency Syndrome (AIDS) had become, according to Margaret Heckler, then Secretary of Health and Human Services, the number one health priority and most critical health problem in the United States.

The CDC publishes a weekly surveillance report on "AIDS Activity" in the United States. Figures from the January 14, 1985 report indicated that there were a total of 7,857 cases in the United States, of which 48% of the people with AIDS were dead. As of January 13, 1986—only one year later—the number of cases reported by the CDC stood at 16,458, of

Dr. Quadland is Assistant Professor of Psychiatry, Mount Sinai Medical School, New York City. He is Consultant for prevention programs to the Gay Men's Health Crisis in New York City, and Director of Research for the "800 Men" Healthy Sex Education Research Program. He is in private practice of psychotherapy and sex therapy in New York City.

Mr. Shattls is currently completing his doctorate in Social Welfare at the Hunter College School of Social Work, CUNY. He is in clinical practice in New York City and is Assistant Director of the "800 Men" Healthy Sex Education Research program. He is a clinical and educational consultant to the Gay Men's Health Crisis in New York City.

Correspondence may be addressed to Dr. Quadland, 69-1/2 Perry Street, New York, NY 10014, or to Mr. Shattls, 75 Bank Street, New York, NY 10014.

which 51% of the people with AIDS were dead (Center for Infectious Diseases, 1986). At that rate of increase, the absolute number of cases is more than doubling every 12 months. It is estimated that by January 1987 there will be approximately 30,000 officially reported cases in the United States, though many experts believe that the actual number of AIDS cases far exceeds the reported incidence. Currently, 73% of the total cases involve homosexual or bisexual men.

Initial perceptions of AIDS as a "gay plague," and the feelings of impunity and apathy within the general public which accompanied these perceptions, are slowly beginning to change. There is justifiable concern that AIDS is spreading out of the originally identified high-risk groups. But, as with any sexually transmitted disease, it is important to recognize that certain sexual practices, and not sexual preference, are the critical factors in determining risk. AIDS is caused by a virus, not by homosexuality or by sexual behavior itself. A good deal of confusion about this issue exists among heterosexuals and even some homosexuals who are eager to blame the horror of AIDS on an alternative lifestyle.

It is estimated that there are perhaps 10 times as many cases of what has been labeled ARC, AIDS Related Complex, as there are cases of full-blown AIDS. ARC is a similar but milder form of immunological deficiency which sometimes develops into AIDS. Dr. James Curran, director of the CDC's AIDS task force, has suggested that there are between 60,000 and 120,000 people in the United States with ARC.

Research findings both in France and the United States suggest that the recently isolated retro-virus LAV, or HTLV-III, is causally related to immunological dysfunction. Some experts suggest that an additional one to two million Americans may be asymptomatic carriers of the virus and that, of these, 5% to 10% are expected to develop AIDS within 5 years (AIDS, A Growing Threat, 1985). Others, however, paint an even more dismal picture, estimating that as many as three million Americans have been infected and that 50% of these may eventually develop and die from AIDS (AIDS in the Future, 1986).

In the spring of 1984, Dr. Robert Gallo and his team at the National Cancer Institute in Maryland announced that they had been successful in producing large quantities of HTLV-III in the laboratory. The development of a test for antibodies followed, making it possible to screen and protect the nation's blood supply. While this development was hailed as a major scientific breakthrough, the use of this test has raised a number of ethical and political questions concerning the possible misuse of test results and a potential for violation of individual rights to privacy. Further, since there are no effective treatments or cures, the knowledge that one has been exposed to HTLV-III is of questionable use, and may serve only to increase stress and concern.

Grim statistics, debates about ethical and political considerations, and a penchant for the sensational have characterized coverage of the AIDS epidemic by the news media. The announcement that American film star Rock Hudson had been stricken with AIDS made headlines around the world. However, the horrors of the AIDS epidemic reach far beyond the personal tragedies of the patients themselves. Although it is devastating to see young, vital people suddenly transformed into terminally ill persons, it is equally painful to witness the despair and anguish of these patients' loved ones—parents, children, lovers, friends, husbands, wives, and acquaintances. Add to this the frustration, helplessness, and often hopelessness of the helping professionals who have few answers, no cures, and ultimately no effective treatments, and the true scope and tragedy of AIDS become apparent.

Given this bleak and frightening picture, it is easy to understand the intense emotion which the AIDS epidemic has engendered both within and outside the homosexual community. Understandably, there has been a precipitous increase in anxiety within the primary risk group, i.e., sexually active homosexual and bisexual men. The ignorance and denial which characterized the early years of the health crisis have given way to frustration and depression about the illness itself, and anxiety and bewilderment about how to live, be sexual, and form relationships in the midst of this epidemic. The traditional association between sexuality and life is being supplanted by a new and devastating association between sexuality and death, a link which has profound influence on the sexual attitudes, values, and behaviors of homosexual men in particular, and all sexually active people in general.

It is essential to remain clearly focused on the facts if the dangers of purely emotional responses to this crisis are to be avoided, to keep clearly in mind that germs and viruses, not sexuality or sexual orientation, cause disease. Secondly, since AIDS is a sexually transmitted disease, "prevention" is possible even though, at present, "cure" is not. However, prevention requires far-reaching changes in sexual behavior. Knowledge of these necessary changes and the ability or willingness to comply with them varies greatly among homosexual men.

Federal, state, and local health agencies, mental health clinics, and private practitioners across the country are greatly concerned about communicability and the development of programs that will be effective in reducing what are believed to be "high-risk" behaviors. During the past few years, guidelines for risk reduction have become more specific, and two categories of high-risk behaviors have been identified. The first relates to sheer numbers of different sexual partners. An individual who has not been exposed to the virus who engages in high-risk sexual activities with multiple partners is at greater risk of exposure than one who is monogamous. The second outlines particular high-risk sexual practices significant for all persons at risk, including those who have already been exposed to the virus and whose sexual behaviors increase the likelihood of immunological vulnerability or breakdown.

However, it has become clear that simply disseminating information regarding risk and recommending changes in sexual practices, while sufficient for some, are not adequate to obtain the desired changes in sexual behavior of many sexually active homosexual and bisexual men. Sexual behavior is a complex and integral aspect of people's lives, both psychologically and socially. Attempts to alter sexual behavior patterns in order to save lives will obviously require very sophisticated educational approaches. Yet the development and implementation of such programs requires equally sophisticated theoretical formulations of the salient issues. It is necessary to examine anew the complex relationships between the intrapsychic, interpersonal, and social underpinnings of sexual behaviors, their meanings, and their significance, as helping professionals attempt to influence these behaviors.

SEXUAL CONTROL: A CONTROVERSIAL ISSUE

Common sense suggests that individuals engaging in high-risk behavior, upon recognition of the danger, would change their behavior. Yet, in the face of strong conflictual motives, the rational does not always prevail. Persons who continue to engage in high-risk sexual practices despite awareness of the possibly mortal danger to themselves and others are apparently responding to a phenomenon more complex than a simple sexual urge. For some, a lack of choice is involved. Terms and concepts sometimes used in relation to continued high-risk sexual behavior include "compulsive," "impulsive," "hypersexual," and "addictive." Although it is tempting to dismiss the distinctions between these terms as semantic, upon close examination genuine conceptual differences do emerge. An understanding of these differences is essential in attempting to specify the dynamics inherent in these behaviors, and for the development of a more concise, etiological theory.

Labels used to define the concept have important theoretical implications. For example, Fenichel (1945) is quite explicit in the distinction he makes between an impulse and a compulsion and in the theoretical and treatment implications which follow from them. The differential use of terms like compulsive and impulsive connote differential hypotheses concerning causality and have implications for interventions designed to achieve behavioral change.

Terms like addiction and dependency are also commonly associated with behaviors that are characterized by their excessive, persistent, self-damaging nature. Traditionally, addictions imply physiological dependence and withdrawal effects following cessation of intake. In regard to the use of substances, the global reference to addiction has been replaced by terms "use," "abuse," and "dependence" to indicate increasing degrees of pathology, although these discriminations are often vague and unreliable (Diagnostic and Statistical Manual, 1980).

It is interesting to note that much of the literature which addresses disorders of sexual desire focuses on problems of inhibited rather than excessive desire (e.g., Kaplan, 1984). Whereas inhibited desire is viewed with compassion as a clinical issue or a medical problem, excessive desire is often viewed as a perversion, frequently linked with issues of morality and sin.

The term promiscuous has been dropped in much of the literature because of its pejorative connotations. However, a brief examination of other labels reveals that they all have a connotation of perversity, immorality, or psychopathology. For example, included among the terms in the literature used to describe excessive sexual behavior are: the Casanova type, compulsive promiscuity, Don Juanism, erotomania, hyperaesthesia, hypereroticism, hyperlibido, and hypersexuality (Orford, 1978). It is noteworthy that these terms were originally used to describe excessive heterosexual behavior. Even so, and despite all of the scientific-sounding jargon, the labels still convey moralism and disdain. Yet we must also acknowledge the extent to which sexuality is admired and valued in our culture, how it is used to sell everything from soap to political candidates. However, this admiration is sexist and heterosexist. In American culture, sexual prowess is admired in heterosexual men, not in women or homosexual men.

If excessive sexual behavior is defined in terms of a lack of adequate control over one's sexual behavior, one must also define what an adequate or reasonable level of control would be. In this regard the issue of frequency becomes important. However, researchers as early as Kinsey, Pomeroy, and Martin in 1948, and others since, have objected to frequency as a criterion for defining what is considered normal.

> It is impossible to separate normal and abnormal sexual behavior in other than an arbitrary way, since the distribution of amount of sexual behavior in a population follows a continuous unbroken curve with no evidence of a separate sub-population of people whose behavior is excessive and qualitatively different from that of others (Kinsey, Pomeroy & Martin, 1948).

If, as Kinsey and his associates suggest, frequency is an untenable concept in defining "compulsive sexuality," one is left with the issue of control as the critical variable. Here again, however, there are difficulties. Any description of uncontrolled behavior implies an all-or-nothing, discrete quality to behavior which, as with frequency, exists along a

continuum. Control is relative, not absolute. One may be more or less out
of control or in control with differences in perception and definition
varying over time and from one individual to another.

In addition to being highly idiopathic, perceptions of control are also
culture-bound and must be looked at in context. Social conventions and
values, formal and informal, have an impact upon one's perception of
normal and one's reaction to deviation. To some degree, deviance, like
beauty, is in the eye of the beholder, and it may not be possible to define
control globally, for all people. From this perspective, it seems clear that
the perception of control is subjective and must be defined by the individual. So long as sexual behavior is not troubling to the individual or does
not infringe upon the rights of others, it need not be defined as problematic.
It is only when there is a self-defined, subjective, or experiential sense of
distress or dissatisfaction that these behaviors become a problem. Idiopathic behavior or lifestyle preferences do not imply pathology simply
because they are unconventional or nonconforming.

In the face of the mortal danger which the AIDS epidemic represents,
many homosexual men have come to perceive sexual behaviors which
before had been unquestioned or even highly valued as no longer
desirable or safe. It is at this point that formerly idiopathic behavior may
be viewed as a psychological or psychosocial problem. Continued
high-risk sexual behavior in the face of a deadly epidemic, when
individuals are well-informed regarding risk, may be an indication of a
problem with sexual control. This is particularly true when individuals
express a sincere desire to change these behavior patterns but, for
whatever reasons, cannot. Reality may be subjective, but it is nevertheless defined by consensus. Most rational people do not choose to put their
lives in jeopardy simply to satisfy a genital urge.

As any clinician can attest, perception of a problem does not
necessarily lead directly or easily to changes in behavior, even when
those changes are viewed as desirable and necessary.

> Changing a specific lifestyle, or altering set patterns of behavior, is
> difficult, time-consuming, requires much effort, and is, at times,
> painful. A man who attempts to evaluate his sexual wishes and acts
> needs to develop a comprehensive understanding of himself and these
> issues before a lasting change can take place. (Gershoni, 1985)

If the AIDS crisis can be seen as having any positive consequences at all,
one is in relation to this new, forced, self-examination and recognition of
the difficulty in effecting even desperately desired changes in sexual
attitudes and behavior.

Recent, less judgmental investigations of "compulsive sexuality" have described this phenomenon as a new category of sexual behavior which involves more than mere frequency of sexual activity (Blanck & Blanck, 1974). Depending in part upon one's theoretical orientation, as well as the way in which one defines the problem, the behavior in question may be viewed as a symptom or as a solution. For example, from a psychoanalytic perspective, "compulsive sexual behavior" might be described as a form of acting out. "Acting out refers to behavior motivated by unconscious, object-related fantasies repressed by an ego capable of employing such high-level defense" (Wachtel, 1977). Compulsive behavior may serve an ego defensive function which operates without conscious awareness. Defense mechanisms serve to protect the ego from anxiety. If, as this model suggests, compulsive sexual behavior is intrapsychically motivated by a need to reduce anxiety, it is important to understand the source of this anxiety. Regardless of whether one views compulsiveness symptomatically, i.e., as a manifestation of an inner conflict, or as an attempt to reduce anxiety, i.e., as an adaptation or solution to an inner conflict, it appears that, from a psychodynamic point of view, compulsive sexual behavior expresses an inner need which goes beyond a simple response to a genital urge.

From a behavioral perspective, problems with sexual control may be viewed as a learned response or a habit in which the sexual behavior reinforces the avoidance of anxiety associated with feelings of loneliness, low self-esteem, problems with intimacy and closeness, and, among homosexual men, with internalized homophobia (Quadland, 1983). Homosexual men who continue to engage in high-risk sexual behaviors despite the potentially mortal danger of doing so may also be responding to learned attitudes, which suggest that a high level of sexual activity with many different partners is a symbol of one's manhood and desirability, and an important part of one's homosexual identity.

THE IMPACT OF AIDS ON SEXUAL BEHAVIOR

The preceding observations suggest that a variety of approaches to facilitate change in sexual attitudes and behavior among those at risk for AIDS is necessary. The fostering of more positive attitudes toward healthy sex may have an impact on the types of sexual activity practiced. Attitudes which place a high value on one's health and the health of one's partners could supplant former values associated with multiple, anonymous, high-risk sexual encounters. For some, including those who have learned to use sex habitually to reduce anxiety, change may be more difficult. Alternative methods to reduce anxiety in conjunction with the development of improved social skills to enhance interpersonal relating may be required, along with far greater understanding of sexual behavior and its varied motivations and reinforcements.

A number of studies were conducted during the early days of the AIDS epidemic to evaluate the impact of AIDS on the sexual behavior of homosexual and bisexual men. In a survey of 655 homosexual men in San Francisco in 1983, McKusick, Horstman, and Coates (1985) found substantial reductions in frequency of sexual contacts. However, men who frequented bathhouses and men who tended to use sex to reduce tension showed little change in frequency or type of sexual behavior. Men in monogamous relationships also showed little change in sexual behavior within their relationship, perhaps because they did not view such change as effecting their risk status. Men in non-monogamous relationships and men not in relationships reported substantial reductions in high-risk sexual activity, but not a corresponding increase in low-risk sexual behavior. Knowledge of healthy sex guidelines was quite high, but changes in sexual practices toward behaviors that would reduce risk for AIDS were not related to this knowledge. Rather, change tended to be associated with the degree to which one perceived himself to be personally at risk for the illness and the extent to which he believed changes in sexual behavior to be efficacious in reducing risk (Morin, 1984). It also appeared that knowledge of risk and of healthy alternatives to high-risk sexual activities were not enough for some men to cause them to make adaptive changes in sexual behavior. Finally, it appeared that some men may have been withdrawing from sex in general. The question arises as to whether such a change in sexual behavior was durable, whether it might contribute to tension and depression, or whether it might lead to occasional lapses into high-risk behavior.

Van Ness and Puchall conducted a survey of homosexual and bisexual men in Washington, D.C. in 1983, a time in which there were few cases of AIDS there, but also about the time media attention to AIDS was becoming more extensive. The climate was one of confusion due to conflicting information about AIDS and its transmission. AIDS generally was seen as something affecting people in areas such as New York and California, and not an immediate threat to residents of the District of Columbia. Reduction of number of different sexual partners had been recommended by authorities as the primary means of reducing risk. Van Ness and Puchall found that most men (54 percent) reported some decrease in their number of different sexual partners; 35 percent showed no change; and 11 percent showed some increase. While this was early on in the epidemic and AIDS was not yet perceived as an immediate threat, still the majority of homosexual men were informed about risk reduction and the need to make appropriate changes. However, there appeared to be a core of persons who might be at higher risk of infection due to the frequency and type of their sexual behavior who were not making recommended changes.

Recently, a risk reduction program called "The 800 Men Study" was conducted in New York City (Quadland, Shattls, Jacobs, & D'Eramo, 1986). It attempted to test several relevant hypotheses, including the expectation that an educational experience which eroticized healthy sex alternatives to high-risk sexual behavior, and which provided small verbal group experiences to enhance social skills and promote emotional sharing and peer support, would be more effective in promoting healthy sexual attitudes and behavior than a simple AIDS information program or a more anxiety-provoking program showing the emotional and physical devastation of AIDS. This hypothesis was based on the premise that compliance with healthy sexual practices includes, as one of its consequences, an inherent sense of loss which may lead to resistance. Therefore, if people are to be influenced to reduce high-risk behavior, they must be offered an alternative to that behavior which is not only healthy, but also attractive and appealing. Further, it was assumed that there is an affective as well as cognitive component to attitude and behavior change. Small group discussions were provided to process affective responses to information, and also to develop the social skills often required to implement healthy sexual experiences. Data analysis is in process at the time of this writing, but preliminary impressions confirm the importance of small group process and support in promoting attitude and behavioral change.

In summary, it appears that AIDS education programs which include guidelines recommending ways in which one can reduce risk of illness through changes in sexual behavior are an effective way to influence the sexual behavior and attitudes of many homosexual men. However, there is a substantial portion of the homosexual and bisexual male population for whom these methods are not adequate. More creative educational programs which address the complex and multi-faceted issues involved in behavioral and attitudinal change are needed. The urgency of this need has become more apparent as evidence has accumulated which suggests that these may also be the men who are at greatest risk of either developing or spreading infection by virtue of their sexual behavior.

A variety of clinical issues emerge here as impediments to the adoption of healthy sex behavior. Different programs must be developed to address the varied needs and capacities of men who are attempting to deal with high levels of anxiety and depression while adjusting to abrupt and frightening changes in their lifestyles. One such program was devised to address the needs of homosexual and bisexual men who have difficulty with sexual control and who found themselves unable to make desired changes in their sexual behavior despite being well-informed about the probable risk.

AN EXPERIMENTAL GROUP PROGRAM

Early AIDS education programs in New York City emphasized reducing the number of different sexual partners and avoiding public places for sexual activity such as bathhouses and backroom bars, as well as avoiding particular sexual activities thought to be of high risk. People were encouraged to get to know a partner and something about his sexual history before having sex, and to form monogamous sexual relationships. Homosexual men were suddenly presented with the prospect of a horrifying and deadly illness which, it appeared, could only be avoided by changes in sexual lifestyle which for some men were quite drastic. Responses to knowledge about AIDS and one's perceived risk of actually becoming ill varied widely. Some men cut back on sex immediately, exercising caution and restraint in their number of different contacts and in the sexual activity itself. At the time, this was considered a moderate or reasonable response to the crisis. Extreme responses also were observed. Some men withdrew from sex entirely which, while it may have reduced anxiety for some, raised anxiety and tension for others, sometimes leading to sprees of overindulgence followed by anxiety and guilt. Others tended to form what were termed "premature relationships"; a monogamous lover relationship formed on or shortly after the first date. Since risk-reduction authorities had not yet defined the exchange of bodily fluids as the primary risk factor, there was a false sense of security and safety from infection among men in monogamous relationships. Many men sought to form them, while others attempted to maintain existing relationships longer than they might have were it not for the AIDS epidemic.

Equally extreme responses to the health crisis, it seemed, were observed in men who made no change at all in their high level of sexual activity. This lack of response was difficult for educators and medical authorities to understand, given the possible severe consequences of continued high-risk sexual activity. Why some people seemed to overreact to the crisis by responding in one extreme way or another, while others responded reasonably and moderately, and still others did not respond at all, is a very complex and important question.

First, it is necessary to place homosexual men's sexual behavior in a socio-cultural context. For homosexual men, sexual identity and the freedom to express one's sexuality as one chooses is a very important aspect of personal identity. Sexuality has been a very important component in the struggle for self and social acceptance, a process that can be long and arduous for many men. It is not surprising, therefore, that homosexual men would be resistant to attempts to influence their sexual behavior. Also, places such as bathhouses or bars provided not only potential sexual contacts but also opportunities for homosexual men to meet and socialize with other homosexual men. Encouraging homosexual men to avoid these places represented a drastic change in and loss of social activities which, for some, increased isolation and depression.

Other explanations were suggested for a lack of change in sexual behavior in response to AIDS. One was denial as a defense against what was realistically a very frightening situation. Denial of risk was rationalized with statements such as "If I don't have it by now, I never will" or "If I just eat well and exercise, I won't get it," or more politically motivated rationalizations such as "This is just a plot to get us to stop having sex." Such denial is often a defense against extreme anxiety and the sense of powerlessness to do anything about one's jeopardy or vulnerability. Because the incubation period for AIDS has been estimated to be 5 years or longer, many homosexual men believe that it is just a matter of time before they become ill, or that the damage to their immune system has already been done. This belief is associated with extreme anxiety which many men express in frequent visits to physicians' and therapists' offices. Others, we suspect, deny their own risk as a defense against overwhelming anxiety and a sense of doom.

A second explanation for not changing sexual behavior was that some people were unable to make desired changes. These were men who, either of their own volition or on recommendation from their medical doctors, had educated themselves about AIDS, believed a high level of sexual activity represented a significant risk of serious illness, and wanted very much to reduce their number of different sexual partners, but found that they could not. In 1982, Michael Quadland, a psychologist and sex therapist, began receiving calls from men who were extremely concerned about their own behavior as a risk for AIDS, had identified themselves as having a problem controlling their sexual behavior, and were seeking help in gaining such control.

After interviewing several men with this complaint, certain common characteristics emerged. In general, these men were highly anxious about AIDS and the risk which their sexual behavior seemed to hold. They reported not feeling in control of their sexual behavior, reported having more sex than they wanted, and reported feeling victimized by their frequent sexual activity, sometimes in a variety of ways besides the risk of AIDS. Many reported spending far too much time, by their own definition, in the pursuit of sex. Some reported putting themselves in danger in order to have sex, while others feared that they jeopardized their primary relationship, the health of their partner, their friendships, or their jobs. For some, the sexual behavior was embarrassing or humiliating to them, and they often emerged from these experiences feeling more lonely or more unattractive than before. Usually they had not discussed the details of their sexual behavior with anyone; friends, lovers, or even therapists. Masturbation seemed not to be associated with the problem;

that is, it did not reduce the felt need for a sexual encounter, and there was little compulsive masturbatory behavior observed among these men. While the sexual experiences reported were genital, the primary motivation and satisfaction seemed often not to be purely sexual. For many, the sexual behavior functioned to reduce anxiety, and this anxiety often had to do with low self-esteem, loneliness and isolation, and in some cases internalized homophobia and fears of an intimate relationship with another man.

A pattern of sexual control emerged which seemed most closely related to that of overeating. Sex, like eating, is a positive and important aspect of life for most people. However, it can be a serious problem when it is out of control. It appears that over-indulgence in both areas is associated with anxiety reduction and a mislabeling of, and diversion from, the anxiety-provoking stimulus.

A typical example illustrates the pattern. An individual is at home and experiences some agitation or restlessness. He labels this feeling "horniness" and decides to go out looking for sex. Immediately he is distracted from the anxiety-provoking stimulus, possibly loneliness in this case, by preparing to go out. This is the first reinforcer (a negative one) for the behavior, the removal of a painful stimulus. Positive reinforcement for the sexual behavior may be derived from the sexual encounter itself, the pleasure of the orgasm, but, perhaps even more importantly, from the affirmation of the individual's sexual, personal, or physical appeal. Unfortunately, such reinforcement is fleeting and is often accompanied by guilt or remorse. The anxiety-provoking stimuli return, tension builds, and the pattern is repeated. (See Figure 1.)

In 1982, Michael Quadland began treating homosexual men who had presented themselves for therapy for problems related to a lack of, or inadequate, sexual control. Groups of no more than eight members met once per week for 90 minutes. Group members committed themselves to

Figure 1

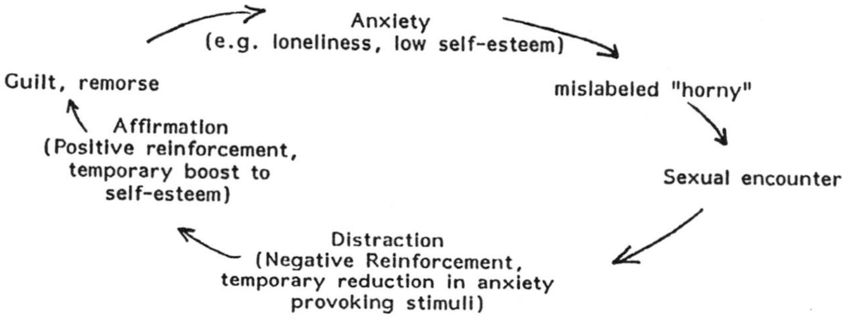

Anxiety
(e.g. loneliness, low self-esteem)

Guilt, remorse

Affirmation
(Positive reinforcement,
temporary boost to
self-esteem)

mislabeled "horny"

Sexual encounter

Distraction
(Negative Reinforcement,
temporary reduction in anxiety
provoking stimuli)

5 weeks of participation and, if they found the experience helpful, committed to a second 5-week period. Average length of stay in the group was slightly more than 20 weeks. The goal of participation in the group was to gain control over one's sexual behavior, not to eliminate sex, and not to conform to any arbitrarily imposed standard of frequency. Each participant defined for himself what control meant to him. Usually, it was the ability to make a conscious, rational choice to have sex, or to be able to choose not to when that seemed best for him. A positive attitude toward sex as a healthy aspect of human behavior was maintained throughout the course of the groups. Only with regard to the self-defined perception that one's sexual behavior was out of control was a problem deemed to exist.

The focus of the group was two-fold. The first was to clarify for each participant the issues involved in his self-defined lack of sexual control. Interpersonal as well as intrapsychic and unconscious issues were explored. What feelings were being expressed in these sexual behaviors, and how were they being articulated? What needs was he attempting to satisfy with his sexual behavior and how effectively was this being accomplished? What fantasies about prospective sexual encounters supported the sexual behavior, and how did the realities of the actual encounter compare? What was accomplished interpersonally with the sexual behavior, and what was avoided or left unfulfilled? How did the sexual behavior function? If it functioned, at least in part, to reduce anxiety, what was that anxiety about? How was it important? How did it affect his sense of himself as an attractive, competent, lovable, or worthwhile person? These issues were explored at length in the group, and participants, who frequently were or had been in psychotherapy elsewhere, seemed eager to challenge and learn from one another, becoming quite skilled in this "analytic" process. It was assumed that increased understanding of the behavior, the motivation for it, and the way that it functioned in an individual's life, would be associated with freer and more rational decision-making in regard to the behavior.

The second approach of the group was behavioral. Many participants perceived their sexual behavior to be life-threatening, and a group norm developed quickly that, whether or not one understood the reasons for the behavior, one set out making changes immediately. Focusing on the behavior meant first to determine exactly what was happening. Group members would ask one another "How often are you having sex?" "Where?" "With whom?" "What are the cues for your sexual response?" "What do you do sexually?" "What is the reward?" "What is avoided by having sex?" Often new participants were not aware of the many elements and components of their sexual behavior. In this regard, all participants were asked to keep logs of their sexual thoughts, feelings, and behavior, recording when they felt sexual, what was happening at the time, what they were feeling, what their fantasy was of having a sexual encounter, what they wanted, what actually happened, and how they felt afterwards. This process was often revealing to the individual about the motivation and the function of his behavior.

At the close of each group session, participants were invited to set a goal for themselves for the following week. The goal might be to reduce or eliminate a certain behavior, such as the number of different sexual encounters, to engage in safer sex practices with their partner, or to employ some new behavior which was seen by the individual as positive though difficult, for example, telephoning someone for a date. Such goals were expressed in terms of voluntary contracts-for-change which individuals made with the group. There was no reproach of those who chose not to make contracts with the group. The subsequent group session began with participants reporting on whether or not they had kept their contracts. The norm that evolved in the group was based on positive reinforcement for individual successes and support, rather than punishment for failures. Those who had not kept their contracts were often reminded of past successes, assured of their general progress, and encouraged to continue their effort.

An intimacy developed among participants, perhaps based on this new verbal sharing of feelings and behavior which in the past had been hidden. Identification with one another occurred as a response to the development of coping strategies and solutions, as well as from the shared problems, behaviors, and the motivations for them. Participants exchanged telephone numbers and were encouraged to contact one another as an alternative to seeking a sexual encounter. Many participants made use of this device borrowed from Alcoholics Anonymous, and friendships did sometimes develop between participants. It is assumed that the trust and intimacy which developed among group members in group sessions tended to defuse some of these issues for participants even when outside the group, and may have facilitated the development of closer and more lasting friendships and relationships. In a few cases, group members did develop romantic and sexual relationships outside the group with men who were not group members. This was viewed as a positive development by the group and members were very supportive of those new relationships.

A CONTROLLED STUDY OF GROUP PARTICIPANTS

From 1982 to 1984, data on demographic characteristics, neurotic symptoms, and frequency and type of sexual behavior of participants were collected in order to answer two questions: (a) Do homosexual and bisexual men who identify themselves as having a problem with sexual control and seek treatment differ from homosexual and bisexual men who do not seek treatment for this problem? and (b) What is the effect of group psychotherapy undertaken for problems of sexual control on the sexual behavior of group participants? Group participation was not contingent on being involved in the research aspects of the program.

Most homosexual men living in New York City during this period were under unusual stress and pressure to change their sexual behavior in response to the AIDS epidemic. Also, given the widespread public education programs about AIDS and its probable transmission via sexual contact, it was imperative that a matched comparison group be used. The comparison group, matched for age, socioeconomic status, and sexual orientation, consisted of men who also had presented themselves for private psychotherapy with the same therapist, but not for an identified sexual control problem or sexual dysfunction or inhibition. It was obvious from clinical interviews that both the experimental and comparison groups were well informed about AIDS. In general, comparison group members had made desired changes in their sexual behavior, though the changes themselves were not uniform. The experimental group, on the other hand, had not been able to make desired changes in their sexual behavior.

The experimental and comparison groups were studied using a pre-post test design (Quadland, 1985). In general, participants in both groups were highly educated and highly functioning men. While problems of interpersonal relating, social isolation, and alienation had been observed clinically among experimental group members, no consistent pattern of greater psychopathology was suggested, and this was confirmed by the study results. The experimental group did show a history of significantly fewer long-term relationships. As was hypothesized, the experimental group also showed a greater number of different sexual partners than the comparison group, both historically and currently. However, when asked in the post-test what they would like their level of sexual activity to be "ideally," given the current health crisis and given their own personal preference, desired levels were very similar for the two groups.

Participants were asked to rate their subjective feelings before, during, and following sexual activity on a Likert scale from 1 to 5, never to always. Of particular interest here was whether the experimental group felt different prior to having sex than did the comparison group. It was predicted that they would score higher than the comparison group on a combination of negative feelings, including anxiety, frustration, boredom, loneliness, and depression, and lower on a cumulative score of positive feelings of love and relaxation. Observed differences were in the predicted direction, but only the difference in the positive feelings was significant.

It was predicted that the experimental group who completed group psychotherapy would show a reduction in their number of different sexual partners. Group members reduced their current mean number of different sexual partners per month from 11.5, at time of entry into group, to 3.3, 6 months after leaving group, whereas the current mean number of different sexual partners for comparison subjects did not change significantly during the same approximate time period. These observations confirmed the clinical impression that group members had reduced their number of different sexual partners during the course of group therapy. They reported a mean of 13.7 different partners per month over the previous 5 years, 11.5 per month over the 6 months prior to group therapy, and 3.3 per month 6 months following therapy. The comparison group, on the other hand, reported a mean of 3.5 partners per month over the previous 5 years, 2.1 per month over the 6-month period prior to entering psychotherapy, and 1.9 per month 6 months after entering psychotherapy, showing a gradual, consistent reduction in the number of different sexual partners, probably due to the threat of AIDS. The experimental group showed an abrupt reduction at the time of group therapy that had not been observed prior to that time.

Questions were also asked which attempted to determine whether the nature of sexual contacts had changed; that is, whether they were one-time encounters, individual or group sex, in a public or private setting, with or without drugs or alcohol. Both groups showed a significant reduction in the number of one-time sexual encounters and the proportion of sexual activity in public settings. The experimental group showed a significant change in the amount of alcohol or drug use in conjunction with sex, whereas the control group did not. Neither group showed significant change in the proportion of individual to group sexual activity. The experimental group showed a change in the proportion of members involved in a primary relationship from 20% prior to joining the group to 40% 6 months after termination from the group. This difference approached significance ($p < .06$). No similar change was observed in the comparison group.

DISCUSSION: SEXUAL CONTROL

When the AIDS crisis linked sexual activity with serious illness and death, as it did in the awareness of most homosexual men in 1982, it triggered in each of them a complex emotional, attitudinal, and behavioral response which mental health professionals, at this time, lack the expertise to decipher or to measure. At a simple level, it seems reasonable to assume that if you learn that a certain activity in which you engage is associated with mortal illness, you reduce or eliminate that activity, or find a somewhat satisfying alternative. Many men made such changes as a result of public education which had included specific suggestions on how to reduce risk by altering sexual activity.

In regards to what it means when a person does not make such changes, we have explored here one possibility; namely, that some people lack sufficient control over their behavior in this area to effect change. Further, we have theorized that this lack of control may be due to the fact that sexual activity for some has assumed a special function of reducing anxiety having to do with loneliness, inadequacy, or insecurity, rather than with genital gratification. We recognize that sexual activity may, at one time or another, reduce anxiety for all people, and that it is important to avoid absolutes in our conceptualization of this problem. People are more or less anxious, adequate, and secure. They are also more or less sexually active or controlled, with all such variables fluctuating simultaneously on a continuum. The critical distinction is that some people are able to act in their own best interest at times when they need to, while others feel compelled to indulge as a diversion from anxiety and find it extremely difficult to make a conscious choice for their own well-being. We have explored theoretical conceptualizations which might lead to some understanding of this issue for certain people, and have shared clinical observations of men who defined themselves as having a problem controlling their sexual behavior.

Clinical work with homosexual men who have a problem with sexual control raised for them, and for us as professionals, the crucial issue of freedom of sexual expression—the ability to choose whom to have sex with, how often, and in what social or relationship context. Sexual oppression can occur in many forms in relationships or in the workplace. One can also be oppressed by his own need for sex when sex is being used to divert him from his own interpersonal or intrapsychic problems. It is important to recognize that freedom of sexual expression is accomplished when individuals are not oppressed by their own, as well as society's perceived needs, but rather when they are free to make choices about their sexual lives.

The research reported here supports the hypothesis that persons who have difficulties with sexual control are no more neurotic than people who present themselves for psychotherapy for other conflictual life issues. This finding challenges the many anecdotal reports which attempt to associate a lack of sexual control with neuroticism or psychoticism. (Gerson, 1974; Ellis & Sagarin, 1965).

While the experimental group had a mean number of different sexual partners which was four times that of the comparison group over the 5 years prior to the study, there was a large amount of variation in these figures, particularly in the comparison group. This suggests that some members of the comparison group were choosing to have several different sexual partners. The fact that this monthly mean figure dropped precipitously in the 6-month period just prior to participation in the study, a period of heightened AIDS awareness, suggests that comparison group members chose to have fewer sexual encounters as a means of reducing their health risk. Here we see the importance of defining this problem as one' of control over one's sexual behavior rather than as an arbitrary frequency figure. Some people can and do choose to have a much larger number of sexual contacts with different partners than do others. They make choices about their behavior, and change it when they want to, with relatively little difficulty.

The experimental group, on the other hand, showed no such precipitous drop in frequency of different sexual contacts in the 6 months prior to group participation, despite being well-informed and anxious about the probable risk. After completion of group psychotherapy, however, the mean frequency of sexual contact dropped significantly, and approached that of the comparison group. The group psychotherapy experience was obviously helpful in facilitating a reduction in the number of different sexual contacts. Because number of different sexual partners had been defined as a risk factor for AIDS, this was an important finding. Further, it suggests that a level of control was achieved and had endured for several months following the group. However, there is no direct measure of a sense of control over one's sexual behavior, a shortcoming of studies of this type. After stating unequivocally that issues of sexual control should not be defined in terms of numbers of different sexual partners, it is regrettable that these are the only parameters we have currently to measure change in such behavior. Creation of a measure of self-perceived control over sexual behavior has been a focus of our work recently, and a suitable instrument should be available in the near future.

It was interesting to note the similarity in the levels of sexual activity members of the two groups would choose, given the current health crisis and their own personal preferences. Both groups would choose approximately 14 sexual experiences with a partner per month, with a mean of 1.5 different partners. This suggests that persons who have problems of sexual control do not differ from others in what they want for themselves sexually. They are not, as some have said, simply people who choose to have more sex. Rather, it appears that these are people whose sexual activity is not consistent with their sexual value system.

While some members of the experimental group experienced serious difficulties in their professional lives or with their relationships, such was true of the comparison group seeking general psychotherapy as well. The major difference between the two groups was in the frequency and type of their sexual behavior. It was interesting to note that the proportion of experimental group members involved in a relationship rose from 20% prior to group participation to 40% 6 months after the group. Obviously, this could be due to a number of factors, including the desire to reduce one's risk of AIDS by becoming involved in a monogamous sexual relationship, a strategy that was being recommended in risk-reduction education programs at the time. It is also true, however, that the group experience of sharing problems, along with feelings of anxiety, frustration, and hope, created an intimacy and assertiveness among group members that may have enhanced their ability to negotiate a monogamous relationship and in general reduce inhibition regarding relationships.

Men who have problems with sexual control reported fewer positive feelings of love and relaxation prior to sex than did comparison group members. Their scores were not significantly different on measures of negative feelings such as anxiety, frustration, loneliness, boredom, or depression. It may be that men seeking psychotherapy also score high on negative feelings around having sex, though the feelings may be manifest in a different way.

This study supports professionally led group treatment focused on (a) developing insight and understanding of the problem, and (b) a gradual gaining of control over sexual behavior as a clinical intervention for the problem of sexual control. Because of social attitudes about the problem, individuals tend to be isolated with it. Group treatment reduces this sense of isolation. Participants identify with one another in ways that are useful as well as cathartic. The group provides a support system for members which includes confrontation of resistance as well as acceptance and encouragement of behavior change. Perhaps most importantly, it provides a forum for developing intimacy which may reduce anxiety and inhibition regarding ongoing relationships.

However, it is very important to note that the group model employed here differs markedly from professional and self-help groups which employ the addiction model (Carnes, 1983). The authors believe that to apply the concept of addiction, as it is commonly understood and applied to the abuse of substances such as alcohol, drugs, or cigarettes, to problems of sexual control is inaccurate and presents serious problems in the conceptualization and treatment of sexual control. One problem is that sex is generally a positive and healthy human activity, whereas drugs, alcohol, and cigarettes are generally deleterious to health. Therefore, the goal of treatment for addiction has been to eliminate the substance from the individual's life because it is not necessary for existence or even life-enhancing. Treatment consists of supporting the individual through a withdrawal period, followed by ongoing peer group support to maintain abstinence. The problem is more complicated for issues of sexual control, as it is with problems of overeating, where the goal is not to eliminate the behavior, but rather to manage it in a way that is life-enhancing to the individual. Gaining control over one's behavior and managing it effectively over time is usually more complicated and difficult than elimination of the problem behavior.

Some professional and self-help treatment approaches to problems of sexual control have attempted to apply the addiction model to sexual behavior. There is a great deal of variation in these groups, but in extreme cases, the model is essentially unaltered. "Sobriety" is defined as abstinence from all sexual activity, including masturbation. After a "withdrawal" period, one must continue to avoid masturbation and any sexual activity outside the primary (usually marital) relationship. This approach assumes that there is a need for a withdrawal period from sex, as there is from alcohol or drugs, which has not been demonstrated and which is not supported by the research reported here. It may be, as this research suggests, that a gradual decrease in the frequency of sexual activity is more efficacious. Also, the addiction model often attempts to apply an arbitrary standard of sexual behavior, monogamy, which not all people share.

Further, it should not be assumed that masturbation is directly related to uncontrolled sexual activity with a partner. While some people with problems of sexual control do masturbate compulsively, many participants in the program described here did not, nor did their masturbatory behavior necessarily tend to lead them to seek a sexual encounter, nor did masturbation tend to satisfy their perceived need for a sexual encounter. In the treatment approach reported here, participants gained control over sexual activity without prohibiting or eliminating masturbation. In fact, it may be that to prohibit masturbation during a "withdrawal" period predisposes the treatment to fail, resulting in guilt, remorse, and a sense of failure for the patient.

CONCLUSIONS REGARDING AIDS EDUCATION

Previous investigations suggest that reduction in high-risk sexual behavior is not associated with information dissemination alone. Some authorities argue that many of the major health problems which exist in the United States today result largely from unhealthy lifestyles, and that most health problems are related to behavioral rather than medical problems. (AIDS: A Growing Threat, 1985). Two issues of major interest for future study are the specification of the attitudes which underlie the sexual behavior of homosexual and bisexual men, and the relationship between changes in attitude and reduction in high-risk sexual practices. It is assumed that behavior is a function of individual and social attitudes, values, and beliefs; that attitudes develop as part of a complex socialization process; that attitudes are deeply embedded and an integral part of the social framework within which the individual develops; and that, for all of these reasons, attitudes are extremely resistant to change. However, there is at least theoretical support for the hope that the AIDS health crisis may in fact represent an opportunity to effect behavioral change. Allport

(1935) suggests that periods of emotional disorganization are favorable to attitude change and that new attitudes may emerge during such a period.

A recent *Time* magazine article stated that "There is, in fact, no parallel to the anguish now being endured by America's gay men, who live in every town and city in the U.S. and total perhaps 12 million, as many as the combined population of all eight Mountain States" (AIDS: A Growing Threat, 1985). Described by medical experts as "the disease of the century," AIDS seems all the more frightening because there is no cure or no effective treatment, and because whatever hope there is of developing a vaccine is discussed in terms of years. Current trends indicated that 16,000 new cases would be reported from August of 1985 through December of 1986, with the average life expectancy of a person diagnosed with AIDS still only 18 months. Fear and panic have spread across the country, creating a potentially dangerous socio-political climate for the very people who have been most oppressed by the disease.

There is a pervasive sense of mourning and depression in the homosexual community which effects many aspects of life, including sexuality, and a real risk exists of reverting to more negative attitudes about homosexuality among homosexual as well as heterosexual people. It is extremely important for mental health and other health professionals to convey the message clearly that homosexuality and sexual behavior did not cause AIDS, and that all people concerned with individual human rights and freedom of sexual expression need to continue to dispute those who would use the AIDS epidemic to impugn those who choose an alternative lifestyle. We must not allow society to blame the victims of this tragedy.

There are important bio-psycho-social issues at both extremes of the spectrum of behavioral responses to AIDS among homosexual men. Both the terror which leads some homosexual men to eliminate sex from their lives totally and the hopelessness which leaves others at risk because they cannot or will not change their sexual practices must be addressed. The fact that sexual attitudes and behavior are resistant to change represents a challenge to health professionals. Future efforts must be designed to meet this challenge through the development of creative healthy sex education programs which will enable homosexual men, and ultimately others, to enjoy gratifying and healthy sex lives without jeopardizing their health and the health of their partners.

REFERENCES

AIDS: A growing threat (1985, August 12). *Time*, pp. 40–47.

AIDS in the future: Experts say deaths will climb sharply (1986, January 14). *New York Times*, Sec. C, p. 1.

Allport, G. W. (1935). Attitudes. In C. Murchison (Ed.), *Handbook of social psychology* (pp. 798–884). Worcester, MA: Clark University Press.

American Psychiatric Association (1980). *Diagnostic and statistical manual of mental disorders* (3rd Ed.). Washington, DC: Author.

Blanck, G., & Blanck, R. (1974). *Ego psychology: Theory and practice.* New York: Columbia University Press.

Carnes, P. (1983). *The sexual addiction.* Minneapolis: Compcare.

Center for Infectious Diseases (1986). *Acquired immunodeficiency syndrome (AIDS) weekly surveillance report—United States.* (AIDS Activity Reports of January 14, 1985 and January 13, 1986). Washington, DC: Centers for Disease Control.

Ellis, A., & Sagarin, E. (1965). *Nymphomania, a study of oversexed women.* London: Ortolan.

Fenichel, O. (1945). *The psychoanalytic theory of neurosis.* New York: W. W. Norton.

Gershoni, Y. (1985, February 11–24). Overcoming sexual compulsion. *New York Native,* p. 24.

Gerson, A. (1974). Promiscuity as a function of the father-daughter relationship. *Psychological Reprints, 34*(3).

Kaplan, H. S. (1984). *Comprehensive evaluation of disorders of sexual desire.* Washington, DC: American Psychiatric Press.

Kinsey, A., Pomeroy, W., & Martin, C. (1948). *Sexual behavior in the human male.* Philadelphia: W. B. Saunders.

McKusick, L., Horstman, W., & Coates, T. (1985). AIDS and sexual behavior reported by gay men in San Francisco. *American Journal of Public Health, 75,* 493–496.

Morin, S. F. (1984). *AIDS risk reduction: The relationship to personal beliefs.* Position paper prepared for the symposium, The AIDS Epidemic: Development of Strategies for High Risk Behavior, University of California, San Francisco.

Orford, J. (1978). Implications for a theory of dependence. *British Journal of Addiction, 73,* 299–310.

Quadland, M. (1983, November 7–20). Overcoming sexual compulsion. *New York Native,* pp. 25–26.

Quadland, M. (1985, February 11–24). Compulsive sexuality and sexual freedom. *New York Native,* p. 26.

Quadland, M. C., Shattls, W. D., Jacobs, R., & D'Eramo, J. (1986). "800 men": A safer sex education program. Unpublished report in progress. New York: Gay Men's Health Crisis, Inc.

Van Ness, P. N. & Puchall, L. B. (1983). *A survey of the sexual behavior of gay men in Washington, DC.* Unpublished manuscript.

Wachtel, P. L. (1977). *Psychoanalysis and behavior therapy: Toward an integration.* New York: Basic Books.

The Worried Well: Maximizing Coping in the Face of AIDS

Kathy J. Harowski, PhD

University of Minnesota

SUMMARY. This paper discusses the AIDS epidemic in terms of its impact on the psychology of individuals and their relationships. Special emphasis is given to treatment strategies that therapists may find useful in working with the worried well presenting with psychological and sexual difficulties in reaction to AIDS anxiety. Issues of denial, control, and compliance will be presented as central to working with this population.

For at least the past 3 years, Acquired Immune Deficiency Syndrome (AIDS) has been unavoidable news. Even casual attention to newspapers or other media bombards one with "the latest" data on the medical, social, and political controversy surrounding the syndrome. While this bombardment of information alleviates irrational fears and provides information about prevention, for many it increases anxiety. Adding to the anxiety produced by this constant stream of information is the fact that much of it is ever-changing and occasionally contradictory, making a planful, rational approach to the threat of AIDS difficult for at-risk individuals to achieve. The cold, hard realities of the syndrome—a death rate of approximately 50 percent, a doubling of cases every 9 to 12 months—fuel panic and anxiety among the homosexual, bisexual, and heterosexual population.

With better delineation of the etiology of the syndrome, it has become possible to define certain groups as "at risk" and describe specific sexual behaviors that increase risk. The mechanism of contagion for AIDS has been discovered: a virus, HTLV III, found in body fluids such as blood and semen of those infected. The main method of transmission is through sexual behaviors that involve the exchange of body fluids, particularly unprotected anal intercourse.

This "at-risk" group, the worried well, are defined as persons at risk for AIDS because of past or present sexual activity or intravenous (IV)

Dr. Harowski is Assistant Professor, Program in Human Sexuality, Department of Family Practice and Community Health, University of Minnesota Medical School, 2630 University Avenue, SE, Minneapolis, MN 55416. Correspondence may be sent to the author at the above address.

drug use without a known exposure to the AIDS virus (Forstein, 1984). This definition can be expanded to include those who test positive on HTLV III antibody testing and who have not developed Aids Related Complex (ARC) or AIDS. While these individuals can be given specific guidelines about sexual behavior designed to prevent them from spreading the HTLV III virus, they are left with considerable anxiety about their own future health.

While the above definition makes it clear that the worried well include men and women, heterosexuals, bisexuals, and homosexuals, the group earliest impacted by the syndrome was gay males. The Center for Disease Control statistics currently place 75 percent of known AIDS cases in this population.

SOCIAL AND POLITICAL PRESSURES
AFFECTING THE WORRIED WELL

Cultural perspective frequently defines a society's view of and reaction to an illness (Sontag, 1978). The fact that AIDS initially appeared in the wake of the sexual revolution, and in populations typically scapegoated, has only added to the uproar. Indeed, this syndrome has been viewed as everything from an illness of the "me generation" to "divine retribution" for sexual promiscuity and homosexuality. In *Illness As Metaphor* (1978), Sontag states that metaphor and illness become interwoven when a metaphor connects with a "disease [so] overlayed with mystification, [so] charged with the fantasy of inescapable fatality" (p. 87). The illness thus becomes politicized and viewed as embodying many of the evils of a society. This abstract notion becomes very real when considering how people with the illness are viewed and treated by others, as well as how they feel about themselves. The worried well, then, cope with the double burden of the realities of AIDS as a medical concern and the psychological pressures created by the social use of this illness as a metaphor.

Of course, Sontag's point is that illness is not metaphor. In her words, the "healthiest way of being ill is one most purified of, most resistant to, metaphoric thinking" (p. 3). This approach to AIDS, viewing the syndrome for what it is and removing its emotional/political overlay, is admittedly difficult in the current social climate. Attempting it is a vital step in psychotherapy with the worried well.

The AIDS pandemic is occurring at a time when American society is changing its view of homosexuality. Homosexual men are "coming out" and gaining rights and acceptance in increasing numbers. Currently, same-sex preference is viewed as a normal variant of sexual expression rather than a psychiatric illness or abnormality. AIDS has appeared, then, at a time when a homosexual orientation is becoming somewhat more comfortable for the individual and his or her society. For some groups and individuals, this devastating syndrome serves to justify anti-homosexual beliefs and homophobia. This backlash has resulted in some bitterness and despair in the gay community. Joseph, et al. (1984) describe the pain and rage of homosexual men who feel as if hard-earned gains and increased acceptance may slip away in the face of the AIDS phenomenon. This fear of backlash and increasing homophobia is not without justification. A recent survey of health professionals (Douglas, Kalman, & Kalman, 1985) concluded that "a disturbingly high percentage of the health professionals [we] studied acknowledged more negative, even overtly hostile feelings towards homosexuals than they had before the emergence of the AIDS epidemic" (p. 1311). Even more striking was the finding that one-third of the caregivers surveyed felt that AIDS patients received inferior care while hospitalized.

In addition to examining our own feelings about homosexuality and AIDS, it is the responsibility of therapists who work with the worried well to be aware of the realities of homosexual lifestyles and not be prey to stereotypes and generalities. This is particularly pertinent in the areas of sexual behaviors and relationships (Batchelor, 1984), central issues of concern for many of the worried well. Many surveys and research studies can provide accurate information and help therapists deal with their own homophobia and exposure to misinformation and stereotypes (e.g., Bell & Weinberg, 1978; Bell, Weinberg, & Hammersmith, 1981; Coleman, 1981/1982).

Finally, therapists must keep in mind the historically difficult relationship between the gay community and health care providers. For example, homosexual individuals have frequently chosen to not disclose their sexual preference to physicians in order to avoid moralistic judgments and the possibility of poor health care (Dardick & Grady, 1980). In particular, mental health care was sometimes avoided by the gay community because of the traditional view of homosexuality as a pathological, psychological condition. Homosexual men who seek out information and medical treatment for AIDS-related concerns may find themselves in a peculiar situation; sexual behaviors that they were previously warned against for moral reasons may now be described as dangerous for medical reasons. Homosexual men are still reluctant to venture out of their community for medical or mental health care; a recent survey indicates that information and counseling regarding AIDS are initially sought via gay organizations and self-help groups rather than mental health professionals (Harowski, 1986).

INDIVIDUAL PSYCHOLOGICAL REACTIONS TO AIDS ANXIETY

For many homosexual men, the stresses of being different in a non-accepting, non-understanding society are intensified by the AIDS health crisis. The host of external or "social environment" issues noted above certainly have an impact on the worried well client, above and beyond individual issues and coping. The most prevalent reaction to AIDS-induced anxiety is that of denial (Forstein, 1984). Believing that "it can't happen to me" is in many ways an adaptive reaction to the anxiety and uncertainty of the current situation. This defense becomes less adaptive when individuals manifest a counterphobic or risk-taking approach to binding their anxiety. Other typical psychological reactions include depression, anger, and the reawakening of negative internalized homophobic feelings. Hypochondrical concerns, somatic reactions, and generalized panic attacks have been reported as well (Morin, Charles, & Malyon, 1984).

In examining psychological reactions to AIDS, it becomes clear that coping mechanisms and geography interact. In cities with a high and more visible number of men becoming sick and dying from AIDS, the worried well report panic attacks, somatic preoccupations, and difficulty in functioning on the job because of depression or obsessional worrying about the syndrome (Morin, et al., 1984). This is in contrast to areas with smaller numbers of the actually ill/dying, where denial and depression seem more prevalent. Forstein (1984) highlights the brittle nature of this denial by stating: "Although powerful, denial is a primitive defense that often breaks down dramatically when AIDS is diagnosed in a friend or acquaintance" (p. 55). This pattern of initial denial replaced by more overt anxiety syndromes is predictive of the future concerns of clients in areas currently less affected by AIDS.

AIDS-induced anxiety may exacerbate preexisting psychiatric illness. For example, paranoid states may develop in vulnerable individuals who become preoccupied with "dangerous" sexual behaviors and potential "contamination." Mild dysphoria and social withdrawal may escalate to become depression, low self-esteem, and isolation in dysthymic clients.

A special situation exists for homosexual men in the process of "coming out" and consolidating a gay identity. These men are especially affected by the social environment issues raised by the AIDS epidemic, and may experience increased difficulty in forming a positive gay identity. Development of an integrated homosexual identity often includes a stage of sexual exploration and experimentation that researchers compare to the heterosexual adolescent experience (Coleman, 1981/1982). AIDS-related anxieties and realities may have a significant impact on the number of partners and specific sexual behaviors of individuals in this phase. The generally high level of anxiety and uncertainty around coming out is certainly exacerbated for those currently in the process of defining their sexual orientation as homosexual. Clinically, this author has had these men present with increased generalized anxiety, some decrease in sexual desire, and over-concern with health and bodily functioning. A number of other therapists have reported this phenomenon to the author as well.

ISSUES IN PSYCHOTHERAPY

A typical concern in therapy with the worried well is that of anxiety management and control. The client's view of his ability to control his fate in an uncertain situation becomes a central treatment issue. For those overwhelmed by denial, depression, or anxiety, feelings of control over their lives are often at a minimum.

The question of modifying sexual behaviors to engage in "safer sex" may mean significant lifestyle changes for homosexual men. Being asked to stop or modify favorite activities may increase feelings of control (e.g., I can protect myself from AIDS by using condoms), or simply increase distress (e.g., I'm being asked to give up a pleasurable activity because it might affect my health). Additionally, decreasing risk-related behaviors may result in a change in important patterns of social behavior for certain homosexual men (Martin & Vance, 1984). These clinical issues must be worked through with clients to insure a compromise comfortable in a physical and psychological sense.

The Cleveland Men's Survey highlights the interaction between feelings of control and modifying behavior (Harowski, 1986). In this survey, homosexual men were administered a multi-dimensional, health-related locus of control scale (Wallston, Wallston, & DeVellis, 1978) to evaluate attitudes about health and determine whether they perceived their health as controlled by their behavior, by powerful others such as physicians, or by chance. The men were also asked about specific sexual behaviors. The worried well surveyed in this sample described themselves as strongly internally controlled and viewed their behavior as having an impact on their health. These men reported minimal psychological reactions to AIDS anxiety. Their strong belief that they were "in charge" of their health reinforced their denial about the threat of AIDS. However, the internally controlled attitude was correlated only very weakly with actual behaviors such as condom use, reducing one's number of partners, and modifying specific behaviors.

The use of denial as a coping strategy is of concern to therapists who work with the worried well in an attempt to break down denial and encourage education in safer sex techniques and taking responsibility for behaviors that impact on one's self and others. Cognitive restructuring strategies can be especially useful in helping these men problem solve and analyze their own behavior. The technique of behavioral analysis, breaking down difficult or anxiety-producing situations into specific steps, aids in clarifying and resolving conflict. For example, discussing sexual activities with a new partner can be broken down into steps such as deciding when to discuss comfortable limits, educating about HTLV III transmission, presenting one's rationale for sexual limits, and so forth. Each of these steps can be discussed and prepared for, with the end result being decreased overall anxiety about setting sexual limits. Redefining "caring" to emphasize taking responsibility for oneself and others in sexual relationships is a particularly useful restructuring strategy for the worried well.

Sexual dysfunction is also a common concern of the worried well. Anxiety is a key etiologic factor in many models of sexual dysfunction (Masters & Johnson, 1970). "Spectatoring," the process of worrying during sexual encounters to the point of decreasing pleasure and creating actual dysfunction, frequently develops in response to sexually experienced anxiety. Clinicians should assess the sexual functioning of homosexual men presenting with AIDS-related concerns. In particular, decreases in sexual desire may be a factor for those men presenting as depressed or anxious. Hypnosis and guided imagery may be useful to heighten relaxation and arousal in these instances. In his book, *Hypnosis and Sex Therapy*, Araoz (1982) presents a comprehensive overview of the use of hypnosis as a cognitive restructuring strategy in sex therapy. He presents specific hypnotic techniques for male dysfunction such as low desire and lack of sexual pleasure. An example is his "becoming alive" exercise (pp. 143–144), which uses hypnosis and imagery to allow clients to view all parts of their body, including their genitals, as alive and joyful. This technique can be combined with sexual fantasy to increase pleasure in sexuality. Araoz also places emphasis on the ego strengthening and enhancing power of hypnosis and guided imagery, certainly of benefit to homosexual men who feel vulnerable regarding their sexuality.

A client presenting with a more counterphobic adaptation might experience an increase in compulsive sexual activity to bind and manage anxiety. This can also be viewed as a reflection of the client's perceived invulnerability to an external threat such as AIDS. Breaking through denial by emphasizing individual responsibility, pointing out the dangers of such risk-taking, and providing alternatives based on problem solving and cognitive restructuring can lead to increased control. When this approach is not successful, a more intensive therapy might be needed to address issues of sexual control and eliminate this destructive behavior pattern (Quadland, this issue).

In working with men with counterphobic concerns, therapists may find themselves in the dilemma of managing their own feelings when faced with clients who make potentially dangerous sexual choices. Morin, et al. (1984) highlight the balancing act presented to therapists who must "remain sex positive and gay affirmative while at the same time working toward an educational model of safe sex" (p. 1291).

Concerns about sexuality lead to a consideration of relationships and intimacy, another area of concern for the worried well. Talking about sexuality assumes new relevance and urgency in the face of AIDS. Relationship issues typically addressed include assertiveness, sexual limit-setting, and making requests of partners. Group work, including role playing of appropriate limit-setting, provides direct, immediate feedback to homosexual men as they learn and practice an important new social skill (Morin, et al., 1984).

Talking about sexuality increases intimacy between partners and allows the worried well to explore levels of comfort and discomfort with closeness. This focus can provide a useful beginning point in relationship definition and redirection for many of the worried well. Issues of trust, affection, and sexuality emerge when working through dilemmas related to intimacy. Nichols (1984) describes the "adjustment process" to an AIDS diagnosis as one in which the patients experience increasing calmness and serenity as they come to feel more in control and more responsible for their lives. A similar process may occur in the worried well as they redefine relationships and intimacy in ways supportive of increasing personal growth and control.

As the AIDS crisis extends across the country, gay communities are organizing to provide support, education, and help for the worried well. Encouraging community involvement is another useful therapeutic approach. Besides decreasing isolation and withdrawal, community participation decreases the sense of powerlessness often experienced by the worried well, provides them access to accurate information, and allows them to perceive themselves as effective, in-control people. The fact that the gay community is organizing around the issue of AIDS should not be used, however, as a release from responsibility by "mainstream" or non-gay mental health practitioners and institutions.

The AIDS epidemic has allowed the gay community to coalesce in significant ways. Homosexual men, individually and via organizations, have worked to provide support and caring for one another in non-sexual ways. Isolation from "mainstream" medical care has been reduced, and homosexual individuals now more openly acknowledge their sexual orientation to health care professionals. As AIDS is viewed not as a metaphor but more clearly as a devastating illness, the response of the worried well, especially in the gay community, will be seen as instrumental in understanding, containing, and managing the syndrome. Sexual and psychological functioning have not been, and do not have to be, victims of the AIDS epidemic. Clinicians can continue building bridges through the process of increasing communication, providing education, decreasing anxiety and depression, and maximizing coping through work with the worried well.

REFERENCES

Araoz, D. (1982). *Hypnosis and sex therapy.* New York: Brunner/Mazel.

Batchelor, W. (1984). AIDS: A public health and psychological emergency. *American Psychologist,* *39,* 1279–1284.

Bell, A. P., & Weinberg, M. S. (1978). *Homosexualities: A study of diversity among men and women.* New York: Simon & Schuster.

Bell, A. P., Weinberg, M. S., In: Hammersmith, S. K. (1981). *Sexual preference.* Bloomington: Indiana University Press.

Coleman, E. (1981/82). Developmental stages of the coming out process. *Journal of Homosexuality,* *7*(2/3), 31–43.

Dardick, L., & Grady, K. (1980). Openness between gay persons and health professionals. *Annals of Internal Medicine, 93,* 115–119.

Douglas, C., Kalman, C., & Kalman, T. (1985). Homophobia among physicians and nurses: An empirical study. *Hospital-Community Psychiatry, 36,* 1309–1311.

Forstein, M. (1984). AIDS anxiety in the "worried well." In S. Nichols & D. Ostrow (Eds.), *Psychiatric implications of acquired immune deficiency syndrome* (pp. 50–60). Monograph Series of the American Psychiatric Press.

Harowski, K. (1986, March). *AIDS and sexual functioning: A survey of homosexual men.* Paper presented at the Society for Sex Therapy and Research Convention, Philadelphia, PA.

Joseph, J., Emmons, C., Kessler, R., Wortman, C., O'Brien, K., Hocher, W., & Schafer, C. (1984). Coping with the threat of AIDS: An approach to psychosocial assessment. *American Psychologist, 39,* 1297–1302.

Martin, J., & Vance, C. (1984). Behavioral and psychosocial factors in AIDS. *American Psychologist, 39,* 1303–1308.

Masters, W., & Johnson, V. (1970). *Human sexual inadequacy.* Boston: Little, Brown.

Morin, S., Charles, K., & Malyon, A. (1984). The psychological impact of AIDS on gay men. *American Psychologist, 39,* 1288–1293.

Nichols, S. (1984). Social and support groups for patients with acquired immune deficiency syndrome. In S. Nichols & D. Ostrow (Eds.), *Psychiatric implications of acquired immune deficiency syndrome* (pp. 78–82). Monograph Series of the American Psychiatric Press.

Quadlund, M., & Shattls, W. (1987). AIDS, sexuality, and sexual control. *Journal of Homosexuality, 14*(1/2), 277–298.

Sontag, S. (1978). *Illness as metaphor.* New York: Farrar, Straus, & Giroux.

Wallston, K., Wallston, B., & DeVellis, R. (1978). Development of the multidimensional health locus of control (MHLC) scales. *Health Education Monographs, 6,* 160–243.

The Individual and Social Psychology of Aging: Clinical Implications for Lesbians and Gay Men

Richard A. Friend, PhD
University of Pennsylvania

SUMMARY. This article examines issues regarding aging for homosexual people in an attempt to provide a more comprehensive understanding and appreciation of the meaning age has for women and men in our society. Through the use of case examples, clinical concerns and interventions are discussed as they relate to three broad areas. Specifically, the interrelated effects of ageism and heterosexism, normal changes in sexual response with age, and "accelerated aging" are explored. The relationship between social context and individual psychology provides the framework for this discussion. As the literature reviewed here indicates, there is a great deal of diversity among homosexual women and men in their experiences with aging. The strengths and insights which characterize many older homosexual men and women, however, provide valuable lessons for all men and women.

During a busy schedule recently, the author saw the following three clients. Albert, a 72-year-old male, sought therapy after the death of his lover with whom he had lived for over 35 years. Troubled by his feelings regarding Sam's death, Albert also needed support in managing concerns about his own future. Loretta and Phyllis were both in their 50's and recently began experiencing anger and sexual problems in their relationship. Brian, 36, had been lonely, depressed, and feeling hopeless about the future. His attitude about most things was "Why bother? It's all down hill from here."

On the surface, these three case studies may appear unrelated. However, Albert, Loretta, Phyllis, and Brian all have something significant in common. For each of them, the issue of what it means to live in an ageist and heterosexist environment has generated special problems.

This paper reviews the literature on older lesbians and gay men in an

Dr. Friend is Director of External Education for the Human Sexuality Program, Graduate School of Education C1, University of Pennsylvania, 3700 Walnut Street, Philadelphia, PA 19104. Correspondence may be directed to the author at that address.

attempt to provide a fuller and more complete appreciation of the meaning age has for women and men in our society. Through the use of case examples, particular attention is paid to clinical issues and interventions as they apply to age related issues. Specifically, the interrelated effects of ageism, the assumption that the young and the old are "less than" those of other age groups, and heterosexism, the assumption that everyone is heterosexual and if they are not, they should be, on lesbians and gay men are addressed. Also, normal changes in sexual response with age and their effect on relationships is examined. Finally, "accelerated aging," defined as the experiencing of oneself as old at a time before one's chronological age peers define themselves as old (Friend, 1980) and its effects is explored here. This latter issue is examined in detail, as it provides valuable insights into the goal of understanding the meanings of age in our society.

Each of the above cases individually illustrates the three broad areas addressed here. Albert's experience managing heterosexist oppression and loss is discussed first. Phyllis and Loretta's relationship is examined next as an example of the potential psychological and relationship difficulties which can arise as a result of normal physiological changes with age. Brian's concern about the future is used as an example of common issues related to accelerated aging.

AGEISM AND HETEROSEXISM

For more than 35 years, Albert and Sam built a life together. When Sam died suddenly one spring from a bout with cancer, not only was Albert left struggling to mourn his lover's death, but many unexpected issues arose for him which triggered a variety of emotions. Sam's family questioned the financial arrangements of his estate and tried to bar Albert from participating in funeral arrangements. Albert was able to find comfort and support from his and Sam's close circle of friends, who helped him validate his anger as well as grieve his loss. In therapy Albert began to address the difficult issues of his own mortality and how to maintain control in living out his life in a self-determined fashion.

Despite a tremendous increase in research on sexual orientation in general, studies of older gay men and lesbians are still very uncommon. The current body of research on older homosexual adults is primarily descriptive in nature, examining myths and stereotypes. The descriptive data has managed to challenge many of the assumptions about older homosexuals, while trying to understand and present a more complete view of the aging and adjustment process as experienced by this population (Almvig, 1982; Berger, 1980, 1982-a, 1982-b; Francher & Henkin, 1973; Kimmel, 1978; Minnegerode & Adelman, 1978; Raphael

& Robinson, 1980). A small number of studies have gone beyond descriptive analysis in an attempt to examine more specific issues such as psychological adaptation (Friend, 1980; Weinberg, 1970; Weinberg & Williams, 1975), age-status labeling (Minnegerode, 1976), partner age preference, accelerated aging (Laner, 1978, 1979), and length of time engaged in homosexual activity, in an attempt to understand aging among gay males (Gray & Dressel, 1985). Within this body of research a great deal more attention is paid to older gay men than to lesbians, an imbalance consistent with the research on sexual orientation in general.

Dawson (1982) estimates that there are 3.5 million homosexual men and women over the age of 60 currently living in the United States. Kimmel (1977) describes at least three general lifestyle patterns among the older gay men he studied. The first style represents those men, like Albert, who are or have been in a long-term relationship. Another lifestyle pattern is the previously married gay who may have children and grandchildren. Last are the loners, described by Kimmel as men who are fearful that their sexual orientation will be discovered and who experience relatively little sexual and social intimacy. Today's older homosexuals face the special problem of invisibility (Almvig, 1982; Kimmel, 1978). Because the majority of their lives were spent in a time where they were forced to hide and conceal their sexual orientation, they may be more isolated from both their age peers and younger homosexuals.

While the stereotype of the older homosexual person conforms to this lonely, isolated pattern, this image and lifestyle pattern does not appear to be representative of most older homosexual men (Friend, 1980; Kelly, 1977; Kimmel, 1977, 1978). Dawson (1982) also reports that growing old in isolation represents the lifestyle of a small minority of the homosexuals with whom he works.

Like Albert, many older homosexual adults are faced with the double stigmatization and oppression of both age and an unpopular sexual orientation (Dawson, 1982; Friend, 1984; Kimmel, 1978). These social arrangements (ageism and heterosexism) create unique conflicts and problems, as well as coping mechanisms, for lesbians and gay men. Lesbians who are coupled, for example, have to contend with the pressure of having a combined female income, i.e., this is a distinct disadvantage as compared with male couples or heterosexual couples and illustrates the relationship between ageism, heterosexism, and sexism.

Clinical issues to consider include managing the compounded effects of traditional age-related issues and oppression. The process of managing terminal or chronic illness can be complicated by the fact that in many hospitals intensive care units exclude everyone except blood relatives (Kimmel, 1978). The attitudes of nursing staff and physicians may create an unaccepting atmosphere (Anderson, 1981; Lief, 1973), and the expression of affection between lovers or same sex friends in the hospital may be discouraged (Weinberg, 1982). An oppressive atmosphere certainly does not facilitate convalescence and may, in fact, interfere with appropriate treatment if a patient withholds information out of fear that this may effect their care. The fear of institutionalization in nursing homes or other rehabilitation centers is great. Not only are these places perceived as unsupportive of the sexual lives of older heterosexual people, but older homosexuals may fairly assume their sexuality will receive even less attention and respect.

The end of a long-term relationship due to the death of a partner can be particularly traumatic, especially if counseling and support is minimal. Kimmel (1978) reports that the lover and homosexual friends of a person who dies are often excluded from funeral planning and participation in other aspects of the bereavement process. For Albert, these were real issues which added anger to his grief.

Counseling and support services are essential in managing and preparing for potential problems in old age. Legal and inheritance issues often magnify and compound the grievance period. The surviving partner may have to manage the possibility of not being recognized as the beneficiary of insurance policies, real estate, or other inheritance. While such is relatively uncommon, careful planning with good legal counsel can help protect homosexuals from these forms of discrimination. It is appropriate for the therapist to address these issues with clients as a way of anticipating and planning for the future. Following the death of a lesbian or gay lover, unsupportive family or insurance companies or both may be sources of significant emotional strain, which must also be managed in therapy.

The potential problems and conflicts of growing older in our culture can prompt the development of many coping mechanisms which manage these problems and serve as valuable resources. The research indicates that being homosexual can facilitate successful aging (Dawson, 1982; Francher & Henkin, 1973; Friend, 1980, 1984; Kimmel, 1978). In counseling it is useful to capitalize on these resources and remind the older homosexual client of these strengths and how to make best use of them.

Homosexuality is reported to be functional in adjusting to old age in several ways. Martin (1982) reports that it is during adolescence that homosexual people become aware of their sexual orientation and begin to manage what this means. According to Kimmel (1978), this early life crisis is:

> one that can involve extensive family disruption, intense feelings and sometimes alienation from the family—maybe one of the most significant a gay person will face. Once resolved, it may provide a

perspective on major life crises and a sense of crisis competence that buffers the person against later crises (p. 117).

This concept of "crisis competence" suggests that successful management of the coming out process provides the individual with coping mechanisms which generalize to other crises later in life. Some of these coping mechanisms are identified as additional factors associated with the facilitation of successful aging.

Gender role flexibility can also be functional to the aging process (Dawson, 1982; Francher & Henkin, 1973; Friend, 1980, 1984). According to Francher and Henkin (1973):

> One of the functions of the hypernarcissism and involuntary self-containment of the homosexual world is the development among homosexuals of interests and pursuits that are not only contradictory to our societal sex-role typifications but that also require a more self-indulgent use of time, not generally acceptable within the heterosexual community (p. 672).

More flexible gender roles may function to allow the older homosexual to develop ways of taking care of themselves that feel comfortable and appropriate. These skills may not be developed to the same degree among heterosexual men or women, who may be used to having or expecting a wife or husband to look after them.

If part of the coming out process involves challenging some of the arbitrary ways in which "appropriate" sexual feelings get defined, this same analysis may be applied to the social construction of gender roles. Rigid gender role definitions may mean a recently widowed heterosexual woman has to learn to balance a checkbook or a heterosexual man may have to learn to cook. For older homosexual men and women, throughout their life there has been the potential for greater freedom to learn skills which may be considered non-traditional. Challenging the social construction of gender roles may not pose a significant threat to the sexual identity of older homosexuals in ways that it might for older heterosexuals. The issues of gender roles and sexual orientation have been managed earlier in life, leaving many older homosexuals feeling intact when it comes to engaging in non-traditional gender-role behaviors. Greater flexibility in gender roles among older homosexuals also suggests that they are not traumatized by living alone, or by the "role loss" of children leaving home and retirement, which are difficult for many heterosexuals (Dawson, 1982; Francher & Henkin, 1973; Friend, 1980). Skills for managing the loss of family and independent living are more likely to be part of the lesbian or gay man's repertoire.

Dawson (1982) also reports that many adults grow old believing that their children or extended family will provide for them or help them in their old age. Given that changing family patterns no longer insure that the elderly are provided for by their family, Dawson says, "gay people have been less likely to assume that their families would provide for them in old age" (p. 6) and are more likely to have planned for their own future security. Having addressed imagined or real loss of family support earlier in life, homosexual people thus may be better prepared for the realities of old age.

Related to the issue of family support is the role of friends as a family network. Francher and Henkin (1973) report that older homosexual men exchange the family supports which were lost when they came out with a strong network of friendships. Bell and Weinberg (1978) describe these friendships as functioning as a "surrogate family." In fact, it is reported that homosexual men have significantly more close friends than do heterosexual men (Cotton, 1972; Saghir & Robins, 1973; Bell & Weinberg, 1978). Friend (1980) reports that there was no zero-gain exchange of family for friends in his sample when they came out; instead, there was a net gain of reinforcing family supports with the support of friends. According to Friend, many subjects anticipated a loss of family supports when they came out which later did not occur. "This in turn facilitate[s] adjustment for older gay men and gives them a broad network on which to rely in times of instrumental or socioemotional need." (Friend, 1980, p. 244).

The strengths of a family of friends can also be bolstered by the presence of an empowering community. In many places, the lesbian and gay communities provide many cultural, social, political, and religious opportunities. In the larger urban areas there may even be organizations like the New York-based Senior Action in a Gay Environment (SAGE), which provides a variety of social and support services for older lesbians and gay men. An important clinical intervention is being aware of such community resources and encouraging clients to explore these possible supports.

Crisis competence, gender role flexibility, and a broad family and community network all provide support for homosexual men and women later in life. Albert had the support of his friends and therapy which helped him with many issues, including coping with Sam's death, being angry at and interacting with Sam's family, making sure that his own insurance policy, will, and property were managed as he wanted, and the hope that his own future would continue to contain people and activities he cared about. In therapy Albert gained additional support and permission to go through his grieving process, as well as insight into the skill he had for maintaining and insuring his future independence.

NORMAL PHYSIOLOGICAL CHANGES IN SEXUAL RESPONSE WITH AGE

In addition to managing the special issues identified above, many older people experience problems which can result from the normal physiological changes in sexual response which occur with age. For example, Phyllis and Loretta's relationship had been very strained lately. Phyllis felt angry and upset because Loretta did not seem to respond sexually like she had previously in their relationship, and Loretta took longer to become aroused, and even when lubricated did not seem to be as wet as before. Loretta was also upset, claiming that Phyllis pressured her to behave in ways which were beyond her control. Loretta said sex still felt good to her and that she would enjoy it even more if Phyllis would leave her alone about her response. Both of them examined Loretta's reactions so much that neither were enjoying sex.

Both men and women experience normal physiological changes and common psychological reactions associated with aging. As men age, they normally find that it takes longer and requires more direct physical stimulation of the penis to achieve an erection, although once achieved they can maintain it longer (Kinsey, Pomeroy, & Martin, 1948; Masters & Johnson, 1966). Masters and Johnson (1966) also report that there is a reduction in the amount and force of the ejaculant, as well as a decrease in ejaculatory demand. In other words, many men find that they no longer experience a driving urge to ejaculate with each sexual encounter. Along with diminished ejaculatory demand is a reduction in the goal orientation of sex which values ejaculation and orgasm as the measure of sexual pleasure. As a result, while every sexual relationship may not lead to orgasm and ejaculation, these experiences are still subjectively experienced as positive. There is also an increase in the length of the refractory period following orgasm, according to Masters and Johnson. That is, many men will not be able to become erect as soon after ejaculation as they have in the past. These changes are usually gradual but noticeable.

Given that there is less of a "need" to ejaculate for many older men, the potential exists for older men to maintain sexual contact for longer periods of time than their younger counterparts. The too-rapid ejaculation frequently found in younger men may no longer be a problem. Instead, the older man may experience a certain freedom to explore and experiment sexually without the fear of ejaculating before he and his partner wish. However, if a homosexual man or his partner believe the myths that sex requires an erection and must end in orgasm and ejaculation, conflicts may develop. Zilbergeld (1978) reports that these goal-directed orientations which characterize male sexuality are related to sexual and relationship difficulties. In therapy it is useful to examine male socialization as it relates to sexual functioning and behaviors.

Women also experience physiological changes in sexual response, many of which are associated with menopause and the climacteric period. Vaginal lubrication tends to decrease and a more prolonged period of stimulation may be required than before (Masters & Johnson, 1966). In some cases, the insertion of anything into the vagina (fingers, vibrators, and so on) may be painful due to decreased lubrication—this is most often corrected by the use of an artificial water soluble lubricant such as KY jelly (Weinberg, 1982). For some women, physicians recommend estrogen replacement therapy (ERT) for managing the changes associated with decreased hormone levels. (Hammond and Maxson [1982] reviewed and evaluated the potential benefits and risks of this treatment approach). Given that the risks of such therapy include a possible link between it and uterine cancer, the potential risks must be balanced against the benefits before implementing ERT.

Decreased lubrication need not indicate a lack of response or desire. In fact many women, like Loretta, may be unaware of the physiological changes until their partner brings them to their attention. Unlike men, women retain the ability to achieve orgasms similar to their previous orgasmic patterns (Masters & Johnson, 1966).

In response to these physical changes, many older homosexuals may begin to avoid sex. This avoidance pattern may develop from the fear that natural age-related changes indicate a sexual dysfunction, which in turn can create a self-fulfilling prophecy. Older homosexual men may avoid sex or become extremely anxious when they are with a sexual partner. The fear that they are becoming impotent, when in fact slower and less firm erections are normal for older men, can create enough anxiety that erectile difficulties do develop. This performance anxiety can be so great that impotence does become a real problem (Masters & Johnson, 1970). Educating individuals about the natural age-related changes in sexual physiology can help to alleviate many of these fears.

For Loretta and Phyllis, education was valuable in managing their sexual and relationship issues. They were also encouraged by knowing that although sexual frequency does seem to decrease somewhat with age, it remains relatively constant throughout the life span (Newman & Nichols, 1960). Given good health and an available and willing partner, those who are sexually active when they were young remain so when they are older. Accepting the myth that sex ends with menopause or at a certain age limit may unwittingly sabotage future possibilities for enjoyable sexual relationships. Many older homosexuals benefit from counseling and education which allow them to feel more secure with their sexuality and relationships, and to improve their interpersonal communication. These interventions help prevent turning natural age-related changes in sexuality into problems.

ACCELERATED AGING

Another age-related issue for which homosexual men may seek therapy is the experience of accelerated aging. Feeling "over the hill" and devalued for not appearing youthful contributed to Brian's depression and loneliness. He would frequently stay home and isolate himself out of his fear that no one would like him now that he was approaching 40 years old. For Brian, internalized homophobia and low self-esteem combined to create a problem whereby he negatively defined himself as old.

Accelerated aging is a concept which has emerged out of the research on older homosexuals, and is defined as experiencing oneself as old at an earlier age than one's chronological age peers define themselves as old (Friend, 1980; Laner, 1978; Minnegerode, 1976). While a great deal of literature on homosexual men assumes or infers the presence of acceler-ated aging, only a small number of studies have addressed this issue directly. The research to date provides conflicting results regarding both the presence of accelerated aging among homosexual men, and the meaning this experience has on their lives.

The construct of accelerated aging within the context of sexual identity is examined here. First, the research on aging among men and women who are homosexual and heterosexual is evaluated as it relates to accelerated aging. Next, a framework focusing on gender, gender roles, and sexual orientation as separate socially constructed components of sexual identity is presented as an explanation and description of acceler-ated aging as a concept of individual psychology. This sexual identity framework suggests that accelerated aging is a function of a specific gender role expression, *not* of sexual orientation per se. Finally, this theory of accelerated aging based on gender is discussed as it relates to clinical interventions.

In describing the gay male community, Gagnon and Simon (1973) write that: "While American society places an inordinate positive emphasis on youth, the homosexual community, by and large, places a still greater emphasis on this fleeting characteristic. . . . In addition, the crisis of aging comes later to the heterosexual" (p. 149). They go on to suggest that society is less concerned with the repression of lesbianism, and therefore has less of a need to conceptualize it so narrowly, allowing the lesbian a more labile and less age-restricted stereotype.

Bell (1971) contends that:

Of all the personal factors that might worry the homosexual there is probably none more psychologically upsetting for many than aging. Because such a great importance is attached to appearing youthful and attractive to successfully compete he often worries as he feels he is losing his youth (p. 272).

In their descriptive comparison between lesbians and gay men, Martin and Lyon (1979) contend that there is less emphasis on youth and physical attractiveness among the former group. Similarly, compared with lesbians, Thoresen (1984) writes, "Male couples are apt to live in a more youth-oriented subculture; as someone has put it, old age begins to set in at seventeen" (p. 2). Additionally, she suggests many lesbians have children and develop a family-based or pseudo-kin based network and as a result "may fear aging less as a time when they fear being alone. This is probably a greater problem for males" (p. 2). Because lesbians do not compete in the same highly physical marketplaces as gay men, Bell (1971) concludes that aging is less traumatic for them.

Berger (1982a) describes the popular view of the older homosexual man as alienated and effeminate, someone who is old at the age of 30. Unlike the previous authors, he goes on to suggest that:

> The old lesbian painted in equally unflattering terms is seen as heartless and unemotional. Like the older male homosexual, her aging is accelerated and she is lonely because younger lesbians find her unattractive. . . . These stereotypes serve the function of social control. They deter young people from choosing a homosexual life-style (p. 237).

Based on personal observations and research, Berger finds evidence to contradict the above stereotypes.

Francher and Henkin (1973) interviewed 10 homosexual men over the age of 50 and concluded that the "male social role as defined by the homosexual subculture is predicated on a greater degree of narcissism and youth orientation than the heterosexual male role" (p. 673). Reporting on a pilot study of 11 older homosexuals, Minnegerode and Adelman (1978) concluded that gay men evaluate age changes in physical appearance more negatively than lesbians.

The overall conclusion drawn from these authors is that aging is more stressful and occurs earlier for gay men than for lesbians. For homosexuals as a group, then, this reflects a within-group gender difference in terms of accelerated aging. Fewer studies have addressed accelerated aging in a more direct fashion. It is interesting to note, however, that this smaller body of research does not attempt to compare homosexual men to homosexual women, but homosexual men to presumed heterosexual men, and homosexual women to presumed heterosexual women. In addition, it is important to note, with the exception of Laner's (1978, 1979) studies, no comparable control groups are used to make these between-group comparisons. In fact, some of these authors base their impressions on either personal experiences or contacts with the gay and lesbian communities. The lack of controlled research casts doubt on the validity of these conclusions because informal impressions are not appropriately utilized as conclusive research findings.

The research which examines this issue directly provides conflicting results regarding the presence of accelerated aging among homosexual men as compared to heterosexual men. Some research suggests homosexual men do define themselves as old at an earlier age than do heterosexual men (Friend, 1980; Kelly, 1977), whereas other studies report no differences between heterosexual and homosexual men (Laner, 1978; Minnegerode, 1976). The only study which examines this issue for women concludes that heterosexual women experience accelerated aging more than homosexual women (Laner, 1979).

Friend (1980) surveyed subjects self-identified as older homosexual men. Old age for men is generally seen by the population as occurring around age 65 (Atchley, 1977; Neugarten, Moore, & Lowe, 1965). The respondents' mean age in the Friend (1980) study was 48. Additionally, 39 of the 43 men were below age 64 while still identifying themselves as "older." According to Friend (1980), "This would support the presence of accelerated aging, at least for the current sample of self-identified older gay men" (p. 239). In Kelly's (1977) sample, most of the 241 homosexual men reported age 50 as the end of middle age and the beginning of old age. Again, in terms of the age norms developed by Atchley (1977) and Neugarten, et al. (1965), the onset of old age is seen as some 15 years earlier by the homosexual men surveyed, supporting the presence of accelerated aging. Minnegerode (1976) conducted the only research specifically directed at examining the issue of accelerated aging among homosexual men. Ninety-five homosexual men between the ages of 25 and 68 years classified themselves as young, middle-aged, or old. Minnegerode (1976) finds no significant differences in the age-status labels of his sample as compared with Neugarten, et al. (1965).

There are serious limitations in the Friend (1980), Kelly (1977), and Minnegerode (1976) research. Comparing self-reported definitions of age with definitions applied to the general population may restrict the ability to draw conclusions about accelerated aging. Accelerated aging refers to between-group differences in self-definitions of age, rather than those differences between self-definitions and group norms.

Laner (1978, 1979) used an interesting approach in looking at the issue of accelerated aging by examining the "personals" advertisements of both heterosexual and homosexual men as a non-reactive data base for autoperceptions and relationship goals. Assuming both the presence of accelerated aging and that younger people are less likely to seek partners through the "personals," Laner (1978) hypothesized "disproportionately more early middle-aged homosexual advertisers will be found, in comparison to heterosexual advertisers" (p. 498).

Laner's (1978) data do not support the hypothesis of accelerated aging. However, more homosexual men than other men did not state their age in the advertisements. Laner (1978) offers two very diverse explanations to interpret her results. Either chronological age is less important to homosexual men, or "age is *so* important among homosexuals, as theorized, that many older advertisers fear to mention it lest they risk rejection on that basis" (p. 499). Not only are there no definitive conclusions which can be drawn from her research, Laner's interpretations can also support arguments for both the presence and absence of accelerated aging among homosexual men.

In a similar study of women, Laner (1979) concludes that "age differences between groups did indicate support for 'accelerated aging' among heterosexual women" (p. 267). Additionally, more than 98% of the homosexual women stated their age in the advertisements, compared to approximately 76% of the heterosexual women. According to Laner, "This appears to be an additional indication of the tendency of heterosexual women to hide their chronological age and, therefore, of the higher negative valence of age for heterosexual, as compared with homosexually oriented women" (p. 272). It is interesting to note that Laner chooses this interpretation for the women's ads she studied, and offers two divergent interpretations for the same of men's ads.

Laner's (1979) finding of accelerated aging among heterosexual women and not among homosexual women led her to the conclusion that in terms of aging, homosexual women may have an advantage over heterosexual women. Laner states:

> Lesbians do not experience the accelerated aging as early, nor is the age of their partners as important as in the heterosexual world. This means that the field of eligibles for lesbians, even though they are a minority among women in general, may be effectively larger than the experienced field of eligibles for heterosexual women who continue to seek the traditional "male older/female younger" age distribution in relationships (p. 273).

Some of the research reviewed here appears to support a particular value orientation toward aging. Typically in our society aging is viewed negatively (Francher, 1962). With this perceptual bias in mind, some literature seems to assume that those who define themselves as older feel negatively about this experience (Gagnon & Simon, 1973; Bell, 1971). It is still unclear from this review of the literature how those who define themselves as old feel about this self-perception.

In summary, a dominant theme in the research suggests that, as compared with homosexual women, homosexual men seem to have more concerns regarding aging and these concerns appear to be expressed earlier in the life cycle. Also, as a group, homosexual women seem less likely than heterosexual women to experience accelerated aging, and the data regarding homosexual men as compared to heterosexual men on this issue is conflicting. One must keep in mind the serious limitations in the interpretations and conclusions drawn from the research reviewed. There is still a great need for further research given these shortcomings and conflicting results. The author is currently collecting data regarding accelerated aging in an attempt to fill some of the gaps in the current body of literature.

Another crucial distinction between these two sets of data is made by Harry (1982), who argues that there are two age-related issues being described which are conceptually different. One highlights the youth orientation of the gay male community, which is said to create a crisis for homosexual men as they age because they perceive diminished ability to compete in the sexual marketplace of the future. Harry compares this to the mid-life transition which "appears to be one during which the individual realizes that the remaining time for doing this [achievement] is growing limited and he questions the direction of his life or lack thereof" (p. 219). The second issue concerns self-perceptions of age. The age changes under consideration here have to do with viewing one's self as "old." According to Harry, "The transition to old age is one in which the individual comes to see his active life of achieving or accomplishing things as largely over," as compared to mid-life transition where the major issue "appears to be what to do with one's remaining life rather than whether there is any active life remaining" (p. 219).

If in fact the data do reflect two different experiences in terms of age-related changes, it is necessary to distinguish between them in the discussion of accelerated aging. To this end, Harry (1982) argues that:

> The concept of accelerated aging seems to imply that gay men go through aging changes similar to those of heterosexual men but do it earlier. If this is so, one must ask whether this early aging refers to an early growing old or to an early mid-life crisis (p. 219).

In examining whether accelerated aging reflects mid-life concerns or a premature self-labeling as old, Harry (1982) makes a strong argument for the former. His data, which include a control group comparison, indicate that homosexual men in their early 40s were more concerned about growing old and looking youthful than either younger or older respondents. The data also indicate that these concerns are especially salient among single homosexual men where "the crisis of aging appears to be more common, to occur earlier, and to last longer than among the coupled" (p. 222). Harry argues that preferred age of partner also compounds these concerns. He says that men who define success in the gay sexual marketplace in terms of attracting significantly younger men may experience a crisis of aging early if they are unsuccessful. The data qualify the relationship between desire for younger partners and aging concerns by indicating that actual number of sexual partners was not significantly related to interest in younger men. Harry concludes that it is not so much success in the sexual marketplace, but the anticipation of decreased sexual rewards in a homosexual man who has internalized the youth-oriented values of parts of the gay world "which sets the stage for an aging crisis and defines what is to be considered a crisis" (p. 226).

Harry's (1982) research also indicates that attachments to work tend to inhibit mid-life concerns among respondents in the same way that attachments to another person reduce concerns for coupled homosexual men. According to Harry, "These data strongly suggest that the mid-life crisis is a crisis of meaning which occurs when the psychological hold of one's environment has weakened" (p. 232). These psychological attachments which provide meaning and interest for some individuals influence the experiencing of a mid-life crisis for others.

Crisis of meaning appears then to be different from labeling one's self as old. The latter reflects a concern over the perceived lack of remaining time, whereas the former is a concern over what to do meaningfully with remaining time. In this way the apparent weaknesses in the existing literature may simply reflect the measurement of two different experiences with life changes (Friend, 1980; Harry, 1982; Kelly, 1977; Laner, 1978; Minnegerode, 1976). Hence, accelerated aging is modified here to mean experiencing concerns over continued meaningful connections with valued parts of one's world, rather than a premature self-labeling as "old."

This revised definition of accelerated aging reflects an existential crisis of meaning for an individual. If, as Harry suggests, there is a perceived reduction in a man's ability to engage successfully in the sexual marketplace of the gay world, which is seen as accessible primarily through attractiveness and youthful appearance, accelerated aging may be experienced. Harry's analysis, while limited to men, for the purposes of this paper is applied to women as well. While gay men may experience accelerated aging as described above, heterosexual women may experience a similar conflict in terms of their sense of diminished access to relationships with men. Given current demographic patterns whereby women outlive men, older men are more likely to be heterosexually married than are older women.

This now raises the question of the ways in which homosexual women and heterosexual men are different from homosexual men and heterosexual women as groups in terms of accelerated aging. If the latter two groups experience accelerated aging due to actual and perceived changes in their interpersonal relationships, homosexual women may not sense the same diminished potential for future relationships with other women, given the reality that women outlive men today. Heterosexual men, on the other hand, may in fact experience a crisis similar to accelerated aging, wherein the value of meaningfulness seems to be centered primarily around occupational concerns related to achievement rather than physical appearance. This career related conflict may simply be labeled mid-life crisis (Levinson, et al., 1978) and is a more stable crisis compared with youthful appearance, which begins to diminish earlier in the life span and continues to diminish through out the course of one's life.

Additionally, homosexual women seem to value physical appearance less than homosexual men (Almvig, 1982; Bell, 1971; Bell & Weinberg, 1978; Gagnon & Simon, 1973; Minnegerode & Adelman, 1978) and see their 30's and 40's as a time of career development and achievement, which promotes a sense of confidence and appeal to others (Thoresen, 1984). Gagnon and Simon (1973) also describe the serious commitment homosexual women have to their jobs as compared to heterosexual women. Hence, homosexual women's experience of mid-life accelerated aging (defined in terms of interpersonal relationships and career concerns) appears minimal compared to that of some homosexual men and heterosexual women, while perhaps more similar to heterosexual men.

In summary, the revised definition of accelerated aging refers to the perception of diminished meaningful attachments for the remainder of one's life. Some of these dimensions of meaning include physical appearance, interpersonal relationships, and vocational concerns. These factors also improve or diminish at different rates over the lifespan. While certainly not an exhaustive list, these factors are highlighted in the literature and provide a clearer and more precise understanding of the dynamics of accelerated aging.

It is also important to note that the language used in this discussion may unintentionally imply certain values about the above dimensions, such as the use of the term "sexual marketplace" versus "interpersonal relationships." It is often assumed that participation in the sexual marketplace excludes interpersonal relationships and is negative in and of itself. The author does not make these assumptions, given the fact that many homosexual men form interpersonal relationships within the so-called sexual marketplace (McWhirter & Mattison, 1984). Additionally, the author is not placing a value on sexual relationships devoid of additional interpersonal qualities, or on interpersonal relationships which do not include sexual components.

Harry's analysis of the accelerated aging concept as an expression of mid-life crisis, and not a premature self-labeling as old, points to some very salient questions regarding the context in which this concept has appeared in the literature. If the finding that accelerated aging occurs among homosexual men is simply a research creation effected by sampling problems, the question arises as to what the implications of this are for the clinician.

If it is assumed that being single and valuing youthfulness facilitate the experience of accelerated aging as defined here, then perhaps those segments of the homosexual male population which reflect these positions are over represented in the literature data bases. Harry and DeVall (1978) argue that independent of sexual orientation, single people are more likely than coupled people to place a greater value on youthfulness and physical characteristics. They conclude that "the reason the notion of the youth-orientedness of gay culture has received such widespread acceptance is that most of the research supporting this notion has been based on those selected gay settings that are most youth-oriented" (p. 123).

Furthermore, if the 40s is an age period in which mid-life issues, if they occur, are highlighted, then perhaps as a group this age bracket is also over represented in the literature on older homosexual men. Berger (1980, 1982a, 1982b), for example, studied older homosexual men in South Florida. Eligible respondents for his study were defined as any self-identified homosexual 40 years of age or older. Like Berger, Kelly (1977) used respondents' definitions of "older" (age 50) to determine his age cut-off point. Out of his total number of older respondents, slightly fewer than 19% were over age 65. Over 90% of Friend's (1980) sample were below age 64.

The difficulty in obtaining significantly older homosexual male respondents for participation in research has by necessity created a lowering of age limits. As a result, those people falling in the age group where mid-life issues or accelerated aging are most likely to occur may be over represented. Hence, the impression of accelerated aging as a predominant experience for homosexual men may reflect an issue of sampling bias.

Harry (1982) further qualifies this methodological issue:

> If some gay men withdraw from the gay world during their forties this means that, when one samples gays from that world, one will disproportionately acquire respondents who have resolved their aging concerns within that world. Hence, those gay men who found other, non-gay-world solutions to their aging crisis may appear rather different from those obtainable from the gay world. This problem arises out of the fact the students of homosexuality remain forever haunted by questions of whether their results are due to their sampling methods (p. 235).

For an excellent review of sampling issues in research involving homosexual male subjects, see Harry (1986).

SEXUAL IDENTITY AND ACCELERATED AGING

Given the assumption that accelerated aging among homosexual men reflects concerns about their future, and that this may not be a common experience but instead a research creation, some additional issues require consideration. Framing this discussion is a sexual identity framework for conceptualizing between group differences and similarities with regard to accelerated aging.

Sexual identity is comprised of four separate but somewhat interrelated components; biological sex, gender identity, social sex roles, and sexual orientation (Shively & De Cecco, 1977). Sex is the biological state of being male or female. Gender identity is the internal conviction of being female or male. Social sex roles are the behaviors and attitudes which are culturally defined as masculine and feminine. Sexual orientation refers to an individual's erotic potential; their feelings of attraction for members of the other sex, same sex, or both sexes. The four components of the sexual identity framework presented here seem to influence the individual aging process in terms of accelerated aging. While these interrelated components may effect accelerated aging in different ways, the focus here is on the individual psychology of aging as effected by social sex roles and sexual orientation, *not* by biological sex or gender identity.

Given the general biological dichotomy of sex into male and female populations, certain role behaviors and attitudes are socialized as appropriate primarily for one sex more so than the other. While these role behaviors are distributed based on sex, they need not be strictly a function of this biological state. It has been argued by many that masculinity and femininity constitute separate and independent dimensions, as opposed to polar opposites of a single dichotomous continuum (Bem, 1974; Block, 1973; Heilbrun, 1976; Larson, 1981; Spence & Helmreich, 1978). This could be taken one step further by suggesting that sex-role behaviors and attitudes, which collectively get labeled as masculine or feminine, constitute separate independent continuums. In this way, individuals may express high or low degrees of assertiveness or narcissism, for example, while also expressing various degrees of other gender-role qualities.

Using this sexual identity framework, it is believed that accelerated aging is a function of certain specific gender-role attributes. These include the association of physical appearance with interpersonal success, which is labeled as "feminine" in our society and is partially expressed as narcissism. Narcissism is defined here as an over-concern with physical attractiveness and as self-centeredness. This is only *one* sex-role attribute and does not necessarily imply that those who exhibit narcissism have an entire sex-role identity which is feminine, although some might. Using narcissism as a socially constructed personality trait and gender-role behavior, each of the four sexual orientation groups are examined next on this dimension.

There is a great deal of support in our culture for a double standard of aging between men and women, whereby women are seen as older at an earlier age than men (Bell, 1976; Fischer, 1977; Harris & Cole, 1980; Jacobs, 1979; Neugarten, et al., 1965; Palmore, 1971; Preston, 1975).

This double standard of aging reflects a socially constructed system of rewards for youthful appearance. Given the strength of this reward system, some individuals may internalize this value as the personality trait of narcissism, a phenomenon which speaks to the need for research that explores the relationship between issues of the social construction of aging and youth, and the individual psychology of these social dimensions. In this discussion of the four groups, an attempt is made to differentiate between social construction and individual psychology. Weaknesses which exist in this theoretical analysis support the need for this type of analysis.

Heterosexual women are reported to be valued primarily for their physical appearance (Frumkin, 1973). Therefore, success and achievement for heterosexual women as it is associated with physical appearance seems related to youth and their appeal to heterosexual men (Bell, 1976; Fischer, 1977; Frumkin, 1973).

Sontag (1975) argues that the youth orientedness of modern urban societies support the values of industrial productivity by creating "a new sense of the rhythms of life in order to incite people to buy more, to consume and throw away faster," and that commercialized images of happiness and personal well-being are "designed to stimulate even more avid levels of consumption, the most popular metaphor for happiness is 'youth.'" (p. 32). These social arrangements which value youth and beauty as a socio-sexual commodity for heterosexual women gets translated into the role behavior of narcissism. In fact, Sontag argues that "a woman who is not narcissistic is considered unfeminine" (p. 36). Narcissism is a dimension of individual psychology created by our society which values youth and beauty.

The physical appearance of heterosexual men, on the other hand, receives much less attention through the life cycle (Frumkin, 1973). Success for a heterosexual male in the socio-sexual marketplace seems more related to his functions of achievement, success, personality, and intelligence rather than his physical appearance (Bell, 1976; Frumkin, 1973; Harris & Cole, 1980; Sontag, 1975). As a social reward system, these measures of male success are not perceived as diminishing with age in the same way as physical appearance does for heterosexual women. In fact, they may increase in value with age (Fischer, 1977; Sontag, 1975).

In terms of social construction, heterosexual men are valued on dimensions other than physical appearance in a manner which may uniquely affect their individual psychology. It is not clear whether heterosexual men care less about their physical appearance than the other groups, even though, given the social construction of age and gender, it has a different value. These double standards around physical appearance set the stage for group differences in individual psychology as it relates to accelerated aging.

There is evidence that like heterosexual women, homosexual men who internalize the values of youthful beauty as a measure of success express this behaviorally as narcissism (Francher & Henkin, 1973). These may be homosexual men with a somewhat feminine sex-role identity, and as a group, they may differ from other homosexual men who have a somewhat masculine sex-role identity in terms of accelerated aging.

This narcissistic valuing of youthful beauty, as it relates to one's perception of potential future attachments with the valued single gay world, may in part explain the accelerated aging reported among some of the homosexual men studied (Friend, 1980; Harry, 1982; Kelly, 1977). For example, Harry (1982) argues that being single facilitates the experience of accelerated aging as defined here. If the single homosexual man assumes that male relationships do not last, or does not see himself in one in the future, then concern with his physical appearance may reflect his perceived need to retain physical appearance as a valued commodity in the gay sexual marketplace. This perception may be highlighted if his assumptions about relationships result in him seeing himself as actively participating in the gay sexual marketplace throughout the life cycle. Again, this highlights the relationship between the individual psychology as the internalization of social arrangements.

To summarize briefly, narcissism is seen as a gender-role expression which may function to facilitate accelerated aging among some homosexual men and heterosexual women. The individual psychology of accelerated aging may be similar among these two groups as it may result from similar social constructions of aging which value youth and physical appearance. For homosexual men, valuing youth and beauty results from the social construction which assumes a future of singlehood necessitating retaining one's physical appearance. It is important to note that these assumptions need not be true, but simply believed.

Similarly, the disproportionate number of older women to men create unique social arrangements for interpersonal relationships. As Laner (1979) explains, heterosexual women may continue to value their physical appearance given their competition for interpersonal relationships with fewer available men. Aging among heterosexual men appears to be related to concerns about future productivity and achievement, and less associated with narcissism and concerns over physical appearance. Hence, these concerns occur at a later period in the life cycle.

As mentioned earlier, homosexual women as a group seem to place less value on physical appearance than homosexual men and greater emphasis on interpersonal relationships than homosexual men. This relational quality is consistent with their childrearing and socialization processes as females in our society (Chodorow, 1978; Gilligan, 1982; Rubin, 1975). While heterosexual women are socialized in the same way, their attraction to male partners may influence their valuing of physical appearance. Accelerated aging, to the extent that it is expressed among homosexual men and heterosexual women, may suggest something important about the gender of these two groups' intimate partners. Both groups are attracted to men. Given that men appear to be more visually oriented than women in terms of eroticism (Money, 1978), the physical appearance of their heterosexual female partners and homosexual male partners may be of special significance in a way which it is not for lesbians and heterosexual women. Additionally, if it is men who have the power to establish the accepted measures of beauty in a culture, they may do so based on youthful standards to which they are visually attracted.

To this end, it appears that homosexual women value interpersonal qualities and relationships as measures of success more so than the physical appearance valued by heterosexual women and homosexual men. According to Bell (1971),

> It appears that aging is less traumatic for the lesbian because she does not operate in the same highly physical setting of competitiveness as does the male homosexual. There is some irony in a society where aging is generally more crucial and resisted more by women insofar as physical attractiveness is concerned that the reverse may be true among homosexuals. This difference is also in part explained because the women do place greater stress on interpersonal factors than do men. In general it would appear that aging is easier for the lesbian to handle psychologically than it is for the male homosexual (p. 298).

According to Almvig (1982), more than 50% of the older lesbians surveyed thought they were either just as attractive as they always were, or more attractive than they used to be. She writes:

> Some lesbians, especially those who have been affected by feminism, have chosen to separate themselves from the stereotypical symbols of female attractiveness in society. Accepting themselves for what they are. . . . a sense of natural attractiveness and comfort with their sexuality may develop (p. 74).

In response to what they look for in a lover, Almvig's subjects as a rule responded to the question regarding personality or status, and least frequently to questions having to do with attraction to parts of the body. This last observation illustrates a different social construction of aging for some homosexual women compared with heterosexual men as a group and homosexual men as a group. In terms of individual psychology, homosexual women do not attach the same meanings to physical appearance and youth as do homosexual and heterosexual men. Additionally, given that there are more aged women than men, homosexual women are at an advantage in a way that heterosexual women are not.

Thoresen (1984) argues that homosexual women see the adult years of the 30s and the 40s as times of career achievement and success. Based on this, it is assumed that as with heterosexual men, their identity is more defined in terms of achievement and success than on youth and physical attractiveness.

While the concept of accelerated aging has emerged out of the literature on older homosexuals, its impact reaches beyond this group and speaks to life span issues for everyone. The evidence reviewed and evaluated here suggests that accelerated aging is not a function of sexual orientation per se, but reflects a specific gender-role expression developing out of particular social constructions. Homosexual men and heterosexual women expressing narcissistic role behavior from the internalization of the value judgment that youth and physical appearance are the criteria of interpersonal success may experience accelerated aging due to their perception that few meaningful attachments remain for the future.

Examining the concept of accelerated aging as it relates to gender roles and sexual orientation provides a fuller and more complete appreciation of the meaning age has for men and women in our society. As examined here, accelerated aging is expressed through the gender-role behavior of narcissism for some homosexual men and heterosexual women. For some heterosexual men and homosexual women, experience with accelerated aging appears minimal due to their expectations of being coupled in the future. Additionally, the partners of these heterosexual men and homosexual women may value other things, including vocational achievement over physical appearance, in a way which minimizes accelerated aging.

ACCELERATED AGING: CLINICAL IMPLICATIONS

One of the purposes of this paper is to understand more clearly how individuals who see themselves as older feel about this perception. As stated earlier, it is common to assume that those who define themselves as old feel negatively about this. There is evidence to challenge the generalization that this negative value orientation toward aging is applicable to most people who define themselves as old. The research also provides support for the notion that individual psychology is closely related to the social construction of reality. Some of the assumptions and attitudes about aging and sexual orientation do not appear to be true, yet the extent to which they are believed seems to effect the process of accelerated aging.

Additional research is needed to determine how common accelerated aging is among certain groups. As suggested here, there is reason to believe that the impression that accelerated aging is a common experience among homosexual men may be a result of sampling bias. Research is needed based more on sex-role identity rather than on sex or sexual orientation.

While not necessarily a common experience, concerns about aging are reported among some relatively young men like Brian. Clinicians whose client populations are drawn from sources similar to those reflected in the current body of research may see clients whose concerns reflect accelerated aging. For Brian, his concerns reflected low self-esteem and internalized homophobia as much as they did accelerated aging.

The popular stereotype of older homosexual men as lonely and pathetic individuals functions as a form of social control. Such heterosexist myths may be used to oppose homosexuality, and to deter people from "choosing" to be homosexual. Heterosexist arrangements and messages promote homophobia (the irrational fear of homosexuality in self and others). For Brian, the ageist and heterosexist messages he heard and believed (such as, "Nobody loves an old queen" and "If you choose that lifestyle you'll be alone, unhappy, and will molest young boys") generated great self-hatred.

Several important clinical interventions were helpful in treating Brian's internalized homophobia and concerns about aging. First, challenging myths and misconceptions with accurate information was very important. Affirmative books such as *The Male Couple*, by McWhirter and Mattison (1984), *Gay and Gray*, by Berger (1982b), *Loving Someone Gay*, by Clark (1977), and *Rubyfruit Jungle*, by Brown (1973), were helpful.

Aging concerns can be addressed both through traditional verbal therapy, whereby the underlying fears and concerns are uncovered and explored, and through encouraging cross-generational interactions. Involvement with homosexual men and women of different ages provides useful social stimulation, as well as diverse role models.

Low self-esteem and homophobia, as they are voiced through concerns about aging, can also be managed using cognitive restructuring exercises. Logging automatic critical thoughts and their subsequent emotional responses provides clients with an opportunity to develop more positive and self-defensive ways of thinking about their lives. Cognitive restructuring, positive role models, and an empathic, supportive therapeutic relationship all function to validate the client's self-worth and build self-esteem. For Brian, these tools were very valuable.

CONCLUSION

Through reviewing the literature on older homosexuals, various meanings as to the significance of age and aging have been discussed. One thing is certain: There is great deal of diversity among homosexual men and women in their experiences with aging. While most seem to be well-adjusted, happy members of the community, support is often helpful in maintaining and developing their personal and group resources. The strengths and insights which characterize older homosexual men and women provide important lessons for all men and women.

REFERENCES

Almvig, C. (1982). *The invisible minority: Aging and lesbianism.* New York: Utica College of Syracuse University Press.

Anderson, C. L. (1981). The effect of a workshop on attitudes of female nursing students toward male homosexuality. *Journal of Homosexuality, 7*(1), 57–70.

Atchley, R. C. (1977). *The social forces in later life.* Belmont, CA: Wadsworth.

Batya, B. (1978). In G. Vida (Ed.), *Our right to love.* Englewood Cliffs, NJ: Prentice-Hall.

Bell, A. P., & Weinberg, M. S. (1978). *Homosexualities.* New York: Simon and Schuster.

Bell, I. P. (1976). The double standard. In B. B. Hess (Ed.), *Growing old in America* (pp. 150–162). New Brunswick, NJ: Transaction Books.

Bell, R. R. (1971). *Social deviance.* Homewood, IL: Dorsey Press.

Bem, S. L. (1974). The measurement of psychological androgyny. *Journal of Consulting and Clinical Psychology, 42,* 162–166.

Berger, R. M. (1980). Psychological adaptation of the older homosexual male. *Journal of Homosexuality, 5,* 161–175.

Berger, R. M. (1982a). The unseen minority: Older gays and lesbians. *Social Work, 27,* 236–242.

Berger, R. M. (1982b). *Gay and gray.* Urbana, IL: University of Illinois Press.

Block, J. (1973). Conceptions of sex role: Some cross-cultural and longitudinal perspectives. *American Psychologist, 4,* 154–161.

Brown, R. (1973). *Rubyfruit jungle.* New York: Daughters, Inc.

Chodorow, N. (1978). *The reproduction of mothering.* Berkeley: University of California Press.

Clark, D. (1977). *Loving someone gay.* New York: Signet.

Cotton, W. L. (1972). Role playing substitutions among male homosexuals. *Journal of Sex Research, 8,* 310–323.

Dawson, K. (1982, November). Serving the older community. *SIECUS Report,* pp. 5–6. New York: Sex Education and Information Council of the United States.

Fischer, D. H. (1977). *Growing old in America.* New York: Oxford University Press.

Francher, S. J. (1962). American values and the disenfranchisement of the aged. *Eastern Anthropologist, 22,* 29–36.

Francher, S. J., & Henkin, J. (1973). The menopausal queen. *American Journal of Orthopsychiatry, 43,* 670–674.

Friend, R. A. (1980). GAYging: Adjustment and the older gay male. *Alternative Lifestyles, 3,* 231–248.

Friend, R. A. (1984, June). *A theory of accelerated aging among lesbians and gay men.* Paper presented to the combined annual meeting of American Association of Sex Educators, Counselors and Therapists, and The Society for the Scientific Study of Sex, Boston.

Frumkin, L. W. (1973). Beauty. In A. Ellis & A. Abarbanel (Eds.), *The encyclopedia of sexual behavior* (pp. 216–227). New York: Jason, Aronson.

Gagnon, J. H., & Simon, W. (1973). *Sexual conduct: The social sources of human sexuality.* Chicago: Aldine.

Gilligan, C. (1982). *In a different voice.* Cambridge, MA: Harvard University Press.

Gray, H., & Dressel, P. (1985). Alternative interpretations of aging among gay males. *The Gerontologist, 25,* 83–87.

Hammond, C. B., & Maxson, W. S. (1982). Current status of estrogen therapy for the menopause. *Fertility and Sterility, 37,* 5–25.

Harris, D. K., & Cole, W. E. (1980). *Sociology of aging.* Boston: Houghton Mifflin.

Harry, J. (1982). *Gay children grown up.* New York: Praeger.

Harry, J. (1986). Sampling gay men. *The Journal of Sex Research, 22*(1), 21–34.

Harry, J., & DeVall, W. B. (1978). *The social organization of gay males.* New York: Praeger.

Heilbrun, A. B. (1976). Measurement of masculine and feminine sex role identities as independent dimensions. *Journal of Consulting and Clinical Psychology, 44*, 183–190.

Jacobs, R. H. (1979). *Life after youth.* Boston: Beacon Press.

Kelly, J. (1977). The aging male homosexual: Myth and reality. *The Gerontologist, 17*, 328–332.

Kimmel, D. C. (1977). Psychotherapy and the older gay male. *Psychotherapy: Theory, Research and Practice, 14*, 386–393.

Kimmel, D. C. (1978). Adult development and aging: A gay perspective. *Journal of Social Issues, 34*, 113–130.

Kinsey, A. C., Pomeroy, W. B., & Martin, C. E. (1948). *Sexual behavior in the human male.* Philadelphia: W. B. Saunders.

Laner, M. R. (1978). Growing older male: Heterosexual and homosexual. *The Gerontologist, 18*, 496–501.

Laner, M. R. (1979). Growing older female: Heterosexual and homosexual. *Journal of Homosexuality, 4*, 267–273.

Larson, P. C. (1981). Sexual identity and self-concept. *Journal of Homosexuality, 7*(1), 15–32.

Levinson, D., Darrow, C., Klein, E., Levinson, M., & McKee, B. (1978). *The seasons of a man's life.* New York: Knopf.

Lief, H. I. (1973). Obstacles to the ideal and complete sex education of the medical student and physician. In J. Money & J. Zuben (Eds.), *Contemporary sexual behavior: Critical issues in the 1970's* (pp. 441–453). Baltimore: The Johns Hopkins University Press.

Martin, D. (1982). Learning to hide: The socialization of the gay adolescent. *Adolescent Psychiatry, 10*, 52–65.

Martin, D., & Lyon, P. (1979). The older lesbian. In B. Berzon (Ed.), *Positively gay* (pp. 134–145). Millbrae, CA: Celestial Arts.

Masters, W. H., & Johnson, V. E. (1966). *Human sexual response.* Boston: Little, Brown.

Masters, W. H., & Johnson, V. E. (1970). *Human sexual inadequacy.* Boston: Little, Brown.

McWhirter, D. P., & Mattison, A. M. (1984). *The male couple.* Englewood Cliffs, NJ: Prentice-Hall.

Minnegerode, F. A. 91976). Age status labeling in homosexual men. *Journal of Homosexuality, 1*, 273–276.

Minnegerode, F. A., & Adelman, M. R. (1978). Elderly homosexual women and men: Report on a pilot study. *The Family Coordinator, 27*, 451–456.

Money, J. (1978). Imagery in sexual hang-ups. *The Humanist, 38*, 13–15.

Neugarten, B. L., Moore, J. W., & Lowe, J. C. (1965). Age norms, constraints and adult socialization. *American Journal of Sociology, 70*, 710–717.

Newman, G., & Nichols, C. R. (1960). Sexual activities and attitudes in older persons. *Journal of the American Medical Association, 173*, 33–35.

Palmore, E. (1971). Attitudes toward aging as shown by humor. *The Gerontologist, 11*, 181–186.

Preston, C. E. (1975). An old bag: The stereotype of the older female. In *No longer young: The older women in America* (pp. 41–45). Proceedings of the 26th Annual Conference on Aging, Institute of Gerontology, University of Michigan and Wayne State University.

Raphael, S. M., & Robinson, M. K. (1980). The older lesbian. *Alternative Lifestyles, 3*, 207–229.

Rubin, G. (1975). The traffic in women: Notes on the "political economy" of sex. In R. Reiter (Ed.), *Toward an anthropology of women* (pp. 157–210). New York: Monthly Review Press.

Saghir, M. T., & Robins, E. (1973). *Male and female homosexuality: A comprehensive investigation.* Baltimore: Williams & Wilkins.

Shively, M. G., & De Cecco, J. P. (1977). Components of sexual identity. *Journal of Homosexuality, 3*, 41–48.

Sontag, S. (1975). The double standard of aging. In *No longer young: The older woman in America* (pp. 31–39). Proceedings of the 26th Annual Conference on Aging, University of Michigan and Wayne State University.

Spence, J. T., & Helmreich, R. L. (1978). *Masculinity and femininity: Their psychological dimensions, correlates and antecedents.* Austin, TX: University of Texas Press.

Thoresen, J. (1984, April). *Lesbians and gay men: Complements and contrasts.* Paper presented at the Annual Meeting of the Society for the Scientific Study of Sex, Philadelphia.

Weinberg, J. S. (1982). *Sexuality: Human needs and nursing practice.* Philadelphia: W. B. Saunders.

Weinberg, M. S. (1970). The male homosexual: Age-related variations in social and psychological characteristics. *Social Problems, 17,* 527–537.

Weinberg, M. S., & Williams, C. J. (1975). *Male homosexuals: Their problems and adaptations.* New York: Penguin Books.

Zilbergeld, B. (1978). *Male sexuality.* New York: Bantam Books.

Index